THE T.V.A.

LESSONS FOR INTERNATIONAL APPLICATION

A Da Capo Press Reprint Series

FRANKLIN D. ROOSEVELT
AND THE ERA OF THE NEW DEAL

GENERAL EDITOR: FRANK FREIDEL
Harvard University

THE T.V.A.
LESSONS FOR
INTERNATIONAL APPLICATION

BY HERMAN FINER

DA CAPO PRESS · NEW YORK · 1972

Library of Congress Cataloging in Publication Data

Finer, Herman, 1898-1969.
   The T.V.A.
   (Franklin D. Roosevelt and the era of the New Deal)
   "An unabridged republication of the first edition published . . . in 1944
as Series B (Economic conditions), number 37, of the Studies and reports
of the International Labour Office."
   1. Tennessee Valley Authority. I. Series.
HN79.A135F5   330.9768   77-172008
ISBN 0-306-70378-5

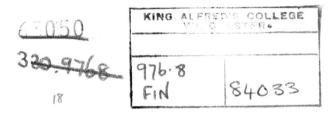
This Da Capo Press edition of *The T.V.A., Lessons for International Application* is an unabridged republication of the first edition published in Montreal in 1944 as Series B (Economic Conditions), Number 37, of the *Studies and Reports of the International Labour Office*. It is reprinted by permission from a copy of the original edition in the collection of the Alderman Library, University of Virginia.

Published by Da Capo Press, Inc.
A Subsidiary of Plenum Publishing Corporation
227 West 17th Street, New York, New York 10011

THE T.V.A.: LESSONS FOR INTERNATIONAL APPLICATION

INTERNATIONAL LABOUR OFFICE

THE T.V.A.

LESSONS

FOR

INTERNATIONAL APPLICATION

by

Herman FINER

MONTREAL
1944

Studies and Reports, Series B (Economic Conditions), No. 37

PUBLISHED BY THE INTERNATIONAL LABOUR OFFICE,
3480 University Street, Montreal, Canada

———————

Published in the United Kingdom for the INTERNATIONAL LABOUR OFFICE
by P. S. King & Staples, Ltd., London.

———————

Distributed in the United States by the INTERNATIONAL LABOUR OFFICE,
Washington Branch, 734 Jackson Place, Washington, D.C.

PREFACE

The idea of a "Tennessee Valley Authority" on an international scale has spread widely. The term is now so commonly used that it has acquired a meaning of its own, independent of the experiment from which it took its name. The T.V.A., after its first ten years, came to be looked upon both as a model and as a preliminary to wider developments elsewhere. In 1942, for instance, at a British Association Conference on agricultural reconstruction, a speaker advocated a "D.V.A. for the Danube Valley", to provide electrical power, transport and irrigation. *The Advancement of Science*, recently published by the British Association discusses the same proposal:

> The application of this idea in the Danube Valley seems to have much to commend it. It presupposes a regional authority with clearly defined powers derived from the various central political authorities in whose territory it operates.
> ... It would, however, only be possible for the countries of south-eastern Europe to carry out the sort of programme indicated at a very slow rate unless they could be assisted by some external agency.

Similar proposals have been made for the Amazon and Yangtse Valleys. But some of the suggestions go much further and recommend regional development through a wider form of organisation. Mr. E. H. Carr in his book *Conditions of Peace* writes: "Side by side with a European Relief . . . we shall need hardly less urgently a European Reconstruction and Public Works Corporation, whose task will be to get on foot such major works of construction or reconstruction as are too extensive and cover too wide an area to be handled by local initiative."

Other writers and speakers have urged the creation of a United Nations or a world development organisation. The Commission to Study the Organization of Peace, for instance, suggests that:

> . . . a United Nations development authority might be set up, working through regional authorities, to deal with economic development and the investment connected therewith . . . Vice-President H. A. Wallace, in a speech in 1942, said "there must be an international bank and an international T.V.A".

In the *New Republic* in 1941, Dr. Julian Huxley wrote:

> What is required is clear. It is the establishment of international organisations for the development of various backward areas of the world. Concretely, we need at the very outset an eastern European and an east Asian development agency.

These quotations will suffice to show that an "international T.V.A." is a conception that, in various forms, is receiving very wide support.

In the development of the standard of living in our own time three things emerge clearly.

1. That the strikingly large increases have occurred in the course of the last two generations, roughly 60 years, especially in countries which initially had a very low standard by comparison with Great Britain and the U.S.A.

2. That the most remarkable gains have been made in those countries which have created or borrowed capital and acquired general education and technical knowledge to enable them to proceed beyond the primary to the secondary and tertiary industries.

3. That unless capital comes from outside, progress depends upon home savings. Without international assistance it is therefore difficult for a region with a very low margin of existence and only a hand-to-mouth economy to make a productive start (the effects of which are cumulative).

A flying productive start can be of immense benefit; and an international resource development authority can help to give that start and, for some time, to guide the subsequent course.

Ever since, ten years ago, the brushwood was cleared away to make room for the first gigantic dam at Norris, the T.V.A. has attracted the interest and aroused the speculations of many minds in the worlds of science, technology, economics and government. Its work has been widely reported, and multitudes of experts have examined its operations on the spot. As the thousands of tons of cement were poured, and the tens of thousands of workers progressed with their tasks, the T.V.A.'s aims and methods increasingly impressed observers. It was conceived on a great scale and its procedure was novel and resourceful.

The Authority was established in the United States of America at a time of economic distress, in the gravest world-wide economic depression ever recorded. It came into being when governments were taking the desperate course of restricting production and destroying produce in the hope of restoring economic welfare. The T.V.A. represented an altogether different conception of the management of a modern nation's economic resources: that of enterprise on a large scale, deliberately undertaken by the public authorities, with certain social and economic purposes clearly in mind from the beginning. It represented an economic policy of hope and expansion in which the Government would play a dynamic part.

As an organisation of the United States Government in an American setting, the T.V.A. has attempted to raise the economic level of a great depressed region and to develop integrally its various resources. The most spectacular as well as the most important single resource is water power. The T.V.A. therefore applied itself to harnessing the existing water resources in the unruly Tennessee River. The river has been tamed by a system of gigantic dams; it has been made almost completely fit for navigation as part of some 5,000 miles of inland waterways; and its tendency to destructive flooding has been reduced. The waters that the T.V.A. caught and then spilled over a score of linked dams have been exploited to make vast quantities of cheap electric power, which has been distributed through non-profit-making municipal or co-operative undertakings, and its uses have been encouraged by educational methods. Especially valuable concentrated phosphatic fertiliser has been experimentally produced, and applied in widespread demonstrations, by means of which the farmers have been educated in better agricultural methods so as to increase their produce, diversify their crops and yet restore and conserve the soil. Rural life has been rendered both agreeable and productive. The T.V.A. has shown steady and active concern for the region's forestry and mineral resources, for the promotion of agricultural and other industries and for the health and general welfare of the people.

In short, the T.V.A. was entrusted, not with a scheme based on the making of a profit, but with the establishment and execution of an integrated resources development plan, using specific undeveloped or underdeveloped natural and human resources. It has fulfilled that trust, and fulfilled it well. Moreover, its operations have brought benefit to private industries and have even stimulated the sales and profits of the electric companies.

The general interest aroused by the T.V.A. has not been confined to its aims. Its methods have also deserved special attention, since they constituted an attempt to fashion an administrative instrument adapted to its particular purpose, and unencumbered by traditional and possibly hampering procedures. The enterprise is public in ownership and management. No single private venture nor even a federation of private companies even if possessed of the necessary authority could have covered such a diversity of operations, in sympathy with the ends in view. Nor could private enterprise, looking to profits, have found or risked the capital involved. The T.V.A. is democratic, in that it derives its statute from, and is financed by, a democratically chosen Congress and Executive, while its local operations have always depended on the free co-operation of local institutions. It is regional in the sense that it was given authority in, and responsibility for, an area two thirds the size of England, which comprised portions and transcended the boundaries of seven States within the watershed—the valley of the Tennessee River. It is decentralised. Administration was, with considerable autonomy, lodged in the Valley itself, and not conducted from Washington, the distant capital of the country. It is a public corporation, enjoying wide delegated powers and many of the attributes of an ordinary business corporation, so that it may act both with responsibility and flexibility and in independence of customary controls by the central departments of the United States Government. It has received the financial resources—no less than 600 million dollars—necessary to a unified plan of works (including over 20 dams), the execution of which required a decade or more of continuous integrated building to yield the amplest economic return of which technology was capable.[1]

It has already been pointed out that consideration of the problems that peace may be expected to bring has spread the idea that there should be many "T.V.A.'s" in lands of undeveloped economy, aided where necessary by an international body. It is important to know, then, what the T.V.A. is and what it has accomplished and what its problems and difficulties have been; and to consider under what conditions and by what adaptation its experience may be applicable elsewhere, particularly in an international setting.

---

[1] For other discussions of the T.V.A., the reader may be referred to the vivid account by D. S. LILIENTHAL (Chairman of the T.V.A.) in *T.V.A.-Democracy on the March* (New York, 1944); and the administrative survey by Professor C. H. PRITCHETT: *The Tennessee Valley Authority* (University of North Carolina Press, 1943).

CONTENTS

CHAPTER I

RETARDED DEVELOPMENT AND WASTING ASSETS

The vital question, to which the Tennessee Valley Authority attempts an answer, is whether an industrious and capable people, though settled in a region which contains substantial natural resources, must continue to endure a low living standard. By what means is it feasible, if at all, to assist a people fairly rich in primary resources and available skills to achieve higher productivity and an increase in their level of consumption and possessions? The significance and worth of the T.V.A. derive from this principal object of enquiry, and from the predominant physico-economic and social characteristics of the Valley region which is their distinctive setting. A brief review of these factors is therefore an indispensable stage towards fuller consideration of the T.V.A.'s various purposes, its many problems of function and method, and its not unimportant achievements.

The Tennessee Valley is a great river basin draining a territory of 40,600 square miles, or four fifths the size of England; the river and its tributaries drain an area shaped like a butterfly, a thousand miles long with a very narrow waist and a maximum width of about 150 miles. The Valley includes portions of seven States— Tennessee, Alabama, Kentucky, North Carolina, Virginia, Georgia, and Mississippi.[1] In 1933 this Valley had a population of about 3,000,000, mainly of English, Scotch, Irish and German descent; some 10 per cent. were Negroes. Nature had originally provided very considerable resources of soil, forest, water and minerals. These resources had been neglected and wasted, and to some extent had suffered destruction. What still existed, however, was of very considerable value. Though much was in danger of loss, much also was capable of rehabilitation.

The signs of human welfare in the Valley were not encouraging. There was a percentage of rural population of 76.8 as compared with 43.8 in the nation as a whole. The gross value of farm products

---

[1] The proportion of each of the seven so-called Valley States lying within the watershed of the Tennessee River is as follows: Alabama, 13 per cent.; Georgia, 2.7 per cent.; Kentucky, 2.7 per cent.; Mississippi, 0.9 per cent.; North Carolina, 11.2 per cent.; Tennessee, 53.8 per cent.; and Virginia, 8.4 per cent.

per capita of farm population was $154 as compared with $362 for the whole of the United States.[1] The standard of nutrition, both in quantity and kind, was extremely low[2]; educational provision was among the worst in the nation[3]; and certain key indices of mortality were serious.[4] Yet the population rates were considerably higher than the average of the whole United States. The fertility rate was one third higher[5]; the size of the family was greater[6]; the number of dependants per family was considerably larger.[7] There was, as in most rural areas, an appreciable regular exodus of the young and able-bodied to employment opportunities, usually industrial, elsewhere in the United States.[8]

To restore this Valley to prosperity two things were needed— the conversion of its potential into actual resources, and the preservation and reconstitution of existing resources which were steadily depreciating and were still in danger of complete destruction. Both these things could be done through the application of science, the vast resources of which were amply available; but the prime requirement was a spirit of enterprise and a form of administration appropriate to ensure success.

The principal special resource of the Valley is its waterpower. The river falls rapidly from a height of 3,000 feet at its source in the Smoky Mountains (the highest range east of the Rockies) and the Blue Ridge Mountains to the point at about 300 feet where at Paducah, Kentucky, it enters the Ohio River, which then flows into the Mississippi. There is a heavy rainfall, ranging up to 80 inches at some places and averaging 51 inches for the Valley as a whole, which normally ensures a swift flow; but it is a "flashy" river, and at the same season varies much in character from year to

[1] In 1934 the average spendable income per person (farm and otherwise) was $211 as compared with $486 for the United States. (Computed by the T.V.A. from *Sales Management*, Apr. 1935.)

[2] In 1934 consumption fell short of the national average by 27 per cent. in white potatoes; 30 per cent. in hay; 45 per cent. in livestock; 77 per cent. in wheat; 92 per cent. in oats, barley and rye. It exceeded the national average in corn by 25 per cent. and in sweet potatoes by 244 per cent.

[3] Average expenditures per child between 7 and 17 were $23.35 compared with $68.02 in the United States as a whole.

[4] There were 7.6 deaths per 100,000 from typhoid and paratyphoid, as compared with 3.9 for the United States; 79.4 per 100,000 from tuberculosis as compared with 63.2 for the United States.

[5] In 1930, 531 children under five per 1,000 women of childbearing age, as compared with 391 for the United States.

[6] Average number of persons, 4.6 compared with a United States average of 4.1.

[7] For every 100 persons of productive age (20-64) there were 122 dependants (people under 20 and over 60), as compared with 90 in the United States.

[8] Nearly one half of the gainfully occupied people were in agriculture; 3.2 per cent. in mining, chiefly coal; 16 per cent. in manufactures; 2.9 per cent. in construction; 6.4 per cent. in transportation and communication; 7.3 per cent. in trade; 5.4 per cent. in professional and public service; and 7.3 per cent. in personal service.

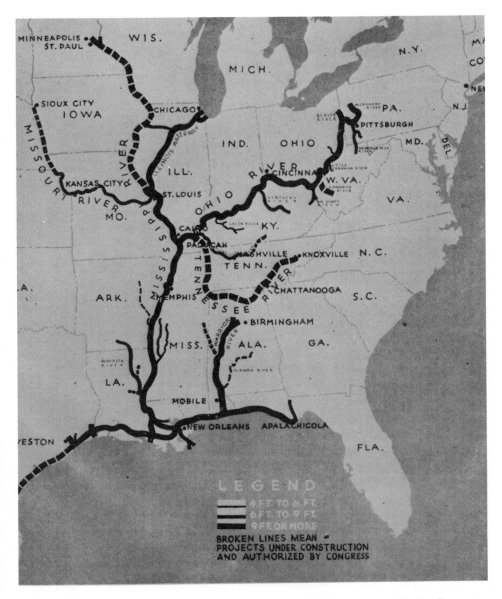

LEGEND: ——— 4 ft. to 6 ft.; ▬▬▬ 6 ft. to 9 ft.; ▬▬▬ 9 ft. or more. Broken lines mean projects under construction and authorised by Congress.

year. The principal stretch of the Tennessee River runs some 650 miles from Knoxville, Tennessee, to Paducah on the Ohio River. In that distance the fall is 500 feet; it is irregular, and at certain points precipitous. Properly harnessed, this great volume of water falling so heavily from one level to another can be the source of enormous electric power, and science has made it possible to utilise that power for the attainment of a generous variety of human purposes, for production and consumption.

Water, however, is not the only resource of the Valley. The area was originally heavily wooded but a great deal of the forest had been cleared to make way for cultivation, and the timber was rarely replaced with anything like the speed with which it was consumed. The agricultural methods used and the crops produced were such as to destroy the soil, which was treated as an expendable mine rather than as a medium of production which ought to be maintained at least constant in its productive capacity, and if possible improved. Certain consequences had followed with all the rigour of nature's punishment when her laws are not observed. The rainfall, coming precipitously in a region of hills and declivities and not being held by the leafage and roots of the trees, had swept away the soil, so that about one and a half million acres were cropped only intermittently owing to depletion, while four and a half million acres were on the decline and some 300,000 acres were practically destroyed. The top soil had gone into the river, silted it up, and made it less fit for navigation; the process known as leaching had taken the essential nitrogen out of the land. It was once said by Mr. Henry A. Wallace, then United States Secretary of Agriculture, that "no civilisation has ever builded in so short a time what our forefathers have builded in America"; but it may equally well be suggested that no civilisation has in so short a time consumed and destroyed so much of the resources of the earth. But it is possible to apply remedies to this wasting asset, and not only to stop the decline of land resources but actually to develop and enrich them by proper treatment.

Furthermore, the Valley had important mineral resources. These had already given a livelihood to more than three out of every hundred gainfully occupied people in the Valley, and offered prospects of considerably wider employment opportunities.

That the conversion of the water resources into actual social benefits and the restoration and even increase of the soil resources can be achieved has been made manifest by scientists in the course of the past century. The scientific means are available to convert a silted, precipitous river, shallow in many places, deep in others, into a great stream navigable from its headwaters down to the

Ohio, and thence, because of the connection with the Mississippi, down to the Gulf of Mexico with access to all the ports of the world; to take the crest from the floodwaters, which are a perennial threat and often a deadly danger to the cities on the river's banks, by regulating dams; and to convert the falling water into electric power, and send it out in the service of mankind to a distance of 250 miles, and much further still by interconnections with other systems. Anticipating the exhaustion of the soil, science and its experts can apply the appropriate remedies. They can restore the depleted soil by the application of phosphatic food; they can correct the damaging agricultural practices of a single crop economy of cotton or corn; and by diversifying the crops both restore the soil and produce a higher standard of living. Special equipment can be devised to conserve the soil and farm difficult hillsides. And, with navigation and electric power and new agricultural practices, an industry supplemental to the Valley economy can be encouraged, each different factor fitting into a balanced efficient pattern.

In this Valley, the conditions of which have been thus roughly sketched, all these things were potential. Why, then, had they not become actual? The missing factor was enterprise—that is, the energetic, benevolent, and unified intervention of an agency which, grasping the possibilities and being interested in the social objectives and consequences, would apply knowledge to the problem. Of course, in this Valley, as elsewhere, any person or persons with sufficient capital might have entered and undertaken the necessary arrangements. The Valley was wide open to enterprise. There were, indeed, a number of private enterprises operating in the area; there were several electric companies, and one great aluminium manufacturing undertaking. There were a few private dams built to provide electricity. But private enterprise was a very incomplete, piecemeal and unco-ordinated method of development. The fertiliser manufacturers could not engage in farm demonstration on an adequate scale; nor would this have promised to yield profits. The people in the Valley themselves were too poor to lift themselves out of their poverty unassisted. In general, they had hardly enough for comfortable living, let alone a substantial margin of savings which, accumulated, might have provided the investment capital for the extensive works necessary to develop the Valley's abundant resources.

Moreover, the Valley is divided in political jurisdiction among seven States and hundreds of local government units, cities and counties. None of these is charged with responsibility or authority for more than the fraction of the Valley that lies within its area. Nor were the boundaries of the States ever coincident with the most appropriate area of economic organisation. Under the laws, it would have been extremely difficult, and probably quite impossible, to create a single private enterprise which could, as a united organisation, have acquired and administered the water resources of the area as a unit. Yet the potential value of those resources could be developed to the maximum only if the inherent natural need for unity of plan and operation were respected. Any one State, or even several States, any one city, or even all the cities together in joint association, any one private enterprise, or even many acting as a consortium, could have seen the opportunities and introduced the measures only in splintered fashion. The enterprise necessary for developing the Valley had to be such as could see the Valley steadily, and see it whole.

But the unification of vision and agency is by no means all. Of far superior import is purpose, the will to attain the social objectives for the sake of all the people of the Valley, an interest that is keen, consistent and direct—that is basic, and not, as it might be in private enterprise, the casual offspring of a profit-making purpose. The region needed, at least for a time, some one to show solicitude and to assist it. That was the vital missing factor in its welfare.

In 1935 the Government of the United States undertook this task of caring for the Valley. Congress passed a law setting up an agency—the Tennessee Valley Authority—to implement its interest in the people's welfare within that Valley, by furnishing adequate capital for development, together with technical assistance, and by assuming a continuous responsibility for developing the resources both by direct activities and by instructing the local population ultimately to help itself.

FORCES LEADING TO THE ESTABLISHMENT OF THE T.V.A.

However, this solution was not easy to reach, nor was it seen or adopted by the genius of a single person at a single moment. For the problem grew piecemeal; or rather several problems were superimposed on each other and suggestion followed suggestion until a comprehensive answer was needed and found. It is essential, then, to glance at the movement of forces which led to the establishment of the T.V.A., since this deepens the appreciation of its significance.

Five streams of tendency produced the T.V.A. The first was a local interest in the navigability of a short stretch of the river and a wider, but still local, interest in protection from floods in an area continually liable to them. The second was the national interest in electric power development. Thirdly, the policy of conserving national resources led to the idea of an appropriate area of government with multiple and integrated purposes. Fourthly, the national defence plants, built in 1916 at Muscle Shoals, raised the problem of their further use. Fifthly, the economic depression, beginning in 1929, sharpened the already developing realisation that governmental economic planning was essential.

Navigation

Just above the city of Florence, Alabama, on a 37-mile stretch of the Tennessee River, lie Muscle Shoals. In that distance the river falls 134 feet and is bestrewn with natural obstacles which prevented traffic in an age when roads and railways were not available as alternatives. As a consequence of Congressionally authorised surveys of nationally important roads and canals, the Federal authority in 1827 made a grant of land to the State of Alabama for the improvement of Colbert and Muscle Shoals for navigation by means of a canal. Many subsequent local demands for such assistance by Federal grants and new works were made to Congress. The deterioration of the railroads during the Civil War added urgency to the provision of river transport, while the United States Army Corps of Engineers observed that important manufactures could have developed out of the local deposits of minerals if navigation had been improved.

Flood Control

Owing to the location of the river basin in relation to the line of travel of the torrential downpours and storms, and the peculiar topography, there is a continuous likelihood of high, damaging floods. The time-honoured and very widely applied remedies for this were the abandonment of large areas of valuable land and other property and the building of levees. Here again, piecemeal activity in the lower reaches, without co-operation or co-ordinated works on the upper, could not adequately achieve the object sought. It began to be seen that the Mississippi, the Ohio and the lower Tennessee would have to be safeguarded by means of planned controls, more comprehensive and placed further back, and by a radically different method of water control.

Thus, for more than a hundred years before 1933, the improvement of the Tennessee River was an object of local and then national concern. But the many schemes of river improvement, being mostly small and largely unrelated, were correspondingly inadequate. In 1904 Congress authorised certain private interests to establish a dam at Hales Bar, finished in 1913, to canalise the 33-

mile stretch of the river below Chattanooga. The river was further improved by the Widow's Bar lock and dam, authorised in 1916 and completed in 1926. The Wilson dam, authorised in 1916 and completed in 1925, provided a first-class canalised waterway for 15½ miles over the Muscle Shoals. In 1914, 1922, 1925, 1927, and again in 1928, Congress authorised comprehensive surveys of the river. The survey begun in 1928[1] and made, like the others, by the United States Army Corps of Engineers, is a magistral document to which, as will be seen, the T.V.A. later became much indebted for the basis of its own plans. This report, completed in 1930, led Congress to introduce in the Rivers and Harbors Act of 3 July 1930 an authorisation for a 9-foot navigation channel project for the 650-mile stretch of river from Knoxville to Paducah, under which the Wheeler Lock was built by the Army Engineers.

Thus, the broadening of concern from mere local interests to a national interest, the inadequacy of individual local and partial projects, the lack of private enterprise, drive and funds on a sufficient scale, were among the tendencies which ultimately produced the T.V.A. The need for a wider authority was shown by the increasing range of the interests involved.

Hydroelectricity

In 1891 the first hydroelectric plant was built in the United States, introducing a new factor in the situation. In 1890 general licence powers were vested in the United States Chief of Engineers, the Secretary of War and the Secretary of the Interior for the purpose of regulating the establishment of structures on rivers and rights of way in the public domain for bridges, canals, and irrigation reservoirs; the development of electricity was recognised as a subsidiary purpose. In 1898 an Alabama representative submitted a proposal to Congress for consent to the construction of an electric plant at Muscle Shoals by a private corporation. This franchise was granted by Congress to the Muscle Shoals Hydroelectric Power Company in 1899, but lapsed, partly owing to disputes between the Federal and State Governments regarding their respective shares of the charges to be paid by the Company for its privileges. A similar franchise was vetoed by President Theodore Roosevelt in 1903, and again in 1908, on public grounds. For public opinion was developing emphatically against the unconditional alienation to private bodies of natural resources, especially waterpower, which held such promise for the daily welfare of the people. The grounds of this opinion were that resources either were not exploited at all

---

[1] 71st Congress, 2nd Session, House Document No. 328.

by private concessionaires or were not so planned as to give the maximum development of navigation or power, and so were lost to the public as a property which would help to defray the cost of navigation, flood control and other improvements.

Nevertheless, local interests, like the Alabama Power Company (the parent company of the Muscle Shoals Hydroelectric Power Company) and political representatives of Alabama, one of the Valley States, still sought to secure waterpower concessions.

Conservation and Multi-Purpose Development

Thus a local interest and resource emerged into the arena of national principle and policy regarding the whole community's interest in its latent resources. At the turn of the century, the factor of conservation, or the planned preservation of natural resources which were being usefully exploited, and of integrated multiple purpose development entered the stream of tendencies. The "conservationist" movement, beginning with a memorial to Congress from the American Association for the Advancement of Science in 1874, resulted in the creation of Federal administrative departments to take care of the forests, to cope with drainage, irrigation and power[1], and in many other subsequent measures down to the present time, including, indeed, the T.V.A. Linked with this movement was the recognition of the reciprocal value of the several uses of naturally integrated resources. For example, the United States Waterways Commission, charged with fostering co-ordinated development and administration of waterway systems, demonstrated the inseparability of problems of navigation, hydroelectricity, forestry, soil erosion and flood prevention, and related these problems to the conservation of coal and iron.

Again, a United States Army Engineers' report of 1914[2] took a considerable step towards the idea of a public and integrated development authority by showing that, in the specific case of the area of retarded development around Muscle Shoals, the general prosperity would be greatly increased if its mineral, forest and agricultural resources were fully exploited by the use of the power now wasting in the Tennessee River. Raw materials would be used in manufactures; ore deposits could be profitably processed; fertilisers could be made at low cost in the vicinity of the field of use—provided the power supply were ample, continuous, permanent

---

[1] Among the many works of which the United States Reclamation Service was in charge was the building of the great Boulder Dam on the Colorado River (1928) and the Bonneville and Grand Coulee Dams on the Columbia River. Cf. U. S. DEPARTMENT OF THE INTERIOR, BUREAU OF RECLAMATION: *Reclamation Handbook* (Conservation Bulletin No. 32, 1942).

[2] 63rd Congress, 2nd Session, House Document No. 20, pp. 6-7.

and cheap. It was rare, after this report, to hear any opinion voiced except in terms of "the region" or "the basin". Such an outlook raised other problems. What area should be envisaged within which to cope with the problem of the river? Some thought in terms of a boundary line 250 miles each way from Muscle Shoals, since transmission lines were feasible over that distance. It was observed that the Reclamation Service acted on the theory that for its work of developing power and irrigation existing State boundaries must be disregarded.

Again, it was insisted in Congressional debate that every phase of the water problem and of all interests and communities within an area widely conceived must be dovetailed; for example, floods on the Mississippi could be most effectively dealt with by holding back water in the tributary rivers. As for the agency which should undertake such work, it was observed that an economic commission was needed, permanent and not ephemeral, not political or partisan or academic, but compact, uniting representatives of the Federal departments most concerned and binding together in close articulation the attainable benefits of the specific plans of each department.

This leads again to the Army Engineers' report of 1930—"the comprehensive plan . . . for the complete development of the water resources of the Tennessee River for navigation, power development, and flood control". This report presented two plans for development of the Tennessee River. The first was a combination power, navigation and flood control plan requiring the construction of seven high dams at an estimated cost of approximately $250,000,000. It was contemplated that private interests would participate in the cost of these dams at least to the extent of the cost of power facilities. The second plan called for a series of 32 low dams with locks at an estimated cost of $75,000,000, which would give only inferior navigation facilities, and would develop no power. The Chief of Engineers recommended this latter plan with authorisation to private interests, States or municipalities to substitute a high dam for any two or more of the low dams. As already mentioned, the project authorised in the Rivers and Harbors Act of 3 July 1930 for a 9-foot channel in the Tennessee River was based on the recommendations of the Army Engineers.

All these developments were important; but for the transformation of ideas, however sound and socially beneficial, into governmental action, a precipitating agent is needed. In the case of the T.V.A., this was the creation in 1917 of a Government nitrate and electricity producing plant at Muscle Shoals for war purposes and its consequential problems, and later the interest in economic planning developed by the great depression that started in 1929.

The Fertiliser and Munitions Plants

The National Defense Act of 1916 included a section "to provide for the fixation of atmospheric nitrogen by the development of waterpower or any other means necessary to establish an adequate supply of nitrogen", and appropriated the funds for the necessary construction. The purpose was to make the nation independent of foreign sources of nitrogen in time of war. The proposal attracted the interest of various private economic groups. One group asked that after the war the plant should be used for the manufacture of fertiliser, and also that, as the power necessary to make the nitrogen would come from Muscle Shoals, the latter plant should be privately owned. Representatives of the farmers' interests warmly favoured the development of nitrates, hoping that the farmers might get cheap fertiliser; they were rather more in favour of the private utilities' operating the scheme than the Government, alleging that they feared a domestic monopoly as strong as that of their former Chilean suppliers. There was a contest between a group of people who (not necessarily in deliberate relation to the Muscle Shoals problem) had introduced a Bill providing for complete public ownership and operation of a hydroelectric nitrate-making plant or plants, while another group strenuously fought this proposal, which would have excluded Muscle Shoals from private business prospects. All the industrial groups concerned with waterpower, fertiliser and munitions, were strongly opposed to such Government enterprise.

However, the powers which it was proposed the Government should receive were, in substance, granted. The United States Government was given the power to designate sites on navigable or non-navigable rivers for the exclusive use of the United States, and to construct and operate hydroelectric or other plants for the production of nitrate for munitions and fertilisers, and even, by an amendment, of "other useful products". A proposal that the Government might sell surplus electric power as well as other useful products was decisively rejected by the Senate.

Two nitrate plants were built in application of these powers. Nitrate Plant No. 1 at Sheffield, Alabama, was an experimental plant using the Haber process. It cost nearly $13,000,000 to build, and nearly three quarters of a million was spent on its operation before it was abandoned as useless. Nitrate Plant No. 2 at Muscle Shoals which, with its accessories, cost nearly $70,000,000, was to produce ammonium-nitrate by the cyanimid process. It began to produce in November 1918, a little late for the war, and after January 1919 was maintained in a stand-by condition. This plant was located at Muscle Shoals, where it was expected that the proper hydroelectric installation would provide the tremendous amounts of power needed for full development. But speed was necessary, and so the Government contracted with the Alabama Power Company to build a 30,000 kilowatt plant[1] at its Gorgas Steam Plant 89 miles away, while the Government itself constructed a steam plant at Nitrate Plant No. 2 to produce 60,000 and eventually 90,000 kilowatts. To exploit the waterpower, the Corps of Engineers began in 1916 to prepare a scheme of combined navigation and waterpower construction activity. Dam No. 2, later known as Wilson Dam, was to be chief of a trio of dams, and the engineers concentrated on this. But the war ended before substantial construction had begun; appropriations from Congress were intermittent, and the dam was not completed until September 1925, when power began to be generated.

At the end of the war, then, the United States Government had some assets and liabilities at and around Muscle Shoals. What was to be done with this property and the potentialities it represented? This problem was one factor which helped to precipitate the ideas already described, and others yet to be brought into account, and in the end to produce the T.V.A.

Congress began to debate the problem of the disposition of the Muscle Shoals property in 1919, when the then Secretary of War, Mr. Newton D. Baker, proposed the establishment of a Government corporation to operate it. The purpose of the Baker Bill was to produce nitrogen products for sale to the United States Government for military purposes, any surplus to be made available to producers or users of fertiliser. The corporation was also authorised under direction of the President to operate the hydroelectric power plant which was then under construction at Wilson Dam, and to use and sell the power there developed.

This Bill, which was not passed, was followed during the years from 1920 to 1933 by a series of twelve other Bills relating to Muscle Shoals. In view of their proposals regarding fertiliser, all these Bills were referred to the Senate Committee on Agriculture. The Chairman of this Committee, Senator George Norris of Nebraska, thus became responsible for dealing with them and some were initiated by him. His interest, quickened by his experience of rural life, was so strong and unflagging that he is sometimes known as "the father of the T.V.A.".

A much debated Bill, in 1924, came partly as a rejoinder to a remarkable offer which Mr. Henry Ford had made two years before —one of a number of offers made by power companies and industrial promoters for the acquisition of the power potentialities. Mr. Ford

---

[1] This Government plant was later bought by the Company.

proposed to buy the Muscle Shoals nitrate property and steam power plants for $5,000,000, and to manufacture nitrogen and other fertilisers at a profit not exceeding 8 per cent. Moreover, he would complete Wilson Dam and construct the projected Dam No. 3 for the Government at cost price, and lease these dams and power plants for 100 years. The House of Representatives accepted this proposal, which was, in fact, backed by the strong influence of the American Farm Bureau Federation, anxious to have cheap fertiliser and indifferent to the method by which it was produced, even if this involved the surrender of great public resources. Senator Norris, however, was convinced by this time that his original belief in cheap fertiliser—he had proposed a Federal Chemical Corporation—on a commercial basis was unfounded; and his 1924 Bill therefore included only authority for the production of power, while experimentation in fertiliser production was turned over to the Department of Agriculture as the best way of aiding the farmer. Elaborate provisions were also included to regulate the sale of surplus power, all in the direction of giving greater freedom of business initiative to the corporation. There were several counter-proposals and clauses were added designed to make a Government power corporation less dependent upon a single customer (the Alabama Power Company) by authorising the construction or leasing of transmission lines from the dam. By 1928, the two Houses of Congress came to an agreement on a Government corporation to engage in fertiliser experimentation and the sale of surplus power. The corporation was permitted to manufacture fixed nitrogen on a commercial basis, but the production of fertiliser was limited to experiment in order to avoid Government competition with the industry. The Bill was adopted on 25 May 1928, but was vetoed by President Coolidge.

Throughout this period, there were frequent counter-proposals based upon the principle that the United States Government should lease the nitrate plants and the power plant to private agencies; usually a term was included within which such leasing could be effected. In 1931, the 1928 Bill, with some slight financial amendments and with a leasing section added to it, was accepted by Congress, only to be vetoed by President Hoover. The reasons given in the veto message are interesting. The President thought that competent management was not possible, seeing that Congress must intervene to secure democratic responsibility and that such intervention was bound to be damaging to the technical administration of the enterprise. Secondly, he thought that the directors would be bound to have a political complexion, and would therefore be technically inept and certain to choose a staff on a political basis.

Thirdly, he was opposed to the Government's entering into business competition in power manufacturing with its citizens, though he did acknowledge that there were many localities where the Federal Government was justified in coping with navigation, flood control, reclamation, or regulation of streams by constructing dams and reservoirs which were beyond the capacity or purpose of the capital available to private persons or local government.

Social and Economic Planning and the Depression

The fifth and final factor in the social situation leading up to the establishment of the T.V.A. was the idea of planning coupled with experience of distress in the great depression. Towards the end of President Hoover's term he had already set up the Reconstruction Finance Corporation, and instituted the research committee which in 1933 published its report under the title of "Recent Social Trends". The development of the idea of governmental planning of large regions or of the economic life of a whole nation was influenced by the world war, by European developments in the aftermath, and by the idea of public works in the great depression.[1]

The Colorado River compact, under which seven States were to co-operate in a scheme for planned irrigation, water control and agricultural and industrial progress, was established in November 1922 and accepted by Congress in December 1928, and led to the construction of Boulder Dam.[2] In May 1923 the State of Pennsylvania began a survey of the problem of "giant power" (published in February 1925) to relate a power policy with industrial, farm and railroad development. In May 1923 the Legislature of New York State established the Commission of Housing and Regional Planning, with wide powers of research, to study housing needs and to prepare plans to meet them. In its final report[3] this Commission said: "These new forces that have come in to dominate the future may be left free to alter the present mould without direction and without control. They may be directed towards a more effective utilisation of all the resources of the State and thereby profoundly affect the future movement of population."

The outlook and words of the New York Commission as well as the report of the Niagara Frontier Planning Board, established on 9 April 1925, bear a close resemblance to the Message with which

---

[1] Cf. INTERNATIONAL LABOUR OFFICE: *Unemployment and Public Works* (Studies and Reports, Series C, No. 15, Geneva, 1931), and *Public Works Policy* (No. 19, Geneva, 1935).

[2] The method of solving the difficulties of the Colorado River States by interstate compact offers an interesting contrast to the establishment of the T.V.A. by Act of Congress. This subject is briefly discussed in Appendix IV.

[3] *Report of the Commission on Housing and Regional Planning*, State of New York, 7 May 1926, p. 11.

President Roosevelt submitted the T.V.A. Bill to Congress on 10 April 1933.[1] Mr. Roosevelt himself became responsible for problems of power development and land planning on election to the governorship of New York State in 1928. In January 1931, prior to the establishment of a land policy for the State, he inaugurated a State-wide survey, the principal purpose of which was to secure that "every acre of rural land . . . should be used only for that purpose for which it is best fitted and out of which the greatest economic return can be derived".

The depression had plunged the United States into widespread and bitter distress, all the more painful because the public institutions for dealing with unemployment and business failure were hardly developed in any of the States and were practically nonexistent in the Federal Government. Immediate and heroic measures were necessary. Both Senator Norris and Mr. Roosevelt, who became political associates during the Presidential campaign of 1932, believed in the planned use and development of national resources for the benefit of "the forgotten man". Mr. Roosevelt had spoken in favour of regulating electric power utilities by means of public ownership, of conservation and reafforestation.

After touring the Muscle Shoals area with Senator Norris and power and electricity experts in January 1933, he outlined the scope and particulars of his plans for the area to the press, describing the project as a great experiment, which might provide 200,000 jobs. He hoped that schemes similar to this, "the most interesting experiment a Government has ever undertaken", might be established in other areas. He believed that this multiple purpose project would be self-sustaining. "Hitherto", he said, "the Government has attacked the various factors in a piecemeal way. Now is the time, I feel, to tie up all the various developments into one great comprehensive plan within a given area."

At the time of the passage of the T.V.A. Act, the conflict of interests and political opinion was tempered by the universal perception that the Government must step in with public works in a situation where there was so much distress. The depth of that distress itself produced a notable degree of confidence in Government enterprise. Yet certain basic differences of opinion and traditional habits of mind still constituted an opposition, even if it were unexpressed, or temporarily held in reserve.

The Character and Purposes of the T.V.A.

The T.V.A. Act was passed on 18 May 1933. No single document expresses the spirit and nature of this enterprise better than

---

[1] Cf. p. 15.

President Roosevelt's Message of 10 April 1933, asking Congress
to pass the legislation:

The continued idleness of a great national investment in the Tennessee Valley
leads me to ask the Congress for legislation necessary to enlist this project in the
service of the people.

It is clear that the Muscle Shoals development[1] is but a small part of the
potential public usefulness of the entire Tennessee River. Such use, if envisioned
in its entirety, transcends mere power development; it enters the wide fields of
flood control, soil erosion, afforestation, elimination from agricultural use of
marginal lands, and distribution and diversification of industry; in short, this
power development of war days leads logically to national planning for a complete river watershed involving many States and the future lives and welfare of
millions. It touches and gives life to all forms of human concerns.

I therefore suggest to the Congress legislation to create a Tennessee Valley
Authority—a corporation clothed with the power of Government but possessed
of the flexibility and initiative of a private enterprise. It should be charged with
the broadest duty of planning for the proper use, conservation and development
of the natural resources of the Tennessee River drainage basin and its adjoining
territory for the general social and economic welfare of the Nation. This Authority should also be clothed with the necessary power to carry those plans into
effect. Its duty should be the rehabilitation of the Muscle Shoals development
and the co-ordination of it with the wider plan.

Many hard lessons have taught us the human waste that results from lack
of planning. Here and there a few wise cities and countries have looked ahead
and planned. But our Nation has "just grown". It is time to extend planning
to a wider field, in this instance comprehending in one great project many States
directly concerned with the basin of one of our greatest rivers.

This in a true sense is a return to the spirit and vision of the pioneer. If we
are successful here we can march on, step by step, in a like development of other
great natural territorial units within our borders.

In this Message to Congress, the concern for the social welfare
of the people of the Valley is evident, solid and genuine. There is
already included a prevision of achievement and of the kind of
governmental instrument necessary to its purposes. The Authority
came into practical being as soon as the Statute was passed; its
first corporate meeting was held on 16 June 1933.

It is an agency of the Federal Government of the United States
of America, established in the form of a corporation, governed by
a board of three directors[2], appointed by the President of the United
States with the advice and consent of the United States Senate.
Its organisation is peculiar, and especially interesting in that the

---

[1] Cf. p. 10.

[2] The first three directors were Mr. Arthur E. Morgan, a hydraulic engineer
and formerly President of Antioch College; Mr. Harcourt Morgan, an agricul-
turalist and President of the University of Tennessee, and Mr. David E. Lilienthal,
a lawyer and member of the Wisconsin Public Service Commission. The first-
named was chairman from the beginning of the Authority until his removal by
the President in 1938. Mr. Harcourt Morgan was chairman from 23 March 1938
to 15 Sept. 1941, when Mr. Lilienthal was appointed. The place of Mr. A. E.
Morgan on the Board was filled by the appointment of Mr. James P. Pope, a
former Senator, as a director on 12 January 1939.

corporation has a clear local responsibility and a given area of government, and is locally resident in the territory of its administration. It is not, like ordinary agencies of the United States Government, housed in Washington and responsible for a single sector of national life, but is responsible for multiple purposes and a complex of related resources as they concern the one particular region. It has considerable freedom of operation, naturally within limits fixed by the law, which specifies responsibility of various degrees to the Federal authority—that is, the President, some of the departments, and Congress. In order that it may the better attain its objectives, the Authority is, as will be seen, freer than the regular administrative departments from certain controls exercised by agencies within the administration branch itself and by Congress; but it is by no means entirely free. It reports to Congress; its accounts are "audited" by the Controller-General; its capital and operating expenses have, with small exceptions, been voted annually by Congress, and its financial procedure and operations have been settled by that body in considerable detail. It has of set democratic purpose co-operated with the States and the local units in the Valley, and also with the local branches of the Federal Government departments which have functions cognate to its own in order to avoid overlapping and to concentrate, for the Valley's benefit, the best technical assistance available. Further, although it was open to the Authority to carry out the development by giving contracts, it deliberately chose to work through its own direct labour force, thus making it an employer, at its highest peak, of something like 40,000 employees.[1]

The purposes and scope of the Authority's power are defined in the preamble to the Statute:

To improve the navigability and to provide for the flood control of the Tennessee River; to provide for reforestation and the proper use of marginal lands in the Tennessee Valley; to provide for the agricultural and industrial development of said Valley; to provide for the national defence by the creation of a corporation for the operation of Government properties at and near Muscle Shoals in the State of Alabama, and for other purposes.

The body of the Statute amplifies and specifies these powers. The Authority was given, first, direct executive power to construct dams and reservoirs in the river to provide a channel 9-foot deep; to promote navigability and flood control, bearing in mind the impact of the Tennessee on the Mississippi drainage basin; to operate the dams or reservoirs primarily for these purposes, and, consistently with them, to develop electric energy which might be

---

[1] Boulder Dam was built by the Six Companies, Inc., for the Bureau of Reclamation.

sold with preference to public bodies and co-operative organisations of citizens or farmers organised on a non-profit basis; to promote rural electrification; to make fertilisers and demonstrate improvements in farm economy; to furnish nitrogen for national defence. Secondly, in addition to this, the Authority was to have a planning power "to aid further the proper use, conservation and development of the natural resources of the Tennessee River drainage basin" and adjoining territory; and "to provide for the general welfare of the citizens of the said areas". But these were not direct planning powers; they depended on recommendations to the President of the United States who could then recommend the necessary measures to Congress. For the rest, the T.V.A. was to depend for its effectiveness on education and persuasion based on the value of its research and the assembling and furnishing of technical experts who could lead, guide and advise. In the exercise and interpretation of these and of other powers instrumental and incidental thereto, the activities of the Authority have been extended in breadth and detail.

As will be seen later, the spirit of enterprise in which this venture has been undertaken challenges the belief so persistently voiced that public authorities cannot be expected to show initiative, inventiveness, persistence and the technical capacity to master the problems involved in industrial and commercial undertakings. The Authority's own recognition of the responsibility for enterprise placed upon it, and its own perception of the kind of enterprise required are well stated in its Annual Report of 30 June 1936, under the heading "A New Kind of Pioneering":

To compress into a few words what the Authority is doing and is attempting to do, it may be said that the facilities of the controlled river are being used to release the energies of the people. The pioneer of a century and a half·ago could get his living from the new land with axe, rifle and plough. The pioneer of the present day has available a heretofore underdeveloped resource—the potentialities of running water—with which to secure in modern times the equivalent of what his ancestor found ready to hand in the late eighteenth or early nineteenth century. He must tame water so that it will not wash away his land or inundate his home; he must have it available when it is needed to carry his goods; he must take power from it to lighten his burdens and to turn an otherwise valueless rock into a valuable plant food. He must put back into his land, as his pioneer ancestor did not have to do, the equivalent of what he takes out of it.

. He cannot achieve all these things by individual effort but he can achieve them if he acts through his governmental agencies, national, State, and local, and in voluntary co-operation with his neighbours. The principle involved is not new: it is as old as the postal service, the army and the navy, or the pioneer custom of co-operative barn raising. The degree of common action now found necessary is not the result of a governmental mandate; it is determined by the nature and extent of the problem.

CHAPTER II

THE TAMING OF THE WATERWAY

All the powers and potentialities of the T.V.A. have their source in the dams and the chain of lakes made by them as they hold impounded the rains and the tributary waters.

The Authority's first and fundamental responsibility was to build the dams; its first problem was whether they should be low or high, for this involved the issue whether the generation of power should be included. In its 1930 survey[1] the Corps of Engineers of the United States Army had provided the basis of planning and operations upon which the Authority drew heavily. Two alternative plans were available, supported by the investigations and recommendations of the Engineers. One plan, which focussed its attention on navigable depth alone, provided for 32 low-lift dams that would provide a narrow navigable channel not nine, but about six feet deep. This would have had no value for flood control, would have subjected river traffic to erratic levels at the piers, and, of course, would have produced no electricity. The second plan envisaged the construction of seven high dams, which, together with those already existing at Wilson Dam, Lock No. 1, and Hales Bar, would give the depth required, and would have the additional advantages of flood control and of permitting the production of electric energy, as well as helping to regulate the navigable depths in the Lower Ohio and Mississippi Rivers. The Authority chose the latter alternative, although its estimated cost was very much higher.

Although the Authority emphasised navigation and flood control as its primary purposes and the production of electric power as incidental, there is no doubt whatever that the spirit of enterprise in the Authority, in the Chief Executive of the United States and in the legislators who had enacted the Statute was most powerfully moved by the very substantial electricity potentialities. Many nations, indeed, regard the latter as quite as appropriate a purpose of governmentally encouraged economic development as navigation, flood control, and fertiliser experiments, but it happened that under the American constitutional system such a development

---

[1] Cf. p. 7.

must be undertaken as incidental to interstate river control. All the powers assigned to the T.V.A. constitute a set of clearly integrated purposes, which are designed to, and actually do, help each other. Most of the immediate benefits to the Valley, however, must derive from the abundant hydroelectric power capable of being released by the Authority's activities.

Shortly after the passage of the Act, the President, by Executive Order[1], placed the construction of the first of the dams, Cove Creek (later known as Norris Dam), in the hands of Mr. A. E. Morgan, the first chairman of the Authority (and engineers under his direction), on the understanding that the work would be done by and through the Tennessee Valley Authority, that is to say, by its own labour force and engineers. Further, the Authority took over responsibility for the maintenance and operation of Wilson Dam, which had been constructed by the Army Engineers. Later, in October 1933, the construction of Wheeler Dam was transferred from the Army Engineers to the T.V.A. and the plans expanded by provision for the production of electric current, in order to increase employment.

Thus the Authority was launched on its career of taming the river. There may have been in the mind of the T.V.A. directors the unified plan which included the total number of dams required to satisfy the responsibilities imposed by the Statute. Congress had no such plan before it; it did not vote a lump sum of money at the beginning to cover such full development, but only a sum of $50,000,000 in the first year[2], and it required the Authority to come year by year for piecemeal appropriations, on each occasion justifying the steps foreseen. By 1935, the T.V.A. was clear in its own mind regarding the scope and magnitude of its task. Congress, however, which had by then lost some of its initial devotion to the purpose, demanded a long-term survey of the Authority's plans, and in an amendment to the Statute of that year directed that the Authority should report not later than 1 April 1936 its recommendations for the unified development of the Tennessee River System. In this report are outlined the chief problems to be faced by the Authority and its proposals for meeting them.

UNIFIED AND INTEGRATED BUILDING

The construction of a dam is not merely the problem of pouring so many tons of concrete into the river at a given place. A compre-

---

[1] Order of 8 June 1933. Section 17 of the Statute gave the power to construct Cove Creek to the Secretary of War or the Secretary of the Interior; but the President might direct either of them to employ such engineers as he designated.

[2] In fact, in the first and second years, T.V.A. appropriations were assigned by the President from a very large vote for emergency purposes.

hensive process of planning has to precede the decision where, when, and how to build. The multiple uses—navigation, flood control, electricity and malaria control by fluctuation of the water level—are in contest for the water of each and all the dams. The land which has to be bought may be very valuable for agricultural purposes; roads and railways may cross it, and cities and villages may be built on it. Hence, a balance of the economy to be produced by the dam must be struck against the economic waste caused by the inundation, and the site may perhaps have to be reconsidered. This means careful adjustment of site and level of the taking line, with the aid of air mapping and stream-flow prediction. In due order of time, the land must be surveyed and bought, and families, and even churches and cemeteries, must be relocated.

The T.V.A.'s policy has been to take its own labour force and equipment from dam to dam, and work of a similar kind must be so scheduled that equipment and men may go on in due progression from one dam to another. This requires a continuity of operation, and therefore a continuity of financing.

To take one example only, and that a medium work: Chickamauga Dam, completed on 15 July 1940, required the following operations:

Operation	Unit	Total
Dam construction		
Excavation (north embankment)	Cu. yd.	275,003
Earth fill (north embankment)	"	709,828
Excavation (south embankment)	"	507,475
Earth fill (south embankment and switch-yard)	"	1,628,586
Slope protection (crushed rock blanket and riprap)	"	270,853
Excavation (N. Chickamauga Creek Divers)	"	483,664
Excavation (lock, spillway and powerhouse)	"	467,530
Concrete (lock)	"	207,684
Concrete (spillway)	"	108,678
Concrete (intake, powerhouse, and misc.)	"	179,006
Foundation grouting (cement)	Cu. ft.	1,695,000
Land acquisition for reservoir	Acre	63,151
Preparing reservoir for impoundage	"	6,033
Highway adjustments	Mile	82
Railroad adjustments[1]	"	—
Utility adjustments	"	27
Cemetery removal	Grave	425
Family removal	Family	903

Height of dam: 129 feet.
Length of dam: 5,794 feet, including two earth embankments, totalling 4,384 feet, and 1,410 feet of concrete works.

[1] Small amount of slope-protection work only.

Making its plans in times of peace, the Authority had looked to the building of some ten dams by the end of 1943. But after 1939, and more especially after the entry into the war of the United States, the need for power for defence and war production (in particular, aluminium) caused the Federal Government, through

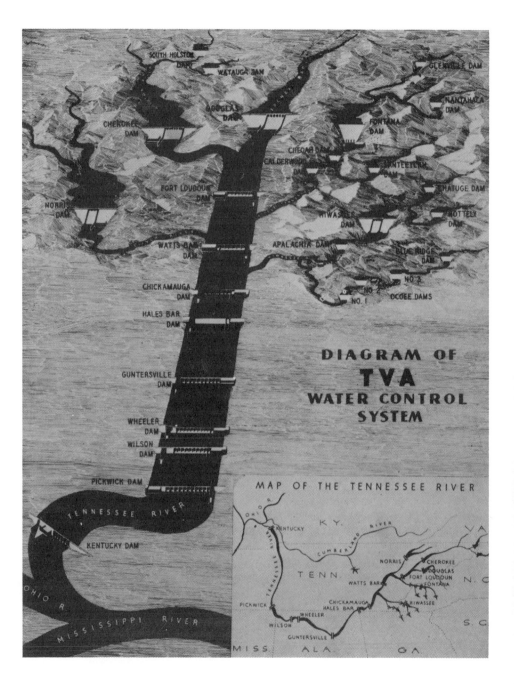

the War Production Board, the War Department and the Federal Power Commission, to propose additional responsibilities for the Authority in regard to rapidity of action and the building of steam plants, and led both to the speeding up of the execution of the Authority's unified plan and to the construction of additional dams outside the plan.

Purchases from the Tennessee Electric Power Company brought within the T.V.A.'s system Hales Bar Dam, Great Falls Dam on the tributary of the Cumberland, and three dams on the Ocoee River. Furthermore, five dams belonging to the Aluminum Company of America on the Little Tennessee River have been included in the operation of the T.V.A. system, though the ownership remains with the Company.

Thus, by 1943, the T.V.A. was master of the integrated operation of some 29 dams— 24 of its own, completed or nearing completion, and the five Alcoa dams under its control. A table showing the characteristics of the system of dams is given later.[1]

NAVIGATION

The part that a fully navigable Tennessee River would play in the inland waterway system of the United States was evidently a great one. The Authority foresaw that its work would be a contribution to the largest inland waterway system in the world, with the possible exception of the fully developed Amazon. The Valley area would be connected by 9-foot channels with Pittsburgh and cities on the Great Lakes, including Chicago, as well as with the Gulf ports. The possibility was constantly borne in mind of co-ordinating navigation on the Lower Tennessee with that on the Ohio, Cumberland and Wabash Rivers by a dam on the Ohio River at the mouth of the Cumberland, a dam across the Tennessee near its mouth, and a connecting channel between the Tennessee and Cumberland Rivers, so as to provide something over 550 miles of continuous navigable water on a single level. It was known that a patchwork development might never result in a completely navigable channel.

While the full 9-foot draught over the whole 652 miles of the river awaits the completion of all the main river dams about 1944, already in March 1943 there was a continuous and commercially useful channel from the mouth of the Tennessee River to Chattanooga, Tennessee, a distance of 464 miles. Below Chattanooga, a minimum depth of 6 feet was available throughout the year, and

---

[1] Cf. Appendix II, table II.

depths of 8 and 9 feet for a considerable portion of the time.[1] Commercial traffic on the river grew from approximately 22 million ton-miles in 1933 to 100 million ton-miles for the year 1941. Products such as wheat, pig iron, automobiles, petroleum, clay, iron, steel, timber, coal and coke, and more recently raw materials for armaments, were moving along the river deep into the Middle West.[2]

As soon as the Authority realised that its dam building progress was bringing it within measurable distance of traffic problems, it began to survey its responsibilities for the provision of terminal and other facilities for the exploitation of the new resources. Private companies became interested in industrial and terminal sites. The Authority took into consideration the problem of tolls at terminals and the conditions of leases for terminals, surveyed the area for possible users of the river, and carefully considered the joint questions of highways supplemental to the river and the arrangement of railway and other freight rates, which affected the exploitability of river transport. In 1938, there was established a Tennessee Valley Waterways Conference, representing the municipalities located on the river, and the Authority has supplied this Conference with research results which, it is expected, will ultimately lead to the arrangement of a unified system of terminals for public use. Traffic estimates have been made, and also attempts to ascertain the commerce that might be transported economically on various types of barge lines; and the T.V.A. collects and disseminates information for the use of public agencies and others interested in utilising the river. In 1940 the Authority undertook a traffic survey of 3,700 business concerns and other shippers and receivers of freight. It was estimated that in 1945 there might be some 2,600,000 tons of traffic on the river, with an annual saving on freight charges of about $3,450,000 and in 1960 some 6,173,000 tons, with a saving of $8,000,000.

FLOOD CONTROL

In planning the height and location of the dams, and therefore the water storage made possible by them, the Authority has looked back many decades for data on floods, in order to find some basis of prediction. The height of the floods at various points on the Tennessee and on the Mississippi are its index of the total amount of water to be held back, and of the points at which that water is to be impounded in order to benefit the threatened places immediately

---

[1] See table in *Hearings, House of Representatives*, Independent Offices Appropriation Bill for 1942, p. 448.
[2] The management of the river for navigation requires the Authority to make special silt studies, prepare navigation charts, and dredge the river.

50 inches of Rain in the Tennessee Valley
Controlled

Speeds Protective Cover Growth

Makes Deep River Channels

Generates Cheap Electricity

50 inches of Rain in the Tennessee Valley
Uncontrolled

Erodes Naked Lands

Floods Town and Country

Makes People Poor

below. Without entering into technicalities, it may be said that the Authority has successfully used the most efficient technical means, and has made a full appraisal of its responsibilities by means of thorough surveys of the Mississippi[1] in order to calculate how many million acre-feet of water taken from the river in flood will reduce the peak in terms of feet of water at various threatened points. The value of the Authority's flood control was first appreciated in 1936. In a flood in March 1936 it was estimated that Chattanooga had been saved some $750,000 by control operations at Norris Dam, and on four occasions in 1937 the Dam reduced flood heights around the same city by an amount varying between 3 and 5 feet. The desperately threatened city of Cairo, Illinois, which protected itself from the flood by mud-boxes on top of the flood wall, was probably saved a loss of some $15,000,000 by the operations of the T.V.A., which reduced the crest of the flood by almost half a foot and thus prevented the dyke from breaking. There were similar benefits all along the river.

In the middle of 1936, when calculating the probable value against costs of the Gilbertsville (now the Kentucky) Dam, the largest of all the Authority's projects, the T.V.A. made a study of the value to the alluvial valley of the Mississippi, from Cairo to the Gulf, of the reduction of flood heights by 2 feet.[2] If a 2-foot measure of reduction were secured, there would then be a 3-foot margin on the levees.[3] A very wide survey was made of all the properties liable to flood damage—cities, railways, highways, unprotected marginal areas, backwater areas, floodways, protected agricultural areas—and allowances were made for levee maintenance and the reduction of damage from seepage. Widespread discussions were undertaken with all the groups concerned, public and private, Federal and local. Calculations based on various reasonable criteria showed that the reduction of flood height by 2 feet could be reasonably appraised at a capital cost of something over $380,000,000, to which the T.V.A.'s contribution by the Kentucky Dam was conservatively estimated at the value of $200,000,000. In the light of subsequent floods in 1937 the calculations were amply confirmed. There is no doubt whatever about the remarkable contribution, present and future, of the Authority to the control of floods in this river system. How much the effect of each dam depends on the cumulative effect of all the dams may be seen from the T.V.A.'s

---

[1] For technical details, cf. 76th Congress, 1st Session, House Document No. 455: *Presidential Message on Value of Flood Height Reduction from T.V.A. Reservoirs.*
[2] *Ibid.*
[3] The levee is the time-honoured method of banking back the waters. There are 1,600 miles of levees along the Mississippi. They actually force upwards the flood heights.

chief engineer's statement in 1939 that with half the total money spent only 15 to 20 per cent. of the flood control expected had so far been obtained.[1]

DEVELOPMENT OF ELECTRICITY OPERATIONS

The development of the electricity operations of the T.V.A. is reserved for full treatment in subsequent chapters, but it is relevant at this point to draw attention to two direct consequences of the construction programme: (a) the magnitude of the installed electric capacity, and (b) the great economies which come about through the complementary operation of the T.V.A.'s system of dams, mainly hydroelectric power, and the steam-generating plants of the private producers who are neighbours of the T.V.A.

With regard to the first point, by the middle of 1943 the T.V.A. had in service some 1,640,000 kilowatt capacity, including steam plants; and on completion of the work authorised it would have some 2,846,000 kilowatt capacity[2] of which about a quarter would be steam-generated. With regard to the second, several arrangements have been made to achieve maximum utilisation of power resources. The steam plants are not as heavily burdened by demand at night and on Sundays as during the day and can produce surplus energy. The T.V.A. takes some of the surplus steam energy and so can reduce generation at its plants, and meanwhile impound substantial amounts of water in its reservoirs for subsequent use. This is particularly important as the opportunity of impounding water is variable, for the river is "flashy". In times of heavy demand this impounded water can be released to meet the requirements of both steam and hydro systems. The result is that steam units with interruptable supply can be assisted; economies are possible in breakdown, in emergency reserves; less plant has to be used because the call on each plant is diversified, and there is provision of emergency service in case of flood. Of course, this complementary operation adds to the difficulty of managing the three main purposes of the system of dams. An electric "grid" of considerable importance is therefore being constructed. A 154 kw. double circuit transmission line, 175 miles long, constitutes the most important tie between the major systems of the north and of the south. It is capable of transferring from one area to another as much as 200,000 kilowatts.

---

[1] The most recent development in flood control is a report made by the Authority concerning the protection of Asheville and the Upper French Broad River Valley, proposing storage reservoirs supplemented by a levee. No power production is feasible. The scheme would cost something over $8,000,000 and the tangible benefits (i.e., increased values of land and other property owing to security) were estimated at a total of $9,000,000.

[2] But some installations were held in abeyance by the War Production Board in order to divert materials to other war uses.

MANAGEMENT OF THE SEVERAL PURPOSES

According to the Statute (Section 9a), the storage of the unified system of lakes formed by the dams must serve three principal purposes, of which navigation and flood control are primary, and the production of electricity incidental. The latter is only legally possible in so far as it is incidentally compatible with the first two. This threefold responsibility in water control operations requires the most careful and considered planning.[1] For one thing, the stored water must be released down the length of the river at the dry season of the year when the natural pools are low in order to maintain the navigable draught, and this involves previous storage. To allow for flood control, the waters must be held back at some times, and released in the intervals between the crests of the flood. Furthermore, in order to secure a substantial basic generation of firm electric power with the maximum use of equipment and continuity of supply, the impoundments of water must be spilled off through the turbines accordingly.[2] Finally, the management of the river is further complicated by the need to vary the level of the river periodically in order to destroy mosquito larvae and thus prevent malaria; this involves notifying and consulting in advance various interests affected by the raising and lowering of the river.

In the process of thus managing the several purposes, a fundamental stage is the prediction of rainfall. This is one example of the co-operative arrangements which the T.V.A. makes with other governmental agencies. In this case the United States Weather Bureau furnishes the T.V.A. with predictions of rainfall, and the United States Geological Survey co-operates with the T.V.A. in the maintenance of an extensive network of rain and stream-gauging stations, furnishing daily reports.

---

[1] The Authority set up the appropriate internal committee arrangements to fulfil its obligations. Since 1937, responsibility for controlling the operation of the reservoirs has been delegated to its Water Control Planning Department, subject to the approval of the chief engineer. Cf. "Multiple Purpose Reservoir Operation", by N. W. BOWDEN, Principal Hydraulic Engineer, T.V.A., in *Civil Engineering*, May-June 1941.

[2] A spilling of water may mean a loss of power, and consequently some of the T.V.A.'s power sales are "secondary", *i.e.*, liable to interruption; some is actually "dump" power, to be sold at any price, since water must be released.

CHAPTER III

MAKING ELECTRICITY AND ACQUIRING MARKETS

When, in 1933, the Tennessee Valley Authority began operations, it was in possession of the power facilities at Wilson Dam and the steam plant at Muscle Shoals. In the course of the first year of its operation, the Authority disposed of 395,842,000 kilowatt hours, mainly by sales. In the year 1942, it sold 5,983,369,534 kilowatt hours, the product of 18 dams and 12 steam plants. In 1933, its revenue from power sales was $833,669; in 1942 it was $25,214,207. It is important to observe that the sales of 1933 had less than doubled by 1938—up to that year the T.V.A. had a financial deficit[1]—and that only from the year 1939 was there the beginning of a very sharp expansion to the considerable total and profits of 1942. Naturally, the chief explanation of this gradual development to 1939 lies in the rate of completion of the dams supplying electric power[2], but contributory factors were the retarding effect of litigation, and the time required to develop organisational momentum. The expansion in the course of some eight years must be regarded as truly remarkable, seeing that the Authority leapt from a very small start to being one of the five largest electricity concerns in the whole United States.

The principal problems confronting the T.V.A. were: (1) the establishment of a policy, especially in relation to the power companies already in the field; (2) the elimination of legal obstacles; (3) the securing of direct access to customers by its own transmission system; (4) encouragement of the acquisition of the local markets by municipalities and co-operatives; (5) the pursuit of a power sales policy, taking into account considerations of price, control on resale by its own distributors, and consumer education. The practical solution of these problems was a most exacting task successfully carried out against heavy opposition. Development is reviewed below in relation to each of these problems, one by one, though it must be remembered that they can only be severed in theory, since all of them together, in varying measure, confronted the Authority from the moment it began operations.

---

[1] Cf. the Annual Reports of the T.V.A.; and Appendix III, table III, 1.
[2] Cf. Appendix III, table III, 2.

THE ESTABLISHMENT OF A POLICY

The T.V.A. had very ample scope in its programme of power utilisation development, since the average consumption of electricity in its area was about 600 kilowatt-hours per residential customer, and only in a few places had a keen promotional policy been followed. The Tennessee Valley had 4.1 electric lights in farms compared with the United States average of 13.4 in farms. Considerable powers to generate electricity and sell the surplus, after the fulfilment of certain obligations, were given to the Authority. Once it has provided for navigation and controlling floods, it may go on to generating electricity; and when its own need for electricity has been satisfied, the surplus may be sold. The Authority was faced by at least two great difficulties: first, it operated in an area served by many utility companies and faced severe competition; and, secondly, there was the possibility that the powers vested in it by the Statute in respect of electricity were unconstitutional, and therefore liable to challenge and perhaps to invalidation, at the instance of the utility companies. Both of these factors retarded the Authority's progress.

However, the Authority attacked its first problem, that of general policy, immediately, and by August 1933 it had produced a policy, which included the following points[1]:

(1) The business of generating and distributing electric power is a public business.

(2) Private and public interests in the business of power are of a different kind and quality and should not be confused.

(3) The interest of the public in the widest possible use of power is superior to any private interest. Where the private interest and this public interest conflict, the public interest must prevail.

(4) Where there is a conflict between public interest and private interest in power which can be reconciled without injury to the public interest such reconciliation should be made.

(5) The right of a community to own and operate its own electric plant is undeniable. This is one of the measures which the people may properly take to protect themselves against unreasonable rates. Such a course of action may take the form of acquiring the existing plant or setting up a competing plant as circumstances may dictate.

(6) The fact that action by the Authority may have an adverse economic effect upon a privately owned utility should be a matter for the serious consideration of the Board in framing and executing its power programme. But it is not the determining factor. The most important considerations are the furthering of the public interest in making power available at the lowest rate consistent with sound financial policy, and the accomplishment of the social objectives which low-cost power makes possible. The Authority cannot decline to take action solely upon the ground that to do so would injure a privately owned utility.

---

[1] *Annual Report*, 1934, p. 24.

Points 7 and 8 express the Authority's intention initially to confine itself to certain regions, including large and small cities, and later to go outside this area if the privately owned utilities in the area did not co-operate in the working out of the programme, or wherever special considerations, like unreasonably high rates for service and failure to protect the public interest, so required. The statement of policy then proceeds as follows:

(9) Every effort will be made by the Authority to avoid the construction of duplicate physical facilities or wasteful competitive practices. Accordingly, where existing lines of privately owned utilities are required to accomplish the Authority's objectives, as outlined above, a genuine effort will be made to purchase such facilities from the private utilities on an equitable basis.

(10) Accounting should show detail of costs and permit a comparison of operations with privately owned plants to supply a "yardstick" and an incentive to both private and public managers.

(11) The accounts and records of the Authority, as they pertain to power, would always be open to inspection by the public.

The Authority immediately set to work in accordance with its policy to market the power produced at Wilson Dam. It made contracts with the Commonwealth and Southern Corporation and its subsidiaries in Alabama, Tennessee, Georgia and Mississippi. At this stage, the power distribution programme of the Authority was carried out by agreement, mainly over the transmission lines of private power systems. The Authority quickly proceeded to the construction of its own transmission system. Forms of contract were worked out with the distribution system, relating to the rates for wholesale supply by the Authority, and the detailed conditions under which the contractor was required to sell the electricity to consumers and to conduct his concern financially and otherwise. The Authority proceeded also to the encouragement of local co-operative power associations in various areas, large and small, as self-governing non-profit corporations.

THE ELIMINATION OF LEGAL OBSTACLES

By the middle of 1934, the power companies realised that the T.V.A. intended to go beyond the generation of electricity and its sale to themselves, and that it regarded with favour the desire of local communities either to purchase a private utility's distribution facilities, or to set up one in competition. They therefore took the stand, first, that it was impossible to sell any part of their own systems without making the remainder uneconomic; and, secondly, that if the Authority could not purchase the whole of their systems on terms satisfactory to them, they would enjoin fulfilment of certain contracts made by the Authority with cities and companies, on the grounds that the T.V.A. Statute was unconstitutional.

In 1934, five suits were pending against the Authority. Among them were an appeal to the Alabama Public Service Commission by coal and ice companies to invalidate the T.V.A. contracts with the Alabama Power Company; another to enjoin the Tennessee Public Service Company from selling properties around Knoxville to the T.V.A. Soon other companies followed suit. They sought, and some obtained, injunctions restraining financial aid by grants and loans from the Federal Emergency Administration of Public Works, popularly known as the Public Works Administration[1], to cities seeking to purchase or construct power plants. Some alleged false representations, attempted boycotts, and unfair competition by the T.V.A. One suit sought restraint of a city from contracting to purchase electricity from the T.V.A. The city of Knoxville itself had voted in March 1936 to construct its own system and purchase from the T.V.A.: it was enjoined. It was in the midst of such opposition[2] which gravely slowed up its operations and involved considerable financial expenses and loss that the Authority proceeded. But the Authority was upheld by the courts in a series of judgments culminating in complete vindication of its powers and the constitutionality of the Statute in 1939 in the case known as "The 18 Companies Case" (*Tennessee Electric Power Co.* vs. *T.V.A.*).[3]

---

[1] The work of this agency terminated on 30 June 1938.

[2] The Authority's operations were much retarded and its expenses increased by litigation. To 30 June 1938, the T.V.A. had been attacked on constitutional grounds in 41 cases, of which 22 were primarily against municipalities or co-operatives. Direct defence expenses amounted to $518,159; wholesale power revenues lost by delay amounted to nearly $5,500,000, and consumers' losses, from not buying at the T.V.A.'s low rates, are estimated at $7,702,100. Cf. 76th Congress, 1st Session, Senate Document, No. 56, *Report of the Joint Committee Investigating the Tennessee Valley Authority*, 1939, pp. 65-66.

[3] The details of the litigation are of interest only in relation to the Constitution of the United States, and would have little bearing on conditions that might arise elsewhere. Readers interested in this aspect of the T.V.A.'s development may be referred to the relevant literature. Here, however, two points need mentioning. First, the courts upheld (a) the T.V.A.'s encouragement of municipalities and co-operatives in seeking to set up their own distribution systems; (b) the T.V.A.'s co-operation with the municipalities and the Public Works Administration to secure the offer of grants by the latter to the municipalities and co-operatives to enable them to set up their own distribution systems (by the time the court was seized with the case in the autumn of 1938, the P.W.A. had made contracts and allotments for loans and grants to 23 municipalities in Alabama, Mississippi and Tennessee, amounting to about $14 million for the construction of municipal systems); (c) the legality of the acts of the T.V.A. regarding their statutory basis; (d) the constitutionality of statutes establishing and empowering the T.V.A.; (e) the legality of the generation of electricity at T.V.A. dams and the consistency thereof with navigation, flood control and national defence; and (f) the propriety and constitutionality of the T.V.A.'s methods of disposing of its electricity. The principal cases were *Ashwander* vs. *T.V.A.*, 297, U.S. 288 (1936); *Tennessee Electric Power Co.* vs. *T.V.A.*, 21F, Supp. 947 (1938); and 306 U.S. 118 (1939). Cf. H. N. MARTELL: "Legal Aspects of the T.V.A.", in *George Washington Law Review*, 1939, pp. 983-1012.

Direct Transmission to Customers

At the beginning, the Authority necessarily sold a large volume of its power to the great private power companies in the vicinity who owned transmission lines and practically all the local distribution facilities: the Alabama Power Company, the Georgia Power Company, the Tennessee Electric Power Company and the Mississippi Power Company. In the fiscal year ending 30 June 1936, for instance, the power sold by the Authority at Wilson Dam went in the following proportions to the various customers:

	Per cent. of total power sales
Municipalities	6.4
Co-operative associations	3.8
Electric utilities	88.5
Industries	—
Direct sales	1.3
Total	100.00

Now, the fulfilment of the Authority's policy of making abundant electricity available at low prices depended upon its ability directly to serve the final distributing agencies. Its necessary procedure therefore came to be, first, to build and acquire its own transmission lines, to avoid becoming dependent on one or two large private companies (mainly the Alabama Power Company) which would then have been in a monopolistic position.[1] The policy of ownership of its own transmission system was also beneficial because any economies effected in costs could be transmitted to the public in prices; and in fact, the T.V.A., by its own independent research work, was able to produce and itself install rural lines much more cheaply than business had hitherto done, yet providing perfectly adequate and reliable service.

Municipal and Co-operative Undertakings

The fullest beneficial development of T.V.A. power operations could be achieved only if the T.V.A. were assured of the local markets, that is to say, if distribution in the cities were under municipal management, and in the rural areas under the co-operatives. Pursuant to this view, the T.V.A. was friendly to these bodies, even to the point of assisting them to acquire distribution systems of their own, though these might compete with the existing

---

[1] The effect of this factor may be observed in sales in 1935. Cf. Appendix III, table III, 2, A.

private distribution systems—not that the T.V.A. pursued a policy of duplicating, but there definitely was a conflict of interest. This was ultimately resolved by the T.V.A. system acquiring, in various ways and by agreement, the distribution systems of the whole area. It should be remembered that the Statute required the authority to sell its power to States, counties, municipalities and non-profit organisations in that order of priority, and individual citizens and other consumers were the residuary purchasers only after these had been satisfied. To implement this stipulation, the Authority lent its good offices to the movement for public acquisition and for the establishment of rural non-profit organisations.

Certain consequential problems then arose, especially that of the financing of the undertakings required by the cities and the co-operatives. As for the former, there were loans and grants from the Public Works Administration; as for the latter, the Rural Electrification Administration (established in Washington by the Federal Government), provided a large proportion of the capital required. This question is discussed at greater length in a later chapter.[1] Here it may merely be said that up to 30 June 1942, of the approximately $90 million required, public bonds had provided about two thirds, loans from the R.E.A. about one fifth, loans made by the T.V.A. about one twentieth, and the P.W.A. and the W.P.A. one tenth.

The Power Sales Policy

By 1938, the removal of all legal obstacles opened out wide possibilities to the Authority. Thereafter it proceeded, in co-operation with the Public Works Administration, and by negotiation with one utility after another, to acquire both transmission properties and outlets for sale.[2] By 1941, the Authority had become almost wholly responsible for the generation and transmission of electric power in Tennessee, and in considerable parts of Mississippi, Alabama and Georgia. The successive stages of this purchase policy and the acquisition of ever more customers is set out in a table, showing the growth of the T.V.A.'s capacity, the growth of the transmission system, the number of public agencies acting as distributors, customers, etc. The net result was the increase in the

---

[1] Cf. Chapter XII.

[2] The largest single purchase was from the Tennessee Electric Power Company, a subsidiary of the Commonwealth and Southern system. The Company sold to the Authority, municipalities and co-operatives, for $78,600,000, a system covering 140,000 customers in the two great cities of Nashville and Chattanooga and in 23 smaller cities and 11 co-operatives. Included in the properties acquired were five dams (cf. Chapter II, p. 21) and a number of steam plants, though the Courts have never pronounced on the constitutionality of the T.V.A.'s producing power by steam generation.

sale of kilowatt hours from less than half a million in 1934 to nearly 6,000,000 in 1942; the increase of retail customers from about 6,000 to nearly 500,000; while 5,000 miles of transmission lines and 5,000 miles of rural lines had been installed by the T.V.A. A more complete and exact display of the T.V.A.'s growth in terms of its capacity, customers, distribution systems, etc., is to be found in Appendix III, table III, 2.

The Authority proceeded in its quest for a market with energy because it wished, as it said in its Annual Report of 1936, to apply the principles of mass production and consumption to this problem in the Valley, in a way which had proved successful in a number of private industries in the United States. It saw that the essential element in mass production was a progressive decrease in unit cost—the more items produced, the less the cost of each item; and in the matter of electricity there was still abundant possibility of decreasing costs and increasing consumption, although private enterprise in the field of electricity supply appeared to be unwilling to make drastic cuts in advance of wider use. Nor was this all. The spirit inspiring the T.V.A. Statute was concern for the rural population. Here was a possibility of doing the maximum amount of good in terms of improving the ease and comfort of farm families, both in their living and in their productive activities, and it was precisely here that the private utilities, owing to the trouble involved and small rate of return, had been disinclined to attempt to develop their business, and thereby the countryside. Indeed, by 1936, analysis of operations by nine municipal and co-operative systems procuring power from the T.V.A. had verified the T.V.A.'s conviction that a drop in price, the use of what in England is called "promotional rate", did in fact promote higher consumption and better revenues.

Breaking the Vicious Circle of High Prices and Low Consumption

Since the war of 1914–1918, many electricity systems have experimented with a variety of rates and methods of charge, with the idea of developing the maximum use of electricity, which in itself leads to a consequential reduction of electricity rates. The T.V.A., uninhibited by certain financial considerations which affect private enterprise in electricity and which had certainly retarded progress in the Tennessee Valley, undertook from the beginning a policy of daring reduction of rates, confident on the basis of its own estimates that the results aimed at would be achieved. Resale prices, therefore, were proposed to the municipalities and other public agencies taking electricity from the Authority, which many critics believed to be either ruinous or subsidised. In fact they were neither, and when the period of litigation had been successfully passed and the Authority had a free run, so that there was no artificial limitation on the demand for its product, the wisdom of its resale policy became evident. An enormously increased consumption followed; the consumers benefited from the very large reduction of rates; and the municipalities and other public agencies, especially the urban agencies, were able to make handsome surpluses. Furthermore, the influence of the Authority's policy was clearly visible on the companies in the vicinity and elsewhere, for they adopted a cognate policy with the same results, namely, reductions in price and considerable increases in consumption with an accompanying increase in profits.

This result was achieved by the combination of two forces: careful attention to cost of production, and diligent promotion of sales. In regard to the cost of production, the Authority could organise the building of dams and the installation of generating machinery to secure the maximum economies on a long-term basis, thanks to its scheme of unified development permitting of the continuous use of equipment and labour experience on successive dams.

INDUSTRIAL SALES

The policy of the Authority in connection with the sale of power and encouragement of the use of electricity in the area presents interesting features, of special importance in the development of a backward area. The figures of kilowatt hour sales for 1942 show that municipalities take 39.2 per cent., co-operatives 4.7 per cent., temporary rural requirements 0.1 per cent. (for dam reservations, or pending co-operative or municipal operation), industrial customers 40.3 per cent., private utilities 11.0 per cent., interdepartmental deliveries 4.5 per cent., and sales to governmental agencies 0.1 per cent. A similar analysis made in 1938 would have shown a strikingly large percentage of deliveries to industrial consumers—a little over 50 per cent.—especially in comparison with those consumers given preference by the Statute, of whom municipalities took only 9 per cent. and co-operatives just under 5 per cent. The Statute, however, empowers the Authority to sell to industrial consumers, on the sound basis of improving the system load factor; and until the development of municipal and co-operative markets reaches the stage of complete absorption of the T.V.A.'s power, not only will the Authority benefit by selling to industrial users, but the municipalities and co-operatives must also benefit as a result of a more economical use of the Authority's properties. Also the economic life of the whole nation benefits by the lowering of manufacturers' production costs made possible by selling power which would otherwise go to waste.

The T.V.A. began selling to industrial consumers in May 1936, but not substantially until 1937. Industrial contracts vary in term from five to twenty years, with provisions for options and cancellations by either side. The companies are given terms reasonably designed to safeguard their capital investment. Up to the time of the war, the public agencies entitled to preference had never suffered shortages from the sales to industrial customers, at any rate, at the price at which the T.V.A. was able to supply. The new war demands were so large that the T.V.A., as already noticed, was spurred on by the Defense Departments and authorised by Congress to produce more power.[1] The Congressional Joint Committee Investigating the T.V.A. of 1938-1939[2] reported that although there had been charges that the T.V.A. had been unduly favourable to the industrial customers, the charges were absurd, and concluded that the rates and contracts conformed with the requirements of the T.V.A. and were advantageous to the Authority. The problem does still remain, however, whether the T.V.A. would not have had much more of the supply taken up by various "public, non-profit" customers, for example, rural co-operatives, if it had been able to charge lower than cost. Universal experience of electric supply shows the extreme difficulty of defining cost to any particular customer, yet the T.V.A. Statute requires supply at not lower than cost.[3]

CONTROLLED RESALE RATES

The Authority sells at wholesale rates, and these are the rates most closely related to its own cost of production and transmission

---

[1] Cf. Chapter II, p. 21. This was accomplished not by legislation adding to or amending T.V.A. powers, but by means of further financial provision in the annual and supplementary appropriations.

[2] Cf. Chapter XII.

[3] There are two stipulations in the Statute which, all in all, permit considerable elasticity of selling policy, so that rates favourable to rural co-operative development would seem to be well within the power of the Authority. Thus, Section 14 says: "To make the power projects self-supporting and self-liquidating, the surplus power shall be sold at rates which, in the opinion of the Board, when applied to the normal capacity of the Authority's power facilities, will produce gross revenues in excess of the cost of production of said power . . . ". Secondly, Section 11 of the Statute requires "that the projects herein provided for shall be considered primarily as for the benefit of the people of the section as a whole and particularly the domestic and rural consumers to whom the power can economically be made available, and accordingly that sale to and use by industry shall be a secondary purpose, to be utilised principally to secure a sufficiently high load factor and revenue returns which will permit domestic and rural use at the lowest possible rates and in such manner as to encourage increased domestic and rural use of electricity".

to the points at which municipalities, co-operatives and industrial consumers can take the power over into their own distribution systems. But, as the T.V.A. observed in a very early Annual Report, by far the greater part of the cost of electricity in the home and on the farm consisted of costs of distribution.[1] If the benefits of the Authority's operation in the Valley were to be passed on to the consumer, therefore, the contract offered by the T.V.A. must state the resale rates.   Hence, the T.V.A. contracts provide certain standard resale rates estimated by the Authority to be reasonable on its analysis of costs of distribution, with lower rates as the earnings of the distributors increase.   A definite procedure is laid down in the contract for the disposal of surplus revenues, the basic principle being that the distribution of electricity will be conducted without profit to any one except the ultimate consumer. The contracts make provision for operating expenses and fixed charges, including, of course, the properly regulated repayment of the debt incurred in the purchase or building of the system, the remaining surplus to be applied to (a) the construction of extensions, (b) repayment of debt before contracted maturity, with the consent of the T.V.A., and (c) further reductions in rates. As the T.V.A. says in its Annual Report of 1941, "These provisions assure retail customers in the Tennessee Valley that the rates they pay will continue to be among the lowest in the nation".

ENCOURAGING SALES

The weightiest factor in the remarkable expansion of the T.V.A. electricity sales was the promotional policy adopted, which brought home to a rather poor, suspicious and fairly unsophisticated body of people, especially in the rural area, the advantages of electricity to the point of inducing them to set up distribution systems and to make contracts committing themselves to purchase so much electricity over a number of years.   This was less necessary in regard to the cities than to rural areas; first, because practically all the cities had electricity, even though they did not own their own distribution systems; and secondly, because the use of electricity for lighting, for the radio, for cooking, and for various home and workshop appliances was well known. In the cities the problem was chiefly whether the citizens could raise their civic spirit to the point of taking action for their own benefit in terms of price and consumption—that is, of establishing their own distribution systems. But in the rural areas a vastly different problem confronted

---

[1] See also H. FINER: *Municipal Trading* (London, 1941), for comparative British experience.

the Authority. Congress had directed it "to promote and encourage the fullest possible use of electric light and power on farms . . . (and) to construct transmission lines to farms and small villages that are not otherwise supplied with electricity at reasonable rates". Furthermore, the President had devolved upon the Authority the responsibility for seeking ways of developing the resources of the Valley and contributing by studies, experiments and demonstrations towards the general welfare of the area.

When the T.V.A. began operations, it found that in 1933 only one farm in 28 received electric service. By 1939, one farm in 7, and at the end of 1940 one in 6, was taking electricity. This important change has come about by reason of four things: the establishment of electric co-operatives, the development of low-cost rural lines, the financing of the co-operatives by the Rural Electrification Administration[1], and the adoption of electric retail rates no higher for rural than for urban consumers. The T.V.A. has taken its responsibility to the rural population very seriously indeed. The fact that one of its directors is a local man is not without importance in this regard. The Authority recognises the value of rural life as a social factor; that the drudgery of the farm and its low income may cause a further drift towards the cities; and that the latest gifts of science and technology ought to be used in order to lighten and make more productive the toil of the farmer.

However, if one farm in six now has electricity, five out of six still have not. It is an issue of public importance whether lower charges and more sales to the rural population would not have been more justifiable than the large sales to industry, even though the latter is in a position (though not compelled) to pass on the benefits of its own reduced costs of power supplied by this great public enterprise.

The T.V.A. had to make the farmers electricity-conscious, and to induce them to form rural electric co-operatives. In order to avoid legal obstacles to development, the Authority, assisted by the Rural Electrification Administration, drafted legislation for the purpose of permitting co-operative electrical associations on a non-profit membership basis to come into existence. The States of Mississippi, Alabama, Tennessee and Georgia soon passed the necessary legislation. The Authority then proceeded to interest

---

[1] This organisation was set up by the Federal Government in 1935 to assist the development of electrification in rural areas all over the United States. Its funds are drawn from Congressional appropriations and it is currently lending money to co-operatives at about 2.46 per cent., with guarantees and conditions of repayment suited to each individual project. For example, the R.E.A. requires each member of the co-operative to lay down a membership fee of $5, and that all easements shall have been obtained, or permission for rights of way promised. For a more detailed discussion of its activities, cf. Chapter VII.

the social and political leaders and the officials of the counties in which it was proposed to set up co-operatives. The newspapers in the area carried information regarding the electricity operations of the T.V.A. At least as effective a contribution was made by the county extension agents[1] and assistant county agents of the United States Department of Agriculture; the fact that they move about the area in their business of encouraging agricultural improvement, gives them easy access to present their views. At a certain point, it was suggested that a meeting of all the interested parties should be called, at which T.V.A. officials would explain the rights and obligations, the rates of wholesale purchase and retail resale. On the Authority's side, there must be regard for the number of consumers and the density of the area covered by the co-operatives. The co-operatives vary from 700 to some 2,000 residential and commercial customers together.

The local co-operative association is composed of a number of consumers and these elect their own board of directors, numbering 5 or 7, or 15, and voluntary officers consisting of a president, vice-presidents, secretaries and treasurer, for the most part unpaid. Each association appoints and pays an attorney and a project superintendent. The R.E.A. requires the submission of the proposed officials for approval, in order that it may secure the appointment of the most competent, or at least be able to give counsel as to where competent people could be obtained.

In order that a co-operative may not be rashly established, the T.V.A. provides instructions in what it calls its Rural Electrification Survey Plan. By following these, its officials can discover whether there will be an adequate and sufficiently persistent demand to repay the costs of the rural electric distribution lines and the day-by-day supply of current. They are instructed that the mere use of electricity on the farm for light and radio will be insufficient to provide a profitable distribution system. The Authority's regulations and instructions guide in considerable detail the discussion of local possibilities, in order that there may be no mistake on either side as a result of eagerness on the part of T.V.A. officials for additional business, and on the part of the co-operative for a new toy, a new pleasure, or an insubstantial bargain. When the local voluntary canvassers, working under the chairman of the committee elected locally, make their tabulation of likely customers, this is checked by the appropriate employee of the T.V.A., the feasibility is determined, and the location of lines is mapped. The Authority has to consider the economic capacity of the district, the rates

---

[1] For the "Extension System", cf. Chapter IV.

which ought to be charged, and the question of rights of way for the lines. At one time, the contracts division of the T.V.A. Department of Power Utilisation made a survey of the proposition; more recently, the T.V.A. and the Rural Electrification Administration have set general standards for area-wide projects, and surveys are made in accordance with them in the same manner as before.

T.V.A. POWER CONTRACTS

The T.V.A., as already indicated, makes a power contract with the co-operative. Such contracts are standard. As the Statute requires, they hold for a maximum of 20 years. They provide for a wholesale rate and binding resale rates. Amortisation is stipulated. Until recently, the Rural Electrification Administration began to collect the repayment of debt 18 months after the first loan, and stipulated 38 half-yearly payments until the debt was liquidated. On recent loans interest payments are delayed for 30 months, and amortisation payments for 48 months, in order to give the co-operative more time to develop sales and revenues. In the course of time, the T.V.A. and the R.E.A. have learned to collaborate and participate in loans, and they work closely together.

The T.V.A. power contract (whether the T.V.A. or R.E.A. finances the loan) contains further conditions for the payment by the distributor of all current operating expenses, including (a) salaries, wages, cost of materials and supplies, taxes, power at wholesale, and insurance; (b) the payment of interest and amortisation; (c) reserves for replacements, new construction, contingencies, and a reasonable amount of cash working capital. Any surplus is then permitted to serve as a basis for the reduction or elimination of amortisation charges and surcharges to consumers, and thereafter of rates; or, if the T.V.A. consents, the co-operative may use all or part of the surplus to purchase or retire the system's debt before maturity. The T.V.A. requires an annual report under a system of accountancy established by the Federal Power Commission, and such additional information as it may from time to time reasonably request. At least two years before the expiration of the contract the T.V.A. agrees to enter into negotiations for renewal or extension. The T.V.A. establishes instruments for measuring demand, energy and power factors. It has the right to inspect any installation before electricity is introduced or later, and may reject any wiring or equipment not in accordance with reasonable standards. The co-operative is responsible for the T.V.A.'s property which is part of its operating system. The Authority lays down the details of financial and accounting policy and renders such advisory accounting service in setting up and administering the accounts as it thinks reasonable. The co-operatives furnish monthly statements to the Authority, and are obliged to allow its inspectors to have free access at all reasonable times to the books and records of the electricity system operations.

The foregoing rules for the administration of the co-operatives are practically identical with those for the municipalities which buy their power from the T.V.A. The chief difference is that, whereas the co-operative must pay a property tax on its distribution system to its county or State, the city treasury receives the equivalent of the State, county, and *ad valorem* tax from the municipal electricity department. The latter may pay into the city treasury' an amount not exceeding 6 per cent. on the municipality's actual investment in the electric system.[1]

The T.V.A. keeps continuous contact of an advisory character with both municipalities and co-operatives. The difficulties of this relationship are somewhat greater with the rural co-operatives since the managers, who are, of course, salaried employees of the co-operative, and by reason of the smallness of the area served cannot be paid a high salary, are not highly experienced. The R.E.A. and the T.V.A. therefore give continual attention to the technical administrative and accounting operations of these local agencies, so that they shall meet their obligations, conduct their operations with a minimum of expense, and not apply to extensions surpluses which should be devoted to meeting loan obligations. An attempt is made to secure the services of competent managers and the retirement of incompetent ones. As is explained in a later chapter, the State Utility Commissioners do not supervise the administration of the municipal electricity systems, and a serious problem is thereby presented to the T.V.A. It knows enough of human nature in business and politics to realise that the quality of the results in sales and service and rates to the customers will continually depend upon clean and efficient municipal administration. Therefore, it cannot wait until some political scandal ruins a local system, but must currently bring home to the municipalities their responsibility. Already the present chairman of the Board has openly declared his deep distress at "indications of an effort to infiltrate politics into the municipalities and co-operatives distributing T.V.A. power".[2] He was afraid of the political determination of contracts, insurance, extensions of lines and service, of inaction

---

[1] Problems arising out of the payment of these taxes are dealt with in Chapter IX.

[2] Cf. T.V.A. Release, remarks of D. E. LILIENTHAL: "Politics and the Management of the Public's Business", 9 July 1942, p. 8.

about unpaid bills, and other similar developments. T.V.A. officials have also warned co-operatives against leaving management entirely to the paid manager.

In the rural areas, it has been found essential to secure a written agreement with the intending consumers. The experience of the T.V.A. has been that the initial enthusiasm which is productive of a promise to purchase may not last. The Authority was therefore compelled to introduce a contract for a minimum consumption for three years, that minimum being set by the customer. It is the Authority's opinion that if electricity is taken for three years its consumption will certainly increase thereafter—an opinion borne out almost everywhere by experience. To give a feeling of security to wiring and appliance contractors, the Authority required the dealers to demand a deposit from the consumer.

EQUALITY OF RURAL AND URBAN ELECTRICITY PRICES

The Tennessee Valley Authority's price policy for power is to eliminate differences between urban and rural rates. Urban and rural rates are the same except that particular contractors have a right to make a surcharge to meet special difficulties of supply, but not above 10 per cent. of the common rate; and, as we have seen, an engagement for a minimum consumption over the first three years must be given by each customer.

From the earliest stages the T.V.A. fostered local initiative. It continues to do so unceasingly through constant personal contact. The T.V.A. regards its work in the extension of electricity to rural areas as a problem not merely of increased sales, but of the beneficial application of electricity to farm life. For example, the principals of the local schools are informed of the Authority's social purposes and induced to give their educational help. Local meetings are arranged at which the purposes of the Authority are explained. To the local wiring contractors the T.V.A. also conducts a mission, on the best technical means of applying electricity to domestic and farm labour, and so on. The T.V.A. induces dealers to arrange displays and demonstrations with the help of the State and county agricultural extension services. Thus, there have been dedication festivals in the High School auditorium, with a display of useful appliances to bring home to the farmer that electricity is not merely the genie of waffle-makers, light and radio; for the emphasis of the Authority is on productive appliances in farm work and in the domestic economy of the farm. The T.V.A. has a staff of home economists who visit the homes to advise on the use of appliances, and also a number of commercial representatives who themselves

help to show the use of farm appliances or bring in farm specialists
for this purpose. These latter induce dealers to come with them
to give demonstrations. The Authority indeed keeps a very watchful eye on the annual sales of electric appliances in its area, as
these are the yardstick of its success. There are some 800 dealers
who send in monthly reports of the number, value and kind of the
appliances sold. The following figures, taken from the Authority's
Annual Reports, illustrate the development in sales of appliances.

Fiscal year	Value of sales of electricity appliances: domestic retail price
	(dollars)
1938	1,612,000
1939	3,688,000
1940	12,500,000
1941	18,500,000

The great increase in 1941 was due to the increase in the number
of customers served by T.V.A. wholesale distributors. The ap-
proximate average was $52.50 per residential customer.

One of the merits of this and other aspects of the development
work of the T.V.A. is the attention given to inventing, or inducing
other agencies, like the local universities and experiment stations
and private firms, to conduct research on, invent and manufacture
appliances especially suited to, the economy of the area.[1]

The T.V.A. does not sell electrical appliances but only electricity.
However, it co-operates with the standard makers of appliances,
gives them lists of rural customers or recommends consumers who
have asked for information to the well-known makers of the best
appliances. It should be said here that in 1933, shortly after the
T.V.A. began to function, the Electric Home and Farm Authority
was set up, a Government corporation to guarantee the credits
given by dealers to purchasers of electrical apparatus. This agency
has strongly stimulated sales in the Tennessee Valley. Its operation
is discussed later.[2]

In 1938 the extension[3] services and their specialists conducted
526 meetings, demonstrations and schools on the farm and home
uses of electricity, attended by 12,600 people; and in 1939, 775
such meetings, attended by 24,517 people. There was a growth
in the number of specialists and additional funds for the extension
services as the number of rural lines and interest in electricity
continued to grow. The extension workers themselves were speci-
ally instructed in rural electrification at 27 training schools.

---

[1] Cf. Chapter IX.
[2] Cf. Chapter IX.
[3] Cf. Chapter IV.

Before leaving this subject, the tremendous benefits obtainable in this branch of the Authority's development of the general welfare of the Valley from the integration of its activities must once again be emphasised. The extension agents are officials, the essence of whose job is to improve agricultural methods and raise the standard of living of those who live by agriculture. Electricity is one element serving this purpose. From another side of its activities, the T.V.A. is directly interested in the same purpose as the extension agents, so that the latter can fully co-ordinate their work in both fields, agriculture and electricity, both lying within the responsibility of the Authority.

PROGRESS IN T.V.A. ELECTRICITY RATES AND THE PROBLEM OF SUBSIDIES

Before the T.V.A. came into the Valley, the average residential customer's consumption was about 55 kilowatt hours per month. Year after year the T.V.A. was beset by the cry of its critics that it would find no market for all the power it was to produce. By 1942, the average residential customer in the Valley area consumed 129 kilowatt hours per month and paid 2.00 cents per kilowatt hour; whereas the average residential customer throughout the country consumed an average of just over 85 kilowatt hours per month at 3.67 cents per kilowatt hour. Add to this the fact that retail sales to small commercial customers in 1942 were at the average rate of 2.14 cents per kilowatt hour, and that the sales to industrial customers were made at an average of 0.77 cents per kilowatt hour, and it is clear that the T.V.A. had to its credit a very considerable achievement. The overall average rate paid by all customers served with T.V.A. power at retail was 1.24 cents per kilowatt hour.

As will have been appreciated, the selling policy of the T.V.A. has a twofold aspect: that of wholesale rates and that of retail rates. As regards the wholesale rates, the main question is whether the Authority sells without subsidising its customers by passing on to them, in some form or another, services and electric power which ultimately and directly or indirectly are paid for by taxpayers. For example, it is important to know whether the interest rate on Tennessee Valley Authority moneys is computed on a fair basis as compared with that which private companies must pay for their capital; whether, again, the T.V.A. makes proper provision for depreciation and for the equivalent of State and local taxation to which private companies are subject, while the T.V.A., being a Federal agency, is given immunity. Secondly, in regard to the resale rates stipulated by the Authority, the question is whether these at least secured the covering of the cost of production while duly accounting for and meeting every item entering into cost. These subjects have been the centre of the most acute and chronic controversy between those who, like the T.V.A., favour public enterprise, and those who are hostile to it. Any claim that the T.V.A. and similar projects could, by force of example, compel private companies to lower rates which were in fact excessive could only be substantiated if the T.V.A.'s own bill of reckoning contained all the items that should properly be included.

The controversy revolving about this question has not always been conducted in a strictly objective spirit.[1]

Whether the T.V.A.'s rates contain subsidies, and whether it is or is not making a profit, depends to a considerable extent on the extremely complicated problem of how to allocate the value of the dams between their various uses, and so properly to allocate the capital valuation of the investment to the generation and transmission of power. In view of the total size of the investment— for ten dams alone it is estimated at $400,000,000—it can readily be understood that a small percentage of difference in dividing up the capital valuation among the three uses—navigation, flood control and power—could make all the difference between a substantial accountancy profit or a considerable loss on operations in any one year. Indeed, such differences rather conservatively regarded and by no means the most extreme suggested, were examined by the Joint Committee Investigating the T.V.A.[2] Based on the estimates of an 11-dam system, one expert postulated an annual loss of $4,039,000, while the chief power engineer of the T.V.A. postulated a profit of $4,624,785. These differences were due to the fact that the total cost of dams as allocated to power in the first estimate was nearly $349,000,000, while the T.V.A. chief power engineer made calculations leading to just under $265,000,000.[3]

The allocation of costs is of basic importance to a development authority like the T.V.A. for three reasons. First, it must know its own cost of production, since otherwise it might in the extreme case (if it were acting benevolently) leave itself at the mercy of all sorts of consumers' demand, and would have no measure of how far it could continue to meet demands on the basis of contracts made with consumers. It would certainly never know whether it were losing or gaining, subsidising or losing business owing to excessive charges. Secondly—and this is very important—without

---

[1] A brief indication of the main problems is given in Appendix VI.
[2] *Report of the Joint Committee Investigating the Tennessee Valley Authority, op. cit.*, p. 170.
[3] Cf. Appendix II.

an allocation of costs, the Authority itself does not know how far to press its continued building of hydroelectric dams and installations, for if the general economy of the surrounding country is considered, it may at a certain point be more economical to produce electricity by alternative methods, such as steam-plant. Thirdly, without the allocation of investment costs, other figures derived therefrom, such as rate of interest, depreciation, and amortisation, cannot find their place in the accounts, and consequently the analysis of operations and the computation of profit and loss become impossible. If, further, it is desired to regard a development authority of this kind as a "yardstick", or in other words, as a mathematically precise demonstration model and index of what could be accomplished in the cost of producing and selling electricity, then of course the "yardstick" must be visible, and the first contribution to that visibility is the exact knowledge of how much capital is being used for the power operations.

Allocation of Costs

This point, of course, was seen by Congress when the Statute was enacted. Consequently, in Section 14 of the Statute there are careful directions requiring the valuation of T.V.A. dams and steam plant and the allocation of the total among the various purposes, namely: (1) flood control, (2) navigation, (3) fertiliser, (4) national defence, and (5) the development of power.[1] The findings were to go to the President, were to be regarded as final upon his approval, and thereafter were to be used in all allocations of value for the purposes of accountancy. This subject and the controversies to which it gave rise are briefly sketched in Appendix VI.[2] But two things may be stated here. The first is that the T.V.A. had to establish its rates as soon as it began and therefore long before a full valuation could be made. It appears that the final allocation, arrived at after years of expert analysis, very closely coincided with this first business appraisal. Secondly, of the various theories of allocation in competition for acceptance, the T.V.A. chose the one known as the "alternative justifiable expenditure" theory. On the basis of this, it reported to the President, in 1938, on the three-dam system of Wilson, Norris and

---

[1] It is interesting to note that the Statute required the allocation "for the purpose of accumulating data useful to the Congress in the formulation of legislative policy in matters relating to the generation, etc., of electric energy and the production of chemicals. . . " As is shown later, the T.V.A. was required to follow the accountancy system for public utilities established by the Federal Power Commission. Cf. Chapter XII.

[2] Cf. also the fullest discussion of allocation by J. S. Ransmeier: *The Tennessee Valley Authority* (Nashville, Vanderbilt University, 1942), especially pp. 305-342.

Wheeler, assigning to navigation 28 per cent., to flood control 20 per cent., and to power 52 per cent. of the total cost. Late in 1940 a further allocation was made, based now upon seven dams as a single system—Wilson, Norris, Wheeler, Pickwick, Guntersville, Chickamauga, and Hiwassee. The respective allocations were: navigation, 21.8 per cent., flood control, 12.4 per cent., and power, 65.8 per cent. of the total investment. Nothing was allocated to national defence or fertiliser. Until the time of the T.V.A.'s allocation there had never been more than a two-purpose project, that is, navigation and power, requiring allocation. The argument regarding valuation and allocation in Appendix VI proves convincingly that the profits claimed by the T.V.A. are true profits and that there are certainly no subsidies. If its power rates are low, this is due to the efficiency and economy of its manufacture and transmission of power and the efficient distributing management of the municipalities and co-operatives, and to the fact that navigation, flood control and electricity properly share the cost of the benefits derived from exploitation of the water resources of the Valley.

CHAPTER IV

THE PROPER USE OF THE LAND

The Land, its Needs and its Problems

The general nature of the sickness of the land in the Tennessee Valley has already been sketched and the need for far-reaching remedies suggested. The subject must now be considered more carefully.

The Tennessee Valley basin contains about 26,160,000 acres.[1] About 18 million acres, or 68 per cent. of the total acreage, are in farms. Nearly one third of this is in farm woodlands, pastured and unpastured. The other 12,000,000 are in open pasture, meadow, and crops. There are 255,000 farm families, with an average of five persons in each. Thus, there are some 48 acres of crops and pasture land per family, or nearly nine acres per person. The average size of all farms in Tennessee is slightly under 75 acres, and has been growing smaller for several decades.[2]

Some other facts are important. The land is located high or low on fairly steep hills; there are many slopes of 20° or more, and some are well over 45°. The annual rainfall, averaging 52 inches, varies from 80 to 40 inches, and the rain is usually heavy. The soil in the Valley is prevailingly of fine texture and dense, so that, though it varies in different parts in use and productivity—there are some 120 soil series and 500 soil types—it absorbs the water slowly, there is a high surface run-off, and if vegetative protection is lacking it erodes very easily.

Of the 26,000,000 acres of forest once covering this region, nearly half has been cleared for tillage and other purposes. Of the 14,000,000 acres of forest left, only 8,700,000 acres now contain trees of saw-timber size, though saw-timber is being cut 1.25 times faster than it is being grown. Nearly three quarters of a million acres are damaged by fire annually. Excessive cutting, burning, grazing, and other deleterious procedures have been so widely practised that much of the Valley's forested area now contains only

---

[1] Details of land ownership and use in the Tennessee Valley are shown in Appendix I, table 1.

[2] But the average farm acreage increased from 74.2 in 1930 to 74.8 in 1940.

inferior stands of young timber. On the land which is being cleared, intensive agriculture has removed or permitted the loss of a large part of the essential nourishment of plant life and the land has been left progressively more open to natural forces of erosion and the washing away of its chemical constituents. About 1,000,000 acres of land, much of which was naturally unsuitable for crops, have been withdrawn from cultivation. A further 1,500,000 are cropped intermittently because of their depleted condition; 4,500,000 acres are on the decline. Steep mountain land has been put into crops in full knowledge that five years of such use would see its destruction. Of something like 12,000,000 acres devoted to the production of crops and pasture, more than one half is in need of substantial change in management and use.

Thus, land which needed very special care was, in fact, by inconsiderate agricultural and lumbering practices, put at a special disadvantage. The growing of so-called row crops, like cotton, maize, and tobacco (peculiarly destructive of soil fertility), stimulated by doses of commercial fertiliser, year after year steadily destroyed the agricultural land, caused the dispersal of the top soil, and then led to the gullying of the hillsides until in some places little remains but exposed rock and gigantic gouges in the soil. The large families, dependent on their small holdings, nevertheless felt compelled to produce these cash crops. These processes had disrupted the cycle of nature, because they did not include the restoration of the land by the use of mineral fertilisers, legumes, and winter cover crops. One of the direct results was a poverty in livestock and milk.

Relation of the T.V.A.'s Powers to Other Government Agencies

The agricultural functions of the T.V.A. are defined, and at the same time restricted, by the Statute: it possesses no universal power of government over agriculture in the Valley. Side by side with the T.V.A. are all the services to agriculture which the Federal Government renders through the United States Department of Agriculture. It is essential to refer here particularly to the functions of two Divisions of that Department, namely, the Federal Security Administration and the Farm Credit Administration, in order to make it clear that other institutions are making an agricultural contribution to the Valley, in total greater than that of the T.V.A., and that the benefits of contractual collaboration between the T.V.A., the land grant colleges, and the two agencies just referred to, may be appreciated.

The Farm Security Administration, established in 1933, has

as its object to help needy and handicapped small- and middle-sized family type farms, by assisting with loans to increase the size of the holding, acquire tools, seed and livestock, to obtain better security of tenure by long-term leases; to help tenants to buy their own land or resettle on better land; and to adjust onerous private and public debts and mortgages. This financial assistance is accompanied by information, advice and guidance for better subsistence and marketable production. There are direct grants to extremely poverty stricken families for basic necessities like food and clothes, and feed for livestock. There are rural medical care schemes in which the family pays a contribution, and co-operatives are encouraged for stock-breeding, tractor use, purchase of machinery equipment, foods, and so forth.

The F.S.A. conducts activities in all the States of the Union, and therefore in the seven Valley States. Hence, its work proceeds simultaneously with the T.V.A. farm demonstration programme. There are no separate figures kept for the Tennessee Valley region, but the seven Valley States receive substantial help.[1]

The connections between the work of the F.S.A. and the T.V.A. programme are clear and cordial. It has already been mentioned that the Department of Agriculture is linked in its work with the land grant colleges and the T.V.A. by a memorandum of understanding. This memorandum includes in its scope the F.S.A. and the F.C.A. and provides for their integration, especially at the county level where the State Extension System finds its daily operation. Legally, the functions of the T.V.A. do not extend to those of the F.S.A., but, linked with the land grant colleges, the programmes are brought into connection. The farm demonstration programme is undertaken with due respect to the work of the F.S.A. and F.C.A. Clients are selected as test-demonstration farmers in about the same proportion that the number of such farmers bears to the total number of farms in a county; more small supervised loans than tenant purchase loans are made. Thus, the F.S.A. assistance is of help in furthering the Valley watershed protection and agricultural development from its angle. There may be, in all this, a certain overlapping in that advice and educational assistance come from both the land grant college officers and the F.S.A. officers; but a complete severance of advice from financial or credit assistance would be difficult to secure.

The purpose of the Farm Credit Administration (set up in 1933, but with a long administrative history), is to provide a complete and co-ordinated credit system for agriculture. It furnishes long-

---

[1] Cf. *Report, Administrator, Farm Security Administration, 1941*, Statistical Appendix. Acknowledgments are due to that Department for information.

and short-term credit to farmers individually or to their co-operative marketing, purchasing, and business service organisations. Substantial use is made of its co-operative credit assistance in the seven Valley States for production, and it is not paradoxical to say that with increased prosperity of the Valley, fostered by the farm demonstration system, it is likely that much more use will be made of the available co-operative credit facilities. Already, observers believe that this beneficial development is on the up-grade. The backwardness hitherto prevailing in regard to agricultural co-operatives has been due to the limited diversification of crops, restriction of tobacco and cotton, and the development of local credit systems and practices based on the latter, for a long standing inter-relationship has developed between merchants, land-owner and tenant. Locally and regionally, strong marketing and purchasing associations have developed, in the last ten years, and this is accounted for, in good measure, by the facilities and services of the Farm Credit Administration. As diversification increases— and this is the T.V.A.'s object—so it may be expected that co-operatives and credit facilities supplied by the F.C.A. will also increase.[1]

The Valley States also benefit by the loans made under the auspices of the federal land banks and Federal Farm Mortgage Corporation to cope with mortgages and emergency situations relating to crops, feed, and droughts.

The T.V.A.'s Agricultural Powers

Nevertheless, the powers of the T.V.A. regarding the land of the Valley are wide in scope and highly important in substance. Like the other specific powers of the Authority, valuable in themselves, they also have a supplementary worth in their integrated relationship with the rest of the Authority's purposes. These powers may be briefly stated: (1) There is the general power stated in the Preamble, "to provide for the agricultural and industrial development of the said Valley". (2) There is the power given in Section 22, "to aid further the proper use, conservation and development of the natural resources . . . all for the purpose of fostering an orderly and proper physical economic and social development . . . " by means of "surveys and general plans" and "to make such studies, experiments or demonstrations as may be necessary and suitable to that end". (3) Section 23 refers to plans and legislation, among other things, for "the proper use of marginal

---

[1] Cf. Annual Reports of the Farm Credit Administration; also L. C. SALTER and E. L. MORGAN: *Farmer Co-operation in Northern Alabama* (Agricultural Experiment Station of the Alabama Polytechnic Institute, Bulletin 249, Mar. 1941).

lands and the proper method of reafforestation of all lands in said drainage basin suitable for reafforestation". The Statute gives certain powers more concrete and specific in relation to the experimental production, testing and demonstration of fertiliser; namely, the Authority may contract with commercial producers for the production of fertiliser as needed for the Government's programme of development; it may arrange with farmers and farm organisations for large-scale practical use of the new forms of fertilisers; it may co-operate with governmental experiment stations or demonstration farms, with farmers, landowners and associations of these for the use of new fertilisers or fertiliser practices in their initial or experimental periods and to promote the prevention of soil erosion by the use of fertilisers and otherwise; it may manufacture fertiliser by such processes as appear wise and profitable to it, in order to improve and cheapen the production of such fertiliser. The T.V.A. further has the power to donate or sell the product of its fertiliser plants so long as it is fairly distributed through the agricultural extension system or otherwise for experimental and educational purposes in co-operation with practical farmers; and to implement these specific powers, the T.V.A. was given authority to establish and operate laboratories and experimental plants and undertake experiments for production in the most economical manner and at the highest standard of efficiency.

It is by the co-ordinated application of these various general and specific powers that the T.V.A. attempts to meet the problem of the proper use of the land in a valley of retarded and sometimes regressive land use.

These powers are permissive; and it must always be borne in mind that the T.V.A. has no power to compel farmers or public authorities to carry out its policy. It must act by persuasion, so far as others are concerned. Out of these provisions the Authority has developed a far-seeing policy of agricultural improvement based on the production of concentrated phosphatic fertiliser and the demonstration of its use on farms with new farm methods. The T.V.A.'s land policy of the highest feasible sustained productivity is based on four factors: first, the physical nature and needs of the land; secondly, the continuation of private ownership of most of the land of the region; thirdly, the establishment of better methods of production than those prevailing when the Authority entered the Valley; and, fourthly, the deliberately chosen method of co-operation with the existing public agencies of the Valley and farmers' clubs, or "soil conservation associations", as they are officially named.

It should be noted at once that while the T.V.A. has statutory power[1] to sell fertiliser and fertiliser ingredients, its policy hitherto has never been to enter the commercial market; it confines itself to giving or to selling to Government or publicly established agencies only.

A Policy for the Soil

Having considered the problems and powers of the T.V.A. in relation to land use, it is necessary now to turn to its policy and activities. Fundamental to the better use of the land is a sound knowledge of the land. The T.V.A.'s many-sided land policy of full utilisation and conservation could only be carried out on the basis of a more exact knowledge than was available when it began operations. However, it is important to remember that its policy and its activities could begin, and did begin, on the basis of such knowledge as existed when it took office. But it has progressively improved that knowledge by a soil survey on which something must be said before proceeding to a consideration of that policy.

The soils of the Tennessee River Basin differ greatly from one another and are scattered in relatively small areas in an intricate geographic pattern. The soil types of a single small farm, or even of a field, may differ greatly from one another as to their use, suitabilities, and management requirements. To organise the soil survey, the State institutions and the Authority had recourse to the United States Soil Survey, the Government agency recognised as best qualified by its 40 years' experience of such work throughout the nation. A memorandum of understanding was drawn up between the Division of Soil Survey of the United States Department of Agriculture, the land grant colleges of the seven Valley States and the Authority to undertake this work as an integral part of the entire Valley programme. The work was started in late 1934 and is still in progress (1943). Beginning in 1935 with the mapping of 352.5 square miles, the annual progress from 1936 to 1941 was between 3,000 and 3,800 square miles. In 1942 it was 1,847 square miles. The total from 1935 to 30 June 1942 amounts to almost 23,000 square miles. Each individual soil type is defined within rather narrow ranges as to its internal characteristics— physical and chemical—and its external characteristics, including slope and erosion. Each soil type has a distinct relationship to crop production and management, and its relative suitability and management requirements are specific.

The soils that are more important to farming can be selected for study in connection with the use of new forms of fertilisers through

---

[1] Section 5 (d) of the Act.

the various steps to be described presently. Of even greater importance is the use of the soil survey as a basis for the interpretation, classification, and extended application of results obtained through experiments and farm experience with fertilisers, crops, and management practices. Besides this, it assists in valuing lands which the T.V.A. must purchase, use or sell, and in the relocation of the several thousand farmers displaced by the building of dams.[1]

LAND IMPROVEMENT BY PHOSPHORUS FERTILISER

The T.V.A.'s immediate problem, then, was to discover the means which would simultaneously prevent erosion and improve the productivity of the land. As regards erosion, of course, there would be a twofold attack—indirect and direct. The former would be implicit in the measures taken to improve the productivity of the land; the latter would, among other things, involve terracing and the planting of shrubs and trees. The former, being fundamentally characteristic of the T.V.A.'s work, is described first.

The T.V.A., on the advice of the land grant colleges, decided that the key to improvement lay in the growing of cover crops. For this a good plant food was necessary. The crucial question was, which should it be? The Statute had left to the T.V.A. a wide discretion regarding the fertilisers it might undertake to produce, its major objective being the improvement of their quality and the cheapening of the cost to farmers. Several choices were possible. Liming materials were plentiful, widely distributed in nature and easily processed for use. Potash fertilisers of high concentration were already available, and there was small prospect of improvement in their quality or price. Further, nitrogen in suitable form for use as fertiliser was, under the stimulus of private initiative (which was not concerned about the erosion of the soil), already available in large quantity at a cost vastly reduced in comparison with earlier years, while the T.V.A.'s Nitrate Plant No. 2 was quite out of date. On the other hand, the phosphate fertiliser in common use was of low concentration and expensive to handle, and there had been little improvement in its manufacture from the beginning of its production a century ago. Moreover, Ten-

---

[1] Of course, any classification of soil—the material basis of agriculture—as detailed and as complete as this has a great many other applications. For example, the effect of building a dam of a certain height upon the land at the back of the dam can be accurately predicted, thus making it possible to arrange in advance some of the necessary rural adjustments. Even alternative locations and heights of dams can be studied in relation to their effect upon agriculture. Through thoughtful generalisation broad areas may be characterised by their agricultural possibilities, and the conclusions are invaluable in the planning of roads, power lines, recreational areas, forest preserves, the location of processing plants, and similar public facilities and institutions.

nessee Valley soil was generally deficient in phosphorus, which is one of the most widely needed fertiliser materials, especially for stimulating the growth of legumes, although the Tennessee Valley contains substantial deposits.

If the soil is well fortified with mineral fertilisers, including phosphate, it is possible to grow legumes, and through these the unlimited quantities of free nitrogen in the air can be absorbed and led into the soil in much larger quantity than through nitrogen fertiliser, and without causing damage as when nitrogen fertiliser is used on row crops unaccompanied by minerals and winter cover crops, the practice which had so largely contributed to waste the soils of the south.[1] At the same time, the growing of legumes, especially as winter cover crops, builds back humus into the soil and protects it from being washed away. The productive capacity of the land is increased, and as soil erosion is reduced, streams and reservoirs are protected from silting. The Department of Agriculture had pioneered with new metaphosphatic fertiliser production processes which lent themselves to use through the ample electrical power facilities of the Authority.[2] The Authority reckoned that if it could produce an improved phosphatic fertiliser at an attractive price, farmers could be led more generally to grow the legumes, clover, alfalfa, lespedeza[3] and vetch, as regular and cover crops, and other leguminous vegetation which would have a high direct value as well as soil-building qualities.

One of the requirements of a good fertiliser was lower cost to the farmer. Half of all the fertiliser used in the United States was phosphatic; but most of it was a superphosphate containing only from 16 to 20 per cent. of available plant food, or about 180 pounds in each 1,000 pounds of mixed fertiliser, the whole bulk of which had nevertheless to be transported from the mine to where it was processed, and then on to the farmers. An improved content of plant food would mean reduction in handling and transport costs, an important step towards making the fertiliser economically acceptable[4], and therefore towards persuading farmers to adopt

---

[1] Two thirds of all the fertiliser sold in the United States of America has gone into the thirteen States of the South to be used largely in this objectionable system of cropping.

[2] The production of superphosphate requires the smelting of phosphate rock with coke and silica in electrical furnaces at a temperature of approximately 2,750° Fahrenheit.

[3] Otherwise known as Japanese clover.

[4] For the year ended 30 June 1942, the cost of power used in the large-scale production of phosphate fertiliser by the T.V.A. was a little over $376,000 as against the total cost of about $2,300,000, that is, roughly one sixth of the total cost. The wholesale cost of power does not markedly differ from that charged by profit utilities for large commercial quantities. The cheapening of the price of fertiliser would therefore need to come from some other factor, and that is why the T.V.A. looks to a reduction of freight costs.

new agricultural practices. There was already a small amount of superphosphate, called triple phosphate, on the market, with a plant food content treble that in ordinary superphosphate; but it had hitherto been difficult (even where attempted) to convince farmers, not usually trained in chemistry, that this was really cheaper to them per unit of plant food, although it cost more per ton.

This is not the place to enter into the intricate technology of the production of superphosphate; the T.V.A.'s technical reports are readily available.[1] Through many researches and experiments, the T.V.A. produced first a 37.1 per cent. P_2O_5 concentration[2] of plant food; then a concentration of 45 per cent., and finally, a concentration of about 63 per cent. in calcium metaphosphate, otherwise known as "metaphos".

Whether the T.V.A. can produce a fertiliser at lower cost than ordinary commercially manufactured fertiliser of the same concentration is as yet problematical. The Joint Investigating Committee found, in 1938, that T.V.A. cost accounting on its fertiliser manufacturing did not sufficiently exclude all expensive experimental procedures and include all cost items on a basis clearly comparable with private industry. Since that time a new accountancy method has been adopted, but the question involved will not be solved until more time has elapsed. However, the savings in freight and handling are manifest.

A calculation of savings in freight and handling costs by the use of concentrated fertiliser carrying 63 per cent. of plant food in comparison with 16 to 20 per cent. in ordinary superphosphates was made by the T.V.A. in 1938. The resultant calculated prices to the farmers were, per ton of available P_2O_5, $81.73 (for 16 2/3 per cent. superphosphates), and $60.59 (for 66 2/3 per cent.) respectively. The country as a whole used only a concentration of mixed fertilisers of the average of 18 per cent. of all three nutrients—nitrogen, phosphorus, and potash.

FERTILISER TESTS AND DEMONSTRATIONS: RESEARCH, EDUCATION, TECHNICAL ADVICE

The Authority could not offer a new highly concentrated phosphorus fertiliser to farmers on the mere assumption that it would give satisfactory results when used on the farm. Each fertiliser goes through a systematic course of experiment, beginning in the

---

[1] Cf. *T.V.A. Fertiliser Processes* (T.V.A. Publication, Oct. 1940).

[2] Phosphorus pentoxide. Further experiments are still in their very early laboratory stages. One is the production of fused phosphate, resulting from the removal of the fluorine from the raw phosphate rock. Another is potassium metaphosphate. This latter analyses about 57 per cent. available P_2O_5 and 34 per cent. K_2O_2, or approximately 91 per cent. plant food.

laboratory, progressing to the State agricultural experiment stations and through greenhouse tests on various soils, on fields and plots, until finally it is tested on farms under practical conditions by farmers themselves. The various stages in this testing procedure are both important and interesting, and especially characteristic of the T.V.A.

The Act establishing the T.V.A. does not limit the application of the fertiliser experiment provisions to the Tennessee Valley, and the Authority has therefore construed the Act to provide for the testing of its fertilisers on a nation-wide scale. As a result, the experiment stations in all but one of the 48 States of the Union and in two outlying possessions have received T.V.A. phosphates for experimental testing. In 1943 this experimental study of T.V.A. fertilisers was actively under way in more than 30 States: the seven Tennessee Valley States, and the rest outside the Valley.[1] The experiment station provides a guide to the State agricultural extension services in the proper use of T.V.A. phosphates under farm conditions.

Privately Owned Farms and Public Test-Demonstrations

The mere demonstration that a highly concentrated fertiliser could be produced was by no means the sole purpose of the Authority's agricultural policy. The grand purpose was the influence that could be exerted on agricultural economy and farm management. The T.V.A. faced the fact that by far the larger part of the land in the Valley (as elsewhere in the United States) was in the private hands of some 250,000 farmers, most frequently in small holdings. Furthermore, for several decades there had already been in operation in each State a system of agricultural education and improvement, administered by the so-called county extension agents who were in the joint employ of the United States Department of Agriculture and the State Agricultural Extension Service, which is an arm of the land grant colleges. This extension system or service is the agency for carrying information to farmers.[2]

---

[1] A table showing the expenditure on the fertiliser programme is to be found in Appendix I.

[2] The extension system, especially concerned with furthering the progress of agriculture in the United States of America, is the organised arrangement for direct local education in agriculture and home economics established by formal co-operation between the United States Department of Agriculture and land grant colleges. The latter are State agricultural colleges subsidised by grants of land and money by the United States Government, under the Morrill Land Grant Act, 1862, the Hatch Act, 1884, and the Smith-Lever Act, 1914. The last-named Act gave a national setting to the system of agricultural education which had been commenced here and there by several States (especially in the South after 1900), operating locally through so-called 'county agents' or 'county extension agents'.

(*Footnote continued overleaf*)

The Authority's basic tenet was necessarily favourable to the continuation and development of individual ownership and free enterprise in farming. Its own financial resources were insufficient by themselves to produce change by purchase on a large enough scale, and therefore it had to try to persuade all the individual parties to participate with a sense of the value of the Authority's policy. This point of view was well stated in the Annual Report of 1939:

Under our system of private ownership far-reaching adjustments in farm and forest practices must largely rest upon the voluntary co-operation and self-interest of those who participate. Such measures must therefore be profitable to those who employ them if the programme is to be widely and enthusiastically adopted. The experience of the T.V.A. during the past year has continued to demonstrate that landowners and farm operators, the community organisations which they have established, and State and local agencies working in their interest are willing and competent in this undertaking. (p. 23.)

And again:

In farm and forest practice under our system of private ownership, the interests of the individual are paramount. Here at once the programme becomes involved in principles of voluntary co-operation and local initiative, which are basic in our democracy. The experience of the Authority has demonstrated that these principles are not barriers. Rather they are the means of succeeding. This programme has been planned, organised, conducted, and to a large extent financed by the farmers themselves. (p. 3.)

Under this programme of combined private ownership and co-operation among governmental and local agencies, the T.V.A. makes the fertiliser available without charge to the farmer through the colleges of agriculture. The agricultural extension arm of the college supplies to the farmer supervision, leadership, and technical information on the use of the fertiliser in the improved system of cropping. Reports on the results of the individual farm demonstrations come to the T.V.A. from the extension services, which obtain them from the associations or clubs of farmers which supervise the demonstration farms.

A rather closer view of the system is essential. In 1934 the T.V.A. began work with the testing of its fertilisers at the various experiment stations. This prepared the way for the farm demonstra-

---

The chief feature of the county extension agent system is the permanent local stationing in a given area of a person trained in agriculture and charged with the establishment of programmes and methods of improving local conditions. The land grant colleges and the State Boards of Agriculture appoint the county agents; the United States Government makes grants to the former, and as a condition requires plans of extension work to be made subject to its approval. The College is required to establish a separate division of extension work, the director of which is chosen by the College subject to the approval of the Department of Agriculture. The agents work with and through farmers' associations, sometimes organised as the Farm Bureau, and various youth clubs, and any other useful approaches. Cf. Gladys BAKER: *The County Agent* (Chicago, 1939).

tion programme which was initiated in 1935, and has gradually extended until, at the end of 1941, forty-seven States had tested T.V.A. phosphatic fertiliser experimentally, and twenty-seven States were conducting test-demonstration programmes.

Contractual Relations with Existing Agencies

In pursuance of the policy laid down in the Statute of arranging with farmers and farm organisations for large-scale practical use of the new forms of fertilisers, under conditions permitting an accurate measure of the economic return they produce, the Authority was empowered, but not obliged, to co-operate with existing agencies or others that might be set up and with the national or local political institutions. A very wide latitude as to the method and agencies through which to work was therefore left to the Authority. Indeed, the Authority could apparently have proceeded in direct contact with the farmers, for even where Section 5 (e) permits operations through county demonstration agents and agricultural colleges, the Statute says, "or otherwise as the Board may direct". And it must always remain a question whether, if this had been tried, it would not have succeeded even better than the course actually taken; at present no-one is in a position to say.

The Authority decided that the situation, the individualistic psychology of the southern farmer, and its own Jeffersonian democratic ideals all required action in co-operation with existing agencies already familiar to the farmers and the other residents of the Valley. This policy is stated in Administrative Bulletin No. 12, Department of Agricultural Relations, which runs as follows:

All feasible means shall be employed to avoid needless duplication or overlapping of funds, facilities, personnel, or programmes of other Government agencies. To this end the activities of the Department shall be undertaken wherever practicable through the medium of existing national, State, and local agencies and institutions, or in co-operation therewith. . .

At each stage in the programme the Department shall: ascertain the nature and objectives of national programmes of soil restoration and maintenance initiated by various competent agencies; co-operate with them in determining the respects in which the proper use of new forms of plant food may contribute thereto; and supply such material as will assist in carrying such programmes into effect. . .

In the conduct of demonstrations and in the widespread application of results, the Department shall work in close co-operation with practical farmers, enlisting their active interest and participation through their national organisations and through local groups capable of assuming responsibility and supervision in their programmes of such readjusted farm-management systems as may be brought about through the proper use of new forms of plant food material.

The system established is based upon two contractual arrangements: (1) a Memorandum of Understanding between the United

States Department of Agriculture, the land grant colleges of the area[1] and the Authority; and (2) contracts between the land grant colleges and the T.V.A. alone.

Under the first Memorandum of Understanding, the national and State institutions established for agricultural teaching, research and extension activities in the States materially affected by the Tennessee Valley Act, having already developed comprehensive training, research and extension projects, established valuable facilities, equipment, and a trained personnel, and accumulated a fund of scientific facts and experience, agree to co-ordinate the phases of research, extension, land-use planning, and educational activities of the experiment stations and extension systems in relation to activities in which the T.V.A. is concerned. These activities are concerned with a unified regional agricultural problem. The agricultural colleges of the Valley States designate a State contact officer selected by the director of the experiment station and the director of extension, financed jointly by these agencies, with contributions from the Department of Agriculture and the T.V.A. This officer has the duty of familiarising himself with the agricultural interests of the T.V.A. and the Department of Agriculture, and passing on the information to the experiment station and extension staffs in his State. The memorandum looks to the creation of joint committees of these staffs in each State, to consider special matters like erosion control, land utilisation, land settlement, and rural electrification. To guide these co-ordinated agencies, there was established a Correlating Committee of three members, one each from the Department of Agriculture, the Valley agricultural colleges *en bloc*, and the T.V.A. This Committee has a full-time executive secretary who divides his time between Washington, the several States, and the T.V.A.

The second phase is the contracts made between the Authority and the seven Valley States (and, as the farm demonstration plan progressed, with a number of States outside the Valley) by which the latter implement the policy of the T.V.A. These contracts also begin with a preamble containing a statement of objectives, as quoted above, and explain that the demonstrations are needed in order to determine the basis for readjustments in farm practices and systems. There is the relationship of mutual benefit, whereby the Authority enlists the personnel facilities and relationships of the colleges in concerted action and without duplication of effort,

---

[1] The University of Tennessee; the Alabama Polytechnic Institute; the University of Kentucky; the North Carolina College of Agriculture; the Virginia Polytechnic Institute; the Georgia State College of Agriculture; and the Mississippi State Extension Department.

while the funds and facilities of these colleges are supplemented by the T.V.A. for the services they perform in co-operation with it.

The contract then binds the parties to undertake to study, determine, and apply principles of rational farm management, and to encourage the widespread adoption thereof. They have to work within the agreement between the Department of Agriculture, the T.V.A. and the colleges. Their chief objectives are clearly stated: readjustment of cropping systems to increase the acreage of soil protecting crops, such as sod-forming legumes, small grains, grasses, and reduce the percentage of bare land and land devoted to tilled crops; the liberal application of phosphatic fertilisers, supplemented with lime when necessary, to promote the growth of ground cover, and especially legumes; the use of mechanical erosion control devices; and the progressive adaptation of these elements of soil management systems into a sound farm business organisation providing adequate farm income.

Furthermore, the contract recognises that to achieve the purposes of the demonstrations, accurate measurement of results is necessary, and therefore must be carried on continuously according to established methods and techniques. This includes careful and deliberate agreement upon the selection of counties to secure a representative variety of soil and climatic conditions, based in part upon the soil surveys. The land grant colleges, through their experiment stations, take the responsibility of interpreting the meaning of the survey and assisting in its use. The T.V.A. reimburses the colleges for funds expended in the expansion of the facilities and personnel needed to complete this survey within a given time, and provides the services of an expert approved by the college, who consults with all agencies concerned in guiding these surveys and in interpreting and applying their results to the programme. Also, the Authority promises to make available its own base maps of the Tennessee Valley area, while the colleges agree to make available their libraries, the results of investigations and experiments, the staff for purposes of interpretation, their research laboratories, experimental farms, facilities and personnel. The T.V.A.'s payments are made as monthly reimbursements to the land grant colleges on receipt of satisfactory records.

In the fiscal year 1941 the number of active test-demonstration farms numbered 26,541. These covered some 5,250,000 acres and were established in 756 counties scattered through 27 States; 85 per cent. were located in the seven Tennessee Valley States.[1]

---

[1] Cf. Appendix I, table 3.

Establishing Farmers' Associations or Clubs

Farm demonstrations require supervision, and they are supervised by the regular county extension agents, but, in addition, within the Tennessee Valley, some 120 assistant county agents and 26 supervisors and special agents are employed and paid by the State Extension Services. The T.V.A. reimburses the colleges for the funds they contribute to the Extension Services for the payment of these agents. "County agricultural associations" are established, and the interest and co-operation of the individual farmers enlisted in the following manner. County agents encourage local meetings of farm communities. Sometimes a simple business meeting of farmers suffices, but in most cases a community meeting, complete with wives and children, is convened, and the proceedings are partly social and partly educational. In the course of the meeting the dangers threatening the land and their remedies are described, sometimes with the aid of lantern slides and films; and it is made clear to the farmers that they should improve the land they now occupy, because the days of the American frontier, when they might have eased their condition by moving to more fertile land elsewhere, have passed away. The appeal is to a better standard of living, and the direct relationship between better farm methods and high income, low individual tax rates, good schools and so on, is brought clearly home.

The farmers are impressed with the need of organising in order to operate the new system, including the use of T.V.A. phosphate. How this can be done is explained. Where no other organisation is available to sponsor the tests, they must establish among themselves voluntary soil conservation or soil improvement associations or clubs, in order to secure a combination of the intelligence of a number of farmers to cope with their concrete problems.[1] The test-demonstration farms are selected by the club according to type of farming, involving differences in combinations of climate, temperature, days of sunshine, length of day, rainfall, humidity, air currents, soil conditions, topography, density of population, and type and proportions of crops and livestock. If the farmers themselves are willing to undertake a demonstration, the college will come in with scientific help and encouragement, and the T.V.A. will make phosphate available. They learn that the T.V.A. will work with them only through the extension system, with which they are already long familiar. Sooner or later, some local leader among the farmers makes contact with the county and assistant county agents and proposes a conservation association.

---

[1] About three quarters of these clubs have a membership of from under 100 up to 300.

The Test-Demonstration in Practice

The farmers' association makes an agreement with the agricultural extension service. The farmer who has been selected as the operator of a test-demonstration is first in the order of those making the agreement, and ,he agrees to carry out certain practices in the use of the phosphate. He will co-operate with the county agent and assistant agent in developing sound methods of agriculture. He will keep adequate farming records; practise methods of erosion control agreed upon; use T.V.A. fertiliser only on soil protecting crops and not on inter-tilled crops, such as corn, tobacco, cotton or potatoes; refrain at least for a period of five years from ploughing under permanent pastures to which fertilisers have been applied; indicate on the map of his farm the acres to which T.V.A. fertilisers have been applied, the dates and amounts per acre of the applications; leave certain portions of each field unfertilised in order to check the effectiveness of the fertiliser; allow free access to his farm to the county agent or his representative for inspection purposes. Although the fertiliser is a donation, the farmer has to pay the freight, handling and other miscellaneous expenses on the fertiliser received from Muscle Shoals.

The T.V.A. considers that when a farmer is a test-demonstrator, he takes on a public responsibility, and the farm, which belongs to him, becomes a semi-public test and demonstration ground. The T.V.A. fertiliser is not given directly to the farmer, but through the college is made over to the association or club, which passes it on to the farmer. The county agents and their specialists participate, not in the sense of "showing the farmer how", but as scientific advisers, since the T.V.A. recognises that the farmer is best acquainted with his local conditions and that each farm has its own character, and is indeed a combination of many diverse agricultural and human factors. The part played by the trained agricultural worker is in applying technical guidance and educational devices, in order that the farmers may the better determine their own course of management.

There is very close and careful consultation between the agents, the extension specialists, and the demonstrator. Each farm is treated as a separate and individual problem, and each factor in its wealth-producing activities—pasture, arable land, dairy, fruit crops, cash crops, timber and recuperative cover growing—must be taken in relationship with the rest since, even in the course of the demonstration, each farmer must meet the demands of the home and his current commitments. The assumption of responsibility as a test-demonstration farmer may involve quite drastic and costly reorganisation and improvements on the farm, such as draining, terracing, fencing, and so on. Home economy may need adjustment to what the farm is producing. Furthermore, the farmer has to pay for the quantities of limestone necessary to supplement the phosphatic fertiliser supplied by the T.V.A. Hence, it is important to overcome the scepticism of the farmer, and persuade him that he will be the better off at the end of the demonstration period and if he continues good methods. The demonstration farmer is under the fairly continual observation of his neighbours who formed the club and helped to designate him because of his good standing and trustworthiness, for they wish to adopt on their own farms those methods that prove beneficial.

The success of the demonstration is not to be measured simply by what happens to this particular tract of land, or the quality of it, but rather by the skill with which it is managed; and by the fact that those in close association may take notice and be convinced. It is not the part of that particular farmer to preach the lessons that he may so profitably have learned; it is rather for the association to take note, and even more for the county agents and other extension workers to bring home the lessons of the demonstration and to encourage all around to take up similar methods. Through the unit farm tests, the way to an "area" test, later to be described, is opened. As farm tests spread, the farms on the periphery tend to start another circle of farms under test, and so the work and influence progress.

The Alabama Extension Service made a study of 290 farms under T.V.A. demonstration over a six-year period. An average of 57 persons had visited each farm in that period, of whom 35 had adopted improved farm practices, and 15 had been influenced to participate in the Agricultural Adjustment Agency's programme.

"An Accurate Measure of the Economic Return"

Naturally, in order that the demonstration may offer lessons, it is important that the farmer should honour his agreement to keep records and that these should be duly analysed from time to time.[1] The T.V.A. does not lay down the course which the farmer has to pursue; the State extension systems advise him on these matters,

---

[1] Section 5 (b) of the Statute says: "To arrange with farmers and farm associations for large-scale practical use of the new forms of fertilisers under conditions permitting an accurate measure of the economic return they produce". Section 5 (e) adds that the donations or sales of fertiliser "for experimentation, education and the introduction of the use of such products in co-operation with practical farmers" is to be conducted "so as to obtain information as to the value, effect and best methods of their use".

occasionally assisted by suggestions from the correlating committee at its half-yearly meetings. Neither does the T.V.A. lay
down the form of records. These are prepared by the land grant
colleges, which means that there is a variation, State by State, in
content and quality. Generally they follow a farm record book
patterned after that of the United States Department of Agriculture in co-operation with the Agricultural Adjustment Administration and the State extension economists. These books are more
or less detailed accountancy analyses for the farm, providing for
an annual recording of stocks, receipts, purchases, expenses, map
of the farm, livestock breeding, note and mortgage transactions,
purchase and sale of real estate, and so on.

It is essential for the success of the demonstration that the
records should be full and accurate. This is, in the first place, a
responsibility of the farmer assisted by the county agents; secondly,
of the State extension services; and, as the procedure has come to
be administered, only in a third and indirect way a responsibility
of the T.V.A. Yet, according to the Statute, the responsibility for
the large-scale practical use of the fertilisers "under conditions permitting an accurate measure of the economic return they produce"
rests first and foremost upon the Authority. It may be that the
full organisation and steady pressure needed to secure full and
accurate returns from the farmers could not, and cannot for some
years, be developed otherwise than through the methods already
adopted by the Authority. The Authority has not yet been able
to develop its co-operative responsibility to such a point as to ensure
that farmers keep records as accurately as desirable, or that the
county agents, the assistant agents, and other representatives of
the State extension services exert swift pressure to this end. It has
been obliged to proceed by gradual educational methods. It is
hoped that the time is not far distant when farm reports will be
complete, exact, and up to date.

The county agents have a complex and difficult job. They must
review the farm record books, and make clear to the demonstration farmer himself and to the other members of the association
the meaning of the results. They must also educate and persuade the farmer himself to understand the meaning of keeping
records.

The fertiliser provided by the T.V.A. is of substantial value.
For example, phosphate is normally made available for soil conserving crops at the rate of 40 pounds of triple superphosphate per
acre per year. The cost may be calculated at 1.9 cents per pound,
that is to say, something like 76 cents per acre, against which the
farmer places his labour, equipment, and hazards. The farms in

the Valley area, though varying very greatly in size, are mainly of about 25 to 50 acres, but 90 per cent. of the demonstration farms are from 51 acres upwards[1], so that year after year quite a substantial contribution to the demonstration system comes from the Authority.[2] Before the T.V.A. came into existence the extension service had urged farmers to undertake such a system of demonstrations, but without the free contribution of fertiliser and the joint effort of farmers the scheme was unsuccessful. Not all the farmers who make an agreement keep it; some use the fertiliser dishonestly for the production of cash crops. The proportion of these backsliders, however, seems to be quite small; this is attributed partly to the good sense of the farmers and partly to the sanction of the public opinion of the local soil conservation association.

Area Tests

Besides conducting the unit farm demonstrations, the Authority also participates in area test-demonstrations, an interesting and highly instructive supplement to demonstration on individual farms. An area test-demonstration includes a number of farms in the same community. The area demonstration is extremely valuable, because an entire community may be affected by a common geographical factor; for example, it may lie in the watershed of a small stream tributary to the river, or the single farms may be conducting their operations as complementary to each other, some producing milk, others crops, others pulse and small grains, others tending herds for breeding. These areas vary from 1,000 to 10,000 acres. In the Tennessee Valley there are some averaging 5,000 acres and containing several score farms. Such area demonstrations are started only where considerable progress has already been made by the test-demonstrations on single or unit farms, and where a considerable proportion of the farmers are interested. From time to time, assisted by the county agents and any necessary specialists, the farmers make changes in the plan originally sketched for each area.

---

[1] About 10 per cent. of test-demonstration farms are 50 acres in size or smaller, 33 per cent. are 51 to 100 acres, and 20 per cent. are 101 to 150 acres. Though some small farms from 25 acres up are included in the demonstrations, the main concern of the county agent is with those of between 51 and 150 acres. This figure has significance when it is considered that the average size of a farm in the State of Tennessee is slightly under 75 acres, and only in Georgia does the average acreage go up to 110.

[2] The T.V.A.'s interpretation of the donations of fertiliser is that they should not be considered as a donation but rather as a partnership arrangement whereby both the farmer and the T.V.A., through the land grant colleges, supply valuable goods and services in order to discover certain fundamental principles affecting agriculture.

Results of Demonstration Programme

After some six years of farm demonstration, the Authority has been able to see results.[1] These appear in reports prepared by the extension services in special areas, based upon a single farm or several, or upon a number of counties, and designed to show what progress, if any, has been made along the lines anticipated by the colleges and the Authority.[2] It is impossible at this stage of the Authority's operations to give a complete survey, but some examples which the colleges have made public are extracted in a later chapter.[3] At this point one widespread sample alone may be cited. It is the record gathered by the Tennessee Agricultural Extension Service of 100 farms.

Seven stages of progress were noted and the number of farms that had advanced to each was set down. On 71 farms that showed greater vigour in livestock (stage II) there was an increase of 9 in the number of calves born per 100 cows. On the 37 farms showing improvement in land use (stage IV), corn acreage was reduced by 20 per cent., while acreage of legumes and hay and pasture grasses was increased by 15 per cent., and acreage of winter cover crops was increased by 26 per cent. Furthermore, on these 37 farms the number of cows was increased by 18 per cent., the number of calves was increased by 49 per cent., the number of cattle and calves purchased was decreased by 25 per cent., and the quantity of dairy products sold was increased by 15 per cent. Other results are shown in the following table.

Number of farms	Stage	Results
		Improved biological adjustments
83	I	More vigorous growth of legumes and grasses treated with lime, phosphate, and other fertilisers.
71	II	Increased vigour of livestock consuming the legumes and grasses.
52	III	Increased yields and quality of crops following the treated legumes and grasses.

[1] The value of the T.V.A. fertiliser at present made available to the farmers for co-operative tests has been assessed by computation of the money value of the nitrogen it puts back into the soil, if that amount of nitrogen had been bought commercially. One pound of phosphate used on legumes, it has been computed, permits the plant to utilise from 3 to 5 pounds of nitrogen from the air. It is estimated that T.V.A. phosphates used in demonstrations would thus equal 124 million pounds of nitrogen drawn from the air, worth $10 to $15 million. Cf. *Budget Justification: Hearings, Independent Offices Appropriation Bill*, 1940; H.R. 1939, p. 1804.

[2] See *Results of Co-operative Tests*, etc., by the Valley States Land Grant Colleges (T.V.A., Nov. 1940), Parts I and II; also Carleton R. BALL: *The Work of the Land Grant Colleges in the Tennessee Valley* (1939).

[3] More detailed figures are given in Chapter XIII.

Number of farms	Stage	Results
		Improved farm management
37	IV	Changes in land use, especially shifting row crops to pasture and hay.
33	V	Adjustments in kinds and numbers of livestock and livestock production practices.
		Improved family welfare
20	VI	Increased security and well-being of the family, or families living on the farm.
		Improved community welfare
9	VII	Increased security and well-being of the people of the neighbourhood, community, county, area, State, region and nation.

T.V.A. PHOSPHATES AND THE NATION

The T.V.A. is interested in concentrated phosphatic fertiliser both because of the special needs of the Valley, and of its general concern for the national good. By 30 June 1939, the T.V.A. had purchased nearly 3,500 acres of phosphate lands in the Tennessee area, costing $1,288,000 (including prospecting and land acquisition costs), as a reserve for its own manufacturing programme.

From the beginning the T.V.A. has shown concern for the national use of phosphatic fertiliser and the ownership of deposits. It has made surveys of the latter, and estimates of the amounts required by the whole United States in a very long-term appreciation of the needs of the soil. It has suggested the purchase of deposits by the United States Government to add to those already governmentally owned (90 per cent. of all) in Idaho, Montana, Wyoming and Utah. These deposits are low grade ore, but T.V.A. discoveries and refinements of production methods, by greatly decreasing transport and handling costs, have given sound promise of their exploitation and distribution if the appropriate hydroelectric or steam plants should be set up on the spot. The T.V.A. has manifested great concern regarding the disastrous consequences which may result from neglect of the problem of dwindling phosphorus reserves. Nearly four million tons of rock phosphate are mined annually (chiefly in Florida and Tennessee, because close to fertiliser consuming areas), of which one million tons are exported. The rest was necessary to meet American needs in 1939. But the T.V.A. observes that many times more than three million tons are needed to make up the annual losses in the quality of American soil, and, at the rate of current extraction, the deposits of Florida and Tennessee will be exhausted in 50 years. Hence, the Authority made recommendations to the President for securing phosphate reserves. The recommendations were passed on by the President to Congress[1], and the matter was taken into consideration by a Congressional Committee. This Committee recommended[2] that a committee should be appointed for further investigation of phosphate deposits, their ownership and use, and other mineral resources; that the Geological Survey be enabled to make a thorough survey of United States phosphate reserves; that the T.V.A. experimental work be continued and extended; that the Agricultural Adjustment Agency programme be extended; that an experimental plant, for education and demonstration, be established in the vicinity of the western State phosphate reserves, and that meanwhile the T.V.A. should conduct experiments with these reserves, especially for use on western soils; and that the United States Government should purchase privately owned phosphate lands now in a non-productive condition.[3]

The T.V.A. does not sell fertiliser except in one case. It made available to the Agricultural Adjustment Administration[4] superphosphate for distribution as a part of the Federal grant-in-aid, implementing the national soil conservation programme. In 1938 some 36,000 tons were so used; in 1939, 45,000. This enables the Authority's influence towards better soil and crop practices to be extended. The A.A.A. reimbursed the Authority on the basis of cost of production based on available plant food, which has varied from 75 cents per unit to 64 cents per unit (20 pounds of P_2O_5).

Fertiliser companies have watched T.V.A. operations with a careful eye, lest, as with its power operations, it should produce on a really large scale for the open market.[5] This the T.V.A. has never attempted. The companies have even complained of the substantial amounts supplied free of cost by the T.V.A. and the A.A.A. under the demonstration scheme. For how long the continued

---

[1] Cf. *Presidential Recommendation to Congress on Production and Conservation of Phosphates*, 20 May 1938.

[2] 76th Congress, 1st Session, House Document No. 21, *Report of Joint Congressional Committee to Investigate. . . Phosphate Resources of U.S.* (17 Jan. 1939).

[3] In November 1942 a consulting committee on western phosphate was appointed, but the war has impeded progress.

[4] The Agricultural Adjustment Administration, a branch of the United States Department of Agriculture, was established in May 1933 to maintain continuous and stable supplies of basic farm products at prices fair to both farmers and consumers, to conserve soil resources and individual farms, and to assist farmers in obtaining an equitable share of the national income. In February 1942 the Agricultural Adjustment Administration was converted into the Agricultural Adjustment Agency of the Department of Agriculture.

[5] Mr. C. J. Brand, Executive Secretary of the National Fertiliser Association giving evidence before the Joint Committee of Investigation (*Hearings*, Part X, p. 4358) said: "The T.V.A. conducts research on new processes and on the testing of new projects and new products, which we certainly do not criticise, in fact which we rather applaud, because we think that the Authority has funds to do things which the private industry has been unable to do".

experimentation on a large scale can be maintained, without doing much more, or much less, is a serious question. As has been said, the T.V.A. has power to sell fertiliser, but does not do so because public opinion would probably not support it. At any rate, one of the results of T.V.A. production of concentrated fertiliser has certainly been to stimulate fertiliser manufacturers to produce more concentrated superphosphate and to hold down its price. This result has not yet assumed large dimensions, but it is perceptible, beneficial, and promises to become ever more important. It is indeed urgent that it should; for supposing that the T.V.A. persuades the farmers to use superphosphate and therefore to demand it, the educative work will have been of little avail if concentrated superphosphate is not manufactured to meet the demand.

Is the T.V.A.'s message, as expressed in its farm demonstration scheme, catching on ? That is the test of its worth; for the forcing quality of phosphates on crops can be tested in the laboratory or in field plots. There are farm demonstrations in some parts of counties, amounting in all to something like 10 per cent. of all the counties in the United States. The appreciable increase in the productivity of land, cattle products and poultry has been amply demonstrated by the comparison of land farmed and fertilised under land grant college guidance and other land.[1] But the T.V.A. has also discovered that converts have been made. For example, in 13 counties of Alabama with three pounds of purchased phosphate for each pound of demonstration phosphate used, the improved pasture area increased from 1935 to 1940 from 2,000 to 29,000 acres; the area of winter legumes from 60,000 to 204,000 acres; the area of perennial legumes from 1,200 acres to 11,000 acres; and the area of lespedeza from 100,000 to 178,000 acres. In south-west Virginia, by 1935, after many years of floating knowledge that phosphate and lime were needed, only 5 per cent. of the farmers had treated their pastures. By 1940, over 70 per cent. of the farmers had adopted this practice and were using 45 per cent. of their A.A.A. payments for lime and phosphate. In 1940, in the North Carolina counties in the T.V.A. area, where the demonstration programme is most intensive, farms applied 56.6 pounds of A.A.A. superphosphate to their cropland and open pasture; but farms in non-demonstration counties applied only 1.6 pounds. There are many other indices of the same nature to show that the lesson is being learned and applied. The research department of the American Farm Bureau Federation reported in November 1940 that the T.V.A. fertiliser production and farm demonstration policy

---

[1] Cf. tables in Chapter XIII.

were sound, and recommended the extension of the use of the improved plant foods, and that Congress further support the programme.

NITRATES AND PHOSPHORUS FOR NATIONAL DEFENCE

It was noticed earlier that an important factor leading to the establishment of the T.V.A. was the building by the United States Government of nitrate plants during the war of 1914-1918 to aid the production of munitions and fertilisers. Section 5 of the T.V.A. Statute put Nitrate Plants Nos. 1 and 2, the steam generating plants connected with them, and the limestone quarry, into the Authority's charge. The Authority was required to maintain in a stand-by condition such portions of Nitrate Plant No. 2 as were not actually used in its fertiliser operations. The Authority, however, as has been seen, found that the production of phosphoric fertiliser was technically and economically preferable to the production of nitrates. Nitrate Plant No. 1 was obsolete; the War Department did not regard it as a military asset; it was fit only for scrap, though the Authority left the problem alone. As regards Nitrate Plant No. 2, the Authority, at the request of the War Department, originally prepared a plan for rehabilitating a part of the plant to produce ammonium-nitrate, at a cost of nearly $1,000,000; but this was rejected, and not until 3 December 1940 did the War Department direct the Authority to recondition the plant. A little earlier than this the Authority had already begun to build a new and modern synthetic ammonia works to replace the cyanimid process installed when the plant was originally built; the War Department provided the funds both for the reconditioning and the new construction. The Authority has planned for the production of 150 tons of anhydrous ammonia a day; when fed into the ammonium nitrate plant this produces 300 tons daily of ingredients for explosives. As in the previous world war, it is proposed that the plant may later be available for experimental work with fertilisers. The phosphorus produced by the Authority is also an important element in the manufacture of munitions, and elemental phosphorus has been sold to the War Department as a constituent of munitions. In order to increase its phosphorus production satisfactorily, the Authority set up a new electric furnace designed to add the equivalent of 50,000 tons per year to the 100,000 of concentrated fertiliser already produced. At Mobile, Alabama, work is planned for a phosphorus and metaphosphate plant, of a capacity equivalent to 75,000 tons of the latter annually, to be ready in 1944, located at Mobile to take advantage of the large reserves of phosphate rock in Florida, easily accessible by water transport.

DIRECT EROSION CONTROL

The farm demonstration work of the T.V.A. serves the indirect prevention of erosion by encouraging the growth of a matting of leguminous and other cover crops. By itself, this is sometimes insufficient to cope with the problem of severe erosion, and the Authority has therefore taken certain other direct and supplementary measures. The first of these is the encouragement of terracing, an ancient method of making trenches and shallow dykes along the contour of the land, to hold the water and reduce the speed at which it runs off, making it "walk" instead of rushing downhill. The Authority was not the pioneer in the introduction of terracing in the Valley. In the State of Alabama, farmers' associations organised on a county basis, encouraged and assisted by the State extension services, had devised an arrangement with manufacturers of terracing machinery for the purchase of large power grading machines, the purchases being underwritten by some responsible local agency. The assistant county agent and the district terracing supervisor manage the machines with the use of local labour and are responsible for the scientific layout of the terraces; the farmers pay the associations between $3 and $4 per hour for the work. The T.V.A., through its agricultural department and the arrangement with the extension services already described, set itself to encourage these operations. The number of power terracing units was 55 in 1935 and 1936; by 1938, there were 70 large units and 5,000 individual and small units. The increase in the area terraced has been shown by the fact that, in the year 1935, 26,000 acres were terraced; by 1941 nearly 700,000 acres had been terraced.[1]

FORESTRY

Soil erosion control, direct and indirect, involves the problem of afforestation, but afforestation goes beyond this in its economic significance. More than half the land area of the Valley is still

---

[1] The figures are as follows:

Year	Cumulative total acres terraced
1935	26,307
1936	92,292
1937	
1938	361,799
1939	468,904
1940	582,669
1941	675,523

In the year 1938-39 large units terraced 41,515 acres and small units 65,590 acres; and the cumulative total of 468,904 acres terraced had been contributed as to 269,637 acres by large units and as to 199,267 acres by small units. In the year ending 30 June 1938, of the large power outfits, 14 were owned commercially and 56 by associations.

under forest, but the timber volume is only about 10 per cent. of the original stand. In the Tennessee Valley, forests are a means of retarding excessive water run-off and of preventing soil erosion and the silting of rivers; and they are an economic resource which produces timber and its by-products and which provides a habitat for wild life.

So far as erosion control and reafforestation are concerned, the Authority's soil and forest surveys and regional land use programme indicate the areas requiring immediate attention. Through the county agents of the State extension services, farmers apply for soil-erosion-control work. If there is merit in the application, a contract is made with the farmer by which he must maintain the improvement of his land for at least five years. Then, year by year, projects are established to construct check dams and diversion ditches, to plough in gully banks, and to mulch and matt sheet eroded areas. This is supplemented by the planting of forest trees, produced by the Authority in its two forest tree crop nurseries maintained at Clinton, Tennessee, and Muscle Shoals, Alabama, and distributed free to farmers with whom it has contracts. In all this work the Authority has been assisted by men from 18 to 36 from Civilian Conservation Corps[1] camps located in the Valley area. From 1933 to 1942 these camps provided approximately 5 million man days of labour on forestry projects sponsored by the Authority, being maintained, of course, by the Federal Government. Altogether some 136,000 seriously eroded and gullied acres on approximately 15,000 farms having a total area of more than two million acres have been protected. Up to the end of 1942 more than 150 million forest trees had been planted in the Valley through this T.V.A. co-operative programme, and of these, 105 million were used for erosion control on farm lands.[2]

Besides the trees mainly on private land in connection with erosion control, the Authority has planted nearly 45 million on 37,000 acres of its own land acquired from its reservoir operations. Thus, it has also established protective strips around the margins of lakes created by its dams.

Protection and development of the forest resources of the watershed naturally promote improved use of land and resources, and thus facilitate the achievement of flood control and navigation objectives. The Authority's activities in reafforestation and forest development are designed to increase the infiltration of rainfall,

---

[1] The Civilian Conservation Corps (C.C.C.) was established in April 1933 to provide employment and vocational training for youthful unemployed citizens. It was abolished in June 1943.

[2] The advent of the war has caused the drastic reduction of these activities.

reduce run-off, and regulate the flow of streams. Fortunately, action taken in this direction also increases the economic value of the forest by making it more productive. Thus the general welfare is served in a dual way through the encouragement and development of forest conservation practices in every possible manner, with and through existing forestry agencies. The agency with which the Authority co-operates and the type of co-operation depend to a considerable extent upon the type of landowner involved. For instance, the extension service is primarily interested in farm forests; the State foresters have an over-all interest; whereas certain public owners are ordinarily interested only in the tracts under their jurisdiction.

Educational Guidance of Private Owners

The problem of ownership, therefore, is a fundamental factor to be considered in the designing of a forestry programme, particularly where co-operation must be conducted with several agencies, each of which is somewhat jealous of its prerogatives in this field. To achieve management conducive to sustained yield among a large group of scattered landowners, each with an individual education and outlook, is a very difficult task.

Farm forests cover 39 per cent. of the forest area of the Tennessee Valley and involve over 150,000 owners. As such a large proportion of the forest resources of the Valley form part of farms, it is realised that (as with the fertiliser programme) private ownership must be encouraged and forestry treated as but one aspect of the total farm economy. Such a programme must necessarily be one of education—issue of educational materials, use of motion picture films, furnishing of free trees for reafforestation demonstrations, making demonstrations of improved forest practices, reducing woodland grazing, and encouraging organisation for adequate fire prevention. Thus, the farm forestry problem is approached as one of educating the landowner to the desirability of so managing the forest that maximum production and resultant income are obtained. The highly expert advisory assistance furnished to the Extension Services by the Authority is having a generally beneficial effect on practices.

Forty-three per cent. of non-farm forest[1] is owned, in large holdings up to several hundred thousand acres, by corporations and individuals, many of whom are non-residents. Although a few such tracts are well managed, most of them are being rapidly exploited for timber, coal, iron and phosphate. These lands become chronic-

---

[1] See Appendix I, table 1.

ally tax delinquent, are subject to timber theft, and present a serious problem in public administration. Where such landowners have an interest in improving practices, an educational approach, through the offices of the various State foresters, is followed. However, lack of interest on the part of these owners makes this one of the remaining urgent problems to be solved.

The public forests represent a permanent and stable type of ownership. These have been acquired by various public agencies, Federal, State, and municipal, for purposes of watershed protection, timber and game development, or recreation. On these areas long-term programmes of improvement directed towards producing the greatest public benefits are possible, and the Authority is assisting these agencies by making available to them the advisory services of specialists in the various forestry fields. Were all the forest land in such stable ownership, sustained industries and employment and the resultant stabilisation of local economy could unquestionably be achieved. However, the Authority believes in preserving private initiative and trusting to the capitalistic incentive of profit, and because of this it has long since given up its original design of solving the forestry problem through the public acquisition of large tracts of forest land and a policy of intense development as practised in some European countries.

Forest Survey and Prospects

As a basis for determining what its programme should be, the Authority has completed a survey of the forest resources on all the 14 million acres of forest within the Tennessee Valley. This survey shows that the 54 per cent. of the Valley which is covered by forests is now producing only one third to one half of the local employment and income which it might produce under prudent management and protection. Even so, the forest industries of the area manufacturing primary products employ 63,000 workers, drawing annual wages in excess of $42 million. These industries manufacture such products as lumber, cross-ties, veneer, fuelwood, pulpwood, and cooperage. Other wood-using industries reprocessing these rough products employ an additional 9,000 workers drawing annual wages of $7,600,000. Thus, inadequately exploited, the forest resources yet furnish employment to 72,000 workers who draw $50 million in wages annually and produce approximately $112 million worth of products.

It is estimated that in time a programme of forest development could at least double the production of the forest, and afford employment to about 150,000 workers producing products valued in excess of $200 million. Such a development is being encouraged by the Authority in forest and factory. In co-operation with State engineering colleges and the United States Forest Products Laboratory, the Authority is investigating methods of producing laminated lumber manufactured from small, defective hardwood trees, tree tops, and logging waste now considered unmerchantable. This investigation has reached the pilot-plant stage and if successful should add to the manufacturing possibilities of the Valley's raw materials. Other investigations looking towards further manufacturing of raw wood are being undertaken, and it is upon the results of such studies and the conclusions drawn from them that the Authority relies to bring home to individuals and public agencies of the area the importance of forest conservation.

Co-operation with other Agencies

At the same time, improved methods of timber culture are being studied and demonstrated. To this end the Authority has a memorandum of understanding with the United States Forest Service, whereby it collaborates with the Appalachian, Southern, and Central States Forest Experiment Stations and the Forest Products Laboratory in co-operative investigations of experimental areas. In addition, data are being collected and studies made on various parts of the forested areas which the Authority has acquired in connection with its dam construction programme. These experiments are designed to determine the most satisfactory species and mixtures of trees to be used for reafforestation, rates of tree growth on different types of soil, determination of the most economical methods of handling stands of timber of various mixtures and stages of growth, and many other studies which have a wide and practical applicability throughout the Valley. The information obtained is then made available to forest landowners and agencies for use on their own lands.

Because of its interest in flood control, the Authority, through investigations such as the above, is also determining the effect of reafforestation and other forestry practices upon the rate of erosion, siltation, and water run-off. Thirteen drainages, ranging from 100 to 17,000 acres, have been equipped for such investigations. Measurements of rainfall, stream flow, and other factors, including ground water, are taken from typical streams before treatment, and are continued over a period of years after erosion control and forestry treatment to determine the exact effectiveness of the measures taken. From the results of such studies it is hoped that a quantitative measure of the effectiveness of forest cover for controlling run-off and erosion and increasing ground water storage may be obtained.

Finally, the Authority is interested in the protection of forests from fire and their care as a haven of wild life. On its own lands, of course, the T.V.A. has an adequate number of fireguards, but its own lands are only a very small proportion of the total acreage to be protected. Hence it co-operates with the States and the United States Forest Service to stimulate concern and the proper measures of organised protection required for some 14 million acres of woodlands. The Authority calculates that less than 20 per cent. of this area is receiving sufficient protection. Surveys show that an average of some 700,000 acres of timberland is burned by some 10,000 fires annually in the Valley, that is, about 5 per cent. of the total is lost each year. From the beginning the Authority encouraged and collaborated with the States in measures of widespread education. From February 1934 to 31 December 1942 about 6,000 educational motion picture programmes were presented to more than three quarters of a million people in the Valley States. Children and teachers have been enlisted in the campaign, and hundreds of thousands of leaflets distributed. It is thought that this has had the effect of producing more organised protection. The Authority has also made a forest fire survey for the entire Valley, going back to 1931, which has been made available to Federal, State, and local authorities and enables them to see the relative local incidence of fires and its relationship to the protection afforded.

USE OF T.V.A.-OWNED LANDS

The T.V.A. has necessarily purchased large areas of the Valley. Most of this land forms the impoundment basin behind each dam, but the so-called "taking line" is so arranged as to include tracts of land along the margin of reservoirs and rivers in order to provide for safety, protection, and measures against soil erosion leading to silting. In 1941 the T.V.A. owned approximately three quarters of a million acres, and this has involved the Authority in the responsibilities of an owner of landed estates. In the first place, as already indicated, some of the non-crop land has been used for reafforestation. Secondly, land which is considered physically suitable has been put into agricultural use. The Authority itself does not act as farmer, but through its Agricultural Relations Department it has entered into contracts with the "soil conservation associations" (farmers' clubs or associations) of a number of reservoir counties providing for payments by the Authority to the association for advice and assistance rendered in licensing Authority controlled land. The associations classify the lands, and recommend what crops could most suitably be grown. They also recommend the tenants (or "licensees" as the Authority prefers to call them) among the neighbouring farmers, and the amount of compensation, or rent, which the Authority ought to charge. Naturally, the Authority's interest in the introduction of better farm practices and improved crop rotation plays a major part in the use of such land. In 1940 there were nearly 2,000 licences, covering about 54,000 acres, and the revenue coming to the Authority from this source was nearly $103,000. In the last two or three years there has been a deliberate reduction of the Authority's intake of land. It prefers not to assume additional responsibilities or take land out of private enterprise, and may even return lands to private ownership and use where this would not interfere with its own essential activities.

Fisheries and Wild Life

The large tracts of land and lake have led to other problems— problems of biological readjustments, as the Authority calls them. The introduction of a number of large lakes and reafforestation in the area are bound to affect the wild life in the river and on the adjoining land. The denudation of the area in the past had been destructive of wild life. The T.V.A. intends to assist the development of fish, game and fur bearing animals. Very early in its career, the Authority began investigations of fishery in the river and lakes to ascertain the effects of impoundment, and it is now clear that most of the species which thrived in the river will do well in the reservoirs. The movement of the water for navigation, flood control, and the production of electricity is one of the problems to be met in fishery production. Stabilisation of water levels during the spawning season has proved feasible and effective. Hitherto the Authority has maintained hatcheries, but these have now been turned over to the United States Fish and Wildlife Service for stocking the lakes where necessary. For the most part it is believed that natural propagation will keep the reservoirs fully productive, after the fish have adjusted themselves to their habitat, and the stocking of the reservoirs from the hatchery will no longer be necessary. A census recently taken shows that in 1940 there were removed from five T.V.A. reservoirs nearly 5 million pounds of fish; the oldest reservoir (Wilson) yielded the most pounds of fish per acre of water.

Studies have been made of the conditions under which fur bearing animals can find a productive home in the Valley, and also of the food of quail. Game food trees and shrubs have been planted in several reservoir areas. Aquatic food plants and waterfowl migration have been surveyed. In July 1938 a refuge of roughly 41,000 acres of land and water, a part of the Wheeler Reservoir area in northern Alabama, was designated by Executive Order of the United States President as a migratory waterfowl refuge. It is assigned for use by the United States Fish and Wildlife Service as a refuge and breeding ground for migratory birds and other wild life.

CHAPTER V

THE ADVANCEMENT OF ECONOMIC OPPORTUNITY

The primary tasks of the T.V.A., tending to develop the Valley's water and soil resources and so raise its standard of living, have now been described. But these by no means exhaust all its efforts or contribution towards the main object. There are a number of related activities which, together with those already described, may properly be called economic planning for the Valley's prosperity. These activities spring from two principal sources which are, of course, connected and complementary, though each also has its own specific objectives. The first of these sources is the attempt to raise the meagre standard of living by making labour easier or more productive on the farm, chiefly by the invention or adaptation of farm apparatus or processes. Incidentally, this assists the fulfilment of other T.V.A. purposes, for example, the increased sale of electricity and the conservation of the soil. Secondly, by what are called the "planning" sections of the Statute, namely, Sections 22 and 23, as well as the implications of the Preamble, the T.V.A. has a more general responsibility for increasing the well-being of the Valley. To this end, it is endowed with powers to make studies, demonstrations, and investigations, and to propose action. This general power has been used in the conduct of investigations into the mineral and other resources (for instance, recreational and tourist possibilities) and their economic exploitation. The belief that the income of the area could most effectively be raised by a measure of industrialisation was an additional spur to research into local resources and industrial processes which could be of use locally.

Perhaps the quickest route to the raising of the standard of living would have been wholesale promotion of industry; but in the climate of opinion outside the Valley and having regard to the deficiency of T.V.A. powers for such a purpose, this course could not be followed. Hence, no large-scale campaign for the promotion of industry was undertaken or considered. But it was believed that if cheap electricity, good transport facilities on the river, and perhaps processes that could be locally handled, were provided, and if this came to be known, industry would establish itself. This would increase traffic on the river, and so again add to the income of the region. With this general destination in mind, then, the T.V.A. has taken the path which will presently be described, particularly emphasising its intimate understanding of, and concern for, the Valley's problems, because the centre of its administration is lodged in the very heart of the Valley itself.[1]

T.V.A. PLANNING POWERS

Before attempting to describe the T.V.A.'s efforts to advance economic opportunity and, in the next chapter, its contributions to the social well-being of the Valley, a few words are necessary on the nature of the powers of economic planning given to the Authority by the Statute. This is most essential if the powers of the T.V.A. are to be seen in their proper proportion. The Statute at first sight appears to give the T.V.A. wide powers of economic planning. Section 22 gives powers to the President, who has transferred the powers to the T.V.A., and these powers are "to aid further the proper use, conservation, and development of the natural resources . . . and to provide for the general welfare of the citizens . . . "; but this power is limited only to the making of surveys and general plans within the limits of appropriations made therefor by Congress. Thus, T.V.A. powers are not designed to reconstruct the area itself forthwith, but only to make surveys and plans, and even then, only so far as Congress has appropriated money therefor. The purpose stated in the same section, namely, "all for the general purpose of fostering an orderly and proper physical, economic and social development of said areas", is wide in scope, but, as we must emphasise once more, is limited to "studies, experiments, or demonstrations as may be necessary and suitable to that end".

These powers to study, experiment, demonstrate, survey, and make general plans—which, by the way, may be undertaken in co-operation with States or their subdivisions, or with co-operative or other organisations—do offer, however, a wide opportunity in its own field of planning, namely, the preparation of schemes, the development of ideas and the making of systematic suggestions for reconstruction and improvement. It is important, then, to observe that the T.V.A.'s powers, though limited in regard to putting plans into action, are wide in regard to the making of plans. If it is not in the position of an absolute practical governor over the area, it is at least in the position of a leader of thought.

---

[1] Cf. 77th Congress, 2nd Session, *T.V.A. Statement* in *Hearings on S. 2721,* 1942; and *Annual Report of the Tennessee Valley Authority,* 1939, p. 82.

Again, there is Section 23 which gives to the President of the United States the obligation of recommending to Congress legislation to carry out the general purposes of Section 22, that is, surveys, experiments, and so forth, and also for the special purpose of bringing about the maximum development of flood control, navigation, manufacture of electric power, the proper use of marginal lands, reafforestation, and the "economic and social well-being of the people living in the said river basin". This section, then, gives to the T.V.A. the opportunity, through the President, of proposing legislation to Congress which might add to its powers to take action, or might lead to other public agencies being given powers for such purposes.

Now, as will be seen, T.V.A. planning powers, in the context of the remarks made above, have been used. But the T.V.A. was established in an area already occupied by a number of governmental agencies, some local and some Federal. The area was already occupied by agriculture, industry, and other interests. In other words, the Authority did not have before it a clear slate on which to draw any planning that it chose. Nor is that all. It will be noticed that the planning powers of the T.V.A. are limited by (a) appropriations which Congress is prepared to make for the necessary surveys and investigations, and (b) the need, in broader matters, for further legislative power. In fact, Congress has consistently shown extreme caution in giving appropriations for purposes of surveys and research. It has been found difficult to secure appropriations for purposes which may be regarded as general planning, and the T.V.A. has had to restrict its scope to those projects which can be shown to be strictly related to its primary tasks. This has seriously limited its scope, as has also the great difficulty of securing the legislative attention of Congress when an addition to the powers of a public enterprise are involved, as they necessarily are with the T.V.A.

In addition to these external limitations on the T.V.A.'s planning power, it is necessary to remember the general character of opinion in the country in which the Authority functions. This is not favourable to general planning.

Secondly, the T.V.A. has had to steer towards the advancement of economic opportunity and the people's social well-being by its cautious interpretation and use of its primary powers and the planning authority referred to above. In spite of all the contributions it has undoubtedly made to the well-being of the Valley, it is necessary to notice that comprehensive planning has not been undertaken; nor, therefore, has there been the drive which would be necessary to implement such plans. Further, once the demonstration period is over, the T.V.A. must simply leave the venture it has initiated to take on, or not, with those groups of the public, such as industry, or farmers' associations, or co-operatives, or States, which may be interested in carrying the results of the plans and demonstrations into effect. There, the responsibility of the T.V.A. necessarily ends, though its interest and concern may not; and because of this limitation, whatever its zeal, the prosecution of wide and comprehensive measures is necessarily restrained.

PROGRESS BY RESOURCES RESEARCH, TECHNICAL ASSISTANCE AND EDUCATION

In view of what has just been said, it is not surprising to find that the T.V.A. has sought to assist economic progress by research, technical assistance and persuasion. As we have already seen in various aspects of the fertiliser, farm demonstration and power programmes, the Authority attaches supreme importance to research into the resources of the region and the conditions under which these may be made economically valuable, and to the invention of processes and apparatus. Though the various resources are generally known as a result of past investigations by private agencies, and public departments like the United States Geological Survey and the Bureau of Mines, none has, or perhaps could have, so persistently and patiently concentrated on the subject as an authority lodged in the locality and vested with a special responsibility. This research work—since the T.V.A. must be careful in its expenditure of public funds—is usually undertaken by arrangement with the laboratories and the local land grant colleges, with the T.V.A. initiating and stimulating the undertaking. The Authority has, however, also conducted some research in its own laboratories entirely. Sometimes it co-operates with the research sections of private industry

As has been shown, the T.V.A. has no power to regiment the region; it must proceed by persuasion and the demonstration of the value of its discoveries. It therefore furnishes initiative, direction, publicity and expert guidance. Further, by stimulating demand for apparatus, it induces private enterprise to manufacture this at cheap enough rates for purchase by the low-income groups of the Valley. Some examples from the principal lines of development may be given to make both purpose and method clearer.

Agricultural Appliances and Processing

One basic objective is the discovery or adaptation of machinery and electrical equipment to permit of the better processing, conserving or marketing of the agricultural products of the area by cheaper and more productive methods. It is essential to discover or invent apparatus adequate to the task, and yet cheap enough for the low-income groups of the Valley.

A combined seed and fertiliser distributor has been developed in co-operation with the Agricultural Experiment Station of the University of Tennessee, under a contractual arrangement, and is now in commercial production and being sold through regular sales channels. The patent in such a case is applied for by and belongs to the T.V.A. A low-cost small-scale thresher has been developed and is now in commercial production by a farm machinery manufacturer. Research is far advanced (with the Georgia Agricultural and Engineering Experiment Stations) into the growing, harvesting and processing of flax. Lespedeza harvesting equipment, as an attachment to an ordinary mowing machine, has been invented, and has allowed a doubling of the recovery of the precious lespedeza seed.

The Authority has also stimulated the development of a general utility half-horsepower feed grinder which is cheaper than a similar unit on the market produced by a manufacturer, and also of an electric curing unit which is subject to automatic control, is cheap, and has practically no fire risk, to cure the sweet potatoes which are grown in large quantities in the Valley and which have hitherto been cured by coal or wood heat. Installing electric heaters in place of the conventional wood stove has increased storage capacity by 10 to 15 per cent. Under demonstration, the unit has shown something like a 7 per cent. increase in repack and the quality of the product is improved. The total gain per 2,000 bushels is $134; the total investment cost of the unit is $95. A similar process of experiment is in progress with electric units for the curing of ham, tobacco and hay, and also for the production of a combined dairy steriliser and water heater.

Hay Drying.

The development of electric hay-drying apparatus gives an instructive insight into T.V.A. research purposes and methods. The humidity of the Valley promotes the growth of a heavy hay crop, but as the hay-drying season tends to be showery, hay curing in the field is very difficult. The T.V.A. and the land grant institutions conferred early in 1942 to select the most important farm problems amenable to solution by equipment. As a result, the

Authority co-operated, in the States of Virginia, North Carolina and Georgia, with State extension services and experiment stations and the Appalachian Electric Power Company (Virginia) to explore the value of a barn hay-drying system adaptable to almost any type of barn, founded on the principle of the circulation of air by electric blowers through a number of air ducts.

Farmers were assisted with designs of the dryers, advice where equipment could be purchased, and supervision of installation. By the end of the 1942 hay season, 34 hay dryers had been installed in the Tennessee Valley States: 27 by farmers and 7 in college and experimental station farms (there would have been more, but for the wartime scarcity of equipment). For 20 dryers installed in 1942, installation costs of all kinds ranged from $80 to $350 each, allowing only a quarter of the cost of the motor, since this is generally used for other jobs also. Excellent results were obtained; the quality of the hay was especially highly rated under United States Department of Agriculture tests. A survey of nine counties in southwest Virginia by the Virginia Polytechnic Institute showed that farmers who relied on field curing lost about half a million dollars of the value of their 1942 hay crop, whereas no losses were reported by farmers owning hay dryers.

Food Processing and Preservation.

Producers of fruits and vegetables in the Tennessee Valley region and other parts of the South have suffered from distance to markets and the lack of properly-developed means of preservation. In view of the growth of quick-freezing in the North and Far West and the lack of it in the South, it was decided to conduct research in that field, and to adapt techniques to agricultural conditions and markets in the South, where producers are generally small and scattered. A new immersion process of quick-freezing, along with suitable equipment, was developed by the Department in co-operation with the University of Tennessee Engineering and Agricultural Experiment Stations. In 1940 this was put into successful commercial use by a farm co-operative in Cleveland, Tennessee. A small portable freezer has also been developed for use in freezer locker plants and in scattered small-scale operations. Research has been conducted on freezing techniques generally in co-operation with Georgia Agricultural Station. Improved methods of cold pack freezing have been developed and tested in field operations. This experience has enabled T.V.A. engineers in the last two years to give technical assistance to packers in Georgia, Alabama, Tennessee, and Virginia in the freezing of over 4,000,000 pounds of strawberries.

In 1938 a refrigerated barge was constructed by the T.V.A. to demonstrate the feasibility of combined storage and transportation facility. It delivered strawberries to customers as far afield as St. Louis and New York. Both this and a second barge are to be used as mobile units for research in complete food preparation and processing. They contain facilities for investigating the problems of preserving local agricultural food products by dehydration, canning, chemical and other means, all of which are being studied with reference to their technical and commercial aspects. The work of the plant is co-ordinated with the research and basic investigations conducted in co-operation with the State Agricultural Experiment Stations and Extension Services, and it will be used to demonstrate the technical and economic feasibility of the processing and equipment thus developed.[1]

Again, the T.V.A., working through the extension system, has assisted in the development of community "walk-in" refrigerators, in order to secure that the meat produced on the farm shall be properly conserved for home use. Owing to the extremely warm climate, the farmers in the Tennessee Valley are unable to keep fresh meat for any length of time, and consequently, where individual refrigerators are not available, pork is preserved by salting. Salt pork is not a good article of continual diet; moreover, about a quarter of the pork slaughtered on southeastern farms is spoiled before it can be cured. If a low-cost community refrigerator could be developed, and operated by 10 to 25 families, fresh rather than cured meat could be consumed; and furthermore, there would be practical inducement to put land into pasture for veal or beef. In the demonstrations, the farmers paid the operating costs. On the basis of the results, which were extremely favourable, literature was prepared and articles published in trade journals, in the hope of stimulating private manufacturers; but blueprints were also given so that any intelligent country shopman could make the unit himself, after buying the parts. By 1941, 19 such refrigerators were in operation independently of T.V.A. aid, on a private basis where space was rented, or on a co-operative arrangement. The T.V.A. is also testing a unit of especially large capacity in which freezer compartments for each family are included, with space allowed for the preparation of meat for storage.

---

[1] A small pilot dehydration unit was constructed and assembled at the Georgia Agricultural Experiment Station where the various methods and techniques in the dehydration of southern agricultural raw materials have been studied. The data taken from this small unit operation are being studied in the design of a larger commercial unit, and supplied to the Agricultural Engineering Development Division for use in their field demonstration programme with four small community-size machines.

Cottonseed Cooking.

Another process developed by T.V.A. methods which may prove of very great ultimate significance is the improved production of cottonseed oil. For something like half a century no progress had been made in the equipment and method of handling cottonseed in the mills. When the cotton fibre and lint have been removed from the pods, seed is left, which is actually worth something like 17 per cent. of the total value of the cotton crop, and from which oil, meal, and hulls are produced. A good deal of the meal and the seed produced in the Valley was sent out to other parts of the United States for processing. The University of Tennessee College of Engineering, which had begun investigations at the instance of local representatives of the industry in 1929, thought that this was due to the existence of many mills too small to employ adequate capital. Big mills had their own research laboratories and could keep up with the times. The problem, then, was to improve the technology of the small local mills, and more especially the major operation of cooking the cottonseed. Through the financial and moral co-operation of the T.V.A., suitable units were designed for use in the small mills. Cooking time was reduced from between 1 and 2 hours to 20 minutes, and the oil yield so increased as to promise an increase in profit of $1.00 a ton, considerably more than the former total profit of the average mill. Some of the devices were invented by the T.V.A. engineers themselves, and others by the University of Tennessee staff. The patents are to be exploited, not by the T.V.A. directly, but by a non-profit research corporation (the directors of which are prominent businessmen) set up by the University of Tennessee. From the small mill, the oil-cake is sold to local farmers as feed for cattle.

The T.V.A.'s interest in this experiment is not a direct money return, although it has supplied about one half of the $90,000 required for research and demonstration, but the possible increase of the Valley's wealth. Only a part of the fees for the use of patents will go to the T.V.A.; the rest will finance further research. By 1942, twelve private mills in the Valley States were using the new cooker, which is now being manufactured under licence by three important firms.

Minerals

From the beginning of the Authority's operations, there has been a keen interest in the possibilities of the Valley's mineral resources, and even further, in the possibility of creating conditions conducive to a substantial degree of industrialisation. Hence careful attention was paid to the primary task of locating, discovering and evaluating the natural resources of the area and to the experimental demonstration of their uses.

The Authority's investigations disclosed reserves of crude china clay or kaolin in the area. Of equal importance, the particular contribution of the T.V.A. Ceramic Laboratory (co-operatively with representatives of the industry) was to develop a superior method of refining the crude clay so that it could compete successfully with imported china clays in the finest translucent whitewares. The result has been that several American ceramic plants are continuing the use of North Carolina primary kaolin or are substituting the clay of improved quality for imported china clay.

In 1939, some 16,000 tons of highly refined clay were thus produced; in 1940, over 30,000 tons. Experts believe that this enterprise may grow to four to five times its previous capacity.

The laboratory also demonstrated the high quality of translucent whiteware which could be made in experimental electrically fired kilns, designed by the Authority. Thus two objectives were achieved simultaneously: demonstrated quality of clays in finished products, and the demonstrated qualifications of high temperature electrically-fired furnaces as an alternative to the traditional methods. The laboratory was subsequently turned over to the United States Bureau of Mines for a continuation of the electro-technical research connected with minerals and for further experiments designed to increase the industrial utilisation of Valley minerals.

In the last decade industrial advance seems to have taken the path of chemical, rather than purely mechanical, progress. The present developments in the Valley may therefore be leading to the creation of new products and the use of new raw materials. Supplying cheap electricity in the T.V.A. region does not merely mean a cheaper source of mechanical power; it also makes possible the development of electro-chemical and electro-metallurgical industries which have heretofore been unprofitable owing to the high cost of electricity employed in the processes. Chemical industrialists and technicians therefore need to reconsider the use of the mineral raw materials of the area.

In the past, one of the most important developments of the region has centred in the coal and iron industries. There are extensive raw material resources for both of these, and their future development is even more promising, since it will include certain advances hitherto impossible. Iron may be utilised largely in the form of special lines of iron and steel in alloys. Scattered deposits of manganese ores, lesser deposits of chromite, and some even scarcer alloy materials indicate that in the future the T.V.A. area may produce ferro-manganese, ferro-chromium, ferro-silicon, and other ferro alloys on an extensive scale. The manufacture of these will be rendered possible by the fact that electro-metallurgical methods supplied by cheap electric power will be available. New technology in ore dressing opens up a new field for the production of mineral resources not hitherto utilisable because the material mined or quarried did not meet the commercial specifications. Examples are the production of ilmenite (titanium), kyanite, and barite concentrates by froth flotation; also, utilisation of low grade phosphate through better means of concentration. Thus, a constant reappraisal and economic study of the minerals of the area is required if the best use is to be made of them.

The development of adequate transportation facilities on the Tennessee River has also opened new possibilities for the development of the raw material resources of the Valley. There are large coal deposits contiguous to the Tennessee River that have been made accessible by the improved navigation facilities. These have been studied and appraised and substantial amounts of coal are now being mined and shipped on the Tennessee River from deposits that till now could not be profitably worked. The movement of limestone from a quarry on the river for the production of calcium carbide is about to start.

Tourist Trade

The Authority has created some pretty lake land, and, mainly under the influence of its Department of Regional Studies has realised the potentialities for recreational use. The States in the region had no recreational programme, and four had no organised park systems. Several demonstration parks were established by the T.V.A., and there are other sites yet to be developed. The parks already established were not constructed by the Authority itself, but, pursuant to its regular policy, through other agencies already in operation in the area—in this case through the National Park Service's materials, technical assistance and counsel and the labour of the Civilian Conservation Corps.

The Authority itself has operated the parks[1], and has attracted masses of people at the week-ends and holidays with its facilities for horseback riding, boating, swimming, camping and vacation cabins. Restaurant facilities are operated under concession.

Other parks are being built, and the Tennessee State Department of Conservation will operate them on standards of develop-

---

[1] In 1934, the T.V.A. was accepted by the United States National Park Service as a "park authority".

ment set by the Authority. The parks, which are on T.V.A. land, will be leased to the State of Tennessee, and, as development proceeds, to other States, at a nominal annual rental.

In an area which includes the Great Smoky Mountains and other fine scenic resources, the Authority has seen the opportunity of attracting visitors. By arrangements with the Tennessee State Planning Board, assistance was given in the creation of a planning commission to serve the counties adjacent to the Tennessee boundary of the Great Smoky Mountains National Park for the development of recreational facilities and business. The Authority does not possess the power to secure that local communities conform to standards of beauty and health necessary to exploit this potentiality, either by itself taking action or by requiring them to do so. But it has done the next best thing by trying to induce the local States, municipalities, and civic organisations to confer with it and with each other in order to secure co-ordinated and adequate action. By the deliberate planning and design of the Authority, the dams are of remarkable beauty, whether as vast structures or as waterfalls. By 1942, 11,000,000 people had visited the dams, from every State and many nations. The Authority has published a work on the scenic resources of the area, and made reports on the opportunities for economic returns from recreational developments. There are great potentialities in this field, especially in the chain of lakes over which the T.V.A. has practically full powers of utilisation. But the Authority itself, as already mentioned, has not had sufficient independent power to put into effect the wider measures it thinks necessary. Its own powers are limited to "demonstrations", and now that it has demonstrated in five parks, and made its surveys, the demonstration period has drawn almost to a close. It now needs more powers, at least over its own lands. In 1940 the Authority recommended to the President, and through him to Congress, the necessary measures.[1] Foremost among these was the broadening of its own powers to construct and operate recreational facilities on the properties acquired for water-control purposes, utilising the labour of the N.Y.A.,[2] W.P.A.,[3] and C.C.C.[4] Yet it may not press

[1] Cf. 76th Congress, 3rd Session, Document No 565, *Report on the Recreation Development of the Tennessee River System*, Jan. 1940.

[2] National Youth Administration, established in June 1935, within the W.P.A., to provide work-training for unemployed youth and part-time work for needy students.

[3] Works Progress Administration, established on 6 May 1935, to co-operate with local State and Federal sponsors in the execution of a programme of public works projects. In July 1939 it was reorganised as Works Projects Administration, when N.Y.A. was put under its aegis. The W.P.A. was abolished in 1943, and the N.Y.A. transferred to the Training Division of the War Manpower Commission.

[4] Cf. p. 71.

for these powers, as an alternative still offers in arrangements with the States. Indeed, late in 1942, the Authority made an agreement with the Tennessee Department of Conservation whereby the latter assumed responsibility for development, operation and maintenance for recreational purposes of Authority-controlled properties in the State, excepting those lands located in dam reservations. The spirit of the agreement was the explicit recognition that the public should be encouraged to look to the State rather than to the Authority in matters of recreation. In connection with its reservoir programme, the T.V.A. may recommend the purchase of, or itself purchase, land for public access and recreation on the advice of the State Department of Conservation. The State Department of Conservation is responsible for advising sponsoring groups on the form, conditions, financing and standards of development and operation; the leases or licences are then made by the Authority, if satisfied with the situation as reported by the Department. The Department becomes responsible for conducting studies and investigations of the recreational value of the Authority's lands.

Industry and Freight Rates

Careful and persistent studies made by the Authority have revealed to what a large extent the system of rates prevailing in the United States in so far as they affect interterritorial economic relationships, discriminates against the South-West, the South-East, and the Interior West. The Chairman of the T.V.A. has declared:

> The system of interterritorial freight rates has handicapped and hamstrung the efforts of these various regions to engage in that measure of manufacturing of their raw materials which is economically sound. At the same time it has stimulated the export in raw or semi-finished form of those natural resources. Thus, the South-West, the South-East and the Interior West have become predominantly raw material areas, whereas the North-East, having an advantage by reason of interterritorial freight rates, has become predominantly industrialised. . . The importance of the interterritorial freight rate system is very great indeed . . . and is only in recent years becoming fully understood and comprehended.[1]

This theme is important to the T.V.A. because it is fundamentally interested in securing a rising standard of living in the Valley. The Authority has been much concerned at the fact that the regions which produce raw materials are also places of low income, whereas those which live by the production of manufactured goods, or the

---

[1] Paper on *Freight Rates and Southwestern Industry*, by D. E. LILIENTHAL (University of Texas, Nov. 1941).

processing of raw materials, are areas of high income. This is strikingly exemplified by the lowness of income in the south-eastern States and in the Tennessee Valley. It is a difficult problem to lift up the economic standards of a region even where all factors, like natural resources and human skill, are to hand, but even more difficult to make anything of an area where these have been allowed to deteriorate. Hence it is of the utmost importance that at least no artificial maladjustments should be permitted to remain a moment longer than is necessary after their discovery. The T.V.A. therefore undertook to make it plain to the public and the agencies of government that the south-eastern States were being subjected to irrational discrimination.

In a number of studies[1], including a report to Congress, the Authority has shown to what a great degree the northeastern States are given a preference in the freight rate system, especially in manufactured articles which might be produced in the South as well as anywhere else. In other words, this artificial obstruction operates as though the northeastern section were protected by a tariff wall as regards imports of manufactures and a subsidy to its competitive cost of production against southeastern rivals, and a bounty on its purchase of raw materials and food.[2]

The T.V.A. has publicised the facts, and this and other forces caused the Interstate Commerce Commission in 1939 to undertake an investigation of class rates in the United States east of the Rockies. In 1940 Congress amended the Interstate Commerce Act to include a prohibition against undue and unjust discrimination among the regions. The T.V.A. has sought and is seeking equality of opportunity among the regions of the United States. At the request of the President, it has co-ordinated the preparation of the economic evidence from the South and West to be put before the Interstate Commerce Commission in its class rate investigation.[3] It bases its appeal on the need to integrate the nation by reform of an unbalance between the workshop regions and the raw materials regions of a single society. It believes that mile for mile equality of rates will make for the decentralisation and diffusion of industry over the whole nation, and so produce greater stability of welfare and assist the diversification of industry which is natural to all areas, but is now thwarted by rate distortions. It argues that regional specialisation, exaggerated by disparity of rates, militates against full production and the maximum national income.

---

[1] *The Interterritorial Freight Rate Problem of the U.S.A.*, 7 June 1937; and *Supplemental Phases of the Interterritorial Freight Rate Problem of the U.S.A.*, 27 Apr. 1939.

[2] Cf. Ford K. EDWARDS: *Territorial Unit Costs for Railroad Freight Service*, 1939 (I.C.C. Docket 28300, Exhibit 13, introduced in Sept. 1942).

[3] Cf. Exhibit and Testimony, I.A.O. Spottswood (I.C.C., Sept. 1942).

Direct Promotion of Industry

It is clear from the foregoing account of the T.V.A.'s economic activities, and even more from its aspirations and continuing concern, that its interest in the economic welfare of the area is intense and, so far as time and possibility go, laudably successful. A rather wider aspect of this subject is the question of a more comprehensive and forceful attempt to secure the development of industry in the area. The present Chairman of the T.V.A. has stated that the South needs an increase in income derivable from greater reliance on manufacturing or processing its raw materials.[1] There are interests which strongly desire this, such as business groups; there are hundreds of thousands who can be said to need it, whether they are articulate or not. When cotton mills were opened, small as the wages were, there was a rush to get work.

A serious problem was whether the Authority should actively encourage the establishment of industry in the area. Another was whether industry would feel the attraction of the opportunities in the Valley, increased by the availability of cheap power. But development was slowed by the fact that electricity was not yet available. Secondly, the Authority, because of its public character and unprecedented position, has been confronted with opposition in this initiative. Thirdly, there is resistance to industrial development by publicists and members of Congress, who fear adverse effects on industries in their own areas.

Some have even challenged navigation activity on the ground that there will be decreased rail traffic, and losses to the coal industry. Fears of losses to coal sales and railway coal haulage from hydroelectric development have been expressed by industrialists and labour unions.[2]

The minority members of the Congressional Joint Committee Investigating the T.V.A. in 1938-1939 viewed industrial development with disfavour. On the T.V.A. ceramic experiments they say:

Moreover, these expenditures have been paid for by tax-payers in other sections of the country where the ceramic industry is more highly developed and where, if such experimentation were made, better results could have been achieved.[3]

---

[1] Cf. D. E. LILIENTHAL: *Restoration of Economic Equality among Regions of the U.S.A.*, 21 Mar. 1940, p. 314.

[2] Yet stimulation of the use of electricity by the T.V.A. has been a clear benefit to coal producers, since in systems other than that of the T.V.A. electricity is chiefly generated by steam. Tennessee, Alabama, Georgia and Mississippi used ten times the coal in the generation of electricity for public use in 1942 as compared with 1933.

[3] *Minority Report*, p. 312. Cf. Chapter IX.

Conscious of such feelings, the T.V.A.'s attitude to industrialisation was to limit its action to the development of the basic resources of the area, river transportation facilities, security from floods, cheap electric power, agriculture, and the study of mineral resources. It is thought that when the advantages are known, and discriminatory freight rates against the region are removed, industry will come of its own accord without a campaign of promotion.

Already there were industries establishing and expanding themselves before the second world war began, and the T.V.A. claims that this was due to its activities as described above. The Authority observes that industrial growth in the Valley between 1933 and 1939 took place at a greater rate than in the southeastern States as a whole or the United States as a whole:

> The Tennessee Valley in 1939 had 721 more manufacturing plants and 40,952 more industrial wage earners than in the depression year 1933, a gain of 53.4 per cent. in plants and 41.7 per cent. in wage earners, according to census figures. The southeastern States as a whole in the same period showed increases of 41.1 per cent. in number of plants and 33.9 per cent. in number of industrial wage earners. The United States as a whole increased 30 per cent. in plants and 30.2 per cent. in wage earners.
>
> The Tennessee Valley also showed an increase in manufacturing since 1929, a boom year, although industrial activity in the nation as a whole declined. The Valley's 122 counties had a total of 139,074 industrial wage earners in 1939, compared to 127,010 ten years earlier, a gain of 9.5 per cent. The South-east's gain was 3.8 per cent. while the nation declined 10.8 per cent. Actually, these gains were somewhat greater and losses less, due to changes in classification omitting certain repair and other industries in the 1939 census that were included in the 1929 census.
>
> Industrial growth in the Tennessee Valley since 1929 has been due partly to expansion of established industries, in chemical, textile, rayon, aluminium and various other branches of manufacturing, and partly to location of new industries in hosiery, garments, shoe, woodworking, phosphorus, and other lines. These gains more than offset the heavy losses in industry suffered during the depression.[1]

There has been a growth in the manufacture of manganese, ferro-alloys, phosphorus, electrodes, aluminium, rubber products, flour, and, under Government sponsorship, warfare chemicals. Such industries have come into the Valley primarily because of low-cost electricity and the availability of mineral resources. Since 1941, other plants have been introduced or expanded, most not requiring a heavy power load. Examples are: textiles, paper tissues, flooring and wooden boxes, medicinal preparations, printing, dairy products, ammunition, steel products.

---

[1] Cf. 77th Congress, 2nd Session, Senate Committee on Agriculture and Forestry, *Hearings on S. 2361*, 16-19 Mar. 1942, p. 300.

The war has stimulated industry in the Valley, as outside it. Some of the plants may stay, and may well be joined by other units, for there will be abundant power now that steam plants have been added to a greatly expanded hydroelectric system.   The Tennessee Valley will be subject to all the hazards of the whole nation, and of all nations, for that matter, in respect of post-war readjustment, and is at present alert to the fact.   The situation will require exceptional clarity of thought and resolution on the part of the Authority; for it involves the relationship of the economy of one region in the process of special development to the economic policy of the whole nation of which it is a part.

At the present stage of the T.V.A.'s work of fostering economic welfare[1], the results may be considered beneficial to the community as a whole, for it has concerned itself not with competition with the production of other regions of the United States but only with increasing the welfare of the Valley's inhabitants.   This it has done by: (a) considerably reducing their electricity costs, and extending the use of electricity; (b) arresting the waste of soil resources and increasing the yield of the earth, thus raising incomes; (c) reducing costs of transport, which must stimulate industry and permit some purchase of commodities from wages or securities or savings; (d) preventing damage from floods, and thereby making the money which would have been spent on repairing it available for constructive activities and purchases; (e) discovering processes and resources which add to the wealth of the area and the whole country, with almost negligible competition with existing interests.

---

[1] The activities described in the foregoing paragraphs, as well as those in the following chapter on the social well-being of the people, fall almost entirely into the T.V.A.'s budgetary classifications of "Development Activities" and "Related Property Operations".   The net expense on these operations (income was negligible in comparison) for 1933-1942 is displayed in Appendix IV, tables 4 and 5.

CHAPTER VI

THE PEOPLE'S SOCIAL WELL-BEING

If, as will by now have been appreciated, the planning powers of the T.V.A. are limited, on the one hand, to studies, proposals, instruction and persuasion, and on the other, to planning in the sense of the wise and far-seeing conduct of its primary tasks, the Authority has, nevertheless, assumed responsibilities and made measurable progress in their fulfilment. Some other activities of a "planning" nature but also of direct executive force result from its general responsibility for the increase of the welfare of the region, as well as for the consequences of its own activities on the life and amenities of the region.

One of the most striking and stirring features of the multifarious activities of the T.V.A. has been the intensity of its regard for human relationships, and its conscientious assumption of responsibilities arising out of a profound feeling for human values. Coming into an area with new ideas, devices and public works, the Authority caused a disturbance, in some cases necessarily severe. It determined that so far as it was in command of the situation it would do everything possible to secure satisfactory readjustment. This aim has been pursued in the T.V.A.'s physico-economic studies and regional planning, in its relationship to the local governing authorities, in its policy of relocation of families, schools and roads, and in its attitude to public health and general education.

REGIONAL STUDIES AND PLANNING

It is evident that the Authority's activities involve readjustment projects which the local agencies must be induced, and in some cases even compelled, to accept. It is useless for the Authority to push ahead regardless of social and economic consequences; and it can only estimate what these will be if it is well-informed. Moreover, the Authority has an interest in and a clear responsibility for raising the general well-being of the area. It therefore makes studies of local administration, and these are available to the local agencies, the States and civic bodies with an interest in improvement. Thus, the Authority has made research studies of municipal government in Mississippi and Tennessee, published by the Mississippi State Planning Commission and the University of Tennessee. Under co-operative agreements with the Authority, the State Universities of Alabama and Georgia have made studies of the municipal government systems of those States. A series of studies emerged from the need to ascertain the feasibility of extending electricity distribution, the justification for taking land for reservoir property, and the effects of this and its operations on the economic situation and public finances of cities and counties. Some study has been made of county organisation and administration in all the seven States, since there is very frequent contact between them and the Authority. In Tennessee and Mississippi the municipal situation of a hundred cities has been analysed.

The social and economic effects of the building of dams on the surrounding area have also been carefully studied. It has been necessary to consider and report upon industrial developments in the South, the problem of municipal government subsidies to industry, occupational distribution and trends, the migration of the population. Information has been collected on the growth and decline of local industries and plants, transportation facilities, schools and many kindred subjects. All in all, these studies contain a large amount of extremely valuable analytical material gathered on a scale more comprehensive, and certainly more purposeful, than ever before. However, they do not, in themselves, furnish a grand design for the economic and social prosperity of the region. The spur to the production of such a design would have to be the possession of the power to implement it and, as has been explained, such power has never been given to the T.V.A.

The specific objectives of the T.V.A., and its general mandate to plan under Sections 22 and 23 of the Statute, have given it an impetus to collaborate with the local authorities in order to foster better planning. In this sphere of physical and physico-economic planning, it is obliged to proceed by means of patient demonstration and persuasion.

Thus, there have been especially close and helpful contacts between the Authority and the Planning Boards of the States. Until 1940, the T.V.A. had no organic relationship with the local authorities concerned with planning, but nevertheless achieved much by personal and continuous contact and the exchange of information and counsel. Various concrete services were rendered, such as the establishment of land-use studies by North Carolina, the creation of county-planning commissions in Tennessee, the furthering of organisations to develop recreational and tourist facilities, studies in a regional highway system, and the purchase of sub-marginal lands. For the State of Tennessee, in 1935 the Authority actually prepared legislative recommendations to promote planning, zoning and conservation.

One illustration is both apt and important. When Guntersville Dam was to be constructed, much fine river-bottom land, the chief resource of the community, was threatened, and it was at first thought that a town of 3,000 people was doomed. The T.V.A. met civic representatives for a discussion of the problems involved in its plans for safeguarding the industrial section and for relocation, which assured the town of a promising future provided it could help to transform itself from a small inland agricultural and trading township into a developing centre of trade and recreation. The city council created a planning commission, which, with the technical assistance and advice of the T.V.A. and a co-operative agreement with the Alabama State Planning Commission, made plans to prevent damage to recreation by industrial development and *vice versa*, and assisted the development of a public park and a harbour for boats. The town has become a trans-shipment point for gasoline, automobiles, wheat, flour, and other bulk commodities. Recently the T.V.A. assisted the planning commission to prepare a waterfront plan covering 20 miles, and in conformity with this the T.V.A. was authorised to build a commercial terminal. The town had 2,836 inhabitants in 1930; by 1940 the population had increased to 4,398.

In the middle of 1940 an addition was made to the community planning work of the T.V.A. by the establishment of a regular planning assistance programme. This system was designed to bring about a more concerted and continuous relationship between the T.V.A. and the local urban communities. The chief purpose was to discharge the responsibility of the T.V.A. for community readjustment in reservoir-affected communities. It was proposed to aid the solution of community readjustment problems and to secure the establishment of planning as a recognised function of local government; and this was to be attempted by stimulating local planning programmes of the State Planning Commissions until sufficient public interest could be secured to assure their continued existence and expansion, and by experimenting with the methods of local planning and of rendering technical planning service to small communities. The Authority also proposed to assist in preparing model planning legislation and instruction material for school curricula.

The usual T.V.A. procedure of co-operative contracts was adopted, and these were made with the Alabama and Tennessee

State Planning Commissions. The Commissions employ resident planning technicians and have the responsibility for initiating and guiding the local planning programmes. The T.V.A. reimburses them for the expenses of this programme and, furthermore, supplies a technical staff of three to five men to assist the Commissions in furnishing technical service to the local planning programmes. In the Tennessee contract, it is provided that the State Planning Commission shall supply equal funds with the T.V.A. for local planning assistance to local communities.

Under this arrangement, both in Alabama and Tennessee a number of urban communities have set up Planning Commissions and begun planning programmes. These Commissions have actively concerned themselves with zoning, sanitation, defence housing, recreation development, improvement in the maintenance of forested lands, highway and waterfront planning, and community relocation.

The usual train of events is for the local Planning Commission to report on its problems to its own community, to define in general the answers to those problems, to make the necessary studies on which solution can be founded, and then to communicate more formally with the T.V.A. department concerned—it may be the Department of Reservoir Property Management, or the T.V.A. Forestry Relations Division, or the Department of Regional Studies. The T.V.A. then either offers observations on a revision of the plan or may actually be asked to produce the chief draft on the basis of the material submitted.

The State Planning Commissions provide funds and technical advisers, and in some cases have been able to utilise the technical help of the National Resources Planning Board. It has been possible also, as a result of conferences between the T.V.A. and the State Planning Commissions, to secure the assistance of planning technicians from the Federal Housing Administration.

It is believed that interest in regular planning as a function of local government can best be stimulated by the demonstration of successful planning, and by making it clear that planning possibilities are a responsibility and opportunity of the community itself, though the State and the T.V.A. may be called upon for technical help. Again, the stimulation of interest in the community itself for its own planning has meant the maintenance of continuous contact with civic groups and all the organs and agencies of public opinion, and this still remains a great problem. Experience points to the need for each community, or group of communities where these are too small for independent financing, to have a full-time paid officer in charge of planning administration and the stimulation of interest in it. Another element of T.V.A. technique is the direct or indirect circulation of model planning and zoning ordinances and material for school use on community planning.

It is possible that the Authority would have made greater progress in such planning activities (for example, in the development of recreation, parks, roadways, improvements in municipal and county government, schools) if it had had the power, not merely to plan and demonstrate and suggest developments to the local authorities and to Congress, but itself to undertake the necessary work through its own officials. That, however, raises the question of the comparative merits of fairly quick achievement by an outside authority, as against the slower action of the inhabitants of the area itself, under the skilled guidance and encouragement of a friendly outside agency.

The Relocation of Families

When a dam is nearing completion, the backwater areas must be scheduled for clearing and flooding; farms and houses will be inundated, and the families living there must be removed. Though the people themselves have always made the decision as to where they will move, at the beginning of the Authority's operations the question arose whether such families should be advised to move out of the area altogether, since some of them lived on very poor land, and the total amount of good land in the area was not great. It was decided that so far as possible the people should be kept in the Valley. Their land (including house, permanent improvements, etc.) is acquired by the Authority at replacement cost on present appraised value. The appraisals are made on the assumption that the seller is not a willing one, and this permits some indirect compensation for disturbance, removal and readjustment.

The Authority has taken the problem of removal, resettlement and readjustment very seriously. Principally in co-operation with the Agricultural Extension Services (by contractual arrangement with the land grant colleges), plans for evacuation of the area and the relocation of the displaced families are formulated well in advance. The county agents give aid to the farm families in their resettlement problems. They discuss with them their economic and social problems; provide lists of farm property for sale or rent; assist in inspecting and selecting new farms and in the wise reinvestment of the price of the old farm; and give realistic and objective advice on these matters and on farm programmes. Once the families are resettled, the county agents keep in touch with them until they are able to continue satisfactorily without help. The Farm Security Administration, Federal Housing, National Youth Administration, Works Progress Administration, Civilian Conservation Corps and Social Security Board, together with the various State Departments of Welfare, are brought in to collaborate where the case so requires. It has also been possible in many cases to assist families by giving them employment on some of the Authority's own projects—the dams, relocation of roads and railways, reservoir clearance—upon satisfactory report as to their qualifications from the personnel department of the Authority.

By 1 February 1943, over 11,272 families had been relocated, most of them to their own satisfaction and advantage. Some families not actually relocated were adversely affected by the purchase of lands they had formerly farmed, or by the closing of roads or flooding of former marketing centres. These too were assisted in their adjustment to new conditions by the assistant county agents.

Relocating Highways

The Tennessee Valley Authority is legally liable to make good the damage done to public as well as private property by flooding or other taking out of use. The Authority, therefore, is responsible for replacing flooded roads with highways of similar character and affording reasonably similar service to the residents.

The Authority has the alternative of paying an agreed sum to the local authority for the replacement of the road, or building the road itself and then handing it to the local government. It has chosen the latter alternative and has taken the improvement view of its obligations, looking at least to replacement of equivalent service, and not merely to calculation of equivalent cost. However, it also has regard to the value of the land served by the road; if the former is unproductive it may pay to buy the land and save the cost of relocation; or, as in one case, the road may be relocated to improve the land-use pattern.

The T.V.A. has on its engineering staff specialists in highway and railroad relocation many of whom, through their previous experience, are familiar with local conditions and with the local governing authorities in the Valley. These engineers study the problems raised by the construction of a reservoir project and prepare an integrated plan of highway adjustment which is carried out after full discussion with each local authority concerned.

The T.V.A. suggests improvements in standards; for example, wider roads, bridges of concrete instead of wood, or better types of pavement. These improvements involve greater capital cost, but pay in the long run because of the reduction in maintenance. The local authorities, of course, must agree to contribute the difference between the cost of replacement in kind and that of the higher standard road. Payment for such improvements is usually made in kind; for example, by construction of pavement or of entire sections of highway.

A typical example of improvement in standards was the construction of a bridge across the Norris Reservoir on the Clinch River. The cost of the bridge desired by the Tennessee State Highway Department was approximately $200,000 in excess of the cost of a bridge equivalent to that which was inundated. The bridge was constructed and paid for by the Authority, and in compensation the State constructed one of the other highway relocations for which the Authority was responsible.

In replacing existing roads of poor type the Authority has frequently improved the standards because its machinery, being adapted to the construction of wider roads, can build them as cheaply as it can build roads as narrow as those replaced. A large proportion of the construction work of highway relocation is carried on by the Authority with its own forces. The remainder is performed under contracts.

Schools

Difficult problems arise in regard to public schools that are either flooded or made inaccessible and worthless because of the relocation of people. After a co-operative survey with the county superintendent and the State Department of Education, the T.V.A. buys the schools by agreement; if this is impossible, as happened in one case, it proceeds by condemnation. The T.V.A. endeavours to contribute to the improvement of the educational situation in the area. Its Department of Personnel (Training Division) decides after the survey which school, if any, or what location, would best serve the school population after readjustment. In one case, at Guntersville Reservoir, it was possible to buy out six schools, and to use the compensation paid to the county to build a single consolidated school on an up-to-date design, a happy solution which the local authorities had long wished, but for which the capital had hitherto been lacking. Similar arrangements were made at several other places.

Some difficulties of inadequate attendance at the schools of a single county caused by the relocation of population have been overcome by arrangements made by the T.V.A. for additional pupils to come from across the county borders. This is seemingly a small problem, but it is difficult because jurisdiction over education invariably arouses the obstinacy of the respective local parties. The T.V.A. has dealt with the problem successfully.

Besides the obligation of the Authority to provide for the relocation of schools, there is another educational responsibility arising from the need to provide schooling at elementary and high school stages for the children of the workers on its dams. State Governments do not recognise a liability for providing tax-supported educational facilities for those on Federal Government property in the same way as they do for their own regular inhabitants. The Authority provides tuition through its own personnel, or induces some local school to supply the courses it requires, making a small contribution to the cost of the teacher.

The T.V.A., following the lines of advanced educational thought, seeks to make the local schools more than an instrument of formal tuition, and therefore encourages the use of the school as a community centre. This connects very well with its programme of education in electrification, and all its agricultural developments like farm demonstration, the control of soil erosion, forestry and fire protection. It encourages education by the use of documentary films, which it circulates.

In the arrangement of school facilities for children of employees in the construction villages, the T.V.A. has only in two cases taken the course of building a school itself. The first was Norris High School, part of a planned community on a permanent basis. The other was at Muscle Shoals (Wilson Dam), which is a Government reservation, where the village was too far from the nearest school facilities. In all other cases, it has been able to carry out the policy it prefers, namely, that of making a contract with schools in the vicinity through the county education authorities whereby the T.V.A. pays a per pupil fee on condition that its pupils are guaranteed a standard of education which will at least put them on a par with other children of the same school age when they move away. Altogether the T.V.A. provided, in 1938, for some 561 elementary school children and 325 high school children in this way. At the same time, the contract provides for job training, general adult education, and recreation.

The Authority may stipulate the length of the school year, the qualifications of the teachers, and the water supply in the school. Moreover, the Authority requires that a member of its training section shall be a member of a committee to be appointed by the local school board to make recommendations to it for improving the educational service and assisting the setting up of standards for, and in the selection and approval of, teachers. These stipulations are made only where necessary. It is the business of the training division of the T.V.A. to safeguard the maintenance of such standards, and the Authority also has a part-time principal supervisor of elementary education who visits the schools and reports to the Authority. On several occasions, the T.V.A. has successfully proposed the dismissal of teachers falling below the standard.

The Authority's intention is ultimately to hand over the direct administration of schools, even on its own properties, to the State and county governments, who, it considers, are and ought to be responsible for schooling. Recently the T.V.A. has sought more continuous co-ordination of its own responsibilities and those of the States of Tennessee and Kentucky. The T.V.A. provides an education officer for each appropriate area, and the States establish a co-ordinating committee of all appropriate agencies for a concerted attack on educational problems.

Public Health

The T.V.A. maintains a Health and Safety Department, the activities of which go beyond mere concern for the health of the Authority's employees, dealt with in a later chapter[1], and reach far out into the well-being of the communities in the Valley.

The work of the Authority in the field of public health falls into two broad classes: public health problems, such as malaria and stream sanitation, caused by changes in environmental hygiene consequent upon the Authority's construction programme and the entry of large bodies of workers from outside; and research and the promotion of public health administration, based upon the Authority's responsibility for plans and studies to raise the general well-being. The T.V.A. must also consider its general legal liability for damage done to third parties by health risks. Furthermore, public health properly forms part of the educational interests of the Authority.

Sanitation and Malaria Control

The Authority is interested in securing clean, sanitary living quarters, wholesome food and a safe water supply in order to safeguard the health of its employees. For this purpose, its own officers at its camps see that the water supplies, the sewerage works and the sanitary facilities of houses and dormitories reach a proper standard; but a wider area needs control, and this is served by T.V.A. inspection and collaboration with the State and local health departments in charge of such services. For control purposes

---

[1] Cf. Chapter XI.

studies have been made of the various effects of pollution of the Tennessee River and its tributaries, in which the T.V.A. Health Department collaborates with other departments, as well as with the State Public Health Departments and the United States Public Health Service.

The vital branch of the Authority's activity is malaria control. As is well known, in various parts of the world malaria has destroyed the economic possibilities of whole regions. If the disease were allowed to run its course, all the navigation possibilities and all the hydroelectric power in the Valley might come to nothing. In more than half the Tennessee Valley malaria is endemic, and there are infection rates from 0 up to 60 per cent. in the samples collected in blood surveys. Whenever water is impounded south of the Ohio River a potential breeding place for the malaria-carrying mosquito is created. It was necessary, therefore, for the Authority to establish expert supervision in the preparation and maintenance of reservoirs, to set up arrangements for controlling the mosquito on the reservoirs already impounded, and to take such further steps of research and collaboration with neighbouring communities as would improve the economy and efficiency of the measures for control. The T.V.A., by thorough collaboration with State health departments, which have for many years treated malaria, has secured useful developments of State regulations for each reservoir. With experience, greater care has come to be spent on reservoir preparation; this has meant slightly larger capital costs, but has considerably reduced the annual costs of maintenance thereafter, while increasing effectiveness.

The Authority has undertaken very extensive investigations into malaria, in co-operation with the Department of Preventive Medicine of the University of Tennessee, which indeed it helped to establish.[1] Its researches, which cover thousands of individuals in different biological and economic contexts, could not possibly have been undertaken without the collaboration of the Health Departments of the States of Alabama and Tennessee. This co-operation is developed in other directions, and co-ordinated with a health educational programme, and so a wide defence belt against the transmission of malaria outward from the reservoirs and the river and inward from the valley communities to its own employees is secured.

Collaboration with Local Health Agencies

In order that there may be mutual service and assistance between the authorities in the area and the T.V.A. in the perspective

---

[1] For some time T.V.A. paid a grant of one third of the salary. Three fifths of the physicians of Tennessee are educated at the school.

sketched above, and especially to make sure of the health protection of employees in the areas of the major construction operations and services, the T.V.A. has other co-operative undertakings, supported by T.V.A. grants-in-aid, with several counties in Tennessee, Alabama, and North Carolina, Mississippi and Kentucky. The agreement is made with the State authority, which then agrees upon a public health programme in the appropriate counties. It undertakes to employ for these services only such persons as are jointly approved by itself and the T.V.A., and to submit progress and financial reports to the Authority. The T.V.A.'s interests are secured by the arrangement that its grant-in-aid shall be made monthly upon receipt of a certificate that the services have been duly performed; and the companies make monthly and annual progress reports.

The official health agencies and the Authority jointly plan a health programme with special emphasis upon environmental sanitation and immunisation against smallpox, typhoid and diphtheria. The Authority reviews the qualifications of health department personnel assigned to its areas. There is such an intimate continuous day-by-day relationship between the T.V.A. staff and that of the local agencies present in the field that the T.V.A. has achieved more than it might have done through inspectors. In certain instances, however, the Authority also appraises the work of the local agencies on the basis of the "Appraisal Form for Rural Health Service", developed by a committee of the American Public Health Association. All the progress reports are discussed very soon after their submission by the T.V.A., the State Department of Health, and the local Health Department. Although the financial sanctions have been utilised on two or three occasions, they have involved only the adjustment of minor administrative routines.

Public Health Education

Beyond such direct health activities, the T.V.A. assisted in the establishment (by contract with the University of Tennessee and the Tennessee State Departments of Health and Education) of a very widespread and thorough attempt to promote public health by promoting popular education on the subject.[1] The system is now altogether in the hands of the State of Tennessee, but the T.V.A. still serves in a consultative capacity. Originally the Authority contributed certain grants to the State of Tennessee to start the provision of a number of health educators and of courses of

---

[1] This further developed a scheme started in Jan. 1931 by the University of Tennessee, then assisted by the Commonwealth Fund, a private agency.

preparation for health educators. At one time, the Authority had
a power of approval of the curriculum, the plan and staff. The
purpose of the scheme is to secure the creation of a widespread
health consciousness through the training of so-called "public
health education co-ordinators", to be certificated by the State
Education Department. Elementary and high school teaching
manuals and a syllabus for a field extension course for elementary
teachers have been written. There is a University Professor of
Public Health Education (to whose salary the T.V.A. originally
contributed) supervised by the University, and a State official
called the Health Education Co-ordinator. A State Committee
representing the University, the State Departments of Health and
Education, and the T.V.A. directs the scheme. There are connections with the extension division and the health departments of
various cities and counties, and many local civic agencies and
social and educational agencies have been brought into the network of co-operating units. Considerable public understanding of
and interest in the work of the public authorities has been awakened
by lectures and field demonstrations. This may be expected to
have practical effect on public hygiene in the near future, for in
public health the authorities cannot possibly secure their results
by mere action and exhortation—they must place heavy reliance
upon the intelligent and loyal co-operation of all the people. A
similar co-operative health project was undertaken in Alabama.
Thus, by a small money grant, the T.V.A. was able to help to start
a much larger effort by the local agencies themselves, and to gain
an influence over an area much more extensive than is available to
it by a rigorous interpretation of its rights and obligations under
the Act. Wide facilities are obtained immediately at relatively
small cost. In the T.V.A. construction villages the Authority continues to make an annual grant to the counties for health services
rendered by them, and it has stimulated three times as large a contribution by the counties themselves, producing a standard which
the Authority itself would otherwise have had to maintain alone.
It is highly possible that with the decline of the Authority's calls
upon their services, and of its grant, the new standards will not
be allowed to sag.

In its health activities, the T.V.A. has been substantially helped
by the United States Public Health Service. It has borrowed consultants from the latter, and continuously sought its advice and
occasionally its supervision. For example, a very far-reaching
enquiry into tuberculosis has been undertaken under its direction
with the assistance of the Valley States and the authorities. Part
of the purpose of this study is to determine the respective causative

parts played by the economic, the social, and the climatic factors. The United States Public Health Service also manages grants to the States in the Valley as elsewhere, and, knowing the connection between the Authority and the States, it can advise accordingly.

The success of the contractual system is partly due to the fact that at the head of the T.V.A. Health and Safety Department there is a distinguished public health administrator, Dr. E. L. Bishop, most of whose professional career has been spent in the service of public health administration in Tennessee.

It is in the outstanding national distinction of its administrators and experts that the T.V.A. finds the way to acceptance of its enterprise and guidance. The previous local service of its own employees is by no means a necessary preliminary to fruitful co-operative relationships, but it is sometimes useful in convincing the local inhabitants that a man's ambition is fully satisfied in the service of their welfare.

General Regional Education and Technical Assistance

The T.V.A. has a special interest in the general education of the people of the Valley, over and above its interest in the education and training of its own employees. The latter has usually, but not always, been the T.V.A.'s point of departure, and various aspects of the subject are discussed in a later chapter. The general education of the Valley, recognised as indeed a vital constituent of sustained economic and social progress and even a pre-condition of the attainment of technical skill, is conducted along two lines: (1) the encouragement of library services; and (2) stimulation of local schools and civic agencies.

In the Tennessee Valley area one half of all the counties have no public library service whatever. The T.V.A. does not supply books to its employees directly from a department of its own excepting the technical works and works relating to the economic, social and other operations of the Authority; these it supplies from its technical library or by loan from National and State libraries as needed. Apart from this, it makes arrangements by contract with State and local public library agencies. The T.V.A., for its part, pays a grant to these agencies, which agree to supply library service to the construction projects and also to work towards the establishment, independently of grants from the Authority, of permanent library facilities for these areas. These arrangements have not only achieved the immediate purpose in supplying collections of books at the dams. They have also encouraged the extension of library service by towns to the surrounding counties; and services have been continued for the general benefit of the area by the local agency after the T.V.A. had withdrawn its financial support. In one case, the county voted a special tax to continue the county-wide library service first begun in response to the needs of T.V.A. employees.

A more concerted attack on the subject of library facilities was made in the spring of 1940, when librarians representing the local State and National agencies upon which the T.V.A. principally depends for its library services met to examine the problems and explore the possibilities of a more effective co-ordination. University of Tennessee and T.V.A. staff members led the discussions. In the spring of 1941 a permanent organisation, the Tennessee Valley Library Council, was established to study the problems, to serve as a liaison group in directing the efforts of libraries towards a solution, and to promote the co-operation of libraries among themselves and with related agencies.

The Authority believes that it is desirable to bring home to the people of the Valley the general significance of its own activities, partly with the practical object of securing the intelligent co-operation of the people in the efforts of the Authority to improve their condition, but also for the general purpose of widening their outlook, and showing the relationship of their traditional local institutions to the work now being done in the regional area and with the Federal authority. Therefore, since 1936, the T.V.A. has sponsored a number of conferences between itself and representatives (usually the presidents) of the Land Grant Colleges in the area, in order to prepare a curriculum and a doctrine, as it were, and an organisation through which it might be taught. The basis is, of course, the powers and purposes of the Authority and the economic and social consequences of its activities, and particular emphasis is laid on democratic participation of the local agencies and inhabitants in the Authority's programme. It is desired to enrich the training and educational programmes at those points where the T.V.A. has specific interests, and identify the mutual interests of all agencies in the Valley in the use of appropriate instructional materials.

In September 1938, an Advisory Panel on Regional Materials of Instruction for the Tennessee Valley was established, composed of representatives from the universities of the Valley States and the heads of certain of the research departments of the T.V.A. This body, served by a Principal Supervisor of Instructional Materials, provides suggestions and materials which may be organically related to the curricula in the Tennessee Valley schools at all levels. Thus, for example, the T.V.A. Department of Forestry Relations supplies material in non-technical language to the Bureau of School Service of the University of Kentucky to illustrate the applied economics of the area, for instance, by bringing home to the pupils the relationship between a more adequate diet and tree-crops. Local school programmes and other materials have also been devised to deal with farm and domestic economy. A series of readers is being prepared by the Bureau on the growth and management and exploitation of tree-crops, for use in the experimental schools. An original emphasis on the production of tree-crops for sale was changed into an emphasis on home-consumption by the farm family. The T.V.A. Department of Regional Planning Studies has produced, with the assistance of the Advisory Panel, a booklet called *Communities for Living*, a collection of popular material on the subject of local planning. The teachers who used the experimental edition assisted in the production of a final revised edition.

The Advisory Panel is thus a kind of clearing house through which its members, all experts in some particular field, and the members of the various teaching institutions and local communities connected therewith, seek the most appropriate pattern and methods of community and regional tuition. The T.V.A. has an enormous amount of information, highly conscious in its marshalling and dissection of social facts, and through the Panel this is made available and adapted to educational use, among the teachers in the Valley, at the universities, as at the lower levels of education, and so permeates the younger generation in the Valley. In this way the T.V.A. makes living contact with the people and needs of the Valley, and the people of the Valley are gradually helped to realise the significance for them of this powerful Federal agency of regional resources development.

Finally, no reader of the preceding chapters on the T.V.A.'s activities can have failed to notice the frequent references to the technical assistance given by the T.V.A. to the region as well as to its concern for education. The farm demonstration programme is almost entirely a process of education and assistance by a body of trained agricultural experts. The rural electricity programme, with its home economists and demonstrators, its T.V.A. accountants to guide the administration of the co-operatives, and the invention and provision of electric apparatus, is another example. The advisory relationship between the T.V.A. power departments and the municipal electricity undertakings is one more aspect of the value of the T.V.A.'s technical knowledge and ability to the public agencies and people of the area. The publication of the T.V.A.'s research studies in the social and the economic field, its advice on physico-economic planning, its encouragement and assistance at

conferences of civic and State agencies, its dissemination of the
facts regarding its own or collaborative inventions of agricultural
apparatus, produce-conserving and processing methods, the extent
and quality of mineral resources, and so on, are further contributions to the raising of the level of technical skill, ability and control
over economic processes. In certain of the agricultural, industrial
and manufacturing processes to which reference has been made,
T.V.A. experts actually demonstrate the manufacture and application of newly invented apparatus and devices.

All this is in addition to the public health education just described, to the fostering of general education by the T.V.A.'s concern
for public libraries and its connection with schools for children and
adults with the object of making clear the relationship of its purchases and programmes to the economy of the region, and to the
Authority's efforts to raise the standard of vocational skill of
its own workers. The Statute wisely provides that the T.V.A. may
call upon the departments of the Federal Government for advice
and assistance, which the latter have an obligation to render at the
President's request. This power has been very amply used, and
so the skill at the disposal of the Federal Government is mobilised
for the Valley's benefit.

This function of bringing to the Valley the assistance of physical
and social science and technology is of supreme importance, since
it is the procedure best calculated to enable the people to stand on
their own feet in the course of time. For all experience of economic
development—and the T.V.A. is consciously guided thereby—
shows that the soundest foundation of progress is knowledge, both
technical and general, possessed and applied first by leaders, and
in the long run, by dissemination through them to the broad masses
of the people. There is indeed a close and causative correlation
between the quality and diffusion of education and expert skills,
and the general level of economic productivity.

CHAPTER VII

THE CORPORATE AGENCY AND ITS METHODS OF OPERATION

After considering in the foregoing chapters the problems faced by the T.V.A. in the fulfilment of its purposes, attention may now be directed to its characteristic methods of operation, and therefore to its most significant administrative features. These are (1) its corporate form; (2) its democratic and contractual collaboration with existing public agencies and the people in the Valley; (3) its "regional" area of responsibility; (4) its integrated resource development and therefore its multi-purpose character; and (5) its method of procedure by technical assistance and education.

THE CORPORATION

The T.V.A. is a *corporate* agency of the United States Government. It is important to consider what was intended by vesting in a corporation the powers which Congress thought necessary for the development of the area. Congress might have lodged the various powers separately in the several departments of the United States Government in Washington, and have arranged for special co-ordination among these departments so far as their activities related to the Tennessee Valley. But the purpose was to treat all the problems of that area as integrated; and this led almost with iron logic to the establishment of an authority on the spot, that is, to territorial decentralisation or regionalisation. The second idea, developing simultaneously with the first, was that a special instrument of administration ought to be devised better adapted to the functions to be exercised than were the traditional departments of the Government. In his Message of 10 April 1933 to Congress, requesting the creation of a Tennessee Valley Authority, the President asked for "a corporation clothed with the power of Government, but possessed of the flexibility and initiative of a private enterprise". This meant:

(1) That it should be endowed with certain specific powers in relation to persons and property and in relation to its own purposes.

(2)   That it should have succession in its corporate name; and the power to sue and the liability to be sued in its corporate name, to adopt and use a corporate seal, to make contracts for the purposes and through the procedures provided in the Statute, to make, amend and repeal by-laws, to purchase or lease and hold real and personal property necessary for its business, and to dispose of any personal property, to exercise the right of eminent domain[1] in the name of the United States, and to proceed by condemnation where necessary for the purposes of the Act.

(3)   That it should be empowered to appoint its personnel with exemption from United States civil service rules and to organise its internal affairs with comparative freedom.

(4)   That, since the Authority must come under some superior national control, it should be assigned special relationships with various of the controlling departments of the Federal Government designed to secure political responsibility, but without subjecting the Authority to a straitjacket.

In the words of the House representatives on the conference committee on the T.V.A. Bill: "We have sought to set up a legislative framework but not to encase it in a legislative straitjacket. We intend that the corporation shall have much of the essential freedom and elasticity of a private business corporation."[2]

Congress seems to have chosen the corporate form for four reasons.   In the first place, those who originally drafted the early Muscle Shoals Bill wished to establish an authority which (a) might be an altogether private corporation, and if not, (b) would have political interference in its administration reduced to a minimum by the corporation's independent power to appoint its own employees; (c) would have its own self-contained financial balance-sheet, which would provide the incentives and correctives of profit and loss necessary to good business effort; and (d) would be able competently to plan for the future, because it would have freedom to buy and sell without having to wait upon annual appropriations from Congress.

Secondly, various analogies were adduced in the course of debate when hydroelectric power began to play a large part in the legislators' mind; for instance, the Ontario Hydroelectric Commission, and electricity administration in places of great repute like Tacoma and Los Angeles.

Thirdly, there were precedents for a corporation owned by the Federal Government.   As far back as 1904 the Panama Railroad

---

[1] To take property compulsorily with compensation.
[2] 73rd Congress, House of Representatives, *Report No. 130*, 1933, p. 19.

Company had been taken over by the United States Government, which had continued to operate it substantially as though it were still a private corporation. The Alaska Railroad had been managed in much the same way since 1914. Then, in the course of the war of 1914-1918, a number of powerful corporations were organised by the United States Government to run emergency fleets, to buy and sell grain, to build houses, and so forth.[1] In 1924 the Inland Waterways Corporation was established to take over from a Bureau of the War Department a commercial transportation service on the Mississippi and Warrior Rivers. This corporation. was endowed with capital stock, and was given power to move funds from one branch of its transactions to another, to establish a reserve against accidents and to borrow additional capital, flexibility in contractual relations, and relaxation of the full degree of audit of its accounts by the Controller-General in order to permit a proper flexibility of business judgment.

Fourthly, since the last war, administrative theory had moved strongly towards the detachment from the traditional controls of administrative agencies which had the characteristics of an industrial or commercial enterprise. This development was due to a questioning whether civil service methods of appointment and the settled procedures of administrative control collectively known as "red tape" could not be improved upon; and whether it was really possible for Congress annually to make a genuine review of the detail of administrative activities, or advisable for it to intervene continuously in rather trivial everyday matters of administration. It was further believed that independent accounting and financing would stimulate responsibility and enterprise, and that if an agency were set up with these characteristics, a special *esprit de corps* might be promoted conducive to the will to increase revenue receipts and keep down expenses. Indeed, the men who drafted the first post-war Bill to deal with Muscle Shoals deliberately adopted the corporate form to meet the foregoing considerations.

These tendencies, which also operated in other countries at the same time, have persisted in the United States. More public corporations were set up during the great depression. Indeed, the most considerable of all, the Reconstruction Finance Corporation, was established in 1932. Later, with the "New Deal" administration,

---

[1] Instances are: The War Insurance Corporation (1918); the United States Shipping Board Emergency Fleet Corporation (1916); the Food Administration Grain Corporation (1917); the United States Housing Corporation (1918); the Sugar Equalisation Board (1917), etc. Cf. H. A. VAN DORN: *Government Owned Corporations* (New York, 1926).

there came in quick succession the T.V.A., the Homeowners' Loan Corporation, and a long succession of others.[1]

It should be observed that the term "public corporation" is a name given to a type of administrative agency and does not imply that all such corporations have identical administrative characteristics. The nature of every public corporation is determined in each particular case by the legislature, which endows it with characteristics appropriate to the functions it is designed to perform.

To sum up the aims pursued by establishing the T.V.A. as a public corporation, it was desired, first, to exclude politics and partisanship in the conduct of its business. This was to be secured principally by having the directors appointed by the President of the United States; by exempting T.V.A. employees from the requirements of civil service regulations and, at the same time, requiring the Authority to set up its own merit system. Secondly, the Authority was to have financial flexibility in obtaining, spending and accounting for its funds, and was to establish its own separate annual accounts to show the state of its business at proper intervals. Thirdly, it was to have a degree of freedom in carrying out certain transactions, such as purchasing land, equipment, and other properties, and the power to make out-of-court settlements in disputes with other parties. Fourthly, to assure the continuity of its policy and activity, it was to have power to appoint and regulate its own staff and set up its own procedures, and also to have a margin of moneys for use in continuing its operations. Fifthly, it was to have power to sue without going through the agency of the Federal Department of Justice in order to ensure flexibility; and liability to be sued directly on much the same basis as any ordinary business, in order to give confidence to its clients.[2]

---

[1] Since the beginning of the second world war, a number of new corporations have been established in the United States under the Reconstruction Finance Corporation for the procurement of stocks of materials necessary to the national defence programme; among these is the second edition of the Export-Import Bank, established in 1940, to promote the development of natural resources in Latin America, leading *inter alia* to the establishment of development corporations in Bolivia, Ecuador and Haiti.

In Great Britain, whose experience in this respect has been as carefully followed by American students as United States' experience has been watched by the British, there are some notable instances of administration by public corporations; for instance, the Port of London Authority (1908), the Central Electricity Board (1926), the British Broadcasting Corporation (1927), and the London Passenger Transport Board (1933). Cf. L. GORDON: *The Public Corporation in Great Britain* (New York, 1938); and T. H. O'BRIEN: *British Experiments in Public Ownership and Control* (London, 1937). In Germany the administration of the railroads and postal services, shortly after the end of the world war, was vested in independent corporations, the *Reichsbahngesellschaft* and the *Reichspost*. Similar developments in the case of railroads occurred in Austria, Belgium, Greece, Poland, Rumania and Switzerland.

[2] Cf. in particular David E. LILIENTHAL and Robert H. MARQUIS: "The Conduct of Business Enterprises by the Federal Government", in *Harvard Law Review*, Feb. 1941, for an interesting analysis of the nature and operation of public corporations, with some special reference to the experiments of the T.V.A.

The T.V.A. cannot do what it likes; it can do only the things which are specifically permitted or commanded in the Statute, and can reasonably be implied from such permission and commands. Its powers are further governed, of course, by the general character of the United States Federal system of government. The Authority stands inside a constitutional system founded upon a basic law and developed by interpretation over 150 years. In that Constitution, the Federal Government (Congress, the President, and the Courts) has powers; the States have powers and rights; individuals are guaranteed certain rights, and, in some cases, immunities from the action of Governments and rights of suit against them. The Authority, therefore, has in the first place to be careful not to overstep the powers vested in it by Statute and Executive Order under the powers derived from the Federal Constitution, nor to deny rights which other agencies and individuals properly possess.

Since the T.V.A. is subject to the law of the land, its actions are subject to control by suit brought against it in the law courts; and the wide extent to which it is open to such challenge has been shown in practice by the number and diversity of the actions brought against it. Its suability, with the right to make settlements out of court, has clearly focussed responsibility upon it and impells it to make settlements wherever feasible and on terms most conducive to its business interests.

DEMOCRATIC COLLABORATION

The T.V.A. entered an area in which local political agencies already existed—the States, the municipalities, the counties. These, and most of the politically conscious citizens, looked with much gratitude and some eagerness to the establishment of the T.V.A. It was evident that, in the fullness of time, considerable benefits would accrue to the region. At the same time, the Board of Directors was given a responsibility which was, as it were, exclusive; that is to say, no provision was made in the Statute (so far as T.V.A. powers were concerned) for self-government by the people of the area, whether through direct nomination of all or one of the directors, or through the election of an executive or advisory body supplementary to the Board. There was, and is, no democratic government in the sense of a locally-elected body of local directors of the T.V.A. responsible to the local constituency. As directors, the President selected three men of energy, capacity and public spirit, fully sensitive to and aware of their responsibilities, and intensely alive to the pioneering opportunities provided. A twofold danger therefore arose. One aspect was that the directors and staff might regard the area as a backward colony, to be adminis- tered, it is true, with unbounded benevolence, but nevertheless from above. The other was that the inhabitants of the Valley, southern people proud of their own institutions and folkways and still affected to some extent by memories of the Civil War, might suspect and resent the intentions and activities of the directors, however well-meaning.

The problem involved was not successfully solved at once. In the first few months of the Authority's advent in the Valley, some resentment was roused by observations made by one or two of the directors which led people, on the whole erroneously, to believe that an alien authority was claiming charitably to improve them. The attitude of the leaders of the Valley people themselves is best expressed in an article written in 1937 by one of themselves, George Fort Milton, as follows:

At the beginning some of us resented rather deeply the paternalistic attitude at the top. These outlanders seemed to have come down here to reform an illiter- ate, godless lot who would not wear shoes; they could teach us that there was really some merit in occasionally employing footgear. . .

However, it soon developed that this was by no means the general purpose and policy of the Authority; there was exhibited at least an equally vigorous idea on the part of some of its controllers that Tennessee Valley Authority's purpose in this Valley was not to redeem a backward race by demonstration; that rather it was to afford opportunity to people who, whenever given oppor- tunity, promptly embrace it. This new tone and attitude, an index to Tennessee Valley Authority's own capacity for self-education, was a happy change. Today one hears fewer whispers of this zeal for reform, but rather a growing under- standing of the merit of the people of the region. And with the change on the part of the Authority has come a companion change of the people's own attitude. Tennessee Valley Authority is now of us and not of others. Its roots have begun to sink. It is no foreign Santa Claus, but the spirit and purpose of the Valley.

The change noted came from several causes. In the first place, it was feared that the co-operation of the local population would not be forthcoming, and that this would stultify the whole pro- gramme. Secondly, one of the three directors was drawn from the community in which the Authority was to operate and was thus in a position to interpret to the Board the attitude of the inhabi- tants. Thirdly, it was realised that for good government, realistic information is necessary, and that such information can never be fully available to the Authority unless it is offered by the people and the agencies of the people themselves. Any process of survey and research based upon the unilateral action of the Authority will not only be more expensive but will be less accurate and full. Fourthly, there are existing interests, for example, the land grant colleges, and the local government units and the States, with influence and with powers (including the police power, that is, the actual power of government), which the T.V.A. does not itself possess, but which are necessarily complementary to its own powers and able to make or mar its policies.

That is not all, however. The Authority came to recognise that perhaps its greatest potential contribution to social well-being lies in stimulating the energies of the people themselves, in assisting their own spirit of self-help and initiative. It cannot be said that ideas ever went as far as a transfer of the authority of the Corporation to the local people themselves; but there is a definite conviction that if the Authority were ever to cease to exist it could do so with the assurance that, so far as its responsibilities are concerned, the local population had been brought to some appreciation of their own civic capacities and obligations. This point of view is expressed in the T.V.A.'s Annual Report for 1936 under the rubric of "Local Self-Reliance".

The T.V.A. operates in fields in which national interests are directly involved and in which nothing short of national action can be effective. The roles of the States, and of cities, counties, districts, and voluntary associations within the States, are enhanced, not diminished, in importance by this recognition of interest and jurisdiction. Co-operation, not destructive competition; Federal responsibility in Federal and inter-State matters, with local initiative and self-reliance in matters of a local nature—these are policies by which the development of the Valley is being and should continue to be guided.

The planning of the river's future is entrusted to the T.V.A. The planning of the Valley's future must be the democratic labour of many agencies and individuals, and final success is as much a matter of general initiative as of general consent. The T.V.A. has no power or desire to impose from above a comprehensive plan for the social and economic life of the Valley. It does desire to carry out its own responsibilities, within its proper legislative and constitutional limits, in such a way as to be consistent with the orderly development of the region, and it therefore needs to be cognisant of the major conditions, forces, needs and purposes of the Tennessee Valley area.

In recent years this conviction has become even more conscious. In a series of addresses and articles the present chairman of the Board has systematised and stressed the democratic, decentralised approach. Many benefits are obtainable by the centralisation of authority, but they may be defeated, and will certainly be reduced, by the centralisation of administration, while they will be enhanced and preserved by the decentralisation of administration.

The T.V.A. was so designed as to permit the Authority to *make its decisions in the field*, close to the people and their problems. It is in the field that adjustments and modifications adapting the Federal programme to meet the actual needs of local situations are more readily developed; it is in the field that citizen participation can be enlisted. That power to decide in the field is, I believe, the heart of any decentralised programme, the quality without which there can never be an administration at the "grass roots".

Our unique contribution has been that both by tested means and by newly adopted practices we have been "self-conscious" in our efforts to discover just how far and how effectively in its administration a Federal programme can be brought closer to the people and their problems, how far a Federal agency can take local and State instrumentalities into active partnership.[1]

Only so will the atrophy of local endeavour and the drying up of initiative be avoided; and reliance on a "diet" of fundamental principles and "*a priori* reasoning" by an absentee Government be replaced by facts and judgment from the grass roots.

The same theme is neatly and responsibly expressed by the present General Manager:

The right to help formulate plans and recommendations, to accept or reject recommended programmes and courses of action, or to seek out alternatives, or to do nothing at all, rests with the local community and its representatives.

The T.V.A. does not share this right; as a democratic institution created by the joint action of all communities it is itself an expression of this right. It does share as a consequence the responsibility of participating with the communities in their educational task of assuring that the exercise of their fundamental right of self-determination shall be increasingly wise and farsighted.[2]

Thus, the Authority cannot and does not abdicate its own elementary responsibilities as defined and controlled by Congress. But, as has been seen, it has most deliberately and painstakingly devised its administrative arrangements so as to share in the making and execution of policies with the States, the municipalities, the land grant colleges, rural electricity co-operatives and farmers' clubs, local commissions of public-spirited citizens and those engaged in business. By a series of contractual and co-operative agreements it has stimulated farm demonstrations, the application of electricity to rural productive activities, the raising of the level of education and school accommodation, the improvement of public health, the physical planning of the area, the extension of libraries, the development of recreational facilities, and many other aspects of social existence in the Valley. "For in the scene of general bigness", says the chairman, "men continue to come about the same size. There is still a limit to the energy and wisdom of the best; and so that many men may share in carrying out the vision of a few, we must learn how to *decentralise administration*."[3]

It may therefore be said that while the T.V.A. is not politically

---

[1] *The T.V.A.: A Step Toward Decentralisation*, Address by David E. LILIEN-THAL, Director, Tennessee Valley Authority, before the University of California, 29 Nov. 1940.

[2] Gordon R. CLAPP: "The T.V.A. Programme", in *Journal of Educational Sociology*, Nov. 1941, p. 147.

[3] David E. LILIENTHAL: "The T.V.A. and Decentralisation", in *Survey Graphic*, June 1940.

removable by the local inhabitants through any agency or procedure they can use, and is accountable only to the Federal legislature and executive, nevertheless it is sensitively responsive to the local inhabitants because (*a*) Congress designed a method of collaboration in the Statute; (*b*) Congressmen continually require the exercise of collaboration; and (*c*) the continuous presence of the T.V.A. directors and staff in the Valley itself inevitably produces responsiveness through every-day meetings, face to face, between government and citizens. Two of the directors have lived in the centre of operations for ten years, since the T.V.A. began. A number of the higher personnel have a like length of residence, and many more employees have lived all their lives in the Valley. They may be presumed to identify themselves with the good of the people of the region.

Yet they are the producers and not the consumers of T.V.A. services, so that the identity cannot be perfect. It must be remembered that there is an alternative form of organisation: a region with a government of its own, locally elected and locally accountable.

Some have asked whether, if one of the first three directors was appointed because of his representative standing in the South, it is not desirable to go further along this path, and appoint several representative directors. There is indeed something to be said for the establishment of a Regional Council, nominated by major political agencies like the States. Such a council, however, would need to be on an advisory basis only, to have no share in sovereign decision, for the latter alternative could only mean dispute and confusion in the development of the programme of an Authority whose finances come from the Federal Government. Political influences have on some occasions (although unsuccessfully) pressed for the building of dams in certain areas, or the early starting of works to coincide with political interests. As things are at present, these are suppliants without a sanction; and that is the most they ought to be. For the funds come from the Federal Government, and there has hitherto been little tenderness on the part of Congress towards special interests in T.V.A. matters. Indubitably, in a sovereign representative council governing the T.V.A. with funds provided by the Federal Government, irreconcilable attitudes and wrangles would be provoked by the problem of the expenditure of funds provided by the Federal Authority. The coal and railway interests, capital and labour, have already challenged various developments of the T.V.A. before Congress. Had they been members of a sovereign council of the Tennessee Valley it is doubtful whether the T.V.A.'s own programme and policy as based on Federal enactment would ever have been undertaken, or even if it had been, what its cost and shape might have been.

A comprehensive advisory council is a different matter. The T. V.A. consults various occasional advisory bodies on special subjects; there is, however, no standing advisory council of local representatives giving comprehensive geographical or functional representation. The emphasis of the T.V.A. on democratic collaboration would be better implemented if such a council were instituted, especially in the operating, planning and development period towards which the T.V.A. is moving now that the major construction work is practically completed.   On a long-run view, great advantages to the Valley could be expected from such an advisory council, for (a) the T.V.A. would not need merely to guess at the relative strengths of local bodies of opinion; (b) a valuable reservoir of information would be made available to it; (c) its own justification of its policies might be more intimately and vividly communicated and broadcast; (d) a sense of participation by the Valley would be fostered; (e) more cohesion between the general and special representative civic bodies would be promoted; and (f) experience in the practice of democratic administration of a whole region would be gained.

Collaboration with other Government Agencies

The theme touched upon above, namely, the T.V.A.'s contractual relationships with other agencies of government, requires some further discussion at this stage.   These contractual relationships are of particular interest in connection with the problems of the relationship between an international resources development authority and development agencies in assisted countries, as well as that between such national agencies and the already existing political areas and institutions, especially where different sovereign States are involved.

When the T.V.A. came into the Valley with its own powers and responsibilities, it met a number of governmental agencies already there.   Some of these were coeval with the beginnings of government in the United States, such as the States, the counties, many cities, and so on.   There were also the local branches of the Federal Government Departments, as for example, the Department of Agriculture, the Bureau of Mines, and the Army Engineers. These, like the T.V.A., had powers and responsibilities. The T.V.A., or rather those who set it up, faced the alternative of establishing a complete new set of departments of its own and ignoring the existing agencies and their functions, or co-operating with them. The first alternative would have meant: (a) overlapping, as for example, in the farm demonstration scheme (T.V.A., Department of Agriculture, and State Extension Services); (b) some gaps, as for example, in the exploitation of the recreational resources of the Valley (T.V.A. and States); (c) actual conflict of purposes, as for example, in respect of the power sales policy of the T.V.A. and that of the cities; and (d) uneconomical, inefficient, or inconvenient administration due to the non-use of the most suitable agency for the function to be fulfilled (e.g., the soil survey).

However, since it was the deliberate policy of the T.V.A. to encourage and assist action by the agencies supported and controlled by the public in the Tennessee Valley, the second alternative was adopted. The T.V.A., as already noted in connection with its agricultural, power and health programmes, for example, has accordingly entered into scores of contractual relationships with States, counties, cities, local co-operatives, Federal departments, academic, civic, and scientific institutions, for specific purposes, and has thus sought to produce a continuous and dynamic interconnection. In this procedure the T.V.A. stands in the centre, as it were, as the co-ordinator of activity, usually giving the lead and planning the joint attack on the connected problems of the region, from the earliest stage on. Its contractual arrangements often imply a sharing of expense with the Federal agencies or a financial grant-in-aid, on conditions, from itself to the local agencies, whether States, counties or universities. By trial and error, but generally with early success, it has solved the problems involved in such a situation. These are: (a) selection of the agency whose legal authority and practical capacity are most appropriate to the power to be exercised—for example, the Bureau of Mines to conduct the later stages of the T.V.A.'s ceramic clay researches; (b) clear definition of the share of responsibility assumed by the T.V.A. and its colleague agencies, as illustrated by the Memoranda of Understanding on farm demonstration or on public health; and (c) where the statutory responsibility for a function is the T.V.A.'s, and especially where the Authority pays a grant-in-aid for example, farm demonstration, public health, laboratories, local schools. The T.V.A. has unquestioned responsibility for the success of the ventures and for the means of securing it, whether by supervision or otherwise. In connection with this latter point, it is possible to value highly the farm demonstration work of the T.V.A. and still speculate that the T.V.A. might achieve more by direct relations with and supervision over the demonstration farms than intermediately through the Extension System.

THE REGIONAL AREA OF RESPONSIBILITY

The Corporation is vested with responsibility for an area of its own. An area drawn most appropriately to fit certain economic needs, it cuts through the boundaries of seven States, boundaries which (like political boundaries throughout the world) were established in historical conditions altogether remote from contemporary economic and technical considerations. There is a demarcation of territory, and the assignment of obligations and powers relating to it. The basis of the unity and identity of this area is the physical fact of the river and the watershed itself. The question arises whether such a conspicuous physical factor and tie is essential to the demarcation of an area of development with special responsibilities, or whether governments can be freer in their choice of area, and yet achieve good technical and social results. Examination of the climatic, topographical and economic characteristics of the Tennessee Valley shows that, though the river is a unifying element, there is considerable diversity in them, and that in regard to economic activity various parts of the Valley are integral parts of agricultural or industrial economies transcending the Valley. For example, south of the river is the Alabama Cotton Belt; up to Nashville, a populous industrial and commercial area, and so on. However, conclusions will best follow an examination of the Statute and the practice developed from it.

The Statute mentions, in the preamble, "the Tennessee River and the Tennessee Valley". The enacting clause looks to "the improvement of navigation in the Tennessee River and Mississippi River Basins". For electricity purposes, real estate may be acquired "at any point along the Tennessee River or any of its tributaries". The navigation clauses, again, envisage "the promotion of navigation on the Tennessee River and its tributaries, the control of the destructive flood waters in the Tennessee and Mississippi Drainage Basins". Then, finally, Section 22 (relating to the planning powers of the Authority for raising the general welfare, and other purposes) seems to widen the area by including "the Tennessee River Drainage Basin and such adjoining territory as may be related to or materially affected by the development consequent to this Act". Moreover, there is the authorisation contained in Section 12 giving the Authority power to sell electricity anywhere "within transmission distance", and power to interconnect with other electricity systems. This, as well as certain points in the other clauses quoted, very substantially extends the range of the powers, responsibilities and administrative interest of the Authority beyond the mere basin, which has an average width of some 50 miles. With this latter index may be compared the economical transmission distance of about 250 miles from any point at which electricity is generated. Some sections of opinion, not over-friendly to public enterprise, were perturbed, when the T.V.A. was asking for new bond-issuing powers in 1939, about the possibility of an even greater widening of the T.V.A.'s area of enterprise in electricity supply.

There is no doubt that the drainage basin is a useful unifying concept for a resources development area, whether in the United States or any other country, but it is not the only one possible.[1] In the case of the Tennessee Valley, it will be recalled that the Federal Government's recognition of the economic and social distress of the Valley drew attention to the region as a subject for public development. Generally speaking, three questions arise in a consideration of the proper area for development: first, what is the area already defined for administration; secondly, for what people and groups, over that area, is the Authority made responsible; and thirdly, and very importantly, what are the established relations by the development authority with the people and agencies inside and outside the demarcated area for carrying out the functions for which it is both directly and indirectly responsible? Development by the Authority has, in a large number of cases, been successful only when the Authority has taken very special care to act as a part of the greater economic and social body within which it has its being.

The importance of the navigation powers of the T.V.A., as already noted, is by no means confined to that stretch of river from Knoxville to Paducah for which the Authority is primarily responsible; the river is linked with the Ohio, the Cumberland and the Mississippi to the Gulf of Mexico. This linkage has many repercussions. The railway and motor transport systems in the vicinity are part of the interest, even if not the primary responsibility, of the Authority; the Authority has already raised the question of river transport and its problems (the establishment of terminals and the planning of roads leading thereto) and the problem of interterritorial freight rates.[2]

So also in regard to flood control. Reference has already been made to the T.V.A.'s contribution in holding back the masses of water in the higher reaches of the Tennessee, so as not only to save the cities on that river, such as Chattanooga, from inundation, but, more important still, to help the Lower Ohio and Mississippi.

The necessary relevance of the Authority's activities, transcending the immediate area of administration, is nowhere more strikingly manifested than in its electricity operations.

---

[1] Cf. for general discussion, UNITED STATES NATIONAL RESOURCES COMMITTEE: *Regional Factors in National Planning*, Dec. 1935.
[2] Cf. p. 89.

Through its own transmission lines and the actual range of its own supply, and the contracts for interconnection with great neighbouring power companies, the Authority already stretches hundreds of miles beyond the immediate area of the Valley.[1] Even that is not all, however, because two questions of economic development have been raised by the T.V.A. rates for electricity: first, the effect of cheap rates upon industries in other parts of the country (and whether such industries may or may not set up in the Valley); and secondly, if it can be demonstrated that these cheap rates are in fact subsidised because the Federal Government has financed the Authority, whether other areas in the country may not justifiably challenge this special benefit. The T.V.A. has a tough problem here, but for the moment it is enough to notice that this is a problem of interregional adjustment which a local authority has to face.

In the fertiliser and farm demonstration programme, the Authority itself gradually realised that experiment would give the truest results if the donations of fertiliser were distributed all over the country and tested under the widest variety of conditions. The fertiliser and farm experts in the Authority have sought to make plain to the whole nation the importance of the phosphatic element in the soil. Here again, the range of interest and concern goes far beyond that of the Valley, and the matter has even been considered in relation to international export policy. The T.V.A. operates its fertiliser and farm demonstration programme outside its own area in connection with the Department of Agriculture and the land grant colleges, and the area of operation of these agencies is of course very wide.

Nor, more narrowly considered, is the Tennessee Valley completely coincident with the T.V.A.'s purposes. The Valley of the Tennessee is regarded by many people as having as its natural complement at least the Cumberland Valley. Indeed, in the course of the 74th and 75th Congresses, Bills were introduced for the addition of the Cumberland to the area of jurisdiction of the T.V.A., and in 1941 Congress was again considering this question. It was reasonably urged that more of the State of Tennessee would fall within the Authority's region, Tennessee being the chief State in

---

[1] In the drought of 1940, the Authority delivered power to the Aluminum Company of America (Alcoa), then deeply engaged in the production of aluminium for defence purposes, brought by it from Arkansas and North Carolina. Also, when the Commonwealth and Southern Companies were drought-stricken, they were helped by the same means. When the Hiwassee Dam was under construction, the T.V.A. had no transmission line of its own in the vicinity. It saved the cost of constructing or buying one by an arrangement with Alcoa which gave power to the T.V.A. on the site in exchange for power to the Alcoa in Tennessee. Extra power needed for defence industries was obtained from steam plants outside the area.

the Authority's field of activity, but, under existing conditions, divided into two disconnected areas; that the portion that would be newly included was extremely important, comprising as it did an area industrially, commercially and agriculturally productive; that there would be added to the resources already under development by the Authority high grade coal, hardwood forests, tobacco areas and agricultural land; that social and economic ties corresponding to the social and economic influences exerted by the area outside would be established; and that there was a kinship of the regions in resources, terrain, and the economic bases of population and culture. The interconnection of the two river basins would be of benefit in relation to floods on the Mississippi, additions to power supply, and ease of navigation.[1]

Since 1933, something like 120 State and city planning boards, occasionally advised by the National Resources Planning Board[2], have been established in the area of the T.V.A. The relationships of the Authority with these agencies, in so far as they fall within its area, have already been considered.[3] The point of present interest is that planning agencies have come into being in an area larger than that of the Authority itself. At the conferences of the southeastern section of the National Resources Planning Board, T.V.A. officers from time to time played a considerable part, and the T.V.A. and N.R.P.B. stimulated each other's ideas and researches. The Authority has principally addressed itself to the stimulation of many agencies inside, on the borders of, and outside the Valley. By these connections, the Authority is enabled to exercise a useful influence on the whole of the seven States, though its own area covers only a part of each.

This discussion of the relationship of the T.V.A.'s own specific area to its concern and responsibility for parts of the United States beyond its boundaries suggests several conclusions. First, that the Authority's area has been necessarily restricted in order to secure a sharp focus of attention upon its resources and problems. Secondly, that while an area of special development need not necessarily be based upon electric power or the control of a river, the development agency must have authority and power to deal with its problems in terms of the area that these problems affect, and there may be sub-areas or trans-areas to meet special problems involved in each of its several powers. A small valley authority may have to fit into a larger entity; an immense valley may need sub-regions;

---

[1] Cf. 77th Congress, 1st Session, *Hearings on S. 1539*, pp. 15 ff.

[2] This agency was established in 1934 as the National Resources Board to prepare and present to the President a programme for the development and use of land, water and other national resources. It was abolished in June 1943.

[3] Cf. p. 119.

plain and country may need division; mountain masses may need a single control though they are under several sovereignties. Thirdly, the delimitation of the area lies, to a very large extent, in the discretion of the Government; it depends upon what the Government wishes to secure. Fourthly, any one area is necessarily embodied in the integument of the total economic system of a nation, is affected by the rest of the economic system, even as it affects and contributes to it; hence, there must always be problems of adjustment. And, finally, the machinery of adjustment may take the form of a voluntary agreement between the development area and its neighbours, but in the last resort must be operated by the Government of the whole nation.

INTEGRATED RESOURCE DEVELOPMENT AND A MULTI-PURPOSE AUTHORITY

The Tennessee Valley Authority places great emphasis and importance upon integrated development. It believes that undue insistence upon one branch of its operations, however important in itself, falls short of the possibilities of its mode of operation. It looks at the area in terms of all its needs and of all its resources together. Manifestly, the several powers vested in the Authority have facets and significance for each other over and above their direct values. It has been seen, for instance, that the electricity programme has its own direct importance, but it also contributes to increasing the productivity of the farms and raising the value of farm produce, by making possible the preservation of locally grown food and thus also contributing to improved diet. Again, reafforestation ministers to the improvement of the soil and of farm economy and the redevelopment of timber industries and, by holding the topsoil on the land, aids in preventing the silting of rivers, and thus assists navigation and the production of electricity. Furthermore, the fertiliser and farm demonstration operations are aided by the electricity programme and, in their turn, aid it, because a wealthier farm community will look to electrical apparatus as part of its production methods and comfort in living. The power to conduct research and demonstrations is useful in promoting the productivity of the area, because it may result in the discovery of valuable mineral resources which may either be sold elsewhere or (as in the case of certain clays processed in the area) used by industry, which may be decentralised by the use of the Authority's supply of electric power. Once again, issuing from the duty of constructing dams, there is a whole host of health problems, the effects of which are not confined to workers on the construction projects and the answers to which have wide repercussions. All these

functions, furthermore, minister individually to the civic education of the people in terms of their domestic economy and farm
practices, and to the art of democratic self-government in the co-
operatives.

It would be possible, of course, for each of these powers to be
exercised by a separate authority, and it has been suggested[1] that
certain of the powers devolved to the T.V.A. might well be administered by separate agencies; for example, its farm demonstration work might be undertaken by the United States Department
of Agriculture. But such a development would mean the loss of
the supplemental values, which are most perceptible and better
capable of being planned and achieved where a single unified authority is responsible for all of them together; and moreover, as has
been suggested earlier, would raise the possibility of parallel agencies
acting either in jealous separation or uneasy co-ordination, although
even such emergent problems are not insoluble.

The Tennessee Valley Authority, then, derives much of its
significance from the fact that it is a multi-purpose authority.[2]
The powers listed were conceived of by those who established it as
a governmentally integrated means of achieving integrated resource
development. They had in mind, and the T.V.A. has had in mind
from the beginning, the comprehensive promotion of all the resources in their interrelationship, each resource being utilised in
companionship with the others and their purposes. The single
powers, therefore, are parts of a well-woven web, and all the parts
together make the strength of the Authority and its value for the
region. Each facet of each resource and power has, besides its
own significance, a supplemental one for the rest of the resources
and powers, and the development of each is consciously managed
from this point of view, so that from the very integration an additional value is obtained which is greater than the sum. No single
power, therefore, can be regarded as standing alone; it is always
a contributor to, and needs contribution from, all the rest. This
has clearly emerged from the description already given of the
various phases of the Authority's work.

---

[1] Cf. *Report of the Joint Committee Investigating the Tennessee Valley Authority,
op. cit., Minority Views*, pp. 275-277.

[2] It should not be forgotten, in the interests of proportion and perspective,
that the great cities of the world, not to speak of the smaller ones, are also multi-
purpose authorities, for instance, the great metropolitan centres of New York,
London, Buenos Aires, Vienna, etc. When it is urged that the T.V.A. is a multi-
purpose authority, the implied contrast is with such public corporations as the
Central Electricity Board or London Passenger Transport Board in Great Britain,
or the Inland Waterways Commission of the United States, which are vested with
responsibility for a single function. But it is all a question of degree, for even
these single functions fall into a plurality of purposes.

CHAPTER VIII

MANAGEMENT AND PERSONNEL

THE BOARD OF DIRECTORS

The chief administrative arrangements of the T.V.A. are exceptionally instructive to those who seek to understand its success, for they attempt to answer the two vital problems of securing administrative and technical efficiency, and excluding the influence of politics from the direction and conduct of the undertaking. The various sections of the Statute establish but meagrely the bare foundations of its administrative system.

Supreme in the direction of the affairs of the corporation is the Board of Directors. The Statute says (Section 2 (g)) that "the Board shall direct the exercise of all the powers of the Corporation". Under this Board there are some thousands of employees, the basic principles of whose selection are stated in the Statute. As to the organisation of departments and committees and councils and the hierarchy of staff by which the executive work of this public enterprise is achieved, the Statute is almost silent; the Board of Directors is free to establish such organisation on the basis of the Statute (Section 3) under the following provision:

The Board shall without regard to the provisions of civil service laws applicable to officers and employees of the United States, appoint such managers, assistant managers, officers, employees, attorneys and agents as are necessary for the transaction of its business, fix their compensation, define their duties, require bonds of such of them as the Board may designate and provide a system of organisation to fix responsibility and promote efficiency. Any appointee of the Board may be removed in the discretion of the Board. No regular officer or employee of the Corporation shall receive a salary in excess of that received by the members of the Board. . .

Thus, the Directors are in a position of paramount importance.

There are three directors, one being chairman. The Board is appointed by the President by and with the advice and consent of the Senate.[1] Directors are removable by Congress at its discretion; they are removable by the President if found guilty by him

---

[1] Section 2 (a).

of applying political tests or qualifications in the appointment and career of officials of the Authority or of acting in such matters otherwise than on a basis of merit and efficiency.[1] By a ruling of the Courts, the President also possesses (and has exercised) the right to remove directors, based upon his constitutional duty to see that the laws are faithfully executed. In appointing the members of the Board, the President is empowered to designate the chairman. The directors are appointed for a term of nine years, but the terms of appointment are arranged so as to stagger the term of each director, those first taking office having been given terms of three, six and nine years. Any two directors are empowered to carry on the affairs of the Corporation in the absence of the third director from board meetings.

When the T.V.A. was being developed, much consideration was given to the question of appointment and qualifications. It was clearly realised that the vesting of such an important trust in the Authority, especially with the latitude permitted to a corporation, meant that the experiment would stand or fall by the quality of the directors. The majority report of the House of Representatives introducing the T.V.A. Bill (H.R. 5081) said:

> It is a great responsibility imposed upon the members of the Board, but it is a great opportunity that will come to those chosen for this great service. For such position of trust and responsibility, undoubtedly the President will search the nation over for the right men to whom to entrust not only this vast investment of money but this great responsibility not only to the people of that section of the country, but to the people of the whole nation. If, through the incapacity or the indifference of the members of the Board, this great humanitarian project should fail, then progress along this line in other parts of the country will be set back for two or three generations.

Congress, then, wished to exclude political appointments and influence, and to secure a clear objective devotion to the purposes of the corporation. As for political impartiality, it was hoped that the long term of office—nine years, which is longer than that of most commissioners in other Government corporations—would exclude partisanship. Further, the fact that the Statute had placed the general power of dismissal in the hands of Congress to some degree encouraged the hope that the Chief Executive would not intrude. Finally, the staggering of the terms of office of the directors was designed to produce a consistency and continuity in policy which might not be possible if the reappointment of all directors fell at one time; a further important consideration was that the staggered terms overlap the normal four-year terms of the President of the United States, and this was expected to frustrate the hostile

---

[1] Section 6.

designs of a new and unfriendly President.[1] It is important not to ignore the effect on the T.V.A.'s speed and attack in its early years of the thought that it might have only four years of a friendly President's term in which to lay its foundations securely. Had it been assured of a succession of benevolent controlling authorities, it would have been less hasty in some important matters of power policy, and would not have made enemies.

As regards administrative competence, Section 2 of the Statute lays down three stipulations. First, no director may have a financial interest in any public utility corporation engaged in the business of distributing and selling power to the public, nor in any corporation engaged in the manufacture, sale, or distribution of fixed nitrogen or fertiliser or any ingredients thereof, nor in any business that might be adversely affected by the success of the corporation as a producer of concentrated fertilisers or electric power.

Secondly, members of the Board are not, while in office, to engage in any other business, but are to devote themselves to the work of the corporation; that is, they are to be full-time officials. This has been rather important as it has meant that the directors have been on the spot most of the time, and a close identification of their views with those of the region has resulted.

Thirdly, "all members of the Board shall be persons who profess a belief in the feasibility and wisdom of this Act". This clause is intended to exclude from consideration those who obviously could not be held to believe in the feasibility and wisdom of this novel public enterprise. Some evidence of loyalty was needed, and a similar declaration has been required of all the officials of the corporation also. Whether this profession can govern those who appoint and those who are appointed is an elusive problem in human psychology. It does not, of course, exclude *bona fide* differences of opinion as to what the Act means and how it should be fulfilled, nor has it done so.

The directors receive a salary of $10,000 a year. Some members of Congress believed that it was impossible to secure men of the requisite ability and character at such a salary when they might earn much more in private enterprise. Some also believed that the directors could not be non-political. But these prognostications have been decisively refuted by experience.

---

[1] It is interesting to observe the comments on this of Mr. Wendell Willkie who, as President of the Commonwealth and Southern Utilities, had found it difficult to reconcile the policy of the T.V.A. and the President with the policy of the utilities. Yet on 14 June 1940 (in a Scripps-Howard Press interview), he declared: "Any President of the United States who tries to turn T.V.A. back to the private utilities would be extremely unrealistic"; and "Now let us give T.V.A. a really honest chance to see what it can do or it cannot do for the benefit of all the people".

Thus, there are three directors, full time, all legally with equal power, though one is chairman. Legal equality soon encouraged a struggle for predominance. This resulted in the early years of the T.V.A. in a threefold division of the Authority's work. The too evident disadvantages[1], *i.e.*, the inability to introduce a logical division and proper co-ordination of departmental activities and the disturbance caused by conflicting loyalties, were overcome by the focussing of management in a general manager under the authority of the Board, to be described later. In a multi-purpose authority coherence in policy and unity and drive in management are more than usually important.

Whether a full-time board of three directors was, or is, necessary is doubtful. It was not the deliberate result of careful congressional meditation on alternatives. Various methods of administration are conceivable for such public enterprises as the T.V.A., for instance, by a single administrator responsible only to the President (or other superior control), and unaided and unaffected by any colleagues, advisory or executive, sharing his responsibility; by a single administrator with the executive power and responsibility, but required to consult an advisory board; by a single administrator subject in all things to direction and control by the board of directors; or, as in the case of the T.V.A., by fully collective administration, yet with the majority of two directors able to overrule the third, even if the third were chairman.

Experience of the first eight years of the T.V.A.'s operation (during which there were moments of confusion, dissension, strain and loss of time) certainly raises the question whether a board of three men each with equal authority could not be better replaced by a single administrator. To this, the Minority Report of the joint congressional investigation answered that it would be better to have five part-time directors paid on a *per diem* basis or by a reasonable annual salary, employing a manager and acting as the directors of an ordinary business corporation.[2] But the Majority Report considered that concentration of responsibility in a single administrator would be inefficient, because the range of interests to which the T.V.A. must give skilled attention was too large for a single person, especially as the T.V.A. was moving along novel and untried paths.[3] The directors of the T.V.A. agree with the latter opinion. Yet it is difficult at the operating stage at which the T.V.A. has arrived, as distinct from the earlier policy-forming

---

[1] See *Report of the Joint Committee Investigating the Tennessee Valley Authority, op. cit.*, and more especially *Hearings*, Vols. 1, 2, 3 and 6.
[2] *Report, op. cit.*, p. 277.
[3] *Ibid.*, p. 26.

stage, to discover what a full-time board does that a part-time board could not do.

Initially, the Board of Directors assumed almost all powers for itself, including administrative detail. This led to confusion, and the Board finally consigned administration to various offices and departments, and, in particular, put a general manager between themselves and the detailed fulfilment of their orders. Consequently, the Board keeps in its own hands the major decisions concerning its exercise and development of the discretion vested in it by Congress and the coherent guidance of the whole enterprise; matters of general policy, such as the relative weight to be given to its various programmes, the speed and scope of each main item of administration within such programmes, the adoption of the annual budget, which, in a sense, is a financial focus of the various lines of enterprise in the Authority as they thrust forward. It approves all appointments carrying salaries above $5,600 a year. It must approve purchases of over $10,000 a year, and it reviews purchases where the lowest bid is not accepted. The directors also represent the Authority on important occasions before the public, the President, and Congress. They direct, and sometimes participate in, the general strategy of relationships with other governmental authorities. They take a leading part in stating to various public bodies the general purpose and standards of enterprise of the Authority; this duty falls especially upon the chairman.

The General Manager

The general manager is the chief administrative officer to whom all departments and officials report. He is responsible for the execution of policies and decisions of the Board subject to the latter's control. He prepares the Board's agenda, issues notice of its meetings, presents subjects for Board action, and notifies the departments of the Board's policies and decisions. It is his business to keep the Board currently informed of the activities of the Authority, to make recommendations, and to prepare special reports upon the Board's request. He exercises considerable unifying power and managerial authority—through his duty to prepare and submit to the Board the annual budget estimates. Naturally, he assists in the process of commending the budget to the United States Bureau of the Budget and the relevant committees of Congress.

The general managers of the Authority have hitherto interpreted their duty as not to assume all the tasks of administration

themselves, but rather to evoke from the various experts in the
employ of the Authority the best that they can give in terms of
advice and action.   They remove obstacles to the free and progressive activity of the departments, funnel information to the
Board (by various forms of reports, oral and written), and transmit
the policies decided upon by the Board to all the various
services and experts employed to do its bidding. They seek to overcome the ignorance of employees at different levels of responsibility
of each other's duties and special part in the T.V.A.'s collective
purpose, in order to reinforce coherence of direction.

There are board-staff conferences arranged at the request of
the Board of Directors, the general manager, or one of the departmental directors in order to provide the Board with information
regarding the fulfilment of a policy already adopted, or to elicit
from it direction regarding policy considerations which may arise
out of the working programme of a department and give concern
to the staff.   At such conferences there are present not only the
chief of the administrative department, but also members of the
departmental staff; and thus an opportunity of direct contact
between the supreme direction and the executants of policy is
provided, with beneficial effects on the understanding and morale
of both parties, and on unity of action and timing.

Consultants

The work of the Authority and the planning of the Board have
been much assisted by the calling in of expert consultants.   These
have sometimes acted as a committee, as with the committee of
three public utility experts who examined and reported upon the
problem of allocation of dam costs, or when hydraulic engineering
experts have been called in to give their opinion on the planning
of a dam or some particularly difficult phase of its construction.
There are very many instances in which an individual who is master
of a special field has been consulted; for instance, on labour policies,
legal questions, power finance policies, health and safety problems,
tax studies, engineering, employee training, and so on.   Advice is
sought in connection either with the preparation of a policy or with
technological improvements in processes or, again, in the form of a
general review and appraisal of work already in progress.

Here again can be seen a further aspect of the T.V.A.'s contribution to the welfare of the region in providing and bringing together
the most expert advisers for the solution of its problems.

The following organisation chart of the Authority shows the
distribution of duties:

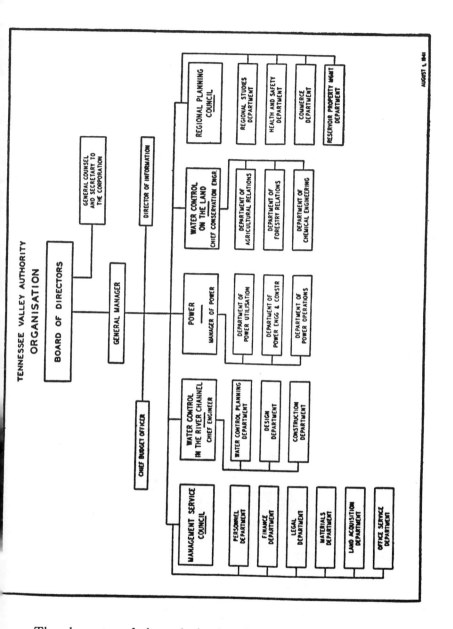

TENNESSEE VALLEY AUTHORITY ORGANISATION

AUGUST 1, 1944

The character of these duties has for the most part been explained indirectly in the various chapters describing the functions of the T.V.A., but a word of explanation is needed in regard to the Management Service and Regional Planning Councils. These councils are meetings of members of the various departments for the discussion of matters common to them, or subjects which, though not requiring a collective decision, may commonly concern the departmental responsibility of each. For example, at the Management Service Council there may be a discussion on T.V.A. publicity, the recruitment of staff, the T.V.A. and industrialisation; and at the Regional Planning Council a review of the significance of all T.V.A. activities, of land-utilisation maps, or malaria control operations, or negro problems. These discussions tend to encourage *esprit de corps* and mutual understanding of each other's problems; they are educational rather than executive or even advisory. Once again, by this device, it is sought to secure in a multi-purpose authority which might easily degenerate into cross-purpose departments, a sense of unified and co-ordinated advance.

PERSONNEL

As with other parts of the system, Congress sought for T.V.A employees the guarantees of political independence and efficiency. Congress had to find the answer to two problems. One was how to secure a defence against political influence; the other was whether the T.V.A. should have its own special procedure to secure merit and efficiency appropriate to its special and local tasks, or be subject to the general procedure of the United States Civil Service Commission. The devices to answer the first question were simple, though difficult to apply. The answer to the second involves issues of great importance in Government undertakings of an economic character, and some brief observations on the long and serious debate which occurred on this question before the T.V.A. was set up, which continued later and has not yet ceased, are necessary at this stage.

Those who were anxious to have the United States Civil Service Commission recruit staff for the T.V.A. and regulate its classification, salaries, its conditions of work, retirement and the rest—in other words, to embody the T.V.A. staff entirely in the one million United States civil servants—wished to exclude patronage and political influence by subjecting the T.V.A. to the regular procedure by which the United States has sought to solve the question of political "spoils". The method generally is universal open competition and (usually) written examinations, with uniformity of treatment for all departments and agencies of the Government, no matter what their function. When there is such uniformity of practice, congressional controls are also easier.

On the other hand, those legislators who wished to endow the T.V.A. with freedom to be its own employing authority aimed at giving the T.V.A. business vitality appropriate to its own special function of economic development.

The legislators sought:

> to write a Bill that would establish a Government Corporation on the same basis of operation as the great industrial corporations of America are run— the United States Steel Corporation in its efficiency, for instance. To accomplish that efficiency the captain of the team has to have absolute command. It is the only way in which efficiency can be obtained.[1]

They were afraid to have the Authority's employees selected by an outside agency (the United States Civil Service Commission), on the ground that this would mean applying a test which no man engaged in that particular business in a private way would apply, and depriving those responsible for the success of a business undertaking of the guarantee of efficiency, the right to hire and fire.[2] Finally, many also believed that if the T.V.A. staff were appointed by the United States Civil Service, then, so long as a candidate could satisfy the usual wholesale tests of ability, he could be appointed to the T.V.A. even if he were an enemy of public economic enterprise and unwilling to work for its success.

The upshot was the inclusion in the Statute of Sections 3 and 6. Section 3 has already been quoted.[3] The amplest creative opportunity was thus afforded the Authority. The power to remove any employee at the discretion of the Board is a clear indication of the flexibility with which Congress, after long argument, decided to endow the Authority in order to meet the problem, so awkward in Government employment, of getting rid of the "deadwood" of incompetent workers.

The Authority's guarantee against political perversion is embodied in Section 6:

> In the appointment of officials and the selection of employees for said Corporation, and in the promotion of any such employees or officials, no political test or qualification should be permitted or given consideration, but all such appointments and promotions shall be given and made on the basis of merit and efficiency. Any member of said Board who is found by the President of the United States to be guilty of a violation of this section shall be removed from office by the President of the United States and any appointee of said Board who is found by the Board to be guilty of a violation of this section shall be removed from office by said Board.

The rule against political considerations is strong and unmistakable. The command that merit and efficiency shall rule is equally firm and clear. What conditions should be established to secure

---

[1] Cf. 66th Congress, 2nd Session, *Congressional Record*, 1 Dec. 1924, pp. 298-299.

[2] *Ibid.*, p. 190.

[3] Cf. p. 1.

the supremacy of merit and efficiency was a matter left freely to
the Board and its properly deputed officers.

Freedom from Political Influence

As regards political intervention in appointments, the Authority
was, from the beginning, subject to heavy pressure. This came
sometimes from the chief party agents, Federal and local, of a
political party, but more frequently from members of Congress
from whom constituents had begged recommendations for jobs.
From the very first, the T.V.A. firmly rejected all attempts at
patronage. In this it was, at its request, assisted by the authoritative influence of the President of the United States. A T.V.A.
report made in 1935, at the most critical period, showed that about
10.1 per cent. of all applicants for jobs had recommendations from
members of Congress, but only 3.2 per cent. of those actually
appointed had such recommendations, and, of course, this latter
figure is no indication that the recommendation was a deciding
factor. Over the whole history of the T.V.A., there is no doubt that,
though subject to pressure, and though sometimes subject to temp-
tation, it has resisted political considerations successfully enough
for their influence to have been negligible.

Originally, the T.V.A. followed the United States Civil Service
rule that officers and employees, while retaining the right to express
their opinions on all political subjects and to vote as they pleased,
should take no "active" part in political management or in political
campaigns. At the employees' request, in accordance with the
Authority's employee relationship policy, to be discussed presently[1], a more liberal rule was adopted. In the first place, an
obligation was put on every employee of the Authority not to use
his authority or official influence, directly or indirectly, to control
or modify the political action of any other person; not to engage
in any form of political activity during the hours of duty, nor at any
other time to take such part in political activities or campaigns as
to impair his effectiveness in his position or the programme of the
Authority, irrespective of party or political issues. It was also
resolved that no officer or employee should be prejudiced in his
career because of his political views or activities, unless these tended
to discredit the integrity of the Authority in carrying out its programme.[2]

---

[1] Cf. Chapter X.

[2] With the passage of the Hatch Law in 1939, the Authority's Political Activity
Policy was supplemented to include the provisions of this law, applicable to employees in all Federal departments and agencies, under which termination of
employment is mandatory for any violation of the specific prohibitions set forth
in the law.

Merit and Efficiency

Though the T.V.A. is free from any geographical limits of selection, it has come about that employees from the Valley States themselves have secured what is perhaps a disproportionate number of the total jobs.[1] This is because of the concentration of the Authority's work in the Valley; and, in regard to industrial hourly workers, because it would be unwise to recruit them from all over the United States with the prospect of their being turned off as soon as a construction job was finished. Although, for example, the salaried employees of the Authority are not required to be residents of the Valley, about 75 per cent. of them are from the Valley States. It is reasonably to be expected that men to fill the highest positions in the T.V.A., being experts with a national reputation, should be sought primarily for their competence, and that the place of their origin should be only a secondary consideration. Familiarity with problems of the region is a definite asset in some types of work. Where this cannot be adequately obtained together with technical competence, subordinate officers with local backgrounds are employed as assistants. The T.V.A. has attracted, trained, and utilised a very able body of personnel officers, whose record of work in providing the skilled professional, administrative and scientific staff, and the thousands of construction workers belonging to 100 different occupations, and in handling the problems of classification and personnel relations, is outstanding in the contemporary public services of the United States.

TOTAL NUMBER OF PERSONS EMPLOYED BY THE T.V.A. FROM YEAR TO YEAR

Year		Annual workers	Hourly workers	Total
30 July	1934	(combined)		7,114
December	1935	(combined)		12,504
"	1936	5,225	9,392	14,617
"	1937	5,715	7,955	13,670
"	1938	5,696	7,219	12,915
"	1939	5,744	6,493	12,237
"	1940	6,953	7,343	14,296
"	1941	8,979	14,548	23,527
January	1942	13,122	20,637	33,759
July	1942	15,032	26,179	41,211

[1] As a concession to the Federal character of the United States, there is an important rule in the United States Civil Service which runs: "Appointment to the public service aforesaid in the departments at Washington shall be apportioned among the several States and territories and the District of Columbia upon the basis of population as ascertained at the last preceding census" (Civil Service Act, 1883, Sec. 2).

NUMBERS AND AVERAGE SALARIES OF ANNUAL EMPLOYEES AT
31 DECEMBER 1941[1]

Classification service	Number of employees	Average salary
Professional and scientific	1,926	$3,373
Sub-professional	1,433	1,618
Clerical, administrative, and fiscal	3,717	1,844
Educational	7	1,960
Inspectional	259	2,145
Custodial	1,260	1,934
Total: Annual employees under the salary policy	8,602	2,167
Trades and labour annual employees	2,097[2]	1,767[2]
Total: All annual employees	10,699	2,092

[1] Hourly employees in the Trades and Labour Service, comprising from one half to two thirds of the total personnel, are excluded from this table.
[2] Figure at 31 Jan. 1942.

Recruitment

To recruit employees for administrative, clerical, scientific and professional grades, the T.V.A. does not, like the United States Civil Service Commission, have regular examinations with a nation-wide announcement of date and requirements and subjects of examinations.[1] Instead, it circularises a number of colleges and institutions of higher learning and invites applications for positions. The applications are reviewed, interviews sometimes held, and a list or register of possible appointees is produced. Those not appointed remain on the register, and are periodically circularised regarding their wish to continue there. In the case of the United States Civil Service the examination results in an order of merit, and when an appointment is to be made the head of the department chooses from three names in the order of merit certified by the Civil Service Commission. Those lower down on the register are considered only later, in their relative order, as vacancies occur. The register is then closed until the next examination. The T.V.A.'s register remains open, however, and any individual may apply at any time for inclusion in it. Since its beginning the T.V.A. has had 600,000 applications for positions of all types.

The personnel department is very dependent on the records of the candidate's previous career. The Authority obtains additional information concerning a candidate through reference enquiries of unusual detail sent to previous employers and to other individuals who know the applicant well. The standing of a candidate, especially for the higher posts, in a particular field can be ascertained from universities, the officers of professional organisations and similar sources.

[1] For certain clerical and custodial positions, the Authority does utilise aptitude tests for the preliminary selection of candidates, and from these tests registers are established. A variety of other factors beside test marks are considered.

When there is a vacancy in the T.V.A., the personnel department provides the records of several of the best qualified applicants listed on the register. It frequently assists the heads of departments and supervisors in analysing the qualifications of candidates. The appointing officer may choose, at his own discretion, any of the names submitted to him, or ask for others. This system renders unnecessary a regular widespread examination with the trouble and expense of making up a numerical order of merit. The officer making the appointment has more latitude in considering ability and the very important personal equation of fitness than where only three names are submitted to him, as in the Civil Service; since selection is based on no predetermined order of merit established by written competition, the possibility is open, though it by no means follows that it is taken, of preferences on the basis of personal friendship or professional or academic relationship. As a matter of fact, complaints of the operation of this factor have been made in a number of cases.[1]

However, it should be remembered that principal officers are held strictly responsible for securing results in the programme under their direction. Moreover, no positions in higher grades are filled until the director of personnel, the general manager and the Board of Directors have approved the appointment. Thus, the procedure followed obviates the choice of incompetents. Of course, in the selection of the T.V.A.'s principal officers, such as the heads of the various departments, very special care is exercised. It is not only recognised ability in the profession that is needed, but some guarantee that the employee will fit in with the purposes and policy of the T.V.A.

Generally speaking, therefore, the T.V.A. approaches business rather than civil service practice in the appointment of its personnel.

Classification and Salaries

The T.V.A. established an elaborate and appropriate classification of its employees, closely following Federal practices, but utilising its autonomy to make suitable modifications. Classification in the T.V.A., like all its personnel services, does not merely consist in putting names and men into a classification of jobs;

---

[1] Professor Leonard White, of the University of Chicago, and sometime United States Civil Service Commissioner, in a report made to the Joint Investigating Committee, says: "There is evidence that the recommendations of foremen and supervisors have as a matter of fact played considerable part in the actual selection for certification for appointment. . . While it does not appear that political influence has been effective in selecting persons for appointment, selection probably has been influenced under the T.V.A. system by personal acquaintance more than would have been the case under the rule of civil service certification."

in the process of classifying jobs and men into the great subdivisions of administrative work, the necessary changes are made in the jobs themselves and the numbers, procedures and personnel relationships required to do a designed task.

Dovetailed into the classification plan is the salary plan. The scale of salaries for clerical, administrative and professional positions in the T.V.A. is generally that obtaining in the Federal Civil Service up to and including $6,500 a year. From that point, the T.V.A. has a larger proportion of higher-paid officers to total personnel than have the Federal departments.[1] Suggestions that salaries should correspond to those of the State of Tennessee cannot stand against the argument that a Federal public policy conducted through a Federal agency provided with Federal funds, and responsible to Congress and the President, can be maintained only on the basis of Federal standards of salary.

For each salary grade there are three rates, known as the entrance, the standard, and the maximum rate. Appointments and promotions are made at entrance rates, and employees receive the standard rate for their grade after a minimum of one year of satisfactory service. After that, they proceed to the maximum, on the basis of a demonstration of superior qualifications and achievement.

A Service Rating Plan calls for semi-annual reports. An unsatisfactory report means transfer, demotion or dismissal. After employees achieve the standard rate for their grade and receive "satisfactory" as their report, the rule is "as you are". Where the rating is "unusually satisfactory", one, two or three merit points are given. It is possible to advance to the maximum grade if six such points are gained in a period of not more than three years. A board of review of members of the personnel department considers all ratings of "unsatisfactory" and "unusually satisfactory", made in the first place by the employee's supervisor. About one in a hundred of the salaried employees is recommended for merit points at the semi-annual ratings. The number of those who achieve the requisite points for the maximum is, of course, very much smaller—in the opinion of some of the employees, unjustifiably small.[2]

Promotion

The Authority has no formal promotion procedures or examinations, but in practice promotions are granted because, under the method of appointment, all employees have a chance of appoint-

---

[1] The T.V.A. goes up to $9,500 a year for its General Manager and one or two other officers; this is much higher than the Federal Civil Service.

[2] For example, on 31 Dec. 1941, among 8,602 employees in all services, 75.9 per cent. were at entrance, 23.9 at standard, and only 0.2 at maximum rates.

ment to vacancies in higher grades. As a matter of fact, in the first few years, development in the T.V.A. was so rapid that some young men who entered it moved upwards at a very early age to new positions of great authority and considerable income. A study made by the T.V.A. itself in January 1941, covering the twelve months from November 1939 to November 1940, showed that there were 2,868 promotions in a total of 6,500 annual employees. This is entirely unparalleled in any civil service.

As the Authority has no special promotions procedure, however, the existence of a vacancy is not drawn to the attention of all those who may legitimately be aspirants for promotion. The employee is not in a position to know whether his record is receiving consideration. This could be overcome by the public announcement of such a vacancy, and the acceptance of application from any qualified employee.

Hourly Workers

The foregoing remarks apply to the employment of the salaried or annual employees. But hitherto, in its years of construction and development, the T.V.A. has had a much larger number of hourly or wage-paid workers of a skilled, semi-skilled or unskilled kind. When the T.V.A. commenced operations in 1933, a time of heavy unemployment, scores of thousands made application for employment. The Authority, true to its ideas regarding efficiency and humane relationships, attempted to proceed by individual interview. The method proved far too expensive, and it was impossible to attract needed types of skill except by specific advertisement. Therefore, the Authority turned to the practice of wholesale examination, based upon tests of ability to understand printed and oral instructions and of mechanical aptitude, devised by the experts of the United States Civil Service Commission. Nearly 39,000 applicants were examined in four days in 138 cities and towns in the Valley under the supervision of local United States Civil Service Boards of Examiners or by local school officials. Trained interviewers, using the ratings at the examination and the experience record, selected the workmen for the first three projects from the register thus established. Under the test of experience carefully analysed, the examination results were found to be highly correlated with efficiency on the job and consequent promotion.

Examinations were held in 1936, 1938 and 1939, as the Authority proceeded with each main stage in its construction plan. Only in the case of the additional projects authorised in the war emergency of 1940 was the examination method dispensed with.[1] It is

---

[1] In this case employees already with the T.V.A. were assigned to 85 per cent. of the supervisory posts of the Cherokee Dam and about 75 per cent. of the skilled workmen posts. Skills were becoming rare in the face of widespread
(Footnote continued overleaf)

clear, upon consideration of the various specialised occupational or trade tests for skilled labour, that the Authority has provided adequate technical tests. The oral interview given to all applicants for skilled labour appointments may perhaps, on the whole, be regarded as superfluous, since it is costly and has had little effect in modifying the result of the written examination.

No part is allotted or allowed to trade unions in the recruitment process, with some slight exceptions to be noticed in the next chapter. The United States Employment Service similarly played no part in the early recruitment, nor has the T.V.A. since then relied upon it other than casually[1], believing that its own direct method gives the desired results better than any alternative.

The T.V.A. does not draw on the country generally for its workers, but defines an area around or contiguous to a construction project. The reason for this limitation is, first, that there is a greater supply of labour than is required in the area defined, and secondly, that if the examination area were unlimited, the cost would be immense, since applicants would expect to be examined in a place convenient to themselves. Furthermore, it is unwise to induce a worker and his family to migrate from one part of the United States to another for a temporary job.

The Authority is not summary in its dismissals, but gives every employee a fair opportunity, through a procedure of appeal up to the Personnel Department, of justifying himself before separating him from its service. It has field personnel officers at the centres of operations to promote good relationship and deal with difficulties at the earliest stage. Its policy is to endeavour to continue the service of its workers, an economical proceeding which avoids the expense of fresh recruitment and retraining in the service. While this policy has not been carried to excess, taken together with the other factors of great care at the stage of recruitment, training workers for other tasks, and sensible practice in regard to transfer, it has kept the turnover of employees small. This is not due to any automatic acquiescence in the retention of incompetent workers, even though the supervisors are reluctant to set down in the semi-annual reports a mark of "unsatisfactory" which might mean dismissal. On the construction projects, where a rather heavy turn-

---

demand, and it became necessary to call for workmen in certain trades (electrician, lineman, boilermaker, steamfitter, machinist and iron-worker) wherever they could be obtained, so that wide publicity was resorted to. 25,000 applications received were rated in four classes on the basis of the candidate's experience; wherever possible, references of prospective employees were checked (frequently verbally), and all individuals hired were selected by skilled interviewers.

[1] Only since the war brought with it emergency demands for labour, widespread transference problems and stringent Government regulations has the T.V.A. entered into co-operation with the local placement machinery of U.S.E.S.

over might be expected, it was in fact only something like 8.8 per cent. in the fiscal year 1942, a figure reflecting an increase due to wartime conditions. The Authority has introduced an "exit interview", a special procedure of interviewing those about to leave its service in order that there should be no misunderstanding of the reasons by either party.

There are extremely strict rules regarding the employment of relations in the Authority. No employee may hold a position involving administrative or supervisory relationship with one to whom he is related by blood or marriage in the first, second, or third degree of consanguinity. Two members of the same household related by blood or marriage in the first, second, or third degree of consanguinity cannot be retained in employment if either receives a salary in excess of $2,000 per annum.

All in all, the personnel of the T.V.A. has been, and is, of very high quality. Though their morale was from time to time subjected to severe strain as a result of the distribution of the Authority's work between three directors, dissensions in the Board, and the litigious hostility of the public utility companies, in the main the employees remained proof against such shocks. During the depression some had been especially attracted to the Authority's service by the public purposes for which the Authority was established; and at the date when it began operations it had the pick of many professional men of great and growing repute. But the intense concern of the directors for the success of their enterprise, leading to meticulous, and sometimes even excessive, care in choosing their staff, whether personally or through their directors of personnel, was also an important factor in building up an efficient service. According to the Joint Congressional Committee:

It appears that the Authority has been able to attract a group of higher administrative personnel whose previous average earning power under normal conditions was considerably higher than the salaries they now receive from the Authority.[1]

There have been several Congressional attempts to bring the staff of the T.V.A. under the United States Civil Service Commission[2], ostensibly on the grounds suggested in our earlier discussion,

[1] *Report of the Joint Committee Investigating the Tennessee Valley Authority, op. cit.*

[2] The Joint Investigating Committee recommended entry into the United States Civil Service Retirement Plan, but the T.VA. has its own scheme, supported by the joint contributions of employees and the T.V.A., which provides the following benefits: service retirement optional at 60 years of age, compulsory at 70; disability retirement for total disability after five years of service; lump sum death benefit of one half year's salary; return of employee's contributions with interest at termination of employment for whatever cause before retirement; and deferred annuity to employees terminated involuntarily after ten years of service, if not discharged for cause (*Management Services Report No. 1*, T.V.A., 1942, p. 27).

not always with the success of the enterprise as the first consideration. A large number of the employees have looked with favour
on the greater security of the Federal Service; the advance within
each grade along seven steps, as compared with the two provided
by the Authority (the second one being highly problematical);
rather wider possibilities of transfer; and the benefits of a Civil
Service retirement plan, which it has been extremely difficult for
the Authority to provide owing to its comparative smallness and
the anticipation of a severe reduction in its staff with the conclusion
of construction development. Futhermore, the United States
Federal Civil Service examinations are notified to the whole country. The Joint Investigating Committee, after careful consideration of the chief aspects of the T.V.A.'s personnel administration,
concluded that the Authority's need for flexibility required that
it should remain master of its personnel policy until the completion
of the period of construction. Subsequently, there might be a
reconsideration of the question of including under the regular Civil
Service the junior and routine positions, but not, be it noted, the
higher officers. The Committee observed:

> The Authority has no easy task. Its success must depend in the future, as in
> the past, on imagination and initiative as in private enterprise. Even more,
> because of its public character and responsibility, the Authority must find means
> to accomplish satisfactory results under limitations of attitude and ethical beha-
> viour far more strict than those commonly expected of a private corporation... The
> Authority has been able to co-operate with other governmental agencies, Federal,
> State and local, sometimes by providing personnel or the means to be used in
> hiring personnel... It has served as a device for obtaining desirable results
> without arbitrary use of Federal power and with a maximum of democratic
> participation. The Civil Service Regulations would have to be carefully limited
> to avoid serious interference with this form of co-operation.[1]

When the Ramspeck Act of 1940 removed all legal obstacles
to the application of Civil Service regulations to all Federally-
owned corporations, the T.V.A. was expressly exempted.

The T.V.A.'s methods and experience hitherto seem to be a fully
satisfactory answer to the question whether public enterprise can
attract to, and retain in its service, men and women who will
continuously work with devotion and initiative. If men are given
work, scientific or organising, in office, laboratory or field, with a
demonstrably high social value; if the work has meaning for them,
and if there is security for the continuance of the service and the
livelihood it provides, then they may be expected to serve with
high, sustained, and ever-developing efficiency, free from undue
envy and acquisitiveness.

---

[1] *Report of the Joint Committee, op. cit.*

CHAPTER IX

FEDERAL CONTROLS AND STATE RELATIONSHIPS

The T.V.A. was endowed with considerable autonomy of management; but since it is a public body with governmental purposes and powers and funds provided by the Government, it was not intended that it should be altogether immune from external controls. The chief aim was to exclude partisan intervention and inessential and obstructive administrative checks and routines. Yet the T.V.A. must come under certain ultimate public controls, and, it must also solve the problem of interrelationships with the States in which it operates, since they possess certain independent powers. The subject of external controls, then, falls into three well-defined divisions: (1) Presidential and congressional controls; (2) Federal administrative departmental controls; and (3) State relationships with the T.V.A.

Presidential and Congressional Controls

From the standpoint of control, the T.V.A.'s most continuous connection with the Federal Government is probably that between it and the President of the United States. This connection derives, in part, from certain directions in the T.V.A. Statute, but on the whole more essentially from the President's constitutional position as Chief Executive. In the latter capacity, the President is vested with the executive power under the Constitution; he is commanded to "take care that the laws are faithfully executed" and he "has the right to acquire the information in writing of the principal officer in each of the executive departments upon any subject relating to the duties of their respective offices".[1] The powers have not been regarded as a mere formality, but in fact the expansion of governmental activities and the development of a vast administration in Washington and in the field have resulted in the President's assumption of the responsibilities of a legislative, political

---

[1] United States Constitution, Section 1, Article 2; Section 3, Article 2; Section 2, Article 2, clause 1.

and administrative leader, executive co-ordinator, arbiter, and disciplinary authority.

The Statute gives the President two rights of supreme importance to the T.V.A.: to appoint the three directors by and with the consent of the Senate, and to designate which among them shall be chairman. In addition to this, the judicial interpretation of his general constitutional power gives him the right to remove directors.[1] The exercise of the joint powers of appointment, designation of chairman and removal has decisively determined the quality of the T.V.A.'s administration. The right of removal and the right to reappoint or not to reappoint at the expiration of directors' terms have, as experience has shown, caused the T.V.A. administration to follow the presidential lead, and to seek his guidance in most matters of supreme policy, for the directors could not avoid looking to him for assistance and direction. Pursuant to his powers, the President continually intervened with encouragement, counsel, assistance, and sometimes command, on major issues, the principal of which were: (1) the speed and magnitude of the construction programme; (2) the power policy, especially in relation to the speed and extent of replacement of the private utilities by public enterprise; (3) the annual financial appropriations to the T.V.A.; (4) the relationship between the T.V.A.'s power programme and economic investment in public utilities in general; (5) the relationship between the T.V.A. and other power enterprises of the United States Government, and the main lines of T.V.A. administration and its standing and prestige before the public. In addition to this, he encouraged the use of the Authority's general social and economic planning powers, helped to defend it against political intervention in its appointment of employees, and gave encouragement by occasional ceremonial visits, and legislative support when the T.V.A. required amendment of its powers.

The removal of the first chairman from office by the President settled a question of crucial importance in the supreme control of a quasi-dependent Government corporation.[2]

Legally, the corporation was clearly put under control of the President, and it was even regarded as in no wise differing, except in degree, from any other administrative office or agency. To this extent, then, its flexibility, which means its power of uninterrupted

---

[1] It must also be noted that Section 6 of the Statute gives the President power to remove any member of the Board he finds to be guilty of a violation of the rule forbidding political tests or qualifications in the appointment of officials and the selection of employees.

As to the general power to remove, the ruling judicial decision is in *Morgan vs. T.V.A.*, 115 Fed. (2d) 990 ff. (Dec. 1940).

[2] Cf. *Report of the Joint Committee Investigating the Tennessee Valley Authority, op. cit.*; also 75th Congress, 3rd Session, House Document No. 155, p. 89.

business initiative, is limited. It is administratively essential to require Federal co-ordination of all Federal agencies. It is essential for the whole nation that there shall be general Federal direction of such important economic activities as those of the Authority, since they must fit into the general economic movement; but T.V.A. experience certainly raises the problem whether immediate supervisory authority, closely exercised by an overburdened Chief Executive, is the best possible arrangement.

In addition to his general right of supervision, the President has a number of specific powers given to him by the Statute. Only permanent provisions are considered here.

The President has power to direct that the assistance, advice and service of any officer, agent or employee of any executive department or independent office of the United States shall be rendered to the corporation for the better execution of its duties. Under this provision, the President has furnished the help of the Corps of Engineers, the United States Geological Survey, the Biological Survey and the Federal Power Commission, and other agencies. The President may provide for the transfer to the Authority of real or personal property of the United States, as he may think necessary, from time to time, for the purposes of the corporation. There is no record of such action. The Board is obliged to file with the President (and with Congress) each December, a financial statement and report on the business of the corporation covering the preceding governmental fiscal year. This has been done regularly. When the Comptroller General has audited the transactions of the corporation, one of the four copies goes to the President. Section 14, which requires that the Board shall allocate and charge to the various programmes the value of its dams, requires the reports to be submitted to the President, whose authorisation is necessary before they become final and can be utilised as the book value of the properties. The first of such reports was submitted in June 1938, the second in November 1940. Section 17 gives the power to investigate whether in the control and management of the dams or properties undue or unfair advantage has been given to private persons, partnerships or corporations by any officials or employees of the Government, or whether in such matters the Government has been injured or unjustly deprived of its rights. As already observed, the President is empowered, by Section 22, to make surveys of and general plans for the Tennessee Basin, and this power was by Executive Order transferred to the T.V.A. He has further the power, under Section 23, of recommending to Congress measures for the better implementing of the purposes of the T.V.A.

Congressional Authority and Control

The power of Congress over the T.V.A. is far greater than that of the President, for Congress established the T.V.A. and has the power to abolish it. Its power is exerted through five principal means. First, Congress has the power to expand, contract, amend, vary and quash the functions and procedures of the Authority by the process of legislation. Secondly, it has the power to grant or deny financial provision, and to apply the procedure, the accounting, and the examination of estimates this entails. Thirdly, there is the power to call for the reports which the Statute requires to be submitted to Congress by the T.V.A. Fourthly, there is the power of criticising the administration of the T.V.A. in the course of debate in Congress; and finally, there is the power of investigation.

The question of Congress's part in the financial provision of the T.V.A. is dealt with later[1]; broadly speaking, Congress has made the T.V.A. almost entirely dependent upon annual appropriations, but has hitherto so respected the argument and claim for administrative latitude that it furnishes lump sums without itemised appropriation, on a kind of gentlemen's agreement that the Authority does not abuse the elasticity thus accorded to it on sufferance.

From the beginning, Congress has watched the T.V.A. with continuous and acute concern. On five occasions the Statute has been amended. On each of these occasions there was not merely a debate on the specific propositions; there was also much discussion and controversy regarding the powers and status of the Authority. Particularly was this so during the amendments made in 1935, when there was a remarkable political onslaught on the Authority. The amendments introduced in May were not passed until late in August, and the Authority was refused the power to issue bonds to the amount it wished, and allowed only half the amount under restrictive conditions. There was an attempt to subject it fully to the audit power of the Comptroller General.

Moreover, the House insisted that the T.V.A. submit to Congress, not later than 1 April 1936, recommendations for the unified development of the Tennessee River system. Again, Congress has had before it, but has never taken a decision on, the inclusion of the Cumberland Valley within the competence of the T.V.A.

Other interventions of Congress have come in its further regulation of the T.V.A.'s obligation to pay sums in lieu of taxes to the States in which it has generating property and in which it operates. In 1941, the relationship between the T.V.A. and the Comptroller General regarding the audit of the Authority's accounts was finally

---

[1] Cf. Chapter XI.

settled by an amendment to the Statute, after very extensive enquiries and animadversions in Congress time and time again from 1933. Once again, in 1942, an attempt was made in the Senate to subject the appropriations of the T.V.A. to the same kind of itemised authorisation as prevails in the ordinary departments.

Utilising its power under the Statute to call for reports, Congress took the opportunity at the time of the amendment of the Statute in 1935 to command that on or before 1 January 1937 an allocation report should be filed with Congress, and that thereafter the T.V.A. should file in its annual reports a statement of the allocation of the value of the newly-completed properties. For reasons already indicated, in spite of frequent congressional questions the T.V.A. could not meet this date, and was compelled to ask Congress for an extension of time; the report was actually submitted in June 1938. When Congress gave the T.V.A. new bond-issuing powers in 1940, it required annual reports on the service of these bonds.

Another opportunity for congressional surveillance of the T.V.A. comes when Congress is debating some aspect of United States Government which converges upon or cuts across the interests of the T.V.A. Thus, in 1935, when Congress was discussing the Public Utilities Holding Bill, one of the directors of the T.V.A. was called to give evidence, and the committee took the opportunity to launch forth on a protracted interrogation about the Authority. Witnesses from the T.V.A. have been called before most of the committees of Congress dealing with various aspects of "Conservation Authorities" included in proposals before Congress. Another example of this method of intervention and comment is the debate on a proposal to make all posts in any independent establishment of the United States Government, paying a compensation of $5,000 or more to its experts or attorneys, subject to appointment by the President and the Senate only. Similarly, in April 1940, when Congress was debating a proposal to extend the civil service system of the United States Government, T.V.A. principles and practices were debated. All in all, such interrogations have kept the Authority alert, because directly or indirectly it has felt a responsibility for answering such comment, in the one sure way of making its administration efficient enough to exhibit at any moment.

The United States Congress has assumed that the power to legislate implies the power to institute committees of enquiry, with power to send for persons and papers under penalty and to require testimony under penalty. Such a power of investigation of course applies also to the T.V.A. When, therefore, disagreements among the directors in 1937, leading to dismissal of the chairman by the

President, became very acute and public, both friends and foes of the T.V.A. urged a congressional investigation.

Congress finally agreed on a series of no less than 19 questions going into most of the chief aspects of the policy and administration of the Board, but also including questions regarding the attacks on the T.V.A. by litigation and the competitive business tactics of the private utilities. Extreme partisans on both sides were not included in the committee. It was voted $50,000 to do its work, a sum insufficient in itself, but the Committee benefited from the services of various Government departments for special investigations, for instance, the Federal Power Commission to analyse the T.V.A.'s accountancy methods. To examine the engineering and power operations of the Authority's work, the then General Manager of the Los Angeles Power Department was appointed. The General Accounting Office lent its services for the examination of the Authority's accounts.

The enquiry lasted from 25 May to 21 December 1938, and was conducted in Washington, Knoxville and Chattanooga. The Committee made an extensive tour of the Valley projects, took 6,200 pages of evidence, and had submitted to it 588 exhibits. It reported in April 1939, the report falling into majority and minority findings. Six members of the Committee presented a majority report; a minority of three members wrote a minority report, while one of the latter also filed a separate report.[1]

The principal findings of the reports have been noted in earlier and later chapters. With very minor exceptions, the majority found that the T.V.A. was economically, efficiently, honestly and constitutionally administered, and praised the social benefits of its activities.[2]

The investigation marked a turning point in the career of the Authority: it was a dividing line between the years of trial and the years of assurance. It had a healthy effect on the whole organisation. While it necessarily threw an enormous burden on the directors and officials of the T.V.A. in the marshalling of information and opinion about their own activities and procedures, clarification of the T.V.A.'s aims and methods resulted from the process of self-justification and cross-examination.

The officials felt the disciplinary energy of Congress, and the effect was substantial, pervasive and lasting.

What has been said about the effect of this investigation holds good also of the other means by which Congress exercises control

---

[1] Cf. 76th Congress, 1st Session, House Document No. 56, Parts 1 and 2, *Report of the Joint Committee Investigating the Tennessee Valley Authority;* Part 3, *Engineering Report; Hearings,* 1939, in 14 Parts.
[2] *Idem,* Part 1, pp. 6-10.

over the T.V.A. It cannot, however, be expected that such control
will be altogether objective and technical; in its nature it is bound
to be political, because it is necessarily exercised or controlled by
party government. But on the whole, the T.V.A. has been given
fair latitude for the fulfilment of its chief tasks.

Federal Administrative Departmental Controls

Audit by the United States Comptroller General

Audit is one of the most usual and essential means of Government control over the actions of departments, agencies or offices.
It normally bears on the legality of the transactions and, either
directly or indirectly, the economy and efficiency of the actions
taken. Questions of law affect efficiency through the sanctioning or
forbidding of certain actions; hence the importance of clarity on
the legal position.

The T.V.A.'s financial transactions require independent external
audit. The main problems are what kind of audit will best further
its purposes and business flexibility, and what agency shall conduct
the audit. The T.V.A. Statute provided that the United States
Comptroller General, an officer of the Federal Government, should
audit the accounts of the T.V.A. not less frequently than each fiscal
year, and through his own personnel.[1] Copies of the audit were to
go to the President, the Chairman of the T.V.A., and Congress,
while another copy was to be available for public inspection at the
T.V.A.'s principal office.

The T.V.A. claimed that it was exempt from the Comptroller
General's audit (as other United States Public Corporations were
exempt by statute or by judicial decision) because Congress had
intended to endow the Authority with the flexibility of private
enterprise. The T.V.A. was prepared to (and actually did) institute
an annual audit of its own by a reputable firm of private accountants. But to submit to the Comptroller General meant that he
would apply to the Authority certain rules applicable to ordinary
United States Government departments which would stultify the
Authority's progress. By virtue of these rules the Comptroller
General could disallow payments made by the T.V.A. not only on
grounds such as fraud or mishandling of funds, but on his officers'
own independent different interpretations of the Authority's statutory powers, and thus make T.V.A. officials personally accountable
for restitution. He could apply the general rules of the United
States Government requiring purchases by competitive bidding,

---

[1] Section 9 (b).

even though these were inappropriate to the T.V.A.'s work and operations. He could require his prior authority for the settlement of claims against the T.V.A. on contracts, transfers of land, and all other transactions, thus depriving the Authority of freedom to take action. He could require that its printing work should be done in the Government Printing Office. His officers, although not trained in business methods, could interpret the T.V.A.'s business powers as conferred by statute, and all books, vouchers and documentary proofs would need to be made available to him, in Washington if he wished, regardless of the inconvenience and obstruction to the T.V.A.'s business. Furthermore, such audit could occur simultaneously with the transactions, and so, by challenging them, delay their completion.

The T.V.A. resisted, but was overborne by the strategic position of the Comptroller General, who could and did enforce his view by refusing to certify transfers of money from the United States Treasury to the T.V.A. Fund, a course which he was able to take owing to the ambiguity of the law as set down in the T.V.A. Statute.

In 1935 the T.V.A.'s claims to flexibility in its purchasing methods were recognised in an amendment to the Statute.[1] It received exemption from the normal rule of advertisement and acceptance of the lowest tender and was allowed to act "in a manner common among business men" in the case of emergencies, repair parts and equipment required for supplies or services previously furnished or contracted for, and items under $500; and it was also permitted to take into account the quality of the goods and services and the bidder's standing as regards finance, responsibility, skill and reliability.

The T.V.A. was also given the right to see any report made by the Comptroller General with a reasonable opportunity to examine his criticisms and compile a statement thereon to the President and Congress.

Another amendment of the law in June 1941 made the T.V.A. specifically liable to audit by the Comptroller General, but at the same time allowed it considerable latitude. The Authority was authorised to spend and make contracts and agreements upon such terms and conditions as it thought necessary, including the final settlement of all claims and litigation so long as the Board considered these to be necessary for the carrying out of its statutory powers. Where the Comptroller General took exception the exception might be conclusively wiped out by the T.V.A. certifying that the expenditure was necessary to carry out the provisions of the Statute.

---

[1] Section 9 (b).

Thus there is supervision over the T.V.A., with latitude. The former has its uses; it produces a general carefulness in the management of public funds, and in some specific cases, such as travel expenses, purchasing procedures, the keeping of accounts and records, the Comptroller's comments have been valuable to the T.V.A. and new forms, regulations and procedures have been adopted on the basis of his suggestions.

The Federal Power Commission

One of the purposes of making the T.V.A. a corporation was to secure independent accounts and accurate analyses of business operations. The Statute obliges the T.V.A. to keep complete and accurate books of accounts.[1] Further, in order to enable data to be accumulated on which to base policy regarding the production and sale of electricity and chemicals, the T.V.A. is obliged to keep accounts showing the major components of its costs[2], to be kept "according to such uniform system of accounting for public utilities" as the Federal Power Commission may prescribe.

The Federal Power Commission is authorised to prescribe accounting systems for public utilities who are directed to comply therewith; the T.V.A. and similar agencies are included.[3] The Commission's accounts were established in June 1936 in consultation with many expert bodies, including the accountants of the T.V.A. Slight modifications were allowed for the T.V.A. to meet peculiarities inherent in its position. For example, the T.V.A. has no "capital stock", an item which appears in this *Uniform System of Accounts;* nor any "investments in Associated Companies". The rules of the Federal Power Commission requires annual reports; and the T.V.A. accordingly has an elaborate system of plant records to satisfy this requirement. In its contracts the Authority requires its own municipal and co-operative customers to follow the Federal Power Commission system of accounts for agencies distributing electricity and to furnish an annual report.

The Federal Power Commission examined the T.V.A.'s power accounting system for the Joint Investigating Committee in 1938.[4] Its report notices some derogations from the Commission's own rules. The Commission thought that "the books lack the completeness, the definiteness and the finality which are to be expected from well-kept books of accounts", though it admitted that this was due in some measure to the fact that construction was the predominant

---

[1] Section 8 (*b*).
[2] Section 14.
[3] Public Utilities Act, 1935.
[4] Cf. p., 150.

activity. It urged that the time had come for improvement. Even at that time the T.V.A. was making changes to satisfy the Commission's criticism, and more has since been done. Thus the corrective power of the Commission fulfills a valuable function. The T.V.A. does not attempt to produce profit and loss accounts to match those of private firms, but makes public analyses of its operations in such a way that the public, which is interested in comparisons, has available all the figures and explanations necessary to construct the appropriate standards. This has certainly been achieved in the T.V.A.'s published annual reports and in the annual analyses of financial conditions of its public power customers.

The United States Government now has a number of hydro-electric plants besides the T.V.A.[1] The important question has been raised whether their rates for power sales should be regulated by the Federal Power Commission so as to introduce some uniformity of public principle. Whatever might be the value of such a regulation, the Federal Power Commission has no authority over the rates set by the T.V.A., which is fully independent in this matter. In this respect the Authority differs from Bonneville (which includes Grand Coulee), which requires the approval of the Commission for its electricity rates.

State Relationships with the T.V.A.

There are two special problems in the relationship between the T.V.A. and the States which require discussion: State or local taxation of the T.V.A.'s properties, operations and employees; and the T.V.A.'s freedom from the jurisdiction of State utility-regulating commissions.

Power of the State to Tax

It is clear that if the seven States had an unfettered right to tax the T.V.A., its operations and its employees, it could be made the victim of extortionate and obstructive charges, and even deliberately crushed. On the other hand, the T.V.A.'s freedom from taxation would deprive the States and the counties of taxable properties and activities. The problem was and still is to discover a just road between the extremes.

A famous judgment in a controlling case says that "the power to tax is the power to destroy".[2] To avoid such implied destruction,

---

[1] These include Boulder Dam, Bonneville and Grand Coulee. Cf. E. A. Abrams, *op. cit.*; also 77th Congress, 2nd Session, United States Senate, Sub-Committee of Committee of Commerce, *Joint Hearings*, 1942, on "Columbia Power Administration".

[2] By Chief Justice Marshall, in *McCulloch* vs. *Maryland*, Supreme Court of the United States, 1819.

the agencies and instrumentalities of the Federal Government have had since the beginning of the American Federal Constitution immunity from measures by the States, among which is taxation, which might obstruct or frustrate the exercise of their powers. The T.V.A. benefits from such immunity, unless Congress should otherwise determine.

When the T.V.A. was in process of formation, the other side of the question was raised. It was argued that the States ought to be compensated for the loss of the waterpower in their rivers and for the flooding of valuable tax-bearing agricultural lands. Some alleviation was sought from the additional burden of taxes which industry would have to bear, or be compelled to migrate to other States.

Consequently, Section 13 of the Statute provided that 5 per cent. of the gross proceeds received by the T.V.A. for the sale of power from hydro-power plants in Alabama should be paid to the State of Alabama, and 5 per cent. of the proceeds from power generated at Norris and any other dams located in the State of Tennessee should similarly be paid to that State. Further, from the gross proceeds of any additional power generated at other dams 2½ per cent. should be paid to the State of Alabama and 2½ per cent. to the State of Tennessee. Such percentages might be revised and changed by the Board upon approval by the President, but not more often than once in five years, and not without giving the States an opportunity to be heard.[1]

The sums involved were not very large. However, the problem was rather the very serious dislocation caused in the finances of government of certain of the counties, especially when the T.V.A. acquired the Tennessee Electric Power Company's properties. The States and the localities had heretofore levied taxes on the electric utilities and reservoir lands which had now come into the possession of the T.V.A. and the municipalities. The total amount of tax was estimated at nearly three and a quarter million dollars, some 92 per cent. of which went to Tennessee, and the rest to Mississippi, Georgia, Alabama, Kentucky, and North Carolina. The losses of the latter States were not great, but were expected to increase as the Authority extended its operations. There was considerable agitation on the subject in the Valley States; politicians and associations—for example, the Tennessee Taxpayers' Association— urged more generous donations by the T.V.A., blaming the public management of power, and especially the T.V.A., for their loss.

As a matter of fact, only about half this amount was actually

---

[1] The order of payments deriving from this provision, for the two States together, was $41,753 in 1933, rising to $527,593 in 1940.

a loss; the rest was diverted to other Government agencies (for example, to the municipality which had become the power distributor) and could be corrected by the State legislature.[1]

The problem was not simple. First, the T.V.A. believed that in view of the substantial annual saving (some $9,000,000) to the consumers resulting from its low price for electricity, the States ought not to be grasping. Secondly, there was the serious issue whether power profits made by the T.V.A. should be used to reduce Federal contributions to the Authority's operations or granted to the States and counties in the Valley. In its wholesale power rates, the T.V.A. allowed for a 12½ per cent. tax equivalent, but the practical tax issue was how much cash should actually be paid over to State and local governments and how much virtually returned to the Federal treasury. Thirdly, there was the parlous financial situation of certain counties which had relied to an extraordinary degree on the single source of taxation—*ad valorem* property tax—for their budget.[2] If the T.V.A. made grants to the States, this would not necessarily mean assistance to the stricken counties; the States might not pass on the grants.[3] Fourthly, the original arrangement applied payment by the T.V.A. to two States alone, but the other States mentioned were also losing taxes. Moreover, the original section of the Statute based the payments upon the place of generation of the electric power, and so gave undue advantages to Alabama, where most of the power was generated, while allotting far less than was lost to Tennessee and other States where the Authority conducted operations through generation and transmission facilities from which revenues had formerly been obtained by the States and local authorities.

The T.V.A. was extremely sensitive to the hardship involved. Had it been able to exercise an influence, it would have attempted to secure some of the overdue economical reorganisation of county government as one ingredient of a final settlement. But, as has been seen, it does not exercise pressure, however enlightened and benevolent.

As a result of conferences with representatives of the States, tax experts, and the men of the counties, the Authority made proposals, embodied in a statutory amendment[4], to deal with the

---

[1] For the figures, cf. A. T. EDELMANN: "Public Ownership and Tax Replacement by the T.V.A.", in *American Political Science Review*, Vol. XXXV, Aug. 1941, pp. 727-737.

[2] Nine counties in Tennessee thereby lost between 10.6 and 28.3 per cent. of their revenues, so drastic a loss as either to ruin their services or to require an impossible increase in taxation or financial assistance from outside.

[3] In 1942 Kentucky passed a law requiring power undertakings to replace county and other taxes.

[4] Section 13, 26 June 1940.

situation. The Authority was to pay to the States and the counties each year certain percentages of the gross proceeds derived from the sale of power, a minimum being guaranteed. The percentage was to be 10 per cent. for the fiscal year 1941, to be reduced by one half per cent. for each of the following years, down to 5 per cent. in 1949, and to remain at that rate[1] annually thereafter. These payments, the Statute said (following certain precedents) were in lieu of taxation, and as a further safeguard to Government immunity it specified that: "The corporation, its property, franchises and income are hereby expressly exempted from taxation in any manner or form by any State, county, municipality or any subdivision or district thereof".[2] One half of the payment would be distributed among the States according to each one's proportion of the gross proceeds of the power sales to the total of all the proceeds of all power sales by the Authority; and the second half according to the percentage of power property held by the corporation in that State compared with the total value of such property held by the Authority. The Statute also stipulated a minimum payment to each State and to the counties.[3]

The T.V.A. is required to report to Congress by 1 January 1945 on the operation of the provisions of this amendment, the benefits received by the States and counties, the effect of their taxable values, and such other information as may be pertinent for future legislation. This is wise, for the policy is as yet only in the making, and the problems are new. Should the States expect to recover all they might have had from private firms? How much should be paid, and for how many years? How far should the benefits conferred by cheap electricity and the navigation, flood control and agricultural programmes be taken into account, for some such account must surely be taken? In the fiscal year 1941, the

---

[1] The reason for the decline of the percentage year by year is to meet the rise in the estimated proceeds from power as the Authority's operations are extended.

[2] Senators were extremely watchful of State encroachments on Federal rights. Cf. 76th Congress, Senate Committee on Agriculture and Forestry, *Hearings on S. 2925*, 1940, p. 33.

[3] Not less than the amount on a two-year average of the State and local *ad valorem* property taxes formerly levied on the power property purchased and operated by the Authority, and on the portion of reservoir lands related to the dams held or operated by the T.V.A. and allocated or allocable to power; and further, a guaranteed minimum annual payment of not less than $10,000 to each State where the Authority owns and operates power property. The share of the counties was to be paid directly, by deducting from the total due to each State the average of county *ad valorem* property taxes. The justification for this minimum payment is that in the early stages of a construction project the State or local health departments, highway and education authorities must take certain action involving expenditure, and therefore a $10,000 payment gives assurance of substantial compensation when needs are likely to be most urgent and the loss of tax basis keenly felt. Actually, the minimum payment proviso has not been invoked, as construction of the power system has been so rapid as to bring the States substantially more than the minimum.

T.V.A. paid $1,499,417; in 1942, $1,859,416. A further $1,850,000 of tax and tax equivalents were provided by municipalities and co-operatives distributing T.V.A. power. In so far as T.V.A. activity improves the general economic development of the region, the general fiscal strength of the States and local bodies is improved. And when the sums replacing State and local property taxes are added, the compensation seems generous indeed.

So far, the counties have resisted any reforms, by consolidation or otherwise, which would rationalise their organisational functions in the light of modern services and administrative science, though they are poor and though the State of Tennessee has authorised and facilitated consolidation.

Taxation of T.V.A. Employees by the States

Until 1939 the incomes of employees of the Federal Government were not taxable by States in which they resided and worked, and this immunity applied to T.V.A. employees. Immunity followed the judgment which declared unconstitutional discriminatory taxation against instruments of the Federal Government. The gravamen of that judgment, however, lay in the issue whether the taxation was or was not destructive of the objectives of the Federal Government. With the passage of time it was realised that the issue of reciprocal immunity of State and Federal officials from income tax was a matter of expediency and degree rather than an absolute principle.[1]

The heavy Governmental burdens of the 'thirties raised anew the question whether the State and Federal Governments should continue to deprive themselves of a considerable revenue basis, and in April 1938 the President recommended to Congress the termination of tax exemptions. In 1939 the Supreme Court allowed the taxation of a Federal Government employee by the State of New York.[2]

Hence, the States in the Tennessee Valley which have an income tax on earnings, such as Kentucky, now tax T.V.A. employees who are resident in the State on the same basis as all other residents. The income tax on the employees has not proved a burden on the operation of the T.V.A.

The United States Supreme Court is, of course, available to protect the T.V.A., like any other agency of the Federal Govern-

---

[1] The establishment of the Federal Reserve Bank system, with many branches, was followed by congressional authorisation for State taxation of these national banks at a rate not greater than that assessed upon moneyed capital in the hands of individuals coming into competition with them. (Iowa—*Des Moines National Bank* vs. *Bennett*, 284 U.S. 239, 1931.)

[2] *Graves* vs. *People of State of New York*, 306 U.S. 466, 1939.

ment, should any tax threaten the due fulfilment of its purposes by "undue interference". For, as Mr. Justice Holmes (qualifying the opinion of 1819) said in a Supreme Court judgment: "The power to tax is *not* the power to destroy while this court sits".[1]

It should be noted that the issue has not been raised in the courts whether a Government corporation, as an entity, can be constitutionally made liable to taxation by the States or the other local government units in which it may operate.

Immunity from Control by State Utility Commissions

Just as the T.V.A. has successfully proceeded upon the assumption that it is properly free from the power of the States to tax, it has also preserved its immunity from interference by the States in pursuance of their right to regulate the public utilities which operate in their areas. There are public service commissions in all the Valley States except Mississippi. All except Virginia require a public utility to obtain a certificate of necessity and convenience as a condition of doing business. In order to preclude the possibility of legal challenge to the freedom of the T.V.A. by interested persons[2] on these grounds, statutes were passed by Alabama and Tennessee in 1935 exempting from all control by the Public Service Commissions Federal agencies owned by the United States or joint stock companies in which the United States held more than 50 per cent. of the voting shares or stocks. These were deemed "non-utilities". The municipalities operating power undertakings were also exempted from control. Kentucky followed suit only in 1942.[3]

This immunity has been essential to the development of the T.V.A. The Commissions exercise a jurisdiction over purchases, leases, extensions, rates and services, accounting practices, security and reserves, records, properties, and management, and can charge inspection and supervision fees. Their power could be used to cripple, even to kill. The utility commissioners are popularly elected, and are fully in the cockpit of State and local politics. Unfriendly commissioners could damage and retard T.V.A. development, if not frustrate it altogether.

One other point needs mention. While the T.V.A. is not subject to regulation by the commissions, it itself regulates the municipalities and co-operatives by the terms of its contracts. This regulating authority (among other things) was challenged on the ground that

---

[1] *Panhandle Oil Company* vs. *Mississippi*, 277 U.S., 1927.

[2] Some annoying suits had been brought by coal and ice companies in 1934.

[3] In Kentucky it was argued that to waive the power of the State Utility Commissions over the T.V.A. would be "in complete abdication of local authority that is unwise, unhealthy and unpatriotic". Cf. article by Prof. A. T. EDELMANN, in *Journal of Land and Public Utility Economics*, Nov. 1942, pp. 481 *et seq.*

it was an invasion of the sovereignty of the States[1], but the Authority's power was sustained by the courts and established in various State laws.

Thus, the Authority has acquired good standing by its immunity from regulation, and the power granted to it by the States to do business with the municipalities and co-operatives and to regulate their practices through the making and enforcement of contracts. Since it has this free scope of power it also has the responsibility for sound municipal and co-operative administration of power undertakings.

———

---

[1] *Tennessee Electric Power Co. et al* vs. *T.V.A. et al.*

CHAPTER X

THE EMPLOYEE RELATIONSHIP POLICY AND LABOUR

When the T.V.A. decided to construct its dams and other plant by its own direct labour force, rather than have the system built for it by the United States Corps of Army Engineers, or under contract with private firms, it assumed responsibility for the solution of the usual economic and social labour problems, and the special problems of a public authority. Organisation of labour among the occupations on the construction jobs was quite strong from the beginning, through membership of the national and international unions; some 90 per cent. of the skilled workers on the construction projects were members of trade unions. In the United States, construction work has often been notorious for rough labour relationships, and the T.V.A. was determined to set a good example. This was necessary even for the sake of obtaining results.

The T.V.A. has instituted organised relationships with its employees, including among other things recognition of their voluntary associations, collective bargaining and grievance procedures, wage settlement, and co-operation of management and workers in certain managerial spheres. The T.V.A. was established at the inception of the New Deal, a time of liberal hopes and experiments in labour relations in the United States.[1] From the beginning, the Authority built up its relationship policy and machinery, with the full, continuous, active and genuine collaboration of labour representatives.

The T.V.A. Employee Relationship Policy, established after joint discussion, became effective on 1 September 1935. It was a policy of the Board, and not a bipartite agreement between Board and workers; the latter came only in 1940. Its importance in the eyes of the directors was well stated by the chairman of the Board, Mr. Lilienthal:

If we fail to establish fair and decent relations between the human beings working on that job the whole project in my judgment would be a failure, even if every other objective were reached. What permanent good will it do to our

---

[1] Cf. INTERNATIONAL LABOUR OFFICE: *National Recovery Measures in the United States*, Studies and Reports, Series B (Economic Conditions), No. 19 (Geneva, 1933); and *Social, and Economic Reconstruction in the United States*, Studies and Reports, Series B, No. 20 (Geneva, 1934), Chapters VI and VIII.

country to save our soil, to control floods and to distribute cheap electricity, if those goals are reached through the exploitation of labour? That wouldn't be progress—it would be reaction. Unless T.V.A.'s labour policies are just, the whole programme is wrong.[1]

Attention must be drawn to the principal features of this policy, and to some of the most important issues involved in it. In the first place, the Authority is an agency of the Government of the United States, and therefore is not as free as a private employer to develop the relationship between employees and management; it must conform to national policy, and the Federal Government, which supplies the funds gathered from the people of the United States in taxation, must be in final control. Within this limitation, the governing principles of a progressive programme of employee relations could be established: "The Authority will support as favourable labour standards and employment conditions as are consistent with the national welfare". Rules on labour standards and conditions of employment were not to be adopted or changed without thirty days' published notice of what was proposed, and until the duly authorised representatives of the employees had had reasonable opportunity to confer with the supervisory staff and the Personnel Division.

THE RIGHT TO ORGANISE AND BARGAIN

The Policy requires management and supervisory staff and all employees to give honest, efficient, and economical service, and this applies to their organisations and associations.

Members of the management and supervisory staff and the supervised employees of the T.V.A. together comprise an organisation for public service. The wholehearted co-operation of all members . . . is essential.

The right of employees to organise and designate their own representatives, free from any restraint by the management, for the purpose of collective bargaining and employee-management co-operation, is established. Union membership is favoured; but neither membership nor non-membership as a condition of employment or career as an employee is required, and discrimination among employees or their representatives on this account is forbidden.

The majority of the employees have the right to determine the agency or person to represent them as a whole. In case of dispute about this, the Personnel Department of the Authority must attempt to adjust the dispute on its merits. If the parties agree, the representative may be determined by an election. If the Per-

---
[1] Speech made at Detroit Labour Day Celebration, 2 Sept. 1935.

sonnel Department cannot adjust this type of dispute, either party may call in the National Labor Relations Board.[1] It was thought that the good will of the T.V.A. towards organised labour might result in the establishment of the "closed shop", but the T.V.A. has carefully safeguarded itself on this matter. The Authority, as representative of the public, felt that it could not permit any other agency to determine who should and who should not obtain employment, and it could not maintain that membership in a union was by itself evidence of that "merit and efficiency" which the Statute prescribes as the exclusive title to a job and career with the Authority.[2] Yet, in considering questions of appointment and promotion, membership of an association which fosters the collective interests of a body of workers is taken into account as one of the many elements making for efficiency; it is regarded as an index of co-operativeness.

WORKING CONDITIONS

Grievances regarding labour standards, pay, classification, hours, conditions, and so forth must be and are handled by the employee or his representative up through the various levels of the organisation to the chief supervisory officer, whence there is an appeal to the Personnel Division.

A procedure is set for the determination of the hourly and annual rates of pay, to be discussed later. The eight-hour day is established[3]; overtime rate is fixed at one and a half times ordinary pay, excessive overtime being regarded as indicative of inefficient supervision and workmanship; and one day of rest in seven is provided. Periods of marked unemployment are met by the reduction of hours to the minimum consistent with efficiency of production and a reasonable minimum income. The Authority does not permit employment of persons under 16 at all, or the employment in hazardous occupations of persons under 18. As sound public policy requires that the most efficient should be employed, the T.V.A.

---

[1] In practice, the Board has refused to accept such disputes for adjudication unless the parties agree in advance to abide by the decision, since the National Labor Relations Act does not give the Board jurisdiction over Government agencies.

[2] In the course of negotiations in 1940, the Tennessee Trades and Labor Council once again raised the question of the "closed shop". The proposal was rejected on the same grounds as before, though negatively, that is, on the grounds that non-membership of a labour union does not demonstrate lack of merit and efficiency. Cf. *Collective Bargaining in a Federal Agency*, address by G. R. CLAPP, Nov. 1941.

[3] By a revision of the E.R.P., effective on 1 June 1938, and for hourly employees only up to 1 Jan. 1938, the scheduled work week for hourly employees was 40 hours or less; but it was possible to require employees to work an extra day at regular pay-rates. For annual employees the work week ranged from 39 to 48 hours, but was in the main a 5-day, 40-hour week.

policy is to bring in fresh blood as it sees fit, and to offer equal opportunities for raising the standards of those already in its service. "Employment is not a vested right." Employees may be suspended from pay status by supervisors, subject to a written statement of the reason; no discharge, however, may be made without the prior fair hearing of the employee or his representative, at his request, and the approval of the Personnel Department. As already mentioned, the Authority keeps personnel records as a recorded and challengeable basis for appraisals of merit and efficiency. It promises (and provides) adequate provision for health and safety.[1]

EFFECTIVENESS OF COLLECTIVE BARGAINING

It can be said that the T.V.A. has amply fulfilled the conditions of its Employee Relationship Policy in every respect. This has been done consciously, and with considerable pride. The Authority is a "model", but not a lax, employer. The stipulations and the general tenor of the document show that it has instituted "collective bargaining". There is every reason, indeed, why public services should establish rules binding them in their pay and service relationships with their employees. But for various reasons such arrangements are rare in the United States, though not in other nations, where experience has shown the objections commonly raised to be groundless, especially where the governmental unit corresponds to that of a very large firm, and, like the T.V.A., conducts business operations, and not general services in relation to the whole of the public which were the main function of the basic and older departments of government. Yet the T.V.A. has safeguarded itself in the Introductory Statement, for it bears a first duty to the public. It does not surrender its final authority, any more than the employees surrender their right to strike. But each party has agreed to a relationship which will avoid the irrational insistence on "public authority" on the one side, and the strike on the other, and arrangements have been made to utilise every reasonable device for securing justice to the claims of both sides.

The implementing of the Policy and the safeguarding of labour's rights have on labour's side been carried out by the unions. The trade and labour workers of the T.V.A. are highly organised in craft unions, and affiliated with the American Federation of Labor. In 1937, 13 of these labour organisations, representing some 85 local unions of T.V.A. employees, set up the Tennessee Valley Trades and Labour Council. The Council, formally recognised by both the Authority and the affiliated unions, represents labour at

---

[1] Cf. Chapter XI.

the annual wage conference (to be described presently) and on various joint committees, and plays a considerable part in formulating and facilitating employee relationships. The clerical, professional, and other "white collar" workers have been slower to organise. There is the Tennessee Valley Engineers Association, which is without national affiliation. The American Federation of Federal Employees, the National Federation of Federal Employees, and the United Federal Workers of America include some T.V.A. employees. The Public Safety Service Employees Union, affiliated with the American Federation of Labor, was acknowledged late in 1940 as collective bargaining agent for T.V.A. guides and guards. Finally, the general office employees made the American Federation of Office Employees their union in March 1942.

Although the Authority has evinced its clear intention to deal justly and amicably with its employees, some of the latter have occasionally gone on strike, and both sides have admitted dangerous friction from time to time. The T.V.A. has been troubled by the usual clash of management and labour interests and by personal grievances, but on the whole the record of ten years is smooth adjustment. The Tennessee Valley Trades and Labor Council, in its statement to the Joint Investigating Committee in 1938[1], expressed great satisfaction with the working of the system of collective bargaining, in spite of real conflicts of interest and opinion.

There have been four strikes in eight years. None of these was authorised by the Tennessee Valley Trades and Labor Council, and only one was approved by the international union concerned. The longest strike, which occurred in July 1939 and lasted from three days to a week at the various projects, was in protest at a jurisdictional assignment and was called by a single craft organisation. The dispute between the two crafts was settled within a week by the President of the Tennessee Valley Trades and Labor Council, who was delegated to act as his representative by the President of the A. F. of L. The second strike was caused by inter-racial antagonism at the Kentucky project in November 1940. The officials of the labour unions and officers of the Tennessee Valley Trades and Labor Council urged the local union members to adhere to the procedures for orderly settlement embodied in the agreement with the Authority signed in August of the same year, and the men went back to the job after $3\frac{1}{2}$ days, although the local situation had been extremely tense. The other two strikes were confined to one trade at a single project. One instance was a jurisdictional dispute, and the matter was settled within 48 hours. The second was due to a misunderstanding by a group of men of the cause of

---

[1] *Hearings*, 1939, Part 8, pp. 3362-3365.

dismissal of one of their members, and the stoppage lasted 40 minutes.

The Employee Relationship Policy did not in its first years win the wholehearted acceptance of all the engineers working for the Authority, most of whom had come from jobs and environments where labour organisation and unions were regarded with aversion. Discipline by the supervisor was regarded as an unquestionable sovereign right of management, and appeals against it as subversive. The Authority claims to have modified this attitude considerably by steady education, in which the field officers of the Personnel Department, acting early on the spot, have been effective. The Policy improved morale and co-operativeness, in spite of some lapses on both sides, and, as the T.V.A.'s Chief Engineer declared, paid in excellent unit costs of construction and operation.

The final statement of the Employee Relationship Policy says that the Board of Directors looks forward to the establishment of joint conferences between employees and management to secure systematic co-operation, and recognises that responsible employee organisations are a step towards this development. It proposes that such co-operative conferences might devote themselves to furthering the objectives of the T.V.A. by considering such matters as the elimination of waste in construction and production, the conservation of materials, supplies and energy, the improvement in quality of workmanship and service, the promotion of education and training, the correction of conditions making for grievances and misunderstanding, the encouragement of courtesy in the relations of employees with the public, the prevention of hazards to life and property, the betterment of employment conditions, and the strengthening of the morale of the service. Not until the second world war were such conferences actually established, with the important exception of a conference which helped to establish the T.V.A. apprenticeship training system[1], and one in the fertiliser works where fairly frequent meetings for the discussion of conditions of work did much to improve morale and suggest improvements in operation.[2]

WAGE POLICY

With regard to the Authority's wage policy and procedure, the Statute lays down a standard. It requires (Section 3) that all con-

---

[1] Cf. Chapter XI.

[2] The wartime joint councils seem, hitherto, to have been chiefly concerned with absenteeism. They have, however, been valuable in making clear the need for interruption of work due to overriding priorities for T.V.A. equipment transferred elsewhere; in the rearrangement of work time-tables; in offering useful technical suggestions to increase job efficiency; and in raising productive morale. Cf. INTERNATIONAL LABOUR OFFICE: *British Joint Production Machinery*, Studies and Reports, Series A (Industrial Relations), No. 43 (Montreal, 1944).

tracts to which the corporation is a party shall contain a provision that "not less than the prevailing rate of wages for work of a similar nature prevailing in the vicinity" shall be paid to labourers or mechanics. Disputes regarding the prevailing rate are to be referred to the Secretary of Labor, whose decision is final. Further, in determining the prevailing rate, due regard must be had to those rates which have been secured through collective agreement by representatives of employers and employees. Where the Authority itself does the work, the prevailing rate of wages must be paid in the same manner as though such work had been let by contract. For the determination of the prevailing rate of wages, the T.V.A. established a regular annual conference with the various labour unions, and included certain basic regulations, some of which have been mentioned, in the Employee Relationship Policy.

Wage conferences began to be held in 1935, and have since taken place annually. Under the current procedure (1943), the T.V.A. management and the Tennessee Valley Trades and Labor Council, representing the Authority's employees in the trades and labour classifications, have agreed that the statutory term "vicinity", describing the area from which wage data will be secured for consideration at the annual wage conference, should be defined as including the entire watershed area[1], together with certain adjacent urban centres.[2] Wage facts are collected also from major war construction projects in this area, public utility power companies extending into the area, and 21 major companies in the chemical, fertiliser, and related industries operating within the area.

Construction wage data are collected by representatives of the Personnel Department by personal visits to the cities and major war projects. Normally, T.V.A. representatives first meet the local union officers to secure information on wage rates, number of men employed, working conditions, in all occupations at the major contractors and projects in the area, and then meet unionised contractors in each craft from whom they secure like information. The survey of maintenance and operating rates is made through personal contact with all electric power generating companies in the area which have union agreements, and with the major industrial companies doing work most comparable to that performed by the T.V.A. Department of Chemical Engineering. In addition, some data on maintenance rates are secured from em-

---

[1] Including the cities of Asheville, North Carolina; Knoxville, Chattanooga, Bristol, Johnson City, Kingsport, Tennessee; Tri-Cities, Alabama (Tuscumbia, Florence, and Sheffield).

[2] Atlanta, Georgia; Birmingham, Alabama; Memphis, Tennessee; Louisville, Kentucky; Jackson, Nashville, Tennessee; and Paducah, Kentucky.

ployers whose names are furnished by the local union representatives met in connection with the construction survey.

All wage data thus secured, as well as facts furnished by the labour organisations, are submitted to a Joint Committee (T.V.A. management and labour) on Wage Data, which in open meeting reviews the information and, without evaluating it, certifies its authenticity to the Wage Conference. This weeds out inaccuracies and resolves conflicts regarding the basis and nature of the information. The Wage Conference itself, which lasts about three days, deliberates on each specific wage request made by the unions on the basis of the facts thus tabled, and the management's proposed schedule. There are, after all, various rates paid in the vicinity in the 200 trades and labour classifications employed with the Authority. Intensive discussion between T.V.A. supervisory officers, personnel technicians and employee representatives results in a schedule. Some of these rates may not be acceptable to members of the Tennessee Valley Trades and Labor Council, but most will be. The schedule is submitted to the Board of Directors for approval on the understanding that appeal may be made against those rates not accepted. The Council and any disapproving international union is free to appeal to the United States Secretary of Labor for a finding of fact regarding any rate not accepted; the rate stands in the absence of a finding of fact which revises it. The T.V.A. has never pursued a policy undercutting the best known wage rates.

Two points may be mentioned in regard to the wage conferences. First, the conferences are genuine in the sense that the Authority is prepared to be and is influenced by the arguments. There are fierce and earnestly stated differences of view, and from time to time the workers call in especially able representatives to advocate their case. They have, indeed, appealed to the Secretary of Labor on two occasions, on both of which the International Association of Machinists challenged the management's interpretation of prevailing wage facts.[1] Secondly, the T.V.A. has had to meet the question of the representation of the workers. Some who were not affiliated with the American Federation of Labor have on occasion put in an appearance at the conferences, but have been compelled by the consensus of opinion to withdraw. One union affiliated to the Congress of Industrial Organizations was consequently accommodated by a separate conference so long as it actually represented a unit of employees.

Out of the experience of collective bargaining, there arose the

---

[1] In the first case (Nov. 1938), the Association's view was upheld; the second difference (Nov. 1941) is not yet decided.

feeling that the Authority might carry its arrangements with labour further. Some matters, such as classification, hours of work, leave, and working conditions, were removed from the jurisdiction of the Wage Conference, after various devices had been tried to relieve it, including subcommittees or special sessions. In 1941, classification was removed to a standing joint committee to act as and when questions arose. For changes in working conditions, direct negotiation at the request of either party was prescribed. Such special joint procedure came to be regulated by the General Agreement made in August 1940.

The General Agreement

The genesis of the agreement is described by the present General Manager, formerly Director of Personnel and, as such, presiding officer at the wage conferences, as follows:

Labour relations in the T.V.A. between 1935 and 1940 moved into a programme of active and two-way co-operation under this (the Employment Relationship) policy. But it was soon apparent that something was missing. Labour, through the Tennessee Valley Trades and Labor Council, a body created by the various unions in the Valley with which the Authority has dealings, proposed that the Employee Relationship Policy of the Board be supplemented by a signed agreement to be negotiated and formally executed by employees through their organisations and by the Authority.

Negotiations went forward and proceeded to a mutually satisfactory conclusion. On August 6, 1940, the Authority and fifteen unions representing T.V.A. employees in the trades and labour services of the Authority pledged their agreement to principles and devices of collective bargaining in a great public enterprise.[1]

The Employee Relationship Policy was rather in the nature of a set of principles by which the Authority bound itself; the agreement binds both sides to its principles and procedures. The former, though established by consultation, was unilateral; the latter is bilateral. A permanent joint conference was established to determine conditions of work and pay, to adjust all disputes growing out of grievances or out of the interpretation or application of established labour standards, and to promote intensive labour-management co-operation between the Authority and its employees. This joint conference was held to be indispensable to the fulfilment of the T.V.A.'s public purposes and required a clear-cut mutual understanding between the Authority and its employees, through the processes of collective bargaining.

[1] *Public Works Employee Relations*, Address by Gordon R. Clapp, General Manager, T.V.A., before the 1942 Public Works Congress, Cleveland, Ohio, 20 Oct. 1942.

The Agreement, which embodies the Employee Relationship Policy with a few modifications and additional clauses, is self-renewable, except that after one year it may be reopened at any time by the Authority or by the Joint Council in joint conference on 90 days' notice by either side. While the agreement remains in force, then, the principles are binding on the T.V.A. as well as the workers; and the Council and its members agree not to encourage or sanction employees leaving their service, but rather to comply with the agreed procedures to resolve all disputes and difficulties. The Authority rejects responsibility for settling jurisdictional demarcations; however, it asserts the necessity of assigning work to carry out its programme and therefore leaves it to the unions to settle such questions, promising to alter its assignment of work when agreement is subsequently reached among the unions. Where disputes between employees and the Authority cannot be settled by the procedure provided under the Employee Relationship Policy, a joint conference may be established to attempt settlement. There is also provision for a joint board of adjustment to make a further attempt at settlement; the members of the board of adjustment have annual office and the chairman and secretary are alternately a member of the Council and a member of the Authority. Beyond this, the parties agree to go to arbitration before an impartial person from a regular panel designated by the board of adjustment.

Joint co-operative committees are to be set up representing the Authority and the employees at convenient points in the Valley to consider the matters enumerated in the concluding statement of the Employee Relationship Policy, and conclusions reached by unanimous decision will be referred for action to the appropriate officers of either or both parties. A joint Valley-wide co-operative conference will meet at least twice a year to review the conclusions reached and action taken by these committees, and in general to promote discussion and action on the subject matter indicated. A central joint council on apprenticeship is provided for to lay down minimum standards conforming to the standards of the Federal Committee on Apprenticeship or subject to its approval. A set of supplementary schedules on hours of service, holidays, days of rest, overtime and call work, and other matters is appended to the Agreement, covering a large number of points which often give rise to bad temper and disturbing disputes.

Thus the T.V.A., working on the assumption that the skill of the workers will be fully enlisted only when there are institutional mechanisms through which they can appreciate that they are fairly treated, and that this is the key to good morale, has successfully operated its system of collective bargaining, unshaken by the pessimistic theories of doubters. A tribute to the success of this policy was paid by President Roosevelt at the dedication of Chickamauga Dam on Labour Day, 1940, in the following words:

This dam, all the dams built in this short space of years, stands as a monument to a productive partnership between management and labour, between citizens of all kinds working together in the public weal. Collective bargaining and efficiency have proceeded hand in hand. . .

CHAPTER XI

SOME EMPLOYEE WELFARE SERVICES

HEALTH AND SAFETY

The T.V.A. employs a medical staff who examine the health of all employees before admission to employment, provide treatment for occupational injuries, make periodical re-examinations and reports, especially as regards communicable diseases, give typhoid, smallpox and other immunisations, and minor treatment. There are medical units at each construction project to deal with minor injuries and the emergency treatment of major injuries. In construction villages remotely situated, the Authority provides general medical care, for which employees and their families pay a fee to meet cost.[1]

The T.V.A. co-operates with the United States Employees' Compensation Commission in regard to employees who suffer disablement, and where the services of specialists are required, the facilities of the United States Marine Hospitals or other places indicated by the Commission are available.

Dam construction is complicated and heavy work, involving the use of dangerous machinery like tractors and drills and cement pourers, often on sloping and broken ground, and the possibility of injury is very great. There is also much danger in electricity operations, and special anxieties arise out of the toxic dust of the fertiliser powdering process.

The T.V.A. has secured a remarkable improvement in accident rates, as regards both number and severity. This has been achieved by careful attention to design and operation of equipment by safety devices, assignment of workers to jobs least dangerous to themselves and others, records and investigations of accidents, the safety education of all workers for awareness of danger, and first-aid training. In all this it has constantly called upon the

---

[1] To 30 June 1942, there had been 253,257 alleged service-connected injuries; the Authority's medical units had administered 576,561 treatments; 13,500 initial compensation claims had been prepared and submitted to the Compensation Commission. Not a single case of smallpox had been reported, and only two certified cases of typhoid had occurred in about four years, though a yearly average of 15,700 employees had been exposed to a fair degree of hazard.

advice of such other departments of the United States Government as the Bureau of Mines, the Bureau of Marine Inspection and Navigation, and the Army Corps of Engineers.

The Authority's safety record[1] compares very favourably with national averages as reported to the National Safety Council. In 1942, T.V.A. accidents were below the national average in frequency to an extent varying from nearly four times on reservoir clearance and more than twice in dam construction to 10 per cent. less in chemical engineering. In accident severity T.V.A. accidents are nearly 14 times less severe than the national average in power-house operations, just under half as severe in dam construction, and a third as severe in reservoir clearance; with twice the severity in construction and maintenance.

The National Safety Council in its publication of country-wide accident rates for the construction industry gives the relative rank of various units in relation to other organisations doing similar work. For 1941 the 17 units of the Authority's Construction Department took 13 first, second or third places in merit.

JOB TRAINING AND ADULT EDUCATION

As a direct outcome of its interest in the welfare of its employees, the T.V.A. has training courses in or near the job. The general object is to improve the ability of the employee for his own sake, as well as to secure greater efficiency in his T.V.A. work. The Authority promotes courses in the local universities, with the same object, but also to assist the vocational or professional advancement of the employees. For example, by arrangement with the T.V.A. the University of Tennessee provides various courses for employees needing education in such subjects as engineering or public administration. Again, the T.V.A. provides for adult education, by arrangement with the local schools at various stages and at its own cost, that is to say, for more general tuition in social and economic subjects and by means of discussion forums, besides initiating the measures already described for securing the interest of the schools of the area in the T.V.A. regional idea and purposes.[2]

T.V.A. policy regarding training has shifted since its inception, though the general object has remained much the same. From the beginning, the T.V.A. has been extremely anxious to provide such

---

[1] In the first fiscal year of the Authority's operations (1933-1934), the accident frequency rate (number of lost time accidents per million manhours) was 55.7, and the accident severity rate (number of days lost per thousand manhours) was 5.06. By the ninth year (1941-1942) accident frequency had been reduced to 14.1, or a little over one fourth the frequency in the first year, and accident severity to 1.95, a total reduction of almost two thirds.

[2] Cf. Chapter VI.

training as would better fit the man for his job, prepare him for promotion, and also render him more capable by increased versatility to take other jobs if necessary, once a construction job had finished. There was to some extent the desire to carry the experience of able workers from project to project. But originally, the Authority pursued particularly far-reaching aims, introducing, for example, a dairy and pasteurising plant and creamery, and including all sorts of what may be called "white-collar" subjects as well as a large variety of trades. The result was excessive expenditure proportionately to the small numbers who could possibly attend the various courses. The programme was carried on without reference to the needs and standards of private industry, and lacked the independent support of the employees. Therefore, without losing sight of the original main purpose, the Authority redefined its procedure to meet the expressed wishes of the employees and the needs of the towns in which they lived. The policy of the Authority is now directed more narrowly than at first to the improvement of skill in relation to present and future jobs with the Authority. It may be mentioned that this redefinition of the T.V.A.'s educational training programme was stimulated by Congressional criticism.

The job training scheme includes the provision of classes, either by the Authority itself within the community buildings on the job, or, as at the cities of Knoxville and Chattanooga, by contractual arrangement with the local technical schools or colleges. All classes are voluntary and come into existence whenever a sufficient number of workers or their organisation requests them, and the programmes are fitted to the shifts of work. They are conducted by voluntary instructors selected by the employees in consultation with the T.V.A.'s training representative. On 28 February 1942, 1,354 employees were enrolled in 76 courses, covering a wide range of subjects, and at the same time 1,036 employees were participating in a formal recruitment training programme. Less than 10 per cent. of all employees are enrolled at any one time, but about one fourth of all the employees take at least one course during the year.[1] As is to be expected, not all the employees take advantage of the facilities provided for their welfare. Moreover, the fact that the Valley is an area of scattered communities complicates the problem of providing education and increases the expense involved.

The training programme includes definite apprenticeship training, on the basis of plans made jointly by T.V.A. management and labour. Before the T.V.A. began its operations, apprenticeship

---

[1] For analysis of training activities for 1934-41, see *Hearings*, Sub-Committee on Appropriations, House of Representatives, Independent Offices Appropriation Bill for 1941, p. 1691.

training in the south-east of the United States hardly existed. But after two or three years of construction by the Authority, when a fairly long period of work could be foreseen, the organised crafts realised the value of an apprenticeship programme, and in 1936 asked for its establishment. The State Departments of Education and the Federal Committee on Apprenticeship gave their advice and assistance. At first, the programmes of apprenticeship were planned by each craft and locally administered by a committee consisting of representatives of the craft union and the T.V.A. management, the personnel officer, the training staff, and the local vocational education agency. These committees agreed on a proportion of apprentices to journeymen, the methods and standards of selection and a plan of instruction, selected candidates for apprenticeship, supervised their progress, and then, after final examination, accredited them as journeymen.

It was soon seen that co-ordination among the various local plans was necessary, and joint committees were set up for each project. In 1938 further co-ordination was brought about on the suggestion of a Federal Committee on Apprenticeship by the creation of a Central Joint Council. This Council on Apprenticeship has ten members, five representing organised craft employees, three representing supervisory management, and two representing the personnel department. Minimum apprenticeship standards for all T.V.A. programmes have been established by the Council. In mid-1941 there were 284 men enrolled in apprenticeship programmes for seven crafts. At the end of the fifth year of operation, the programme had produced 201 journeymen, all of them acceptable to their craft unions and to private employers.

Since practically all the T.V.A. projects are located in rural areas, the community centre which forms part of the village is a very important unit in the whole scheme of recreation and general adult education. Here again, individual volunteers and employee groups or associations conduct a large number of activities including discussion groups, forums, educational and recreational films, and classes in languages, literature, psychology, and other subjects, under the organising supervision of the training division.

CONSTRUCTION VILLAGES AND LOW-COST HOUSING

On all project sites, excepting Chickamauga, which is within easy distance of Chattanooga, the Authority has been compelled to provide housing for its employees. Although low cost has been a serious consideration, since normally the accommodation is valuable only for the time it takes to build a dam (*i.e.*, three or four years), it has not been the only one. The T.V.A. has taken into account how many permanent dwellings are needed for the operating personnel once the construction period is over, and of these dwellings, the great majority have been built at a cost in labour and materials of a little over $5,000 each. Where temporary dwellings were concerned, it has built in an open, spacious layout houses of four to five rooms of very good quality at about $975 a house. The houses are rented on the basis of the governing rate in the neighbourhood for like facilities. Failure to provide the houses would necessitate long-distance travel for the workers, which would not be conducive to their punctuality or freshness on the job. The usual municipal services and utilities are provided under T.V.A. management, and the Authority also operates commissaries and cafeterias. There are construction camp dormitories for single men. There are club rooms at these centres and the library collections referred to earlier are lodged there. Facilities for games, gymnastics, meetings, lectures and the showing of motion pictures are provided. On the whole, there is a very small bookkeeping loss on total operations, but this is regarded as justified on the grounds that the conditions attract good workers, keep them fit, raise work morale, and so conduce to a net economy on construction costs. Losses are charged to construction costs.

In the building of the construction villages, the T.V.A. took the opportunity of adopting special methods of constructing the workmen's cottages to provide a demonstration of sound building and domestic equipment with low costs.[1] The project aroused nation-wide interest because it provided a 5-room cottage for less than $1,000 and a duplex house of two 4-room, 2-bedroom units at less than $900 per family unit. When war conditions began urgently to demand additional housing, the T.V.A. was made agent of the Federal Works Administration to build 150 houses of a demountable type. These constitute a radical departure in method of construction, invented by the T.V.A. In appearance, durability and habitability they are in no wise inferior to the conventional house. Houses to accommodate a single family are made of three sections, and duplex cottages accommodating two families are made of four sections. They are constructed in slices, that is, of uniform-sized portable sections, with all their fittings in them. These are made and assembled at T.V.A. assembly lines at Sheffield, Alabama; each section is on small wheels to facilitate assembly. When they have been fitted together as a complete house and equipped inside, they are unbolted and each section is taken by truck trailer to its permanent foundations, where the sec-

---

[1] Cf. *T.V.A. Memorandum:* "Housing at Hiwassee", 16 May 1938.

tions are set up, bolted and meshed together. The advantage of this demountable house is that it can be taken down to meet a new housing need elsewhere, or to replace existing substandard housing. Further, the house is permanent in value, for it is not designed to last only a few years. If the need remains, the house can serve durably on its original location. The houses cost (at wartime prices) about $1900 each, including electric stoves, hot water heaters, refrigerators and oil-burning space heaters. Moving costs to a distance of 30 or 40 miles are some $300 per house.[1]

EMPLOYMENT AND TRAINING OF NEGRO WORKERS

In the Tennessee Valley, according to the census of 1930 and subsequent calculations, negroes number about 10 per cent. of the population, though the proportion varies from one place to another. Negro workers would like employment on the same terms as the white employees of the T.V.A.; that is, in strict relation to their individual merit and efficiency in open competition with all candidates for jobs, by the process described in a later chapter. They would wish not to be regarded as a separate community or as a labour commodity, separate from the general body of working men and women. The T.V.A. entered an area in which there are traditional and inveterate social patterns regarding race, and whatever the private feelings of individual members of its administration, as a Federal agency it did not feel that it could at one stroke change an obstinate situation. Within these limits, however, the T.V.A. has done a great deal to give employment opportunities to negroes and to help them to benefit from its educational and social programmes.

Whereas negro spokesmen have asked for full equality of opportunity, especially as the T.V.A. is a Federal project and not a private company, the T.V.A. has felt it possible only to proceed gradually. Its general principle is to employ negroes in the proportion they bear to the total population, that is, some 10 per cent. This, of course, has to vary a little according to the local situation. In some places—at dams in the centre of negro population—a somewhat higher proportion is employed; in others—for example, at Hiwassee, where there were no negro residents and special housing facilities would have been required—no negroes were employed. The very large majority of negroes are employed on unskilled labour, but in the last few years the T.V.A. has made progress in giving some semi-skilled and skilled jobs to negroes. There are some negro foremen; there are several white collar workers, clerks,

[1] Cf. *T.V.A. Report:* "T.V.A. Demountable Houses for Defense Workers", 8 July 1941; and "Portable Housing", in *Pencil Points*, July 1942.

laboratory helpers and instructors. Negro personnel officers of the
T.V.A. handle the interviewing, placement and training of negro
personnel. Some negro county extension agents are employed by
the State Extension Services and so assist in accomplishing the
agricultural programme of the T.V.A.

Before 1938, there were cases of maltreatment of negroes by
supervisors on the construction jobs, by threats, violent language,
and, in some cases, physical violence. There had been harsh disciplinary action, arbitrary transfers, dismissals and cutting down to
lower paid work. Investigations by the T.V.A. and subsequent
disciplinary and educational measures have very much reduced
such incidents, and the improvement has been aided by the better
assimilation of the Employee Relationship Policy.

Negroes are not included in the T.V.A. apprenticeship system
in the same way as white workers, but an agreement has been
reached with labour unions whereby negro apprentices are to be
placed in the lineman and carpenter apprenticeship programme.
In operator training for operations in the Wilson Dam Chemical
Works, negroes have full access to this training and are being
promoted on the basis of it.

At each project, where the family units or dormitory space
for single employees have been available for negroes, they are equal
in every respect to those provided for white employees. It is the
policy of the T.V.A. to provide accommodation for recreational
activities here and there throughout the Valley and the facilities
are placed where there is the greatest need. Thus, there are no
recreational facilities for negroes at Norristown or Big Ridge Park,
but a separate park for negroes has been developed at Chickamauga, which has a large negro population.

In the T.V.A. villages there are negro sections and these have
their own organisations, assisted by the T.V.A., for welfare purposes, for recreation, for community services, for adult education;
and the provision for them is as liberal as for other T.V.A. workers.
Special attention has been paid to the particular interests of the
negroes, with the co-operation of local associations or clubs founded
and managed by the negro workers themselves, and sometimes
assisted by college-trained friends and instructors who happen to
live or work in the vicinity. Some examples may be given of the
activities referred to. At Wheeler Dam, training programmes
embraced health and sanitation, carpentry, brickmasonry, home
mechanics, tool subjects, music, job training, games, and library
service. Community gardens were planted and play areas developed. Courses in general adult education gave an elementary
knowledge of farm budgeting and the use of business forms, like

money orders, cheques, notes and contracts. To meet the needs of those who worked at the dams but lived in nearby communities, T.V.A. clubs were organised in the latter. There are weekly meetings of these clubs, their programmes including home mechanics and improvement, handicrafts, gardening and farming, health, poultry raising, canning, the showing of documentary and other films, plays and music. At Pickwick, a negro community building, school and workshop were provided. Here, the negro labour association helped to conduct a programme similar to that outlined above. There were also classes in home making, and parent education. The workers who are employed at Chickamauga mainly come from Chattanooga. The T.V.A. therefore assisted in the formation of a Chattanooga Community Council on Adult Education, on which a large variety of civic agencies were represented, to be advised and assisted by the T.V.A. Training Division and its negro staff member. This body administered in Chattanooga a negro programme of job training, recreation, a Little Theatre, health education and library service. Naturally, a proportion of the financing was supplied by the T.V.A. As a result of these activities the Tennessee State Department of Education appointed a negro director of vocational trade education. At Guntersville, another device was adopted. Many negro workers lived at Huntsville, some miles away. The T.V.A. contracted with the agricultural and mechanical college for negroes to conduct the negro training programme. It established a council on community study and service to discover procedures and disseminate information. A special member of the Faculty directs the various teachers who conduct the training activities. Library service has been provided, and also classes in social studies, job training for workers and other citizens of Huntsville, and recreation for workers and citizens, with a chorus of 100 voices.

Little headway has been made against the social prejudices of the labour unions in the Tennessee Valley. There are negro members of some unions at Wilson Dam in the fertiliser operations but otherwise they are almost entirely excluded. It is in the hands of the labour unions to prevent ill-treatment of negroes and to make a place for their negro fellow-workers to get skilled or foremen's jobs, and if this co-operation were forthcoming, no doubt the hand of the T.V.A. would be strengthened.

CHAPTER XII

THE FINANCING OF THE T.V.A.'s ACTIVITIES

The financing of the T.V.A. multi-purpose system has two chief aspects: (1) the T.V.A.'s own financial basis; and (2) the financing of the municipalities and co-operatives which are the distributors of T.V.A. electric power. Each of these aspects involves interesting problems for development works, and substantial sums are involved in both.

In nearly 10 years of operation, the T.V.A. has administered very considerable sums of money. By 30 June 1942, the financing of its activities had cost almost $600 million.[1] Of this total sum, $570 million had gone to the construction and acquisition of navigation, flood control and electric power assets; some $8.25 million to fertiliser assets, that is, plant, equipment, phosphate lands and rights, and fertiliser stocks; and there were $12 million in general assets. The combined municipal and co-operative capital amounted, on 30 June 1942, to nearly $107 million.

T.V.A. Financing

The T.V.A.'s current operations have been substantial.[2] Its financial turnover and the revolving nature of the funds it uses in power operations have already been noticed[3], and also the characteristics of its expenditures on the fertiliser, reservoir property and

---

[1] To be exact, $591,402,239. Cf. Budget Summary for 1944, Appropriations Sub-Committee, Independent Offices, *Hearings*, p. 457.

[2] Cf. Tables of net income or net expense in Appendix No. I. In summary, these current operations for the period 1933-1942 are as follows:

	$ in millions
Power sold	70
Profit on power	16
Navigability of the river	5
Flood control	3¼
Power losses (1933–1938)	¾
Power profits (1933–1942)	16
Fertiliser and farm demonstration programme	16 [a]
Reservoir properties operation	6 [a]
Development activities	12½ [a]

[a] Net expense.

[3] Cf. Chapter III.

development programmes. The relatively small revenues which the T.V.A.[1] receives serve to offset the expenditures which come out of T.V.A. general funds, replenished when necessary by Congressional appropriations. How the long-term financing of the activities of the Authority, especially the construction of the dams and river works, is effected, and the procedure by which the funds are applied to its purposes, are highly important questions, especially in the case of a public corporation, since the value of this form of organisation lies in the extent to which it provides security for business latitude and initiative. The experience of the T.V.A. in this respect may have a particular interest for governments contemplating the several or joint financing of development works of any magnitude.

Bonds or Appropriations?

Two principal methods of financing the T.V.A. were open to Congress. The Authority might have been empowered to borrow the necessary capital and the amount required for current expenses during development, the debt and dividends to be repaid from its earnings in due course; and in this case it could either have sold bonds on the open market, or have borrowed the whole or part of the funds from the United States Treasury. The other method was for the T.V.A. to be financed entirely by Congressional appropriations in much the same way as the ordinary activities of the Government are financed—that is, by coming to Congress annually, offering estimates of need and then, after cross-examination, being awarded what Congress believed to be adequate. For reasons which are explained below, the latter method (with a slight qualification) was adopted.

However, the T.V.A. did receive some bond-issuing powers, that is, the power to raise loans for specific purposes. The problems at issue, whether and how far the T.V.A. should have such loan-raising power, were clearly stated in discussions in Congress or its committees; both the T.V.A. and Congress found a mixture of advantage and disadvantage in the use of such a power. On the one hand, the Congress would have liked relief from the need of finding appropriations annually, year after year, for a long period, but realised that if the T.V.A. were given a loan-raising power, it would escape from Congressional control over its activities, exercised through the Authority's need to go to Congress annually for fresh money. Congress was extremely sensitive on the question of allowing the T.V.A. excessive latitude of operation and expansion. On the other hand, the T.V.A. favoured the possession of a bond-

[1] Cf. Chapter IV.

issuing power, because it would thereby obtain freedom and business latitude; and because, being obliged to make provision for the payment of interest and the repayment of the debt, it would acquire business independence and its own internal, disciplinary power over its operations and administration based on an independent balance sheet. Again, there was the T.V.A.'s need for a sufficient sum to buy out the property of the private power companies *en bloc* and not piecemeal, since the latter course would necessarily have meant the destruction of their economy. But against these considerations was the great fact that the T.V.A.'s total unified programme was going to cost a very large sum of money which Congress could not be expected to give all at once; and more important, that until the T.V.A. showed signs of being able to repay, the investment market would hardly be ready to advance the substantial funds required, and the T.V.A. must necessarily wait several years before the fruits of its work could even begin to materialise.[1] Finally, there were some T.V.A. activities, such as its planning, its agricultural programme, its public health work, flood control, transportation, forestry, and the rest, which were not of a business character like the power undertaking, but were more in the nature of the ordinary social benevolent activities normally financed by Governments, not out of loans, but from tax revenues.

Therefore, the principal means of financing came to be by Congressional appropriations, and only very small latitude was allowed in the bond-issuing or loan-raising powers of the T.V.A.

Section 15 of the Statute authorised the Board to issue serial bonds to the amount of $50 million running 50 years at 3½ per cent., to be issued and sold on the credit of the United States with the approval of the Secretary of the Treasury. The money was to be used "in the construction of any future dam, steam-plant or other facility to be used in whole or in part for the generation or transmission of electric power".

In 1935, the Authority itself put forward an amendment to the Statute, providing for additional powers to raise funds. The Authority asked for power to issue $100 million in 50-year 3½ per cent. bonds over five years, for the purpose of acquiring existing electric distribution systems and transmission lines. Thus provided, the Authority could have bought the entire system of any private company, and could then have resold individual parts to municipalities or other bodies. Congress rejected the proposal and the T.V.A. received only the limited power of issuing bonds up to $50 million (Section 15 (*a*)), this power being further restricted by the

---

[1] It will be recalled that until and including the fiscal year 1938, the T.V.A. bore a loss on its power operations.

stipulation that such funds should be used for making loans to States, counties and municipalities, and non-profit organisations for a period not exceeding five years (Section 12 (a)).[1]

Hence, the T.V.A. was partly compelled and partly chose to move along the line of annual Congressional appropriations until, as it were, it came of age.[2] And in fact, when by 1939 the major litigation had resulted in fortifying its authority, the T.V.A. was able to ask Congress successfully for a further power of borrowing in order to buy out the principal system operating in its area (the Tennessee Electric Power Company) and other smaller systems. But here again it may be observed that Congress did not give the Authority power to borrow an unlimited amount, nor even to raise $100 million[3] as it wished, but deliberately meted out only the right to raise the exact amounts required for the relevant contracts. Congress was resolved not to permit any free expansion which might have followed a large and unconditional grant. Under Section 15 (c), therefore, amending the Statute, the T.V.A. was authorised, with the approval of the Secretary of the Treasury, to issue bonds not to exceed $61 million, and the purposes and amounts were specifically stated.[4] The bonds were not to bear more than $3\frac{1}{2}$ per cent. interest—the rate needed the approval of the Treasury—nor to be sold at such price as would return more than $3\frac{1}{2}$ per cent. on the investment. They were guaranteed by the Treasury. A complete statement on expenditure of the funds derived from the sale of bonds was to be filed every December with the President and Congress. The proceeds could not be utilised for loans until the contract had been approved by the Federal Power Commission. The authority to issue bonds was limited to 1 January 1941.

Simultaneously with the grant of this bond-issuing power, Congress provided for the extinction in July 1939 of the other bond-issuing power of the T.V.A. already mentioned.

---

[1] Cf. Chapter II.

[2] In fact, the T.V.A. made use of its bond-issuing powers only in a minor degree. In 1938-1939 it issued $8,300,000 in bonds at $2\frac{1}{2}$ per cent. falling due on various dates up to 1961. These were sold at par to the Reconstruction Finance Corporation. The purpose of the bonds was the acquisition of properties from various electric utility companies in the Valley. The Reconstruction Finance Corporation is a United States Government Corporation, established in Jan. 1932 to extend credit to agriculture, commerce and industry.

[3] This was not to be an addition to, but a replacement of, the existing power to borrow $50 million under Section 15 and $50 million under Section 15 (a).

[4] Not more than $46 million for the Tennessee Electric Power Company and Southern Tennessee Power Company; not more than $6.5 million for certain named parts of the Alabama and Mississippi Power Companies; not more than $3.5 million for rebuilding, replacing and repair of the utilities thus purchased; not more than $3.5 million for construction of various facilities to connect the properties bought with the T.V.A.'s power system; and not more than $2 million for loans to public distributors to buy any of the properties concerned.

Lump Sum Appropriations

The T.V.A. has, therefore, been obliged to come to Congress annually for its financial provision, except for an annual sum of $1,000,000 secured to it by the Statute, which it may retain for the specific purpose of defraying emergency expenses and ensuring continuous operation.

Up to 1 July 1942, the T.V.A. had received through Congressional appropriations (mainly annual) $667,969,270.

The annual appropriations have been provided as lump sums in general terms. The annual Congressional formula votes money merely for the purpose of carrying out the provisions of the T.V.A. Act of 1933, as amended from time to time, including the continued construction and the beginning of certain named dams, investigation of sites therefor, the acquisition and clearing of the necessary land, highway relocation, the construction and purchase of transmission lines and other facilities, and all other necessary works authorised by such acts, for printing, for vehicles, for rents, and all necessary salaries and expenses.

This lump sum method, which has been followed from the beginning, differs very widely from the usual method of appropriation by minute itemisation of purposes and sums for expenditure. The lump sum method, which permits financial flexibility within each year, has often been challenged in the Appropriations Committees of Congress and in the course of debate in Congress itself; yet there remains what may be called a respectful, if not unreserved, acceptance by the majority of the view that, since the T.V.A. is so much of a business enterprise and has so many experimental and developmental features, it should be given a reasonable latitude.

This does not, however, mean that the Authority has been or is able, or desires, to do as it likes without submission to Congress's wishes. In fact, the T.V.A., like every other agency of the United States Government, is subject to the Budget and Accounting Act of 1921, and is obliged annually to submit its estimates to the United States Bureau of the Budget. Occasionally this agency sends a field agent to the Authority's offices to make investigations, to ask questions on such items of the estimates as seem to him to require it, and to report to the Bureau. Normally, the Bureau exercises its review by scrutinising documents submitted annually by the T.V.A. and at supplemental hearings of its officials before the Bureau in Washington. How much is to be assigned to the T.V.A. as a whole, and how much to each particular item of its work within that total, is then recommended by the Bureau to the

President, who passes on the recommendation in the United States Budget to Congress, after having required the Bureau to make any amendment he personally may consider appropriate. At the three stages—upon inspection of the estimates by the field agent of the Bureau of the Budget, the Director of the Bureau, and the President—the Authority is obliged fully to justify its request by evidence or argument, and is given ample opportunity to offer alternatives. It may happen, and has happened, that the claims of the special needs of the Valley, sound in themselves, must in a year of economic and budgetary difficulty be reduced to meet the general national stringency.

Consequently, the T.V.A. has given special attention to the problem of displaying the work of the Authority to show clearly to Congress its purposes, its plans and the expenditure in relation to each. In the latest development (fiscal year 1943), this "Budget Justification" appears in the form of programmes, thus:

    I. Navigation, Flood Control and Power,
    II. Fertiliser,
    III. Related Property Operations,
    IV. Related Development Activities,
    V. General Asset Accounts.

Then, under each programme, there is a subdivision into projects, as for example:

Programme III
    1. Reservoir Area Operations,
    2. Village Operations,
    3. Maintenance of National Defence Properties,
    4. General and Administrative Overhead Expenses.

To each of these programmes, projects and items, a very painstaking explanation is furnished, together with statistical tables and other supporting material, so that Congress may have a thoroughly vivid and realistic account of what the Authority is doing and hopes to do. It should be noted again, however, that Congress does not vote the budget in this itemised form, but as a lump sum.

Congress, in accepting this method, nevertheless presses its own specific recommendations where it thinks them necessary. It has from time to time intervened in the administration of the Authority by the device of decreasing the amounts requested[1]; and in some cases has threatened to take very drastic measures. Congress could at any time change its method of granting from a lump

---

[1] Congress has not been friendly to "planning" and "studies" activities unless, these are inseparably and demonstrably connected with the T.V.A.'s primary and immediate duties.

sum to itemised appropriation. It has not done so, because the general idea of the public corporation was that the T.V.A. should be tethered by as few strings as possible, and because T.V.A. administration has been regarded as satisfactory. But, where Congress, as now, votes a lump sum, is it permissible for the Authority to expend all or any portion of that lump sum on *any* activity authorised by the provisions of the T.V.A. Statute, even though the Appropriations Committee might have indicated (but not legislated) by items the specific amounts that should be spent on the different projects? The answer is that the T.V.A., as a matter of law, is not bound by the clearly expressed intent of the Committee. But, as a matter of policy and with a sense of responsibility, the Board does its best to adhere to this intent, which is plainly expressed by full debate and qualified acceptance of the T.V.A.'s budget in the House of Representatives Appropriations Sub-Committee, and to a lesser degree in that of the Senate. Where, therefore, the Appropriations Committee has thus steadily and deliberately made its will known—for example, to slow down regional studies and aerial mapping, and to widen the area of farm demonstrations and fertiliser distribution beyond the States of the Valley—the Authority conforms, acting in the spirit of Congressional recommendation, but it does not regard the penny index as the mark of its duty. It tries to meet Congress's wishes, and where this is technically impossible, conscientiously expends the minimum required by the situation. The result is that the Authority has a practical power of what is known in public financial parlance as *virement*, that is, of diversion of moneys to and from the different items, to an extent never tolerated in the case of ordinary Government departments. Examples of Congressional reductions in the amounts asked for by the T.V.A. are very limited and, in addition, have only a restricted interest. What is interesting is, first, that there is the regular sum of $1 million already mentioned to meet unforeseen contingencies, and secondly, that in its estimates the Authority naturally makes an allowance for contingencies which the Congress may and usually does accept. For example, the power estimates for 1943 contained an item: "Allowances for changes in revenues and decreased production expense in event of a dry year . . . 1,500,000 dollars".

It is a fact of the first magnitude, however, that the T.V.A. cannot always be certain that it will get the amounts of money it requires at the time that it makes the demand. But as a general rule, the appropriations it has deemed necessary have substantially been accorded, and even where, as in a few cases, Congress was at first inclined to reduce the amount demanded, the Authority was ultimately able to justify its demands to the satisfaction of both Houses.

The Appropriations Committee subjects the Authority's officials and directors to a quite extensive and detailed cross-examination year by year both as to policy and the tempo of its execution. The value of its scrutiny lies in its regular attention to: (1) the speed, progress and economy of the construction programme; (2) the development and cost of the specific programmes and the search for criteria of their effectiveness; (3) the direct and indirect cost of the T.V.A. to the United States as a whole and the place of the T.V.A. in the total economy of the United States, in other words what other parts of the United States are getting in return for the tax contribution; (4) publicity operations of the T.V.A.; (5) the quality, size and payment of the staff; (6) specific problems like land purchases, the allocation of costs, the location of particular dam sites, the respective economy of steam plant and hydroelectric plant. The T.V.A. does not, indeed, have scope for any substantial mistake or illegality. This process has quite a salutary effect, though sometimes, as in the case of anybody under cross-examination, it may be uncomfortable for the officers and directors who may have to battle for their point of view against a hostile policy. At any rate, the method clarifies for Congress and the public the implications of the T.V.A.'s policy, and may even sometimes make these implications clearer to the Authority itself. There is a certain weakness in the procedure, for the membership of the Appropriations Committee changes and the same ground may therefore have to be gone over year by year. The strength of the supervision lies in the fact that though a cross-examination takes place only once a year, its effect lasts all round the year both as a result of strictures and praise, and anticipation of what the Committee is likely to say at the next session.

The T.V.A. possesses one further element of elasticity. In Section 26 of the original Statute, the Authority was permitted to retain its earned revenues from power and the other services it might render, and was not, as in the case of other Government agencies, required to turn the money over monthly to the United States Treasury. When ordinary Government agencies and departments turn their funds in to the United States Treasury, they fall under administrative and legislative control, because funds cannot then be drawn out to spend without a special Treasury warrant, and that warrant must be based upon a legislative appropriation. Section 26 required the Authority to pay into the Treasury not all its proceeds, but only its net proceeds, and even so to pay them in only at the end of each calendar year. The latitude thus permitted to the Authority can be appreciated when it is considered that the definition of net proceeds in Section 26 means proceeds after deducting from gross revenues "the cost of operation, maintenance, depreciation, amortisation and an amount deemed by the Board as necessary to withhold as operating capital or devoted by the Board to new construction". This text was so liberal, and left so much to the discretion of the Board regarding the magnitude and timing of its construction, that in the period of construction there could be no net proceeds to turn over to the Treasury.

This section of the Statute came under very heavy criticism in 1935, when the T.V.A. was seeking to have the Act amended to give it greater bond-issuing power. In place of the original section another Section 26 was written, which requires the T.V.A. to pay its revenues from the sale of power or any other products it manufactures and from any other activities, including the disposition of property, into the Treasury at the end of each calendar year, excepting for the amount the T.V.A. considers necessary for operating expenses, and for a continuing fund of $1 million to defray emergency expenses and to ensure continuous operation.[1] This would seem to give the T.V.A. a real latitude on all operating matters; but it excludes the application of moneys to new construction, as formerly permitted. Thus Congress, while allowing the necessary elasticity for continuous operation, reserves to itself the right of annually financing construction activities, except such as might be interpreted as "emergency expenses". Under this sytem, the T.V.A. has actually established and maintained a "T.V.A. Fund" in the Treasury of the United States, in which are placed all the moneys appropriated to it for the year, and the receipts which come to it in that fiscal year. Congress reappropriates to the T.V.A., for use in the succeeding fiscal year, such moneys as still remain in the T.V.A. Fund, including the unexpended appropriations and receipts it has deposited. The T.V.A. subtracts this balance and its estimated receipts for the succeeding fiscal year from the total of its own estimates for both capital and operating expenses, and the amount of the difference is the "new money" requested, which Congress reviews and passes upon as the appropriation for the year. Then the T.V.A. draws its money from the Treasury on the basis of "accountable warrants", countersigned by the Comptroller General, thus transferring amounts it requires to its own cheque accounts.

Thus the Authority has been accorded a considerable amount of flexibility. Flexibility is not freedom, but conditional freedom;

---

[1] It may be noted that many of the corporate agencies of the Federal Government are permitted to use their revenues in their own operations; e.g., the Reconstruction Finance Corporation, the Inland Waterways Corporation, the Commodity Credit Corporation, the U.S. Maritime Commission and the Home Owners' Loan Corporation.

and the amount possessed by the Authority is considerably greater than that possessed in normal times by any ordinary department of the United States Government and by most of the other Government corporations.

There have been proposals to put the T.V.A. on the same footing as ordinary Government departments. The latest came in March 1944, when it was proposed to the Senate that all proceeds derived by the Board from the sale of power or any other products manufactured by it, and any other activities, should be paid in to the Treasury every month and should "not be expended until subsequently appropriated by the Congress". The T.V.A. protested very vigorously against such restrictive proposals, on the grounds that it would be subjected to a financial strait-jacket inappropriate to a business organisation.

The principle of flexibility is very important to any Government corporation likely to be involved in business analogous to that of the T.V.A. If the Authority's right to spend were dependent on items defined in the Appropriation Act, it could not, without illegality, go outside them. It could not get releases of money from the Treasury to meet an emergency, and would need, therefore, to be able to anticipate emergencies, whereas a real emergency is, by definition, impossible of anticipation. The Authority has engaged itself to supply so much firm power, and it has contracts for the non-fulfilment of which it is liable to suit for damages. But hydroelectric power production and transmission are so much affected by weather conditions that between a very wet year and an extremely dry one the difference in T.V.A. generating and operating expense may be as much as $5 million or $6 million. A single storm might do a million dollars' worth of damage to transmission lines. Again, the demand for power may suddenly increase, as happened in September 1939 when the Aluminum Company of America had suddenly to expand its production and asked for additional power. These contingencies cannot be provided for under the United States budget procedure, which obliges the Authority to prepare its annual budget estimates from 14 to 26 months before the date on which expenditures may actually be made. A good instance of the difficulties is provided by the estimates prepared in the early summer of 1939 and filed in December 1939 for the fiscal year ending 30 June 1941. Power revenues for the year were estimated at roughly $14.7 million and the total direct power expenses at $5.6 million, so that the net income would have been about $9 million. Actually, power revenues were just above $21 million, and expenses just below $9 million, with a net income of just over $12 million. If the Authority's revenues had been frozen in Congressional compartments, their utilisation for increased operation resulting from expansion of war industry would have been impossible.

It seems fortunate, then, that Congress retained such elasticity for the T.V.A. Another, although a clumsier, way of achieving the same effect would be to allow a very considerable unallotted sum at the discretion of the Authority. It might be noticed, incidentally, that the T.V.A. does not, as private corporations and some Government corporations do, deposit its moneys in private banks or lodge them in investments; as already stated, the money is placed to the credit of the United States Treasury from time to time.

The T.V.A. power programme is already self-supporting.[1] As a result, there has again been raised in a new form one of the aspects of the problem of financing by issue of bonds. The T.V.A. seeks a feeling of freedom and flexibility. It is strongly aware of the psychological constraint of the method of appropriations and of the ever contingent possibility of attack on its activities and future enterprise. It looks to budgetary practices which will make manifest the self-sustaining character of its business operations. The payment of interest obligations on what was virtually a Congressional loan (*i.e.*, all the appropriations to date) during the construction period, would meet one of the suggestions made fairly often by critics; and the Authority would then feel better able to claim its reasonable degree of administrative autonomy. From time to time, therefore, the Authority has declared its readiness to make interest payments to the Treasury—though so far it has not actually done so. The Joint Committee investigating the T.V.A. in 1938-39[2] recommended that the T.V.A. should pay back to the Treasury the capital advances plus interest.

The Authority has, however, ploughed back an equivalent of such interest payments into the programme each year (after a full disclosure of its intent to Congress) through the budget-review process, and by asking Congress annually for a lesser sum than would have been necessary if the T.V.A. had, for instance, alienated a sum to the Treasury as interest payments.[3]

---

[1] Cf. figures in footnote on p. 191.

[2] Cf. Chapter IX.

[3] According to its latest pronouncement on this subject, the T.V.A. is studying a scheme which, if approved, would permit it to fund all the outstanding appropriations chargeable to power; in other words, 65 per cent. of the amounts appropriated and spent on the water-control programmes. Its object is not only to be self-supporting, but to show that it is self-supporting by presenting a balance sheet that businessmen will recognise, in the usual form, and paying interest on bonds issued against this portion of the programme. When additional funds are needed, they would simply be added to the liabilities in the usual manner. Cf. 77th Congress, 1st Session, Part II, Sub-Committee of the Committee of Appropriations, House of Representatives, *Hearings*, pp. 514-515.

INVESTMENT IN T.V.A. POWER DISTRIBUTORS

T.V.A. municipal and co-operative distributors had, at 30 June 1942, a combined capital of roughly $107 million. As will be seen from the table below[1], some 60 per cent. of this sum had been obtained by bonds sold to the public; some 4 per cent. was lent by the Tennessee Valley Authority; 16 per cent. was lent by the R.E.A.; and some 8 per cent. was composed of grants from Federal agencies, particularly the Public Works Administration. Some observations on the sources of this capital must be made here, as it represents in fact loans made for development, and its nature is therefore important. The Electric Home and Farm Authority's development of sales of appliances is also of interest.

Sale of Bonds to the Public

No special observation needs to be made on the capital derived from the sale of bonds to the public by the municipalities and co-operatives. They are secured on the electric revenues, and the interest rates range from 2.32 per cent. up to 4 per cent.[2] The public very rapidly took up the bonds, having confidence in the capacity of the power undertakings to prosper and therefore to meet their interest payments and loan repayments. It may be noted merely that the establishment of the T.V.A., a public enterprise, and the establishment by the municipalities and co-operatives of power undertakings, gave private enterprise an opportunity of a desirable investment.

[1] The capital structure of T.V.A. power distributors at 30 June 1942 was as follows:

Particulars	$
Long-term debt	
Tennessee Valley Authority	3,777,141.20
Rural Electrification Administration	16,634,916.04
Bonds held by the public	60,675,663.87
	81,087,721.11
Capital	
Investment of municipalities	983,131.36
Memberships of co-operatives	1,038,581.59
Received from consumers	2,284,542.64
Grants from Federal agencies	8,856,272.12
Other capital	111,756.92
	13,274,284.63
Earned surplus	12,587,627.79
Total	106,949,633.53

Cf. *Financial Statements for the Fiscal Year Ended June 30, 1942, Municipalities and Cooperatives Purchasing Power from the Tennessee Valley Authority.*

[2] Memphis sold general obligation bonds, and here the interest rate was as low as 2.19 per cent.

Loans from the T.V.A.

The T.V.A. Statute gave the Authority a variety of powers to make loans. The right to "dispose of surplus power" and "make contracts" and "to exercise such incidental powers as were necessary or appropriate" to the express powers, permitted the transfer of real and personal property to municipalities and co-operatives on an instalment payment plan to enable them to purchase and distribute T.V.A. power. Then, secondly, the T.V.A. had the power, for a period of five years from the enactment date, of "extending credit" to the States, municipalities, counties, and non-profit organisations, for the purpose of enabling such agencies to acquire, improve and operate distribution facilities as well as inter-connecting transmission lines, preserve existing distribution systems as going concerns and avoid their duplication.[1]

Under both the permissions mentioned above, the T.V.A. has made loans to municipalities and co-operatives, in the form of advances of property[2] or work. They were made at the rate of 3½ per cent.; were subject to amortisation in the time and by the periodical payments set by the T.V.A.; and were secured by a lien on the properties and the revenues of the debtor.[3]

Where the property to be purchased from the utilities comprised a distribution system which would go to a municipality and a generation and transmission system which would appropriately become the property of the T.V.A., the Authority bought all the properties in a joint transaction with the municipalities concerned, the costs being shared according to the valuation of the respective properties going to each. The T.V.A. met its share of the biggest transaction of all under the special power given it by Congress in 1939 to issue bonds to the value of $61 million by issuing, in August 1939, bonds to the amount of $50 million to mature not later than 1969, at up to 3½ per cent. interest.[4]

Loans from the Rural Electrification Administration

In a previous chapter[5] reference was made to the promotional assistance obtained by rural co-operatives in the Tennessee Valley

---

[1] Under Section 15 (a) the T.V.A. issued, on 9 Jan. 1939, only obligations in the amount of $272,500 bearing interest at 2 1/8 per cent., due 1948, and sold at par to the United States Treasury. This amount was to enable two electric co-operatives to acquire properties and construct transmission lines.

[2] Another power with the same effect has also been used, though sparingly. This is the strictly time-limited power possessed by the T.V.A. under Section 4 (k) to dispose of real property. Here, however, in order to honour fully Section 12 (a), the T.V.A. did not purchase or construct property for the purpose of resale.

[3] Such loans must be approved by the Federal Power Commission.

[4] This money was first obtained by the T.V.A. from the Treasury, to which interim certificates bearing ½ per cent. interest were issued, pending sale of bonds.

[5] Cf. Chapter III.

area from the Rural Electrification Administration. This Federal organisation was established on 11 May 1935, not for the Tennessee Valley only but for the whole nation, "to initiate, formulate, administer and supervise a programme of approved projects with respect to the generation, transmission and distribution of electrical energy in rural areas". Most of its loan funds as authorised by Congress were provided by the R.F.C. The establishment by President Roosevelt of this Administration was the culmination of a long process leading from the perception, many years before, of the value of electricity to rural production and welfare, and the observation that the private utility companies seriously neglected the rural areas, concentrating only upon the densely populated areas where large and easy profits were to be made. The R.E.A., with a large capital, fosters the establishment of electricity distribution systems by making loans to rural co-operatives. It has officers throughout the country whose business it is to stimulate the establishment of co-operatives and to induce associations of rural people to enter into loan contracts for this purpose. The R.E.A. also concerns itself in various ways with research and other measures for the reduction of distribution costs, for example, by means of cheaper transformers, line construction and accounting, and with the development of cheaper appliances, teaching farmers how to make appliances at home. Of course, in its loan contracts, it insists upon the proper procedures for management and continually seeks to improve their administration, by personal contact between its own officials and the local managers and by correspondence.

As to financing, the co-operatives served by the T.V.A. can be placed in three categories: (a) wholly financed by the T.V.A.; (b) wholly financed by the R.E.A.; and (c) financed jointly by the T.V.A. and R.E.A. Before the R.E.A. was established, all the co-operatives obtained their funds, both for construction and acquisition, from the T.V.A. The R.E.A. is limited by statute to the financing of new rural lines and the acquisition of predominantly rural properties which can be used as a nucleus for the construction of additional new lines. While, therefore, the Authority has withdrawn from the field covered by the R.E.A., it has still been necessary for it to finance acquisitions by the co-operatives when the acquisitions which the R.E.A. was competent to finance did not offer adequate possibilities for additional rural electrification. On 31 December 1942, there were 45 co-operatives receiving service from the Authority. Six of these were wholly financed by the Authority, 28 were wholly financed by R.E.A., and 11 were jointly financed by T.V.A. and R.E.A. Of the six originally wholly financed by the T.V.A., two have already paid off their entire debt.

LOANS FROM THE PUBLIC WORKS ADMINISTRATION

The financial co-operation of the Reconstruction Finance Corporation in the operations of the T.V.A., mentioned above, is only one of a number of financial devices additional to those of Congressional appropriations and the power of the Authority to issue bonds.

Another is the assistance given to municipalities by the Public Works Administration to which reference has already been made.[1] The Public Works Administration, a department of the United States Government, was established under the National Industrial Recovery Act, as modified and continued by the Emergency Relief Appropriation Act of 1935. It was the business of the Administrator of this organisation to prepare and carry through a comprehensive programme of public works, including the construction, repair, and improvement of public highways and parkways, public buildings and any publicly-owned instrumentalities and facilities; the conservation and development of natural resources, including the control, utilisation and purification of waters, prevention of soil or coastal erosion, development of water power, transmission of electrical energy, and so forth. In order to increase employment quickly, the Administrator was empowered to make grants to States, municipalities or other public bodies for the construction, repair or improvement of any such projects. Such grants were to be not in excess of 30 per cent., later increased to 45 per cent., of the cost of the labour and materials employed upon such projects. The Administrator's office, of course, made every enquiry to determine whether the price the municipality was to pay, in constructing a distribution system or in buying it from the utilities, was a reasonable one. In either case, the municipality was encouraged to plan for the lowest price of establishing its own distribution system. Where the utility claimed too high a purchase price, the city was encouraged by the possibility of constructing its own facilities with the assistance of the gift of 45 per cent. and for the rest a very long-term loan with low rates of interest.

With such encouragement, eight cities in Alabama, two in Mississippi, eleven in Tennessee, and one in Kentucky, had been allotted total grants of $7,626,685 and given loans of $6,420,000 down to 1 December 1937, a total aid of some $14 million against the approved estimated cost for construction of electric generation or distribution systems of nearly $24 million. By 30 June 1940, 29 cities in all had actually received $6,302,196 in grants; while something less than $1 million in loans was still outstanding.[2]

---

[1] Cf. Chapter III.
[2] Cf. 77th Congress, 1st Session, House of Representatives, Independent Offices Appropriations Bill for 1942, *Hearings*, p. 512.

The cities usually decided upon the works leading to Public Works Administration, assistance by a special referendum on whether or not they should have a public electricity system. The P.W.A., however, laid down the policy that it would advance no funds until the city had satisfied the Administrator that it was unable, after reasonable efforts made in good faith, to acquire on reasonable terms and conditions the facilities of the existing private utility with which the project would compete.

THE ELECTRIC HOME AND FARM AUTHORITY

As indicated earlier in connection with water power utilisation[1], one very important method of promoting electricity sales is to develop the purchase of appliances. If the appliances are too costly there is a clear limitation on the outlet for electricity, and it is therefore of the greatest interest to a generator of power to influence the cost and purchase of electrical appliances. This can, of course, be done by consultation with the dealers and manufacturers, and the T.V.A. has used this method. But it has also invented an ingenious financial device for promoting the purchase of apparatus, a special form of instalment buying. Under the authority of the President, by Executive Order, there was set up a public corporation (incorporated in the State of Delaware) known as the Electric Home and Farm Authority (E.H.F.A.) which would buy from the dealer in electric appliances (who might be one of the utility companies) the note or bill given him as acknowledgment of debt by a customer who bought appliances from him. In other words, the E.H.F.A. was a financing organisation which, through the dealer, put credit at the disposal of the consumer for the special purpose of electric appliances. The dealer was enabled to do business and receive the price of his appliances at once from the E.H.F.A., which bore the risk. The dealer's part in the transaction was threefold: to collect the instalments on the payment of the debt as arranged and transmit them to the E.H.F.A., and to assume the obligation of the contract; to promote the sale of appliances; and to co-operate with the E.H.F.A. and the T.V.A. in devising cheaper apparatus. This system was fostered by a guarantee of E.H.F.A.'s obligations given by the Reconstruction Finance Corporation, though the T.V.A. looked to the possibility that the credit might eventually come through the commercial banking system.

It happened that the three directors of the T.V.A. were directors of the original E.H.F.A., and some doubt was raised whether the T.V.A. directors could hold this position consistently with their

---

[1] Cf. Chapter III.

obligations under their own statute. They therefore resigned from the E.H.F.A. In 1935 the E.H.F.A. was made national in scope, and afterwards did some remarkable things not only for the Tennessee Valley area, but for the whole country. It had a capital of $850,000, and contracts with 5,000 accredited dealers, to whom it was of great assistance, especially in the case of the smaller firms, by its arrangements for discounting paper. It was especially beneficial in financing electrical and gas equipment. Particular attention was given to financing the more expensive units of electrical apparatus, such as refrigerators, stoves, various cooking devices and cooling units, some of which have a high initial cost, but are of substantial continuing productive value. Down to the middle of 1941, the E.H.F.A. had financed no less than $40 million worth of purchases, with a total loss on collections of only $40,000. It had earned a surplus of $701,000, and had established a reserve for losses of nearly $340,000. Its rate of interest was lower than the market would charge (5 per cent. was its prevailing rate), and it operated in the smaller communities which the larger finance companies usually avoid. Its activity, with a yearly volume of business of about $17 million, was claimed to have helped to hold down interest rates and charges, and was of benefit to all concerned, buyers, utility companies, and dealers. The E.H.F.A. operated in some 37 States, and its contracts on 31 March 1941 numbered 284,000 in round figures. Of these, over 46,000 were in the State of Tennessee, nearly 11,000 in Mississippi, over 6,000 in Alabama, over 26,000 in Georgia, 4,600 in North Carolina, 1,500 in South Carolina—making 95,000 or just about a third of the total in the Valley States. The E.H.F.A. was dissolved in 1943, as war conditions made credit and supply for civilian use an anomaly.

*

*   *

The total capital outlay on the T.V.A.'s own undertaking and its municipal and co-operative power distributors to 30 June 1942 is of the order of $707 million. In the provision of this, Congressional appropriations subscribed by far the largest share (some six sevenths); bonds issued to the public contributed the next largest sum, and Federal credit, development and public works agencies, like the R.E.A., P.W.A. and E.H.F.A., supplied the rest. The last-named devices are particularly interesting as being supplementary to the main form of financing the T.V.A., namely, Congressional annual contributions. They supplied a special fillip to the various dynamic aspects of the T.V.A.'s power business development. Whether it would be wise for development authorities in other countries to depend on the contingent annual grant of fresh appropriations for their work would depend on the steadfastness of the political body responsible for the control of funds. The system worked successfully in the United States. Elsewhere the commitment of a capital sum adequate to a long-term, unified plan of works might require, at the very outset, the grant of a full capital sum or the establishment of some other form of guarantee, in order efficiently to fulfil the entire programme of works.

CHAPTER XIII

INDICES OF PROGRESS

It is clear from the preceding discussion of the activities of the Tennessee Valley Authority that it has considerable achievements to its credit in this first decade of its existence. But its progress cannot be properly appreciated without some understanding of a number of general factors, some of which have contributed to its success, while others have limited its scope. Before stating the record of economic and social advancement, therefore, some attention is directed to these more general factors and particularly to the limitations upon T.V.A. enterprise.

LIMITATIONS ON T.V.A. ENTERPRISE

The T.V.A. operates in the highly developed economic area of the United States of America. This gives it various advantages and subjects it, in a sense, to various disadvantages.

In the first place, the T.V.A. benefits by being able easily to draw on the accumulated knowledge, experience and educated personnel of public and private enterprise and all the institutions of research and training. Again, though it may suffer from railway charges that burden its goods as compared with those of other regions of the nation, at least there are cheap and excellent communications with markets and sources of supply. Furthermore, the T.V.A. operates in a settled country, and is not cut off from its vast economic background by such obstructions as man-made barriers (for example, tariffs) or hampered by natural obstacles (such as jungles, swamps, mountains or insect pests) which stultify economic development in primitive parts of the world. Compared with any authority conducting development works from the beginning in an underdeveloped economy, it enjoys tremendous advantages.

At the same time, however, since the T.V.A. exists in a mature economic society, it is unable to strike out along paths which may seem to it beneficial. It is limited by its Statute; by certain United States constitutional prohibitions; by psychological forces and interests which are expressions of private enterprise. In the prevailing climate of opinion, and having regard to the vested interests in the United States, to have sought to undertake a number of otherwise desirable activities would necessarily have aroused much opposition, and it is important to state clearly some specific things that the T.V.A. has not done nor sought to do before appraising its achievements.

(a) The T.V.A. does not, like commercial concerns, sell the fertiliser it manufactures in the open market, nor seek to produce the quantities to satisfy such a market, although a number of legislators have at various times since 1919 urged that it should do so, and although, judging by the amount of electricity sold to industrial consumers, it has a plentiful surplus of power for such operations after having fulfilled its obligation to give preference to non-profit public agencies and co-operatives. Its fertiliser operations, therefore, beneficial as they are, seem to go beyond the purely experimental, and yet not to reach out for the regional and national economic advantages that might lie in production on a commercial scale.

(b) Rather the same comment applies to T.V.A. experiments and investigations of various minerals and manufacturing and processing methods. It may sell or rent its patent rights; but it does not, either through its own labour forces, or, for instance, through co-operatives, conduct or encourage their local exploitation.

(c) The T.V.A. does not sell electricity below cost. If it had a wider direct responsibility for executing economic plans of its own making as extensive and important as those embodied in Sections 22 and 23 of the Statute, it might very well have chosen to sell less electricity to big industrial consumers and more to rural consumers below cost, even perhaps making free grants for important economic purposes, for example, terracing by power-driven machines, the operation of farming apparatus, or food processing. It sells to the rural consumer at the same prices as to the city consumer, and sometimes the price to the former is even higher by reason of certain surcharges. Can rural rehabilitation and the decentralisation of industry develop as fast as may be desirable in these circumstances?

While it is true that one farm in every six was receiving electric service at the end of 1940 as compared with one in 28 in 1933, it should not be forgotten that there are still five farms out of every six without it. When the Majority Report of the Joint Committee Investigating the T.V.A. asserts that there is no evidence that the preferred consumers have suffered by reason of supplies being sold to industry, the question is raised whether small town and rural productive users could not absorb much more electricity if prices to them were lower.

(*d*)   After a short time the T.V.A. ceased to encourage producers' co-operatives.[1]   There would seem to be substantial scope for
the development of processing, canning, rural crafts and work shops
(for example, in relation to the forestry policy of the T.V.A. and the
woodworking industries) in order to open the way to part-time
employment or opportunities additional to purely agricultural
pursuits.   Such co-operatives have, in many parts of the world[2],
proved to be valuable forms of industrial organisation and particularly responsive to the provision of technical guidance and electric
power.

(*e*)   The T.V.A. has not pursued a policy of acquiring large public
estates for public development.   It has, of course, acquired some
lands, particularly on the margin of the reservoirs, but even in the
latter case it has restricted itself to the minimum and is tending
to reduce its commitments.   It was therefore unable to conduct
certain programmes, for example, the encouragement and organisation of the tourist traffic, and even more, the improvement of forests
and forest management, with the breadth and at the speed which
only public ownership can make possible.

(*f*)   In defining T.V.A. "planning powers" (Sections 22 and 23),
the Statute gave no wide and substantial authority for the "general
purpose of fostering an orderly and proper physical, economic and
social development" of the area, but specified only that such plans
and surveys could be made as "may be useful to the Congress and
the several States".   The President was given power to recommend,
from time to time, legislation for this purpose and, among other
things, for reafforestation and "the economic and social well-being
of the people living in said river basin".   It cannot be said that
there have as yet emanated from the T.V.A. for Presidential and
Congressional consideration any plans of substantial significance in
the sense of these articles, though the services referred to in Chapters V and VI and such reports as those on a phosphatic policy for
the nation and inter-regional freight charges are of great value, as
studies.

Results Achieved

Subject to the foregoing considerations, the T.V.A. has to its
credit some beneficial achievements.   Though it would be valuable
to record the economic and social progress directly attributable to its

---

[1] Cf. *Report of the Joint Committee Investigating the Tennessee Valley Authority*,
in *Hearings*, pp. 1458-1460.

[2] Cf. League of Nations: *Co-operative Action in Rural Life*, Survey Prepared
by the Co-operative Service of the International Labour Office for the Proposed
European Conference on Rural Life, 1939 (Geneva, 1939).

activities arithmetically and unambiguously, this is a very difficult thing to do.

There are three kinds of obstacle to any conclusive appraisal. In the first place, the T.V.A. has existed for barely ten years, and of that time much has been spent in foundation works, the full value of which will accrue only when all are in complete and integrated operation. Thus, all the dams planned and begun are not yet finished, but each additional dam adds a more than proportionate amount to the system's output. Again, the full effect of navigation improvements will only be seen when there is a complete 9-foot system, when terminals have been built, and when all those concerned have become aware of the value of the new means of transport. In the development stage the expenditure is wholly disproportionate to the immediate returns, a fact well known to business promoters; it may be remembered that until 1938 the T.V.A. was "losing" on its power programme. More than this, the first year or two were a time of organisation and preparation, and shortly thereafter T.V.A. efforts were handicapped by legal obstacles. Some features of the scheme require a long time to catch on, but after a deliberate educative process, progress will come cumulatively. The best example of this is the farm demonstration programme.

Hence, the statement of progress to the present, if in terms of immediate statistical records of gain, underrates the contribution of the T.V.A. There are still things in the making, where the work has been and is being done, the foundations have been laid, and the money disbursed, the returns on which will become concrete in a few more years.

Secondly, there are some results which cannot be stated in figures at all, since the figures cannot be gathered. The T.V.A. area is not a closed statistical area like a nation with a guarded and custom-housed frontier over which the corporation exercises the power to command information. The States have this power in some respects; the Federal Government has it in others. But the T.V.A. falls in between. It cannot compel individuals to fill out statistical and other forms. Thus, for example, the T.V.A. cannot gather widespread information about savings or deposits before and since it came; such jurisdiction is in the hands of the other authorities referred to, and is indeed exercised in some respects by the Federal Reserve Bank system, but on a basis which does not at all coincide with the T.V.A. area. Similarly, the T.V.A. cannot verify the effect of its health activities in general, because people move into and out of the T.V.A. portion of the States, and any action by a neighbouring Government agency regarding the gathering of vital statistics is not within the jurisdiction of the

T.V.A. Hence, while some indices of progress are available, others are not, nor can they be deduced from figures collected by other agencies.

Finally, even where the figures are available (for example, regarding the increase in employment since 1933), it is very difficult to segregate the contribution to economic advance of the T.V.A. itself, since the T.V.A. is only one factor among several, and a factor not fully co-ordinated with the existing governmental authorities—Federal, State, county, city, and so forth. Great national, even international, forces may be in operation, of which the T.V.A. becomes an instrument rather than a cause, raising or depressing the welfare of the Valley. The trends of international trade, of domestic investment, of general economic optimism and pessimism, have their influence which affects and screens the effectiveness of the T.V.A. itself. The same applies to the lesser causal effects of the other governmental and social agencies in the Valley. It is well, therefore, that the reader should have in mind the following indices from the United States Statistical Abstract:

Wholesale prices 1926 Average = 100	Farm prices Aug. 1909–July 1914 = 100
1929 — 95.3	1929 — 146
1933 — 65.9	1933 — 70
1934 — 74.9	1934 — 90
1935 — 80.0	1935 — 108
1936 — 80.8	1936 — 114
1937 — 86.3	1937 — 121
1938 — 78.6	1938 — 95
1939 — 77.1	1939 — 93
1940 — 78.6	1940 — 98
1941 — 87.3	1941 — 122

With these warnings in mind, the progress in the Valley since the T.V.A. entered it, may now be appraised with reference to the Authority's various activities.

Electric Power Development

The power operations of the T.V.A. are shown in the table given in an appendix on the basis of the T.V.A.'s own accountancy practice, allocation of costs among the various purposes of the dams, and determination of the items entering into costs.[1] The financial results are very favourable, for electricity revenues now pay not only for electricity operations (including liquidation of debt) but for almost all other T.V.A. activities. In brief, the T.V.A. computes its investment in power facilities (straight line depreciation allowed for)[2] as, roughly, $86 million in 1939, $179 million in 1940, $187

---

[1] Cf. Table in Appendix I. Certain controversial issues arising in this connection are briefly considered in Appendix III.
[2] The most severe method of loading the accounts with charges.

million in 1941, and $250 million in 1942. This means for 1939 a
net return of 1.6 per cent.; for 1940, 2.5 per cent.; for 1941, nearly
4 per cent.; for 1942, 4 per cent.[1]; and for 1943, an estimated 5
per cent.

There are clear benefits from the T.V.A.'s electric power
activities.

The principal benefit is the addition of some 2,000,000 kilowatt
capacity to the already existing resources of the Valley, and the
prospect within two or three years of about 850,000 kilowatts
more. Output was already 6,000 million kilowatt-hours in 1942;
it should be 10,000 million kilowatt-hours in 1944. If this capacity had not been added, and if the existing power companies
had stimulated consumption by T.V.A. methods and at the
T.V.A.'s speed—a hypothesis altogether unlikely, at any rate
as regards speed—consumption might have reached its present
level; but it is more than likely that the amount consumed would
have been generated by steam and not by water power. The hydroelectric capacity would have been wasted; it is now available for
use. When the costs properly attributable to navigation and flood
control are allowed for, the kilowatt-hour production costs much
less than the best competing steam power. There is the long-run
effect, also, that coal is conserved, or may be used for other purposes for which it is indispensable, and is rather cheaper than if
it were still needed for. the competing use. In view of the predicted exhaustion of oil wells in the United States such water
power is an important asset, and in time may even become an
indispensable one.

Secondly, the T.V.A. contributed largely to a rise in the consumption of electricity by residential customers from 55 kilowatt-
hours per month in 1933 to 129 kilowatt-hours in 1944. (The United
States national average was 50 in 1933 and 80 in 1940.) At the
same time, the fall in price meant that by 1942 the average residential customer in the Tennessee Valley was paying 18 per cent.
less for a consumption of 51 per cent. more power as compared
with the United States in general; the fall was from a residential
rate of something like 4 cents and more per kilowatt-hour prevailing in the area to about 2 cents per kilowatt-hour. (The national
average was 3.9 cents per kilowatt-hour.)

Calculated on the basis of what would have had to be paid at
T.V.A. rates for amounts consumed before the introduction of
T.V.A. rates, the estimated annual consumer savings due to the

---

[1] Expenses were greater than normal in 1942, owing to war demands for
power in a year of unusually low-stream flow requiring the use of more expensive
steam-generated power.

T.V.A.'s activities were $9 million a year distributed thus: 36 per cent. to residential customers; 26 per cent. to industrial customers; 35 per cent. to commercial customers; and 3 per cent. to street-lighting customers. Most cities have earned substantial electricity surpluses at the above rates, making it possible to reduce their taxes or give better social services. Thus, in the fiscal year 1941 municipalities and co-operatives earned a combined net income of $4,166,000; in the fiscal year 1942, $3,546,000; the amounts being available for improvement and expansion of the electric systems, retirement of power indebtedness, and the further reduction of taxes, after paying taxes and tax equivalents amounting to 6.54 per cent. and 5.93 per cent. of the power revenues in the two years respectively. Four million dollars is no mean percentage of the total tax revenue of the cities.

Thirdly, the T.V.A. has made cheaper power available for industry, a gain especially important in electro-metallurgical industries. This must mean either cheaper products benefiting the people both inside and outside the Valley, or more wages or more profits (or both); and in either of the latter two cases it cannot fail to result in increased purchasing power on the part of those connected with the industries.

Fourthly, the T.V.A. has brought electric light and power to the farms. Thus, from one farm in 28 with electric service in 1933, there has been a rise to one in six; and the rates are the same as for the cities. The increase has been about fourfold in Tennessee compared with less than double in the whole of the United States. The consequences are that productive activities have been made easier, with a saving of labour and time, and some of the processes and appliances have made it possible to use resources which were wasted before; for example, hay which could not be naturally dried, or sweet potatoes which could not be cured by the stove method; and to preserve farm produce hitherto wasted, such as meat, fruit, vegetables and butter. It can be imagined what this development, when fully exploited, would mean to the Tennessee Valley (and to other countries where terrain or climate make production difficult or the preservation of perishable foods almost impossible), if these appliances, instead of being used by only a small proportion of the farmers, came to be the staple of farm economy. A survey of work methods in all but a few countries of the world shows that by far the majority of mankind, especially in rural areas, are still beasts of burden. Electrical devices offer the opportunity of lightening this toil, and of converting a hand-to-mouth economy, which is a low-standard economy, into a more roundabout process in which the goods produced can be put on a timetable of consumption because in the meanwhile they can be preserved for consumption or marketing.

Electrification of the farms has thus contributed to nutrition improvement. It has also contributed to the farm demonstration programme, which again will have its effects on diet. Moreover, it has added a new social value to rural life, and introduced a factor which to some extent may counteract the drift to the towns. The purchases of electrical apparatus in the T.V.A. area shown in the following table are not entirely or chiefly rural, but they reflect both rural and urban equipment with labour-saving and productive inventions and amenities:

Fiscal year	Sales of electricity appliances, domestic retail price
1938	1,612,000
1939	3,688,000
1940	12,500,000[a]
1941	18,500,000

[a] Sales in the United States in 1940 were $32 per residential customer compared with $46 dollars per residential customer in the T.V.A. area.

Finally, T.V.A. electric policy has acted as a stimulus to the lowering of electricity rates by other agencies in the Valley and outside, as the following table shows:

Electric system	Average rate per kwh. cents					
	1933	1937	1938	1939	1940	1941
U.S. entire industry	5.49	4.39	4.14	4.00	3.84	3.73
Alabama Power Co.	4.62	2.97	2.85	2.76	2.70	2.73
Birmingham Electric Co.	5.92	3.74	3.45	3.23	2.77	2.75
Georgia Power Co.	5.16	3.04	2.93	2.84	2.74	2.74
Kentucky Utilities Co.	6.25	5.05	5.01	4.92	4.64	4.41
Louisville Gas & Electric Co.	5.68	3.77	3.71	3.54	3.28	3.10
Tennessee Valley Authority.	—	1.83	1.95	2.16	2.06	2.05

Navigation Benefits

The development of the river is not yet complete. On completion of the scheme in 1944 there will be a minimum 9-foot draught and the whole Valley will be linked with the great inland waterway system going as far afield as the Great Lakes and the Gulf of Mexico. So far, the T.V.A. has made available a continuous and commercially useful channel 464 miles long from the mouth of the Tennessee to Chattanooga.

Yet even with this incomplete system river traffic is increasing. These are the figures:

TRAFFIC ON THE TENNESSEE RIVER, 1928–1941

Calendar year	Total million tons	Total million ton-miles	Forest products	Petroleum products	Grain	Pig iron	Auto-mobiles
	Totals		Selected commodities *in tons*				
1928	2.17	46.40	228,738	—	—	26,000	
1929	2.04	38.40	197,341	—	—	31,000	—
1930	2.46	46.70	200,832	—	—	—	—
1931	1.24	27.70	94,975	—	—	—	—
1932	.74	16.34	60,566	—	—	—	—
1933	.94	32.65	84,855	—	—	—	—
1934	1.49	43.15	103,222	—	—	—	—
1935	1.89	69.40	111,042	—	—	—	—
1936	2.16	66.40	171,010	—	—	—	—·
1937	1.37	55.33	209,943	—	—	—	—
1938	1.06	55.68	131,859	62,568	—	—	—
1939	1.11	91.31	128,219	103,201	6,001	2,262	—
1940c	2.16	97.42	141,699	90,967	43,140	12,832	175a
1941c	3.09	138.40	166,880	115,375	85,232	16,608	6,180b

a Represents approximately 130 automobiles.
b Represents approximately 4,100 automobiles.
c Preliminary.

This shows a fall in traffic between 1930 and 1939 due, in large part, to the general economic depression, but thereafter a sharp rise in ton-mileage, due in part to the lifting of the depression but also to the improvement of the river channel. There is at present a degree of traffic ascribable directly to the war. Yet, since until the outbreak of the war the trend of traffic in ton-miles was upwards, a permanent benefit may be conceded. Working on a conservative basis, and after a widespread survey, the T.V.A. has estimated an upward trend which in 1945 (the first full year after the improvement is completed) will reach 2,600,000 tons, or over twice the present non-Government movements on the river; and in 1960, 6,173,000 tons. The T.V.A. also estimates savings to those who use the river now at $3,450,000 in 1945 and annually on that basis; and when the river is used on the 1960 basis, at $8,000,000. These developments are postulated on the building of terminals, the establishment of common carrier services, the establishment of truck barge rates, and the growth of the shipment of very miscellaneous cargoes into and out of the Valley.

Flood Control Benefits

To an area afflicted by large and small floods, the T.V.A. has brought a sense of security and relief from damage. So far as can humanly be foreseen, the flood control programme has eliminated the risk of flood; its capitalised value to the alluvial valley of the Mississippi is calculated at some $200 million. Chattanooga can be spared occasional annual damage of some $1 million a year. Besides this, the T.V.A.'s contribution has saved lives, and has averted the stoppage of current business and other activity during floods, and the waste of time and material by many public agencies in taking remedial and rescue measures.

Farm Demonstration Benefits

The number of farms affected by T.V.A. demonstrations in 1942 inside and outside the Valley was some 27,000. The number of farms within the Valley was 23,000. The number of acres concerned in the Valley was nearly 3,300,000, equivalent to one in four of the total farm acreage. If the improvements accomplished on these farms had been all that the T.V.A. intended, they would already have represented a substantial improvement in the standard of living of the Valley; but, as already explained, the farms are demonstrations, and have affected farm methods among neighbours. There is no estimate of the numbers indirectly affected, but some indication of indirect value is shown by the fact that in Alabama about 24,000 farmers visited 81 demonstration farms in a 3-year period.

Detailed results are not yet available on a comprehensive enough basis, but sample studies have been made of which some illustrations are given in Appendix I. They indicate highly favourable trends in all the States. Thus, since 1934, there has been on the demonstration farms quite a substantial decrease in the land left idle and that formerly devoted to destructive crops like corn and cotton. There has been an increase in hay and pasture acreage and in the number and quality of livestock and poultry. A considerable rise in milk and egg production has followed, leading, in Alabama, to the installation of cheese and butter-making plants. A very large advance is noticeable in the per acre yield of cover crops, of hay, and in the saving of seed. Particularly valuable has been the increase in winter legume cultivation. In some cases it is apparent that the chief benefits are yet to come, for many farms have preferred to reduce their cash crops and undertake soil conserving practices which are certain to result in more considerable production and cash crops than before.

Forestry and Fishery Prospects

The T.V.A. has caused the planting of some 150 million trees. Some of these are for timber, others for their crops. Some have been planted with special concern for the arrest of soil erosion and the consequent prevention of the silting up of the river and the reservoirs.

It cannot yet be estimated with accuracy how much silting has been avoided by the plantings, since observations over many years will be needed to verify predictions. It will also be some decades before the improved crop-bearing trees show results, and with them their effects upon local diet and the improvement of livestock.

As for the growth of timber for industrial purposes and uses, here again the full measure of benefit is a matter of the future. But since there is a calculable relationship between trees cut down and planted, it can already be said that the alarming waste of the pre-T.V.A. days has been arrested (although war needs have speeded use abnormally) and that it is clearly foreseeable that the area will once again be a tree-bearing district with an increasing number of trees, based upon a proper timber economy.

If the measures proposed and stimulated by the T.V.A. are carried out, then according to T.V.A. estimates the number of people employed in wood industries will in the course of time be increased from 72,000 to 150,000 and the earnings from these industries will rise from $51 million to $200 million.

It will be realised from what has already been said on forestry prospects that where a development agency is concerned with resources, the growth or the maturity of which (as in the farm demonstration scheme) must depend upon nature, the results of the development plans can only be seen in the span of time which nature imposes. In the present case this span is the time required for the maturity of trees, and the task of the Authority is rather to clear away the obstacles to their planting and natural growth, and to plan for the utilisation of the products as they become available. This takes time.

The average loss of timber by forest fires in the Valley has equalled an area of some 700,000 acres per year, or 5 per cent. of the total forest cover, being equivalent to a total burning every 20 years. Although there is not at present any definite indication of progress in this field, it is expected that the T.V.A. educational and administrative activity will help to reduce this waste in due course.

T.V.A. research and stimulation of attention to fisheries in the river, the sorting out of rough fish and stocking with improved varieties has already brought some addition to the Valley's welfare and is certain to increase this very largely. In 1940, 5 million pounds of fish were taken in five T.V.A. reservoirs.

Benefits from Industrial and other Processes

The processes and equipment for farm and other use produced by the efforts of the T.V.A. were described in the chapters on the advancement of economic opportunity and the people's social well-being, but the benefits may here be summed up in words, if not in figures.

(1) Some resources have been discovered, especially a number of minerals which, with the improvement of technology and contemporary industrial demand, are sure to be of economic benefit to the region and the nation. Among these are: china clay, aluminium-bearing clays, vermiculite, mica, etc.

(2) The T.V.A. has demonstrated the economic availability and use of certain resources, for instance, the processing of clay for porcelain and the processing of cottonseed.

(3) The T.V.A. has demonstrated processes to preserve foods for home use or shipment by freezing or preserving fruit and vegetables, by dehydration, and by refrigeration (community refrigerators, etc.). These processes may have a very great effect upon the economy of the area when they are fully developed. Hitherto, some of the products have been wasted as a result of weather conditions and because of the lack of transport facilities at economical rates. Others, again, have been sent out of the area to be processed elsewhere. The processing will save much of the expense of transport and the waste by spoiling, thus encouraging farm methods more diversified than before, to include cultivation of the hitherto non-storable products.

(4) The T.V.A. has invented or adopted special apparatus, instrumental to agricultural processes, such as the cottonseed cooker, furrower, the seed harvester, the hay dryer, the tobacco dryer, the ham curer, the corn shucker. Its work in this respect has consisted largely in adapting known instruments to the kind of agricultural conditions prevalent in the Valley and to the small cash income of its farmers. By its blueprints it has enabled farmers to make the apparatus; while private manufacturers are already producing equipment on the basis of its designs.

(5) In connection with some of these processes and instruments there are patent rights. Hitherto, the amount annually obtained by the T.V.A. for the use of these rights has been small; but in terms of long-range policy the T.V.A. aims at getting the inventions used rather than making a money revenue from their use.

Employment Opportunity and General Welfare

In discussing the employment opportunities created by the T.V.A.'s activities, the direct employment provided by the T.V.A. itself since it began operations cannot be left out of account. The T.V.A.'s own labour force rose from 7,114 in July 1934 to a peak of 41,211 in July 1942, and was 33,759 in January 1943.

The development of electricity distribution in the co-operatives and the cities has added additional employment opportunities to those existing before. It is true that the T.V.A. system is coincident with the area of operation of the former power companies, and that the major effect has been rather the transfer of management. But the total consumption and number of consumers have increased and there has been a consequent increase in the numbers serving them, and though the exact comparative figures are unobtainable an appreciable increase in employment in the electricity supply trade must also be assumed.

A number of people throughout the United States have also had employment since 1933 producing equipment and raw material used in the construction of the dams, the cement, the cables, the transmission lines, turbines, shovels, concrete mixers, steel sheeting, and all ancillary apparatus. This number cannot be determined, but may be surmised from the figures of T.V.A. annual purchases of materials. Thus, the T.V.A. has spent an annual average of $20 million on materials. Assuming that 70 per cent. of this went to labour, then at $1,500 per year some 10,000 persons would have been employed. A large part of this gain is due to the T.V.A.'s development efforts, even supposing that in its absence others might have done the job.

There has, further, been a perceptible growth of industry in the Valley. The industries which show an increase from 1930 to 1940 in the T.V.A. public power area are: forestry and fishing, construction woodworking, paper, chemicals, textiles and rayon, hosiery, garments, shoes, upholstering, aluminium, food products and public utilities. There has been a decrease in iron and steel. Besides this, there has been an increase in employment in relation to trade, finance, and professional occupations. The extent of increase in urban population and employment in the various industries may be seen in the table opposite from the United States census.

Another measure of industrial activity is provided by the increase of wage earners and their wages and the value added by manufacturing. This is shown for 1929, 1935 and 1939, as follows:

MEASURES OF INDUSTRIAL ACTIVITY, 1929, 1935 AND 1939
T.V.A. PUBLIC POWER AREA

	1929	1935	1939
Wage earners (thousands)	136.4	124.6	147.4
Wages (millions)	$112.4	$ 84.7	$113.8
Value added by manufacturing (millions)	$327.1	$228.5	$316.3

Source: *Census of Manufacturers.*

Again, these data may be set out in a different form in order to give comparison with trends in the seven Valley States and in the United States as a whole.

DISTRIBUTION OF POPULATION, AND DISTRIBUTION OF EMPLOYMENT IN SELECTED CLASSIFICATIONS, 1930 AND 1940, T.V.A. PUBLIC POWER AREA (145 COUNTIES)

(in thousands)

Distribution	1930	1940	Power area	Seven Valley States	United States
			Per cent. change, 1930-40		
Population					
Total:	*3,670.1*	*4,036.8*	*10.0*	*9.6*	*7.2*
Rural farm	2,028.9	2,086.9	2.9	2.5	0.2
Rural non-farm ...	667.5	812.6	21.8	15.9	14.2
Urban: Total.....	973.7	1,137.3	16.8	16.9	7.9
2,500-10,000 ...	269.3	300.3	11.5	18.6	10.3
10,000-100,000 ...	71.8	136.9	90.7	18.4	12.3
100,000 and over ..	632.6	700.1	10.7	13.7	4.6
Employment					
Forestry and fishing....	29.1	31.7	9.0	11.6	
Extraction of minerals..	17.3	16.4	−5.6	−4.0	
Construction	38.1	54.1	42.0	28.8	
Manufacturing: Total..	*155.5*	*164.5*	*5.8.*	*8.3*	
Woodworking	9.1	9.6	5.7	11.0	
Paper	6.7	10.1	49.6	56.5	
Chemicals	10.4	12.3	17.8	16.1	
Iron and steel	23.1	13.9	−40.1	−47.8	
Textiles and apparel..	47.8	68.0	42.4	47.3	
Food products	12.6	17.6	39.7	51.9	
Public utilities	57.3	58.6	2.2	0.3	
Trade	158.7	175.7	10.7	13.6	
Finance	18.4	20.1	9.3	10.6	
Professional	55.5	66.7	20.1	18.6	

Source: *Census of Population*, 1930 and 1940.

COMPARISON OF TRENDS IN MEASURES OF INDUSTRIAL ACTIVITY IN THE T.V.A. PUBLIC POWER AREA (145 COUNTIES), SEVEN VALLEY STATES, AND THE UNITED STATES

(1929 = 100)

Subject	Power area		Seven Valley States		United States	
	1935	1939	1935	1939	1935	1939
Wage earners	91	108	93	114	86	94
Wages	75	101	82	109	67	84
Value added by manufacturing	70	97	65	95	62	81

Some indication of increasing welfare is discernible in the business statistics, that is, sales and receipts of retail and service establishments, although the warning given earlier regarding changes in the price level and the effect of the great nation-wide causes of prosperity or depression must of course be borne in mind. The comparison between the power area, the seven Valley States and the United States figures shows the power area substantially better off than the Valley States and considerably better off than the whole nation.

Since over one half of the State of Tennessee lies inside the T.V.A. area, incomes in Tennessee in the years 1929 to 1941 compared with those of the United States as a whole may be regarded as especially significant in showing a favourable trend. From the standpoint of family income the trend is even more favourable than for the per capita income, since the size of the Tennessee Valley family unit is greater than in the United States in general.

PER CAPITA INCOME PAYMENTS IN ALABAMA, MISSISSIPPI, TENNESSEE, AND IN THE UNITED STATES, 1933 AND 1940

Area	Per capita income		
	1933 (dollars)	1940 (dollars)	Per cent. increase, 1933–40
United States	368	579	57
Three States	149	274	84
Alabama	139	268	93
Mississippi	121	220	82
Tennessee	181	320	77

Source: UNITED STATES DEPARTMENT OF COMMERCE: *Survey of Current Business*, July 1942. Estimates of 1933 population used in computing the 1933 per capita income were taken from *Statistical Abstract of the United States*, 1939.

Perhaps some further indication of increasing welfare, as resulting from the combined power, industrial and agricultural improvements, or at least an increasing confidence in its advent, may be seen in two indices: (a) the fairly sharp rise in new dwelling units, and (b) increased sales and receipts. Between 1935 and 1940, the number of new dwelling units construction as a percentage of the total existing in 1940 was nearly 13 per cent; "urban construction" was 7.2 per cent., "rural non-farm" was 20.5 per cent. and "rural farm" was 13.2 per cent. of the total units in their respective categories. These figures are for the T.V.A. Public Power Area.[1] In sales and receipts the T.V.A. Power Area shows a much more marked rise between 1933 and 1939 than the United States as a whole and the seven Valley States:

[1] *Census of Housing*, 1940, Vol. II.

SALES AND RECEIPTS OF RETAIL AND SERVICE ESTABLISHMENTS,
T.V.A. PUBLIC POWER AREA (145 COUNTIES), SEVEN VALLEY
STATES AND UNITED STATES, 1933 AND 1939
(in thousands)

Region	Total 1933	Total 1939	Per capita 1939	Per cent. change, 1933-1939
Power area	$ 408,435	$ 762,321	$189	86.6
Seven Valley States	2,207,410	3,992,947	198	80.9
United States	26,762,339	45,462,207	345	69.9

Source: *Census of Business.*

The increase in the tourist traffic since the opening of the dams and the installation of recreation facilities should also be counted into the employment opportunities and money turnover. On this it is possible to offer only some arithmetical surmises of the benefit accruing to the Valley. Thus, there has been a stream of visitors to the T.V.A. dams. Registration is not required at all dams, but conservative estimates count these at an average of about one million a year, although since 1937 the numbers have been one and a half million rising to over two million in 1940. According to figures of the United States Travel Bureau, North Carolina received $100 million and Tennessee $81 million from recreation travellers in 1938. Not all of this came to the Tennessee Valley parts of the State, and by no means all can be attributed to the T.V.A. programme. Further, no figures are available from the portions of the other five States falling in the T.V.A. area. But the figures given are an indication of the magnitude of the T.V.A.'s recreational value and of what may be expected when the chain of lakes, the mountains and forests are fully prepared to receive visitors and tourists. It is estimated that recreation travellers in Knoxville in 1939 spent an average of $4 a day per head; and Knoxville's income from recreation travellers in that year was estimated at $3 million. Fishermen spent variably $6 a day. Sporting equipment is being sold much more substantially; fishing tackle and boats, for example. In 1934 there were two small boat-building and repair shops in Knoxville; in 1939 there were nine.

Population and Health

Migration.

It has been noted that the Tennessee Valley was an area of emigration, which would to some extent imply that its younger people were seeking opportunity outside the region. Though it is impossible to isolate figures for the Valley itself, a related computation shows a slowing down of this trend. The figures for Tennessee are more significant than the others, if it is recalled that by far the largest portion of the Valley lies in Tennessee, and that the major operations of the T.V.A. occur in there. The decline in migration from the State in the decade 1930-40 over that of 1920-30 is shown in the following table. From 1920 to 1930 altogether 120,000 (net) migrated from Tennessee; between 1930 and 1940 the figure declined to 31,000.

ESTIMATED NET CIVILIAN MIGRATION IN RELATION TO POPULATION,
1920 TO 1930, AND 1930 TO 1940

Region	Average number of migrants per year		Average yearly migration rate	
	1920-1930	1930-1940	1920-1930	1930-1940
Virginia	23,600	900	1.0	—
North Carolina	1,000	10,000	—	0.3
Georgia	41,900	14,800	1.5	0.5
Kentucky	20,800	11,600	0.8	0.4
Tennessee	12,000	3,100	0.5	0.1
Alabama	15,300	19,800	0.6	0.7
Mississippi	10,500	8,100	0.5	0.4

Source: Henry S. Shryock, Jr., Bureau of the Census: "Internal Migration and the War", in *Journal of the American Statistical Association*, p. 20.

Health.

For reasons given earlier in this chapter it is not possible to offer any statistics to show the effect of T.V.A. activities on the health of the area. The general judgment of those concerned, and of the civic bodies, is that health has at least been maintained; and that, in particular, the measures taken against malaria have prevented any increase in the disease in the face of a grave additional threat.

Recreation.

The T.V.A. has brought to the Valley the opportunity of outdoor recreation and some figures of the extent to which its facilities have been used indicate an increase in welfare from this cause. This does not show itself in monetary terms, as the facilities are free, though it 'is partly reflected in the increased turnover in the sales and receipts of retail and service establishments and in receipts from tourists. Rather is it reflected in the direct benefit that comes from the many outdoor activities made possible by the lakes, and parks built by the T.V.A., or by the States under its stimulus, and the care for scenic opportunities, roads and other facilities for access to them.

Social Gains

How the T.V.A. fosters better educational opportunities, library service, job training, apprenticeship and rural education has already been described. These and its other activities have been conducted in a scientific, humane and up-to-date spirit, and through democratic institutions. It has consciously sought to make clear the meaning of the integrated development of resources to the people of the region and the potential value of such development in raising their standard of living. It has vivified interest in the Valley, and given hopes to the local population. It has contributed to turning the people's attention to the local government institutions of the area by its local government studies and has stimulated the universities by posing problems, suggesting and co-operating in research, and in some cases (for example, in public health) making grants in aid of their work. In an age when social and economic welfare is bound to depend more than ever on the science and art of administration, that is, the organisation, management and application of employees and skill to achieve a collective end without waste of effort and material, the T.V.A., by the conscious planning of its activities and methods, has been a notable experimental model, and its successes have been invaluable demonstrations.

Although it is in the nature of things as yet impossible conclusively to demonstrate in figures the impact of the T.V.A. on every aspect of the Valley's progress, the general feeling of the population cannot be omitted as evidence of improvement. When the T.V.A. entered the Valley, it was met, as it were, by a large question mark. That question mark dwindled under the influence of the farm demonstration programme and of much reduced bills for electricity service. As the full breadth of the T.V.A.'s multi-purpose programme became clearer, and each branch of its benefits became more manifest to the public in practical development, the question mark was replaced by a note of enthusiasm and of co-proprietorship. A very large proportion of the population now talk of "our dams" and "our T.V.A." with pride. The people of the Valley, individually and through their many civic organisations, now believe that their welfare has been increased, that it will be further increased, and that the cause is the T.V.A., and they look with disapproval on any measures which would seem to diminish the powers and strength of the T.V.A. It would be a mistake to ignore testimony of so widespread and steady a nature.

CHAPTER XIV

THE PROBLEM OF AN INTERNATIONAL T.V.A.

THE T.V.A. AS A MODEL

This examination of the functions and operation of the T.V.A. was undertaken for two reasons: to record an experience valuable to those generally interested in the possibilities and conduct of public development works, and, more especially, to distinguish the problems facing an international agency seeking to assist the development of the resources of underdeveloped countries. In the Introduction attention was drawn to the growth of opinion favourable to the establishment of such an agency. The purpose of such an institution—an international resources development authority[1]— would presumably be to contribute to raising the standard of living in underdeveloped countries by means of long-term credits and technical assistance which would foster economic enterprise. In some degree, which would have to be the object of serious enquiry, financial assistance and administrative support of these enterprises would come under the general good offices of such an international agency.

From the facts presented in the body of the study may be deduced the implications of the T.V.A. for international action, and the possible alternative solutions can be appraised. But no demonstration model can be regarded as suitable for adoption in every identical feature by other countries, or even in other areas of the same country, in the expectation that identical results will follow. The T.V.A. is not transplantable without reservations and qualifications; its characteristics merely help to bring out the problems and to suggest alternative solutions.

---

[1] On 24 November 1943 the United States Treasury published a proposal for the establishment of an international bank of reconstruction and development. The "Bank of Reconstruction and Development of the United and Associated Nations" would provide for the establishment of a fund of 10,000 million dollars to be used for collaboration with, and as a supplement to, private long-term investment for the purpose of stimulating the development of productive resources of underdeveloped countries; the fund is to be used either as guarantees of private investment or as direct loans made by the Bank where the borrower has failed to obtain credits from private sources on reasonable terms.

THE VALUE OF DEVELOPMENT SCHEMES

The cardinal feature of the T.V.A. is that it was deliberately established and given responsibility for the welfare of an underdeveloped area.

It was the answer to a complex of economic and social problems, which involved the relationship between a nation and one of its regions, poverty-stricken, but with resources capable of development.[1] National authorities felt that the welfare of any region of the United States was an important contribution to the whole nation, and were convinced that the particular area's own latent wealth should be promoted. The feeling, expressed in the conservation movement, had long been growing that the resources belonged to all the people who made up the U.S.A.; and that this implied the responsibility of all for the development of such resources in whatever area they existed. That the Valley should be ignored and the scope and pace of development set entirely by private enterprise was ruled out.

With this evolution of the T.V.A. in mind, it may be asked whether the richer nations of the world recognise the value to world economy of international assistance to the underdeveloped areas within it. The world is full, as the Tennessee Valley was full, of as yet unexploited or not fully exploited industrial opportunities and the auxiliary transport and distributive facilities. There are mineral resources, agricultural possibilities, and underemployed labour power all over the world awaiting utilisation. There are rivers and canal systems, railway systems, roads, harbours, dock facilities, power resources, and, particularly in our own day, air transport arrangements, awaiting full development.[2] As with the T.V.A., the international problem is not merely one of the discovery and exploitation of resources, but of making them available.[3] As the T.V.A. has proved valuable, instead of harmful, to the whole of the United States of America, international development works may play the same part in the world economy at large.

A very serious problem, among the several which led to the establishment of the T.V.A., was the need to provide employment. It was thought there would be direct opportunities of employment on the construction job itself and that substantial orders for con-

---

[1] Cf. Chapter I.

[2] It has been calculated that two thirds of the world's total output of wealth, that is, economic goods and services, are produced in the industrial countries containing less than one third of the world's population; and that about a half of the world's total production is provided in four countries. Cf. Colin CLARK: *Conditions of Economic Progress* (London, Macmillan, 1940), pp. 2 and 3.

[3] Cf. Chapter V.

struction and operating equipment would support employment in the industries providing it. After the T.V.A. was started the problem was how to use the developed resources to increase the opportunities and profitability of labour and so raise the standard of living.

MIGRATION OF WORKERS OR MIGRATION OF CAPITAL?

One of the results of the stagnation of agriculture and industry in the Tennessee Valley was a steady migration from there to other parts of the United States. The T.V.A. was itself faced with the problem of improving the land of the Valley, assisting the re-located families into new homes, and applying better farm prac-tices or assisting families to settle outside the Valley. Without better land to go to and a knowledge of better methods of farming it was no use taking the second course. Such a course was also regarded as defeatist, since it was believed that the land could be developed and the family made more prosperous; and indeed, side by side with the T.V.A., there was the action of the Farm Security Administration and the Farm Credit Administration, the first assisting the poorer farmers by loans, grants and guidance, and the second by credits.[1] Migration is, of course, a possible, but a difficult solution for the problem of people who live in underdeveloped areas; but, whereas migration to areas of better opportunity in the United States of America was open to the inhabitants of the Ten-nessee Valley because the whole territory was one area of common citizenship, such action is not so simple on a world scale for would-be migrants from underdeveloped countries to countries which will afford them greater opportunities. If peoples in the less developed countries are denied the alternative open to the people of the Tennessee Valley, then Governments may be more easily persuaded to furnish credits and technical assistance.

The T.V.A. is an attempt at intensive cultivation of a particular area now that (as the economists affirm[2]) "extensive" development

---

[1] Cf. Chapter IV.

[2] For example, HANSEN: *Fiscal Policy and Business Cycles*, 1941, Chapter XVI; Temporary National Economic Committee in *Hearings*, Part 9; and *ibid.*, CURRIE, pp. 3520 *et seq.*, where it is argued that the economic opportunities for investment available in the 19th century were the consequence of there being vast uncultivated or semi-cultivated areas and great demand for goods by an increasing population. More recently, it is argued, the basic capital installa-tions—mines, railways, factories, telecommunications, etc., have been provided and required, not total replacement, but only maintenance, repair and improve-ment. Even such improvement, it is argued, gives more productive results with less capital outlay than before. Hence, economic expansion is to be sought by more intensive cultivation, industrial and otherwise, of the opportunities still remaining. Even then it is thought difficult to discover ways of using all the natural savings and feared that in default of a comprehensive fiscal policy some of the savings may be simply sterilised by hoarding.

over the whole country has already established a mature economic structure. Development by the T.V.A. offered a further outlet for the constantly increasing savings of the community, and served, moreover, as a means for the transfer of capital goods from the more to the less developed areas of the U.S.A. Attention may also be drawn to the principle on which the Electric Home and Farm Authority, connected with the T.V.A., operated. The United States Government guaranteed credits (that is, somebody's savings) to dealers in electric apparatus who, in turn, could stimulate sales by granting credit to purchasers of the equipment. The U.S. Government thus, in effect, gave the purchasers of apparatus time in which to save to pay, and contributed to employment opportunities in the electrical apparatus industries.

PUBLIC SUPPLEMENTS TO PRIVATE INVESTMENT IN THE TENNESSEE VALLEY

The usual private channels of investment were, in the case of the T.V.A., unable to supply the capital—600 million dollars— a period long enough to achieve results. In terms well known to readers of *The Wealth of Nations*[1], the problem was not soluble except by deliberate unified planned provision. A large investment had been made in the area by the electric utilities, but that did not at all touch the question of establishing the works necessary to improve navigation, control floods, develop the hydroelectric possibilities, cope with soil erosion, confront the problem of reafforestation, take the risks of encouraging rural electrification, and plan the development of the mineral production and processing work of the area. Mr. Henry Ford's bids for purchase and lease at Muscle Shoals were found unsatisfactory for two instructive reasons: some legislators thought the entrepreneur's reward was an excessive share of the resources to be developed, and others were uncertain whether, even if a single entrepreneur in his own lifetime could successfully conduct the exploitation of such mighty resources, it would be wise to trust to the ability of unknown successors.

WHICH RESOURCES?

The United States Government could have chosen to pay no special attention to the Tennessee Valley at all, and to promote

---

[1] Book IV, Chapter IX. "According to the system of natural liberty the sovereign has only three duties to attend to; three duties of great importance indeed, but plain and intelligible to the common understanding . . . and thirdly, the duty of erecting and maintaining certain public works and certain public institutions which it can never be for the interest of any individual or small number of individuals to erect and maintain; because the profit could never repay the expense to any individual or small number of individuals, though it may frequently do much more than repay it to a great society."

experiments in the manufacture of fertiliser through the United States Department of Agriculture and conduct farm demonstrations all over the country. In the matter of hydroelectric development, the U.S. Government gave priorities to developments in various other parts of the United States. An international agency would have a wide latitude of choice among resources calling for development and since there would still be private investment it could develop its own most useful line among a generous number of alternatives. The choice of the Tennessee Valley was a major political decision taken in response to a number of forces and interests, to benefit both the Valley and the whole country. So, in the case of any development scheme which an international agency might consider, there would be the problem of adjustment between the interests of the lending and the recipient countries. Some resources are complementary to industries already in existence in other parts of the world or in the recipient nations, as for example, rubber which is being produced in Brazil or tung oil in China. The opening up of roads, railways, harbours, docks or airports frees the way to wider markets and reduces the waste connected with the attempts of producer and consumer to make contact with each other. The provision of electric power might be an important boon not only to the countries where it may be generated but to the countries which possess fuel resources that are expendable, like oil, since it lessens the competitive demand for them. Development might, in some cases, involve adjustment in the industrial activities of the contributing countries. For example, in the early history of the T.V.A., coal mining interests and coal miners were perturbed at the extension of the area in which the T.V.A. conducted hydroelectric power operations. Such problems are capable of solution in a variety of ways, but the ways need to be studied and applied.[1]

MULTI-PURPOSE AUTHORITY?

The T.V.A. is a multi-purpose authority, that is, it develops simultaneously a number of naturally related resources. This may or may not be possible elsewhere. No slavish search for precisely what the T.V.A. offers could be commended; still less any restriction to its scope. Each case has its own economic and social merits and difficulties. In the T.V.A.'s case, there was an obvious economic advantage in joint exploitation of the water resources in relation to a number of regional needs. Elsewhere, a single purpose—for example, merely processing milk—might be enough; or, for all

---

[1] Cf. Eugene STALEY: *World Economic Development*, Studies and Reports, Series B (Economic Conditions), No. 36 (International Labour Office, Montreal, 1944), p. 185-199.

Europe, it might be the building and operation of a high-tension electric grid, dependent upon water power (Alps), oil (Rumania), and coal (elsewhere)[1]; or an international sponsor might think it advantageous to attempt the integral and total development of all the resources of an area, on a scale that went beyond that of the T.V.A. This is indeed, what the Chilean Development Corporation does.

THE AREA OF DEVELOPMENT

In an early chapter attention was drawn to the character of the area entrusted to the T.V.A., and it was observed that areas of development, whether financed nationally or internationally, need not be restricted to valleys, although mention has been made of the Danube, Yangtze, and the Jordan Valleys. It happens that in the case of the T.V.A., the resource to be developed was a river, and therefore the watershed was an area which could be delimited for special attention. However, it was observed in the first place that the river was part of a vast inland water transport system some five thousand miles in size. On the other hand, some of the activities of the T.V.A., for example, farm demonstration, experiments in the manufacture of phosphatic fertiliser, soil surveys, etc., were objects not necessarily bound by the physical features of the Valley, and administrable, perhaps even more effectively, over the whole of the United States. The important lesson to be learned from the regional aspect of the T.V.A. is that existing political divisions of the world and their frontiers, whether States or their subdivisions, are not self-sufficient economic units. For resource development the proper area may be less than a square mile (a mine), or it may embrace a whole continent (for transport or power). The character of the resource is the key to the character of the area of development, and since the world's resources are multifarious, so the regions to be developed are multifarious in character. But that is not all. It has already been observed that the choice of that particular Valley, and of a *valley*, was not based solely upon a geological construction, but was a major political decision designed to satisfy a variety of extra-Valley economic interests. The problem involved is the relationship between such a region and the national or world economy of which it is a part.

A RESOURCES SURVEY

The selection of the regions and the resources whose development is to be assisted raises the question of contemporary know-

---

[1] Cf. World Power Conference: Gesamtbericht, Band xix, *Europa's Grosskraftlinien*, by Dr. E. Oskar OLIVEN (Berlin, 1930).

ledge of these resources. It was earlier noticed that until the T.V.A.
set to work with a specific responsibility for the welfare of its region,
several of the Valley's resources had never been persistently and
scientifically investigated in the hope of rendering them available
for use. It may be thought that our knowledge of the resources
of the world is by this time complete. The truth is far otherwise.
Some areas have been very thoroughly prospected and certain
resources, such as oil and tin, have been searched for all over the
world. Their existence and reserves have become well known
through individual owners, financially interested companies or the
scientific departments of Governments. But a very large part of
the mineral, water power and soil resources of the world are actually
unknown.[1] Nor is that all. Where they are known, often only
casual and quite superficial attention has so far been given to their
exploitation. Modern scientific methods and new facilities, like
modern machinery and communications, especially air transport,
might well make them easily available to the world economy as
well as to the country where they are found. The T.V.A. has shown
that a really determined, persistent, intensive search can reveal
unsuspected values. Even if the resources so discovered could not
be initially as productive as similar resources already on the market,
they might still be of more value than the present economic products of the people concerned: to take a purely hypothetical example, new timber occupations might at first be less productive than
the timber industries of other regions already exploited, but though
the labour costs in the new occupations might be higher until industrial techniques have been mastered and the economies of large-
scale production achieved, it is better to have those occupations
rather than the involuntary unemployment which the people of
the region would suffer, if they had no chance of migration on an
economic basis, and if the resources were not exploited.

A geological power and soil survey for all countries which are
underdeveloped would form a "Domesday Book" of existing resources, and make available data on which decisions upon development and priority could be based. Such a world survey might be
undertaken by international action. But it is important that any pros-
pecting authority like the T.V.A. should not suggest the appearance
of the commercial prospector who has been rather too well-known
to countries in need of development. Since economic circumstances
and values are always in a state of change, any survey should be
continuous and should periodically re-assess the resources of various

---

[1] Cf. Canadian House of Commons, Special Committee on Reconstruction and
Re-establishment, *Interim Report, Minutes of Proceedings and Evidence*, No. 23,
pp. iii-v.

countries in relation to their own economic situation and that of the world in general.

PROVISION OF UNIFIED DEVELOPMENT PLANS

An important lesson of the T.V.A. is that whatever the nature of the development or planning agencies in the separate countries, any country seeking international assistance should first furnish a comprehensive scheme of development. On an international scale such a plan would require to include developments (a point not arising in the T.V.A.) which the borrowing country intends to carry out from its own resources, as well as those for which it asks international assistance. It would report the priority, magnitude and time-table of the various works envisaged, much as Congress in the United States required of the T.V.A. the report on its policy known as "Unified Development of the Tennessee River System".[1] This plan would state how the recipient country proposed to finance the various works, and the sources (its own, private foreign investment, or international lending) from which the funds were to come, and what guarantees it would offer to an international agency, so that the agency, in turn, might assure the contributing Governments that their risk on behalf either of their budget in general or their national private investors was justified. The T.V.A. unified plan did not merely concern itself with the financial provision required. Important as that was, its more significant purpose was to survey the economic and social problems to be solved and the value of constructive proposals for a solution. Furthermore, Congress, which passed the law and amended it from time to time, and which decided how such a plan fitted into the broad economic needs and evolution of the whole country, had the general plan in mind from the beginning, though not the unified plan until 1936.

Development schemes could, of course, be prepared at the request of the recipient Government by various technicians provided by the international lenders. Where the schemes were elaborated by the assisted Government's own experts, they might be subject to examination by the engineers of the lending body. As has been seen, the T.V.A. made very ample use of private consultants and assessors and U.S. Government experts, and was glad to receive the resultant encouragement or redirection. Indeed, the T.V.A. was given authority actually to request the assistance of U.S. Government officials "to enable the corporation the better to carry out its powers successfully", and the President of the United States

---

[1] Cf. Chapter II.

was given authority to direct officers to give such assistance if the public interest, service or economy required it.[1] Any scheme would have to define the kind of administrative agency to be put in charge of the work. It would thus become clear how much the recipient country felt it necessary to rely on foreign experts; whether it had made, or could make, provision for training staff in its own technical schools, or whether an arrangement should be made for sending capable candidates abroad for training (as the Bolivian Development Corporation has done); or whether, indeed, with or without international help, an institution for such training might be attached to the development agency.

THE FINANCING OF DEVELOPMENT AUTHORITIES

In financing the T.V.A. the alternatives at hand were bond issues to the public or governmental grants, and, if the latter, then either a block commitment for the whole project, or annual appropriations. The issues thus raised have been explained in a previous chapter.[2] Although the T.V.A. was chiefly financed by annual appropriations, dependent upon the annually variable state of mind of Congress and subject, therefore, to interruptions, Congressional default never obstructed it in the fulfilment of its programme. But there were occasions for anxiety. If an international agency should ever be established to sponsor development works in various parts of the world, the danger of interruption would have to be guarded against.

Dependence on annual grants, either by Governments to an international agency or by the agency for projects in recipient countries, would be an uncertain basis on which to begin works of magnitude and duration. International and national administrators would need some assurance that they could plan and proceed with long-term economies and with the technical demands of the work itself in mind. There are, of course, different kinds of development works. Some can be executed in a year or two and a grant could be made for the whole amount once and for all. But if works were elaborate in plan and required a long term for completion, there would have to be a general commitment for the plan as initially conceived and provision for a margin to cover under-estimates and accidents. The troubled history of Hungarian responsibilities for improving the Iron Gates on the Danube,[3] and of the building of the Panama Canal from the de Lesseps Syndicate down

---

[1] Cf. Chapter IX.
[2] Chapter XII.
[3] See BLOCISZEWSKI: "Le Régime du Danube", in *Recueil des Cours* (Académie de droit international, 1926), Vol. XI, pp. 306 *et seq.*

to its construction by the United States Army Corps of Engineers, under Col. G. W. Goethals[1], shows the need for clear plans, thorough engineering examination, adequate financing, and steady administrative supervision to see that the task is accomplished as planned. In a lesser degree, the failure of Congress to appropriate steadily for the completion of Wilson Dam in the Tennessee Valley shows how much waste may follow from interruption of the progress of such works.[2]

Thus, as with the T.V.A., there are various alternatives in financing international development projects. The basic problem to be solved is to provide certainty in the mind of the assisted country (and the international lending agency itself) that for the necessary period of development as technically determined the requested funds will be available without hesitation. It may be added that in the relationship between the U.S. Export-Import Bank and the Development Corporations of Bolivia, Ecuador and Haiti, a substantial block loan is made on the books (to the Government of the country, virtually to the corporations) but each project proposed by a corporation is the subject of its own specific contract with the Export-Import Bank each time the appropriate sum is released.

The T.V.A.'s financing by annual appropriations throws no light on the problem how to accumulate the international funds to be appropriated: the T.V.A.'s chief funds were derived from the Federal Treasury of the U.S.A. But the T.V.A.'s principal electricity distributing undertakings, the cities, by 30 June 1942, needed for construction and development nearly 107 million dollars. The cities sold bonds on their own credit and the predicted profitability of the undertakings to obtain nearly 61 million dollars and the T.V.A. issued some 50 million dollars worth of bonds, guaranteed by the United States Treasury.[3] The problems of international assistance would at the same time be more complex and several alternative devices and combinations would be available. For example, the United States Treasury's scheme for a United Nations Bank for Reconstruction and Development includes proposals that the Bank may guarantee loans made with private capital to any member Government, and through the Government to any of its political subdivisions and to business and industrial enterprises in the member country. The

---

[1] Cf. Philippe BUNAU-VARILLA: *Panama* (New York, 1914); Barnett SMITH: *Ferdinand de Lesseps* (London, 1895); H. J. SCHARFIELD: *Ferdinand de Lesseps* (London, 1937).
[2] Cf. Chapter I.
[3] Cf. Chapter XI.

Bank may also participate in loans made with private capital or make loans out of its own resources, though, in the last case, only when the borrower is unable to secure funds from private investment sources on reasonable terms.

For the T.V.A. the problems of servicing the debt were relatively simple, once the U.S. Government decided to give its assistance. This meant that the T.V.A. could borrow at a low rate[1] and that its repayments would not be subject to any fluctuation in the rate of exchange. These problems would be more difficult in the case of an international development authority and underdeveloped countries. The establishment of international currency stabilisation arrangements, along the line of recent discussions, would remove one of the difficulties in the way of international loans.[2] The T.V.A. was moreover able to obtain capital assistance actually without obligation to repay to the United States Treasury (in the case of its appropriations, not of its bond issues); and again, it was not faced with an authority outside itself demanding repayment on pain of sanctions. From these facts, an international investment authority might conclude that as regards its loans to foreign countries, there is a case for a period of repayment of about 20 years, in order that the charges on the budget of borrowing countries should not come too early and too heavily for domestic economic and social readjustment.

CLEARLY DEFINED SCOPE OF POWERS

Within its scope any international agency for the development of resources would learn from the T.V.A.'s experience the importance of operating with strict memoranda of understanding so drafted as to minimise any possible anxieties and susceptibilities of recipient States. The T.V.A. does not invade such sovereignty as still belongs to the States within the United States Constitution. Its General Counsel and Legal Department has always been exceedingly careful of any interpretation which might bring the T.V.A. into conflict with the rights of the States, and it may be added, into conflict with

---

[1] In the early stages of greatest risk before the assets and works of a development project begin to yield revenues, the question of the rate of interest on a loan is particularly vexatious. The T.V.A. was able to obtain its capital from the United States Government without interest charge. In its accounts it attributed 3¼ per cent. interest on the funds thus supplied and this was regarded as fair for such works and such an agency as the T.V.A. (cf. Appendix III), but the Minority Report of the Joint Congressional Investigating Committee suggested that 12½ per cent. might have been demanded if the T.V.A. had been in the position of a private firm going to the open market for funds (see also Appendix III).

[2] U.S. Treasury Department Preliminary Draft Outline of a Proposal for an International Stabilization Fund of the United and Associated Nations (Washington, 10 July 1943). British Treasury Proposals for International Clearing Union (London, 1943, Cmd. 6437).

the rights of business interests.[1] In regard to research, demonstrations and planning for example, the T.V.A. Statute is extremely cautious, to the point of requiring the Authority to report its wider plans to the President, who then has to report to Congress, which thereupon may or may not pass legislation to add to the hitherto defined powers of the T.V.A. In the years that have elapsed since the Statute was first passed, the powers of the T.V.A. have been shaped by interpretation and Congressional acceptance thereof directly incidental to the execution of the powers entrusted to it by the Statute. Its general power to undertake such action as is necessary to implement its specific powers has been most cautiously exploited.

Thus, the T.V.A. discovered clay which could be used to make earthenware and it also discovered that the processing could valuably be undertaken in its own designed electric kilns. Yet, it could not proceed further fully to exploit its own discoveries and innovations by becoming an earthenware and porcelain manufacturer, for the Statute did not give this power, and it was operating in an environment in which strong emphasis was laid on private enterprise. Furthermore, its fertiliser operations are carefully watched by private firms which fear competition from public enterprise. Similar problems may arise in the international field.

Two things may be stressed regarding the definition of the T.V.A.'s powers. The first is that the T.V.A. has drawn into collaboration the State and municipal authorities in the region; and it has co-operated with existing Federal departments whose science and skill are of special value. Such collaboration would be even more valuable, and, indeed, inevitable, for an international authority. On the one hand, an international authority would need the assistance of the sovereign national authorities, since its own powers would be limited to its own purposes. It could not possibly displace the national authorities, and even if it were permitted to do so for the better fulfilment of its purposes it would be restricted by conditions set by the recipient Government. On the other hand, its purpose would be to stimulate self-development; and that implies encouragement of the strength of local institutions.

Secondly, the T.V.A.'s powers have been developed to meet specific necessities. The same kind of evolution might be found even more desirable when an international authority has to deal with a number of underdeveloped areas. In order to calm any national sensitiveness, it would be necessary to draft a clear, defined and soberly constructed range of power and activity and to commend its acceptance to all concerned; and then, as the need arose,

---

[1] See Chapter VII.

to explore and arrange for further development by agreement and discussion with the recipient nation. There could be no supra-national agency endowed with unlimited powers and uncovenanted rights of intervention. On the contrary, as the T.V.A. has continuously shown, it would be vital to convey the impression of disinterested helpfulness, advisory character, defined purposes, and clearly-stated procedures. These two basic factors, namely, co-operation with and operation through local institutions, and authority restricted to, but commensurate with, the needs, are illustrated in the development of the T.V.A. as regards health, housing and educational and workers' training functions and in its employee relationship policy.

DEVELOPMENT SCHEMES AND SOCIAL PROGRESS

To fulfil its mandate to promote the general social progress of the region, the T.V.A. must work through various social services. But even the fulfilment of more direct economic works was impossible without certain social services instrumental to them. Its direct object was not only the development of a river and the land, but also the development of men and women: the first was a means to social progress, the second is, in the long run, an element of the first. So, also, the execution of development works in certain under-developed countries may be quite impossible without health provisions—housing, sanitary works, hospitals, doctors, nurses, inspectors, etc. Recent experience in Brazil, Ecuador, Bolivia and Haiti emphatically confirms this point.

The T.V.A. has found education indispensable to the economic and social development of the area for which it is responsible—not only general education, but also education in public health and in nutrition and diet. The T.V.A. rightly perceived, as the example of Denmark's remarkable economic and social development in the last half century conspicuously demonstrates, that the attainment of a high standard of living depended on the education of the people concerned.[1] The plight of the Balkans is a negative demonstration

[1] Cf. P. LAMARTINE YATES: "Factors Affecting Peasant Prosperity", in *Report of the British Association for the Advancement of Science* (1942), pp. 145 *et seq.* "The third great advantage of the Danes is the high general level of education. And here I mean not education in agricultural subjects—their technical schools for farmers are not conspicuously better than similar ones in the Netherlands and elsewhere. I refer to their education in general subjects that the farming community has obtained chiefly at the Folk High Schools. Once an interest in knowledge has been aroused and young people are trained to absorb it, then teaching of specifically agricultural subjects becomes possible and profitable."

of the same idea.[1] It may be considered appropriate that those who administer international financing should give attention to such questions generally, and assist recipient countries and their development authorities by advice on general policy and programmes and technical advisers. It should be remembered that in education of the region, above all, the T.V.A. works in intimate dependence upon the existing public educational and civic agencies and confines itself to inspiration, encouragement, financial assistance and the furnishing of factual material. In no sense does it dictate or dominate. Its dependence on the work of the agricultural extension agents, domestic economists and so forth, is to be noted. In education, even more than in capital investment, there is a "multiplier" which operates cumulatively—for very soon a community learns how to produce its own education in geometrical progression.

Two special kinds of training are desirable: workers' training and managerial training. For workers' training the T.V.A. seeks to bring skills to the Valley, to improve the capacity of the worker on the job, to prepare him for more difficult tasks, and to increase his ability to do other jobs when its own employment opportunity has come to an end. The T.V.A.'s training system is on an entirely voluntary basis, and depends upon, encourages and financially assists the local agencies to meet their wider responsibilities. In an international setting the objects and methods could be similar.

The T.V.A.'s initial experience in managerial training was that at the beginning of operations, some of its leading officers entered the Valley as though to conduct a crusade, and thus aroused resentment and opposition. Through its personnel department the Authority had to undertake a process of education among its construction engineers, who, although highly skilled technically, did not find it easy, after their experience of other parts of the country or labour relationships elsewhere, or in their direction of negro labour, to reach the standard expected in the new area and in the employment of the United States Government. Now the colonial experience of many countries, at different times, and recent experience in the relationship between the United Nations and some countries to the development of whose military resources they made contributions, suggests that, not only are there hardly enough technicians for the various development works required, but that there is also a serious problem in selecting men who will quickly understand the

---

[1] Cf. ANTONÍN BASCH: *The Danube Basin and the German Economic Sphere* (Columbia University, 1943), especially p. 241: "A well-organised system of co-operatives of all kinds could be a great help, especially in furnishing a very badly needed credit organisation. But only among an enlightened peasantry can there be much hope of the kind of co-operative organisation that has become almost essential for prosperous agriculture in Europe."

culture, labour and business practices of the country to which they are assigned, and conduct themselves so as to reduce friction to a minimum. Business habits in various parts of the world are not always exactly those that prevail in Birmingham, England, or Birmingham, Alabama. Religious practices, "mañana", the "unpunctuality of the industrial worker who yesterday was a peasant with no clock but the sun and his stomach", favouritism of various kinds, all must be treated prudently. The present author has seen all the workers in a Bulgarian cigarette factory reduced to collective and uncontrolled weeping because one of their number had received a reprimand for some trivial breach of factory procedure delivered in a tone too peremptory for people fresh from the fields.

By its Statute the T.V.A. was required to pay all its workers on the basis of "prevailing" rates, and the workers had a right of appeal to the U.S. Department of Labor. Legally, it could not undercut. In fact, it found its unit costs beneficially influenced by a genuine, though not extravagant, interpretation of relatively fair conditions. Collective bargaining, health provisions, good housing, education, training, recreation, commissariats, industrial safety, workmen's compensation, annual leave, retirement plans, employee grievance procedures, with access to the highest managerial authority, merit and efficiency in appointments and promotions: the cost of all these was recouped through greater productivity and improved efficiency.

Some Problems of International Assistance

No international lending agency could have that close and dominant relationship to development works in different regions of the world that Congress and the President have in respect to the T.V.A., that is, of a political authority and its subordinate creatures. The relationship would be rather that between lender and borrower. Necessarily there would be loan conditions or criteria which would have to be administered internationally. Such criteria would be different in kind from those applied by private investment in the past; they would be affected, on the one hand, by the recognition of the benefit to the employment situation in the economy of the highly-developed lending nations, and on the other hand, by the purpose of raising the standard of living of underdeveloped countries and making them stronger contributors to the world economy.

Any international agency would be confronted by a number of problems in the relationship between itself and borrowing countries comparable to the problems that emerged in the relationship between the United States Government and the T.V.A., and, via the T.V.A., the seven States of the Valley. Loans would be granted with due regard for the general character, policy and ambition of the economy to be assisted. Not only would the economic advancement of the borrowing country be considered, but also the effect of assistance to it upon the occupations and wealth of its neighbours, for whom, in some cases, the result might be adversity or progress. Again, it would have to be considered whether the bookkeeping loss on a particular development enterprise might not be justifiable because of the project's direct or indirect value to other parts of the country's or region's economy. As has already been suggested, the international agency would keep in mind the desirability of improving those social services for advancing the health, welfare and technical skill of the working population which would be indirectly instrumental in increasing the productivity of the project and the region concerned. Moreover, it would be necessary to limit or prohibit extraordinary charges and taxes on the equipment and personnel of the assisted projects which might otherwise hinder the work of development.[1] It would also be important to provide that proper tax equivalents should be payable by the development projects to the Government or political subdivision normally dependent on it.[2]

The experience of the T.V.A. discloses a dual problem: that of the administrative relationship between the assisting and the assisted authority—that is, the United States Government and the T.V.A.—and the internal arrangements of the regional development agency itself. Similarly, in the case of international lenders, there is the problem of the connection between them and the regional and national development agency assisted, and then the internal questions to be faced by the latter. In the first, the special lesson of the T.V.A. is the freedom of responsibility of the regional or national agency for the "grass roots" development of the area, that is, the direct local concern for decisions and operations on the spot. It happens further that the relationship with the United States Government is direct; supervision and assistance by the Government are distributed among Congress, the President, the Federal Power Commission, the United States Treasury, the Comptroller General, etc. But there are alternatives to this directness of connection. For instance, some nations have special departments, like a Ministry of Planning or a Ministry of National Economy, or a Department of Public Works. Such departments are usually responsible for making comprehensive surveys and plans regarding practically all phases of economic development, for

---

[1] Cf. Chapter IX.
[2] Cf. *ibid.*

marshalling the various demands made by the specialised and operative departments of government and for guiding all these activities in harmony with each other in relationship to the national budget and in general co-relationship to some paramount national need, for example, the lessening of unemployment or the production of some commodity especially needed for the acquisition of foreign exchange. Below such comprehensive economic planning agencies, so to speak, there are again certain special agencies for the development of particular branches of economic activity, as for example, the Brazilian Coffee Department, the Argentine Cotton Board, and the *Corporación de Fomento* (a multi-purpose organisation to be found in Bolivia, Chile and Ecuador, with a parallel in Haiti).

In such development planning practices there is very wide room for diversity. An agency like the T.V.A. is but one of many possibilities. What device is actually adopted must, of course, correspond to the needs and conditions of each country. Whether there shall be special agencies established as the T.V.A. is, on the basis of responsibility for a region (*e.g.*, the Amazon or the Central Valley Region of Bulgaria), or for a function (*e.g.*, development of livestock for the whole of a country) will properly depend upon local circumstances and the balance of administrative advantage. Such considerations would certainly be respected by international lenders, for rational decisions on matters of this kind would be one guarantee of the effectiveness for its purpose of their loan.

PROBLEMS OF DEVELOPMENT SCHEMES WITHIN A SINGLE COUNTRY

Development schemes may fall wholly within a single country or may cut across national boundaries. The conditions and problems of efficiency of management of the former are hardly more complex than those of the T.V.A., but where the economic basis of a scheme requires a region of development including parts of two or more sovereign States, there would be some additional problems to solve.

As the T.V.A. shows, some of the most difficult aspects of schemes falling wholly within the boundary of a single country are: (1) the constitution of the board of directors; (2) the recruitment of staff; (3) demarcation of the area; and (4) the submission wholly, partly, or not at all, of the development agency to its own central parliamentary or executive authority.

(1) In the T.V.A. the Board of Directors is composed of three full-time members, appointed by the Federal Government. There is some *de facto* concession to regional representation in the case of one director appointed for his rather special knowledge of, and

interest in, southern agricultural problems. The room for experimentation and diversity in such matters as the composition of the managerial board is immense. It may attempt a representation of geographic subdivisions, or of the various economic groups, such as labour, management, consumers, etc. It may, as the T.V.A. does not, allow labour a direct place in management; or, as the T.V.A. does, some collaboration where the special interests of labour are concerned. This problem of the collaboration of management and workers has become of more moment in the last two decades in various forms of enterprise, for example, in the British consumers' co-operative movement[1]; in the administration of public utilities by municipalities[2]; and in the administration of armaments factories during World War II.[3] The concessions hitherto made to labour have been of minor significance, though in the war factories the situation has compelled some considerable, but still not decisive, concessions.

(2) In the matter of recruitment of officials, there will be the problem, as the T.V.A. has clearly demonstrated, of recruiting staff for merit and efficiency and of avoiding patronage, favouritism and spoils. The experience of the T.V.A. is notable for its search for the most competent personnel wherever it may be found, whether inside or outside the region. It would be difficult to make a strong case for continued international financial assistance were the meaning of this example misunderstood or neglected.

(3) The lessons of the T.V.A. regarding the problem of the area of administration have already been amply discussed in Chapter VII and on page 221 above.

(4) Finally, as with the T.V.A., it is essential to provide for adequate business flexibility of the local development works management, and yet to secure its conformity to certain broad rules devised in the interests of efficiency as judged by its own national government and the agency of international assistance. The discussion of the situation of the T.V.A. in this context, in Chapters VIII, IX, and X, has shown what a complicated subject this is. It cannot be summarised in a matter of a few lines. For, even the T.V.A.'s relationship to its masters, Congress and the Executive, is only one example in a big class of such relationships in which fall such diverse possibilities as the many other public corporations in the United States and the British examples, like the British Broadcasting Corporation, the Central Electricity Board, the

---

[1] Cf. A. M. CARR-SAUNDERS: *Consumers' Co-operative Movement.*
[2] Herman FINER: *Municipal Trading* (London, 1941).
[3] Cf. INTERNATIONAL LABOUR OFFICE: *British Joint Production Machinery,* Studies and Reports, Series A (Industrial Relations), No. 43 (Montreal, 1944).

London Passenger Transport Board, the Port of London Authority, and others.[1]

DEVELOPMENT SCHEMES CROSSING NATIONAL BOUNDARIES

More difficult problems are likely to be raised where the area to be developed includes parts of several countries. There are areas, for example, like the valley of the Danube, and the Jordan, and others in the Polish-Czech and Alpine regions, where several boundaries converge on the source of hydroelectric capacity, and where the co-operation of two or more peoples would be necessary for the exploitation of resources in the interests of all concerned. In the T.V.A. such a difficulty was overcome, though seven States trench upon the Valley, because the Constitution of the United States gives to the Federal Government full authority over certain resources, such as navigable rivers, and inter-State commerce. Even so, powers were not available to the T.V.A. in the matter of uniform action to preserve the scenic resources, and to make of recreation an amenity saleable to people from outside the area. It had to proceed by collaboration and persuasion, which were not fully effective against the seven separate sovereignties. In the case of the Boulder Dam Project, dependent on an inter-State pact among seven States, and concerning the division of a vital and scarce commodity—water—we have seen that a solution was much more difficult. If there were areas of this kind whose maximum utilisation was possible only by collaboration of several countries, there would have to be organised joint financing, a proportionate distribution of benefits, and an agreement upon collaboration in management and the proportion of employees to come from each district. There would be the question of trade barriers between the national districts, the easing up of passport regulations and crossing permits, and precautions to prevent inferior health administration in one area from causing sickness to those people who come to and fro from other areas. With racial and religious tensions, in addition to the national and political, difficulties of course would increase. It might seem that where joint arrangements for inter-State development works were difficult to establish owing to obstacles of this kind, the minimum solution would require joint management elaborated to a fine degree of detail and fully accepted, after exhaustive discussion, by the collaborating countries and those granting international assistance. The borrowing countries might even consider that the way out of the technical and psychological difficulties that offered the greatest relief from subsequent perplexity, would be for them to devolve the management of the enterprise

---

[1] See Chapter VII.

on internationally appointed managers. In any case, in the light of the T.V.A.'s experience with the seven States, careful arrangements would have to be made to secure the ready collaboration of the several national authorities where their services were necessarily the condition and background of efficient and amicable operation of the inter-State development enterprise.

INTER-RELATIONSHIP BETWEEN REGIONAL AND WORLD ECONOMIC AGENCIES

The T.V.A. is primarily part of a single economy, that of the United States of America. Although there were grounds for special assistance to the Tennessee Valley, that assistance raised problems of the inter-relationship of the region with other interests and the national economy at large.

(1) There were problems in connection with the United States Government's policy on power in relationship to the other uses of the rivers—irrigation, navigation, etc.; the pricing of electricity produced under diverse conditions in different parts of the U.S.A.; and, given revenue and national income, the credits which are proper for public works in general and for each project in particular.

An international development authority would be faced with even more complex problems of the same nature. Hence it would be essential for the development authority's activities and policy to be closely correlated with all other international agencies having an economic and social character. Problems of international relationships would be even more important. Since the economic power of different countries may be diversely affected by an international policy of assistance, the responsible agency must take wide and intelligent views. There is also the special problem of the possible diversion of an apparently innocent economic development scheme to war purposes.

(2) As a department of the United States Government, the T.V.A. was necessarily related to all the other departments of the Government. The departmental arrangement of the whole scope of United States governmental functions had reached a mature condition by the time the T.V.A. was established, and, as frequently noted, it had to be decided what place the T.V.A. should properly occupy in this framework. Departments of world government, regulation, or control, are today only in their incipient stage and hence there must be vagueness on the place and the relationships that a development authority should possess. For international development, the problems of the whole and its parts, which were fairly simple for the T.V.A., are much more complex.

The T.V.A. always took account of the work and jurisdiction of other governmental agencies, whether local or federal, and was fully integrated with them. Quite apart from the legal existence and, therefore, the claims, of existing authorities, there was, as there always is in government of any order, a natural unity of functions which demands a thorough co-ordination of the several specialised agencies responsible for the segments into which the work is broken or by means of which it has grown.

The same general problem faces any international development authority. A number of new international institutions with economic or financial functions may be established after the war. Any international lending agency should be integrated in, and collaborate with, other institutions. Decisions on investment would substantially affect decisions on such matters as labour standards and social welfare, currency exchange, migration, transport, etc. For example, an international migration commission might be confronted with the problem of facilitating the movement of workers into areas of development, of establishing basic conditions for their work, future settlement, or return to their homeland, and of assisting in establishing the basis of good relationships between migrants and the regular residents. Large schemes of this kind might involve international financial assistance. Thus, the connection between the international bodies working towards the same end would be essential to economy and efficiency.

Again, it would be advisable if the international lending agency and the recipient countries had expert counsel and assistance on basic labour standards, the contribution which these might make to the economic efficiency of the enterprise and social progress, and the extent to which, at particular stages of economic advancement, the enterprise could afford them. The T.V.A.'s significance is more than the specific services it has rendered; its psychological, economic and social impact amounts to something more than the sum of its several purposes. The various world economic and social services are intimately related. International lending policies, properly applied, would have a significance greater than any particular financial and economic services that they rendered. They could aid in the building and expansion of a more unified and better balanced world economy.

APPENDIX I

TABLES

I. T.V.A. LAND-USE AND FERTILISER PROGRAMME

1. LAND OWNERSHIP IN THE TENNESSEE VALLEY[1]
(From data available February 1943)

Type of ownership	Number[1] of units	Total land area	Total forest area	Proportion of total forest	Timber producing forest area
		Acres		Per cent.	Acres
Public					
U.S. Forest Service	8	1,567,000	1,567,000		1,559,000
Tennessee Valley Authority	20	412,000	286,000		284,000
U.S. Fish and Wildlife Service	3	17,000	15,000		15,000
National Park Service	7	477,000	456,000		—
Office of Indian Affairs	1	44,000	40,000		40,000
Farm Security Administration	2	36,000	23,000		23,000
States	25	114,000	106,000		94,000
Municipalities	12	30,000	30,000		30,000
War Department	9	113,000	65,000		65,000
Sub-total, public	87	2,810,000	2,588,000	18	2,110,000
Private					
Farm forest	154,000	5,419,000	5,419,000	39	
Private non-farm forest	1,500	6,030,000	6,030,000	43	
Non-forest	—	11,248,000			
Sub-total, private	—	22,697,000	11,449,000		
Water areas		653,000[2]			
Total Valley area		26,160,000	14,037,000	100	

[1] Public: Number of administrative units.
Farm-forest: Number of farms reporting woodland, 1940 census.
Non-farm forest: Number of owners of large tracts, 500 acres or larger, on record by T.V.A.
[2] All water, including T.V.A. reservoirs, except South Holston and Watauga.

[1] Cf. Chapter IV.

2. FERTILISER DISTRIBUTED BY THE T.V.A. IN TEST DEMONSTRATIONS[1]

(In tons)

	Superphosphate		Calcium metaphosphate		Quenched slag		Fused rock phosphate	
	Fiscal year 1941	Cumulative total to 1 July 1941	Fiscal year 1941	Cumulative total to 1 July 1941	Fiscal year 1941	Cumulative total to 1 July 1941	Fiscal year 1941	Cumulative total to 1 July 1941
Grand total	18,352.55	118,336.05	8,948.85	19,958.95	180.30	1,838.80	569.45	573.35
Inside Valley	11,715.10	82,197.50	3,950.25	9,409.00	180.30	1,838.80	562.80	563.50
Outside Valley	6,637.45	36,138.55	4,998.60	10,549.95	—	—	6.65	9.85

3. FARM DEMONSTRATION RESULTS[2]

Experience of Approximately 46 Representative Farms in Virginia, 1934 to 1939

	1934	1939
Average receipts per farm[1]	$2,989	$3,574
Production of beef and dairy cattle		approx. 20 per cent. increase
Average crop yield index	117	158
Acres of pasture per animal unit		approx. 25 per cent. decrease
Length of grazing season		increase of 2 weeks in spring and 2 weeks in fall

[1] Price indices adjusted.

Agricultural Changes 1935-1940 per 100 Acres of Tillable Land in Tennessee

	63 counties (6,000 test demonstration farms)	32 counties (No test demonstration farms)
Increase in hay and pasture acreage	7.23	4.95
Decrease in acreage of cotton	0.81	0.62
Decrease in acres of idle land	0.56	0.00
Increase in egg production	55 dozen	40 dozen
Increase in milk production	237 gallons	27 gallons

Milk Processing and Seed Harvesting in Alabama

	Before 1938	1938–1941
Milk processing plants	None	5 cheese plants 1 butter plant
Value of lespedeza seed, etc., harvested	None (1934)	$418,000 (1941)
Milk market for 1,500 farms	None	100,000 lbs. milk processed

[1] Cf. Chapter II.
[2] Cf. Chapter XIII.

Some Test Farms in 13 Alabama Watershed Counties, 1935 and 1940

	1935	1940	Percentage increase
Improved pasture on farms (acres)	1,969	28,388	1,342
Winter legumes sown (acres)	59,920	204,415	241
Perennial legumes on farms (acres)	1,185	11,311	855
Lespedeza on farms (acres)	99,956	177,766	78
Winter legumes seed saved (lbs.)	663,147	2,389,450	260
Lespedeza seed saved (lbs.)	619,740	1,001,900	62
Basic slag (equivalent) used (tons)	2,214	65,201	2,845

Winter legumes	One unit farm		Community		County	
	1936	1940	1936	1940	1936	1940
Open land sown (per cent.)	18	41	8	42	2.2	14
Seed saved (lbs.)	12,400	50,000	12,400	206,000	42,300	885,000

Farm Management Data for 110 Farm-unit Test Demonstrations in 9 Tennessee Valley Counties of North Georgia in 1934 and 1939

Land-use, crop, and livestock items	1934	1939	Increase or decrease per cent.
Land-use inventory[1]			
Harvested acres	51.5	60.5	17.5
Other cropland	25.2	26.9	6.7
Open permanent pasture	23.0	26.7	16.1
Woodland pasture	17.2	14.5	−15.7
Woodland, not pastured	101.0	95.5	− 5.4
Other land in farms	6.2	5.5	−11.0
Total farm acreage	224.1	229.6	2.4
Crop inventory[1]			
Cotton	5.1	4.3	−15.7
Corn	19.6	18.9	− 3.6
Wheat	2.2	2.6	18.2
Oats	0.9	1.8	100.0
Rye	1.7	2.9	70.0
Hay	14.8	19.0	28.4
Annual legumes	8.0	40.5	406.0
Other crops	7.2	11.0	52.8
Total acres	59.5	101.0	70.0
Livestock inventory[2]			
Cattle, all kinds	13.6	14.5	6.6
Work horses and mules	2.7	2.6 }	20.0
Other horses and mules	0.3	1.0 }	
Sheep and goats	1.3	2.7	107.7
Hogs, all	4.1	7.9	92.7
Fowls, all	64.1	86.4	34.8

[1] Average acres per farm.
Number of livestock per farm on 1 January.

Yield of Non-phosphated and Phosphated Summer and Winter Legume
Crops, and Actual and Percentage Increase due to Phosphates,
on Mississippi Farm-unit and Area Test Demonstration
Farms, 1935 to 1940

Legume crop	Number of field reports	Untreated land	Land treated with triple super phosphate		Increase from phosphate[2]	
		Yield per acre	lbs. applied per acre	Yield[1]	lbs.	Per cent.
Lespedeza	45	2,383	100	3,818	1,435	60
Lespedeza	113	2,578	200	4,077	1,499	58
Cowpea	170	2,244	50	3,455	1,211	54
Cowpea	80	1,815	100	3,179	1,364	70
Soybean	143	2,049	50	3,273	1,224	60
Soybean	90	2,370	100	3,987	1,617	70
Vetch	877	1,986	100	3,626	1,640	82
Austrian pea	116	2,623	100	4,157	1,534	58

[1] Pounds of cured hay per acre.
[2] The increased hay yield has an acre value of $7 to $9, at $12 per ton. The phosphate fertiliser used would cost from $1 to $2 per acre per year at commercial rates. Chemical analyses show that the hay produced by phosphate or lime, or both, contains approximately 20 per cent. more protein and minerals important to livestock production than hay from untreated areas.

Acreages of Different Crops on Farm-unit Test Demonstration Farms
in 15 Tennessee Valley Counties of North Carolina, in
1936 and 1939

Average acreage	1936	1939	Per cent.
Row crops	13.7	12.4	9.5
Small grains	7	6	14.3
Winter legumes	1.8	3.8	111
Summer legumes	11.3	14.9	32

Average Annual Yield of Corn per Acre and Average Daily Production
of Milk per Cow on Farm-unit Test Demonstration Farms in
15 Tennessee Valley Counties of North Carolina, in
1936, 1939 and 1940

	Average annual yield of corn per acre (bushels)			Average daily milk production per cow (lbs.)		
	1936	1939	1940	1936	1939	1940
All farms	30.7	44.0	36.9	15.4	18.8	15.9

Average Numbers of Milk Cows and Poultry Kept per Farm on Farm-unit Test Demonstration Farms in the 15 Tennessee Valley Counties of North Carolina, in 1936, 1939 and 1940

	1936	1939	1940
Milk cows	4.0	4.8	4.2
Poultry	57.3	73.8	65.8

Farm Management Data for 964 Farm-unit Test Demonstration Farms in 55 Counties in the Tennessee River Drainage Area of Tennessee and for all Farms in the Same Districts, 1935 to 1939

1935 = 100

	On 964 unit farms		On all farms in same district	
	1935	1939	1935	1939
Land use, acreages				
Idle and waste land	100	67	[4]	[4]
All crops	100	99	100	96
Row crops	100	87	100	95
Corn	100	89	100	94
Cotton	100	80	100	95
Tobacco	100	129	100	155
Pasture and hay crops				
Open pasture	100	112	[4]	[4]
All hay crops	100	98	100	101
Alfalfa	100	231	100	196
Red clover	100	176	100	109
Acre yields and total production				
Row crops				
Corn, yields per acre	100	118	100	100
Corn, total production	100	103	100	94
Cotton, yields per acre	100	128	100	132
Tobacco, yields per acre	100	116	100	102
Hay crops				
Hay, yields per acre	100	125	100	102
Hay, total production	100	123	100	103
Animal numbers[1]				
Cows	100	103	[4]	[4]
Productive animal units	100	101	100	99
Fertiliser bought[2]	100	194	100	[4]
Total receipts[3]	100	100	100	121

[1] The data on total production of hay during the 5-year period indicate that the farmers could not be sure of the permanence of this increase until the 1938 and 1939 crops had been harvested. Increase in most classes of livestock, especially cattle and horses, is a relatively slow matter. Cattle constitute approximately 60 per cent. of the total number of animal units on these farms. Additional probable reasons why adjustments in livestock, and especially cattle, have not been made on these test demonstration farms are the uncertain or unfavourable outlook for cattle prices in 1939, the low prices received for dairy products in 1938 and 1939, and the decline in farm incomes in the same two years.

[2] Data are for the entire State, instead of only for the districts containing the 964 farms.

[3] Broadly speaking, the farms not following T.V.A. practices have kept the former exploiting methods, with row crops for cash purposes. This has resulted in larger "total receipts" to the latter in the period studied. But when the livestock increases as a result of better feed, cash as well as conservation results may be expected on the demonstration farms.

[4] District data not available.

II. T.V.A. POWER OPERATIONS

1. T.V.A. POWER REVENUES AND EXPENSES[1]

Revenues
(in dollars)

	1938	1939	1940	1941	1942
Power sales					
Outside sales:					
Municipalities and co-operatives	545,690.12	1,516,403.82	7,514,456.43	9,932,982.87	11,144,456.81
Electric utilities	196,767.48	561,315.80	2,183,900.59	2,360,615.68	2,739,427.93
Industrial establishments	918,565.20	2,507,430.75	4,422,533.33	7,780,631.14	10,265,451.24
Rural customers (retail)	154,154.56	347,923.69	396,057.72	179,757.99	158,524.74
Total outside sales	1,815,177.36	4,933,074.06	14,516,948.07	20,253,987.68	24,307,860.72
Interdepartmental sales	490,699.49	512,123.85	693,096.76	798,459.24	906,340.50
Total power sales	2,305,876.85	5,445,197.91	15,210,044.83	21,052,446.92	25,214,201.22
Rents and other revenues					
Outside sources	43,504.33	59,138.23	73,494.46	62,225.94	69,260.93
Interdepartmental rents	5,890.45	2,741.03	1,534.25	22,698.40	46,492.25
Total revenues	2,355,271.63	5,507,077.17	15,285,073.54	21,137,371.26	25,329,954.40

[1] Cf. Chapter XIII.

Expenses

(in dollars)

Production	1,212,432.63	1,553,138.88	6,082,517.72	7,479,441.21	13,578,675.64
Transmission	874,553.26	1,283,448.47	2,667,928.86	3,343,083.76	3,605,262.11
Distribution	56,572.60	122,522.67	101,783.31	59,471.41	51,815.36
Payments to States (1941 and 1942 to counties also)					
Customers' accounting	93,246.69	243,056.14	527,592.63	1,499,394.37	1,859,438.01
Sales promotion	16,621.51	39,021.20	53,008.16	35,692.76	44,608.41
Undistributed power expense	98,377.33	76,997.96	95,983.69	100,294.98	88,806.54
General and administrative	313,639.26	746,011.59	1,168,453.01	1,243,036.11	113,353.59
Miscellaneous income deductions	—	—	—	50,374.19	1,257,742.38
Amortisation of electric plant acquisition adjustments	—	—	—	—	450,000.00
Total expense	2,665,443.28	4,064,196.91	10,697,357.38	13,810,788.79	21,049,702.04
Net income from power programme before interest		1,442,880.26	4,587,716.16	7,326,582.47	4,280,252.36
Difference between interest from municipal, etc., obligations and interest paid on bonds by the Authority		35,474.55	−288,486.73	335,804.27	−606,899.86
Deficit (—) or profit (+)	— 310,171.65	+ 1,478,354.81	+ 4,299,229.43	+ 6,990,778.20	+ 3,673,352.50

Extent to which Net Income of Power Programme Covers Navigation and Flood-control Expenditure

(in dollars)

Total navigation programme expense	Total flood-control programme expense	Total expense	Net income of power programme	Net income from operation of water-control programme
656,453.58	422,785.71	1,079,239.29	1,478,354.81	399,115.52
855,850.45	444,576.61	1,300,427.06	4,299,229.43	2,998,802.37
993,115.26	594,309.54	1,587,424.80	6,990,778.20	5,403,353.40
1,075,707.96	633,420.39	1,709,128.35	3,673,352.50	1,964,224.15

2. GROWTH OF T.V.A. POWER OPERATIONS[1]

A. Capacity, Generation, and Sales

Fiscal year	Installed capacity, 30 June	Kilowatt-hours (thousands)	
		Generated	Sold
1934	184,180	406,868	395,854
1935	184,180	122,370[1]	100,680[1]
1936	184,180	437,450	407,205
1937	347,780	731,588	675,677
1938	383,780	699,094	625,207
1939	421,600	1,733,459	1,618,287
1940	742,800	4,043,377	3,629,676
1941	1,063,905	5,556,000	4,974,057
1942	1,372,980	6,025,147	5,983,369

[1] Private utilities in this year had sufficient water to generate power for their own needs.

B. Number of Retail Customers, Distributors, and Miles of Transmission Lines Operated by the T.V.A. and Rural Lines Operated by Distributors

Fiscal year (end)	Retail customers	Municipalities	Distributing co-operatives	Transmission mileage[1]	Total miles of rural line	
					Constructed by T.V.A.	Operated by T.V.A. and distributors[2]
1934	6,507	3	1	130	—	[3]
1935	11,641	7	3	237	200	—
1936	17,097	10	7	540	729	1,115
1937	30,381	17	15	1,110	2,322	2,905
1938	41,911	21	19	1,422	4,179	4,693
1939	128,536	40	22	2,150	4,891	6,854
1940	391,543	74	32	4,691	5,166	14,621
1941	449,267	76	38	5,016	5,171	19,213
1942	498,335	85	43	5,505	5,171	20,447[4]

[1] Lines of 12 kv. or over operated by Authority.
[2] Includes lines constructed by the T.V.A.
[3] Data not available.
[4] Estimate for 31 December 1941. More recent data not available pending completion of survey.

[1] Cf. Chapter III.

3. DESTINATION OF TENNESSEE VALLEY AUTHORITY SYSTEM OUTPUT[1]

Destination	Millions of kilowatt-hours per month	
	Actual, Sept. 1941	Estimated, Sept. 1943
Industrial:		
Aluminium	155.7	330.0
Phosphorus	62.3	90.0
Ferro-alloys, iron and steel	41.6	80.0
Munitions (including ammonia, nitrates)	.5	50.0
Textiles	18.3	25.0
Cement	7.5	10.0
Foods	9.5	15.0
Rubber	7.2	5.0
Copper and zinc mining	7.7	10.0
Coal mining	3.4	5.0
Miscellaneous industrial	22.6	30.0
Total industrial	336.3	650.0
Other:		
Agriculture (cotton gins, etc.)	3.2	5.0
Transportation	4.8	} 15.0
Communication and miscellaneous utilities	5.1	
Governmental (including miscellaneous, T.V.A.)	9.3	15.0
Large commercial	21.8	30.0
Small commercial	25.5	35.0
Residential	47.7	65.0
Other electric utility systems	68.4	55.0
Distribution losses	18.2	25.0
Transmission losses and unaccounted	51.0	90.0
Total system output	591.3	985.00

4. COMPARISON OF RESIDENTIAL RATES AND CONSUMPTION[2]

Calendar year	U.S. entire industry	Alabama Power Co.	Birming-ham Electric Co.	Georgia Power Co.	Kentucky Utilities Co.	Louisville Gas Electric Co.	Tennessee Valley Authority[2]
Average rate per kilowatt-hour (*in cents*)							
1933	5.49	4.62	5.92	5.16	6.25[1]	5.68	—
1937	4.39	2.97	3.74	3.04	5.05	3.77	1.83
1938	4.14	2.85	3.45	2.93	5.01	3.71	1.95
1939	4.00	2.76	3.23	2.84	4.92	3.54	2.16[3]
1940	3.84	2.70	2.77	2.74	4.64	3.28	2.06
1941	3.73	2.73	2.75	2.74	4.41	3.10	2.05
Average annual consumption No. of kilowatt-hours per customer							
1933	595	793	493	805	566[1]	580	—
1937	793	1,289	760	1,313	666	739	1,427
1938	853	1,362	820	1,399	693	822	1,359
1939	897	1,413	881	1,446	734	849	1,262
1940	952	1,466	956	1,527	781	892	1,425
1941	986	1,440	1,011	1,527	841	945	1,475

[1] Data for 1935.

[2] The variation in average rate and average use from year to year results from the acquisition of a large number of private utility customers. These figures are not comparable with those of the private utilities, since the latter serve mainly the same customers each year.

[3] Large additions to the number of T.V.A. customers meant that initial purchases were still on a rather low level, as when supplied by the utilities, so that purchases came chiefly within the higher price brackets of the scale of rates. In 1942 the average use per consumer was 1,543 kwh. and the average rate 2.00 cents per kwh. At the end of March 1943, 12 months' average use per customer had risen to 1,563 kwh. at 1.99 per kwh.

[1] Cf. Chapter III.   [2] Cf. Chapter III.

III. T.V.A DAMS[1]

STATISTICAL DATA

Main river projects	River	Maximum height (feet)	Length (feet)	Useful storage[1] (acre-feet)	Length of lake (miles)	Area of lake (acres)	Power installation[2] — Authorised (Kilowatts)	Power installation[2] — Possible ultimate (Kilowatts)	Construction started	Construction completed[3]	Cost[4] (Dollars)
Kentucky	Tennessee	166	8,420	4,570,000	184.3	256,000	128,000	160,000	July 1938	June 1938	105,000,000
Pickwick Landing	Tennessee	113	7,715	418,400	50.1	46,800	144,000	216,000	Mar. 1935	Sept. 1925	38,900,000
Wilson	Tennessee	137	4,862	43,000	15.5	15,500	288,000	444,000	Apr. 1918	Nov. 1936	40,700,000
Wheeler	Tennessee	72	6,342	429,000	74.1	68,300	129,600	259,200	Nov. 1933	Nov. 1936	39,900,000
Guntersville	Tennessee	94	3,979	282,000	82.1	70,700	72,900	97,200	Dec. 1935	Aug. 1939	34,200,000
Hales Bar[5]	Tennessee	83	2,315	—	39.9	5,760	50,483	50,483	Oct. 1905	Aug. 1914	—
Chickamauga	Tennessee	129	5,794	377,000	58.9	39,400	81,000	108,000	Jan. 1936	Jan. 1940	37,600,000
Watts Bar	Tennessee	97	2,940	433,000	72.4	41,600	90,000	150,000	July 1939	Mar. 1940	35,900,000
Ford Loudoun	Tennessee	122	3,870	138,500	55.0	15,500	64,000	96,000	July 1940	Feb. 1942	38,500,000
Tributary storage projects											
Norris	Clinch	265	1,860	2,281,000	72-56[5]	40,200	100,800	100,800	Oct. 1933	July 1936	30,900,000
Hiwassee	Hiwassee	307.5	1,287	365,000	22.0	6,280	57,600	115,200	July 1936	May 1940	19,500,000
Cherokee	Holston	175	6,760	1,473,100	58.5	31,100	90,000	120,000	Aug. 1940	Apr. 1942	31,500,000
Apalachia	Hiwassee	150	1,250	36,700	9.8	1,093	75,000	75,000	July 1941		22,200,000
Nottely	Nottely	190	2,305	189,200	23.2	4,430	None	Future	July 1941	Jan. 1942	5,300,000
Ocoee No. 3	Ocoee	110	610	9,090	7.0	518	27,000	27,000	July 1941		8,500,000
Chatuge	Hiwassee	140	2,850	226,500	11.8	7,000	None	Future	Jan. 1941	Feb. 1942	6,900,000
Fontana	Little Tenn.	460	2,330	1,160,000	29.0	10,800	200,000	200,000	Jan. 1942		62,000,000
Watauga	Watauga	318	860	627,000	16.7	7,100	60,000	60,000	Feb. 1942		23,800,000
South Holston	S. Holston	285	1,530	660,000	24.5	9,100	50,000	75,000	Feb. 1942		25,500,000
Douglas	French Broad	161	1,682	1,330,000	43.1	31,600	(100,000)[6]	(100,000)[6]	Feb. 1942		36,500,000
Ocoee No. 1[7]	Ocoee	135	840	33,100	7.5	1,910	18,000	18,000	Aug. 1910	Jan. 1912	—
Ocoee No. 2[7]	Ocoee	30	450	—	—	—	18,800	28,200	May 1912	Oct. 1913	—
Blue Ridge[7]	Toccoa	167	1,000	183,000	10.0	3,290	20,000	20,000	Nov. 1925	July 1931	—
Great Falls[7]	Caney Fork	92	800	49,600	22.0	2,280	29,370	29,370	1915	1916	—

[1] Useful storage is the volume between the lowest operating level of the reservoirs and the top of the spillway or spillway gates.

[2] Power generating facilities provided in all but two projects, Nottely and Chatuge. The T.V.A. total system installed capacity, including steam plants, was 1,493,440 kw. on 16 Nov. 1942.

[3] Construction completed means first unit on line.

[4] Cost includes presently authorised units but is exclusive of switchyards, the total cost of which is estimated to be $36,211,000 for all plants.

[5] 72 miles on Clinch River; 56 miles on Powell River.

[6] Estimate; no official figure released.

[7] Purchased with other electric properties from the Tennessee Electric Power Company.

[1] Cf. Chapter II.

IV. EXPENSE TABLES, OTHER T.V.A. ACTIVITIES, 1933-1942

1. NAVIGATION PROGRAMME 1933-1942[1]

(in dollars)

	1933-1938	1939	1940	1941	1942	Total
Studies and development	19,771	50,191	89,922	82,137	92,149	334,170
Operations	449,932	170,349	198,585	263,343	304,562	1,386,771
Maintenance	18,997	20,411	18,116	9,326	14,221	81,071
Depreciation	845,967	343,724	461,965	550,222	593,701	2,795,579
Administration		71,778	87,262	88,087	71,075	318,202
Total	1,334,667	656,453	855,850	993,115	1,075,708	4,915,793

2. FLOOD CONTROL PROGRAMME 1933-42[2]

(in dollars)

	1933-1938	1939	1940	1941	1942	Total
Studies	180,834	24,517	—	10,141	11,952	227,444
Operations	483,152[1]	163,719	193,672	258,497	299,624	1,398,664
Maintenance	13,569	13,607	9,755	6,217	9,236	52,384
Depreciation	480,388	165,801	178,709	253,931	259,373	1,338,202
Administration		55,141	62,441	65,524	53,235	236,341
Total	1,157,943	422,785	444,577	594,310	633,420	3,253,035

[1] Includes emergency flood relief of $213,654 in 1937.

3. FERTILISER PROGRAMME, NET EXPENSE, 1933-42[3]

(in dollars)

	1933-1938	1939	1940	1941	1942	Total
Experimental large-scale production, sold to A.A.A., and used in farm demonstration, etc.	2,057,325	2,250,406	2,879,478	3,088,632	2,207,786	12,483,627
Manufacturing cost[1], bagging, shipping, disintegration, administrative and other costs	4,570,132	2,207,264	2,794,503	2,982,604	2,297,727	14,852,230
Net income (—) or expense	2,512,807	−43,142	−84,975	−106,028	89,941	2,368,603
Tests and demonstrations and related activities	2,054,429	1,374,963	1,716,219	1,701,528	1,946,899	8,794,038
Research and development of fertiliser production	1,799,673	870,397	995,021	654,718	550,373	4,870,182
Profit on sale of land			− 152,788		−3,055	− 155,843
Net expense	6,366,909	2,202,218	2,473,477	2,250,218	2,584,158	15,876,980

[1] Manufacturing cost (4,200,888) (1,962,416) (2,209,951) (2,939,392) (2,305,656) (13,618,303).

[1] Cf. Chapter II.   [2] Cf. Chapter II.   [3] Cf. Chapter IV.

4. DEVELOPMENT ACTIVITIES

(*Net expense in dollars, year ended 30 June*[1])

	1933-1938	1939	1940	1941	1942	Total
Mapping	2,442,891	256,119	298,300	246,974	203,944	3,448,228
Forestry development and erosion control	1,102,077	220,172	239,185	266,988	307,886	2,136,308
Mineral resources development	770,265	96,383	89,422	181,620	525,398	1,663,088
Public health	403,809	123,572	128,374	127,492	108,091	891,338
Agricultural industries	965,555	188,590	218,313	176,834	164,676	1,713,968
Transportation studies	119,728	6,376	8,357	12,602	—	147,063
General studies	507,622	132,636	119,425	100,195	118,171	978,049
Recreational studies regional	106,653	—	—	—	—	106,653
Administration	—	291,293	307,334	285,741	296,116	1,180,484
Total	6,418,600	1,315,141	1,408,710	1,398,446	1,724,282	12,265,179

5. RELATED PROPERTY OPERATIONS[2]

(*Net expense in dollars*)

	1933-1938	1939	1940	1941	1942	Total
Operation, reservoir lands	207,373	63,513	85,112	58,820	47,628	462,446
Design, grounds and buildings	—	—	—	—	45,097	45,097
Recreational facilities, development	184,491	21,941	94,836	201,316	130,805	633,389
Recreational facilities, operation, net expense	34,173	760	12,866	16,107	32	63,938
Reafforestation and erosion control	298,618	66,463	61,090	58,702	61,905	546,778
Fish and game conservation	201,960	193,332	93,246	61,514	59,223	609,275
Village operations	812,717	219,676	161,525	164,723	139,059	1,497,700
National defence properties	446,686	48,082	3,399	24,548	18,902	541,617
Administration	—	349,971	335,123	367,221	295,520	1,347,835
Total	2,186,018	963,738	847,197	952,951	798,171	5,748,075

[1] Cf. Chapter V.
[2] Cf. Chapter V.

6. CONGRESSIONAL APPROPRIATIONS TO T.V.A.[1]

(*in dollars*)

Fiscal year	Appropriation[1]
1934	50,000,000
1935	25,000,000
1936	36,000,000
1937	39,900,000
1938	40,166,270
1939	40,000,000
1940	39,003,000
1941	40,000,000
1942	79,800,000
1943	136,100,000

	Supplementary appropriation[2]
1941	25,000,000
1942	40,000,000
1942	47,000,000
1942	30,000,000

Total	667,969,270

[1] In 1934 and 1935 the amounts were allotted by the President from large funds voted by Congress to meet the economic emergency. In 1936 and 1937 the appropriations were voted by Congress under the technical form of Deficiency Appropriation Bills; from 1938 to the present they have been voted as a part of the Independent Offices Appropriations Bills, as it was arranged that many United States departments similar to the T.V.A. (*e.g.*, the National Housing Agency, the Federal Power Commission, the Maritime Commission) should be considered by a single Congressional Committee.

[2] Four supplementary appropriations amounting to $142,000,000 were voted in 1941-42 for the additional works and operations imposed by the war. In addition, to 1 July 1942, the Authority had made cash expenditures of approximately $10,000,000 out of funds advanced to it by other Federal agencies (*e.g.*, for the War Department, for Defence Housing, etc.).

[1] Cf. Chapter XII.

APPENDIX II

MINERALS FOUND IN THE TENNESSEE VALLEY[1]

The most important minerals found in the Tennessee Valley and adjacent regions from the standpoint of value, tonnage, and men employed in their production, are as follows: coal, iron (hematite and limonite), sand and gravel, limestone and dolomite, clay (brick, refractory, filler, and miscellaneous), phosphate, pyrite (sulphuric acid). Of these minerals, the first five have a wide distribution in the Valley area. Phosphate occurs in Middle Tennessee, while pyrite and other sulphide minerals used for the production of sulphuric acid occur in the Copperhill-Ducktown district of Tennessee.

The minerals which probably rank next in importance are feldspar, fluorite, mica and zinc (concentrates). Some of these, such as fluorite and mica, are important because they do not occur plentifully in other parts of the United States. Feldspar and mica are produced in western North Carolina; fluorite in the Kentucky-Illinois fields in the vicinity of Rosiclare, Illinois; zinc in east Tennessee near Knoxville.

The following minerals are in active, sustained production, and while their value in the aggregate is very large, individually they are not as important as those mentioned in the two classes above: asphalt rock, ball clay, barite, copper (limited), sulphide ores, granite, kaolin, kyanite, marble, quartz pebbles, sandstone, talc, vermiculite.

The Tennessee Valley area produces a substantial part of the country's ball clay, and much of the best marble. Use of North Carolina kaolin is increasing rapidly as a result of new processes improving its quality and of difficulty in obtaining supplies from England, formerly the chief source. Vermiculite from North Carolina is a comparatively new mineral that is in increasing demand as a lightweight insulation material for construction and insulation uses. The only other commercial vermiculite field is in Montana. Copper is produced in limited quantity at the Copperhill-Ducktown field, where the by-products of the mining operations are used to produce sulphuric acid.

The following minerals are produced in small amounts, or intermittently: bauxite (limited), bentonite, fullers earth, garnet, gold, lead concentrates (limited), manganese (limited), ochre, oil and gas (limited), olivine, pyrophyllite, quartz, quartzite, salt and gypsum, shale, slate, soapstone, titanium (rutile and ilmenite), tripoli, spodumene.

The following minerals, although occurring in this area, are not in production: asbestos (short fibre), chromite, corundum and emery, graphite (amorphous), nickel.

---

[1] Cf. Chapter I.

THE ALLOCATION OF T.V.A. POWER COSTS,
THE PROFITABILITY OF T.V.A. POWER OPERATIONS,
AND THE "YARDSTICK"

The Statute required that the T.V.A. should make a valuation of the first dam (Wilson Dam) which came into its possession, and the power from which was the first available for sale, and thereafter that other plant and other dams should be similarly valued and the valuation allocated between their several uses. But through a series of accidents and difficulties, and some differences within the Board itself as to the theory of allocation, the valuation of Wilson Dam was not actually made until January 1937. Even then, it was concluded and reported to the President under the stimulus of a peremptory amendment passed when Congress reconsidered the Statute in 1935 and discovered that the Authority had not yet produced a valuation.

But the Authority had electric power to sell from the moment it took over Wilson Dam, and it could not wait until a valuation and allocation were made before beginning to make contracts. In other words, it had to set up a rate-schedule before it had made the final and minute mathematical analysis which the Statute demanded of it, and its valuation had therefore to be made on the basis of estimates. This was done by September 1933, in consultation with a number of the most distinguished utility economists in the United States. It was by no means an easy task. Wilson Dam had cost about $46 million to build, but the building operations had not been continuous, a fact which had added to the expense, and they had been carried out at a time of abnormally high prices; furthermore, the dam was already some seven years old when the Authority received it. The Authority therefore made calculations, as the Statute required, of its "present value". On the basis of that valuation—some $30 million—a rough allocation was made of the proportions due to navigation, and to power operations, and the Authority then proceeded on well-known bases of promotional electricity rating to set schedules of prices for its power. It appears that the final allocation, arrived at after years of expert analysis, very closely coincided with this first business appraisal.

Six theories competed for acceptance as the basis of allocation in the total investment as the new dams were constructed. The first was the "no-allocation theory", advanced by Mr. C. W. Kellog, President of the Edison Electric Institute, which required the whole cost of the dams to be attributed to the single purpose of power production. This theory the majority report of the Joint Committee Investigating the T.V.A. regarded as being not consistent, and not objective, but largely controlled by the desire of its sponsors to show that the yardstick was unfair and based on too small an allocation to power.[1] Moreover, this theory seemed directly contrary to the Statute, which directs that the dams and reservoirs shall be operated primarily for navigation and flood control (Section 9 (a)).

A second, which was advanced by the first chairman of the T.V.A., may be called the "proportionate benefit" theory. The fundamental notion here was that the direct costs clearly attributable to each programme—for example, power or power turbines—should at once be allocated to that programme. Beyond that, each of the programmes—navigation, flood control and power, fertiliser and defence—enjoyed a benefit in the common use of the dams and other works. If the benefit receivable in terms of money by each of these programmes separately could be computed, or rather guessed, and then added together, the proportion of the benefit accruing to each to the total obtained by all would then be the proportion of known capital costs which should be allocated to each. Ingenious as this theory was, its great difficulty was the highly hypothetical, imaginary result of the attempt to evaluate benefits.

Thirdly, there were people who said that the basis must be arbitrary; let direct costs be specifically attributed, but an equal one third share of common costs should be borne by the three great programmes. This solution would have satisfied nobody.

Fourthly, there was the "incremental power-investment" theory, advanced by Dean Moreland[2] when a witness for the Commonwealth and Southern Corporation. Here again, the allocation principle referred to the common costs; power was to be charged with the balance of total investment, after deducting the estimated cost of the most economical alternative plan for accomplishing the other purposes. The difficulty here was to assign a cost to each purpose subsequently where this had not been done originally, although three or more purposes were taken into account in the original design, construction and total cost. This necessarily involves hypothesis, and the hypothesis can differ very widely, according to the type of navigation or flood control systems that might have been built; so that under this particular method of allocation the costs and valuation might vary enormously even as between different witnesses who accepted it. Furthermore, this method took as its starting point alternative navigation and flood control systems that would not have accomplished the purposes specified in the T.V.A. Statute.[3]

Fifthly, it appears that while this was never considered as a practical solution of the problem, counsel for the Authority contended that the theory most consistent with the Statute would be to charge directly to power only the cost of the power plant and to allocate to navigation and flood control the common costs of the dams excluding the power-house section. This is referred to as the "by-product" theory, power being considered as nothing more than a by-product of the dams which were built to satisfy the general

---

[1] Op. cit., p. 156.
[2] Dean Edward L. Moreland, of the Massachusetts Institute of Technology.
[3] Cf. Findings of District Court in Tennessee Electric Power Co. et al. v. Tennessee Valley Authority.

public benefit by navigation and flood control, as directed in the
Statute.

The Alternate Justifiable Expenditure Theory

The T.V.A., working through an expert committee of public
utility economists, rejected all these methods as unworkable in
practice, and used as the principal guide to its final decision the
"alternate justifiable expenditure" theory. The briefest and most
authoritative explanation is given in the Report of the Joint Investigating Committee[1]; it refers to a 10-dam cost system, and runs
as follows:

The total cost of the 10 dams, with an installed electric capacity of 1,401,500
kilowatts, is estimated at $407,809,864.

1. The direct costs of navigation, flood control, and power were computed
separately, as being the amount that could be saved by eliminating that function
from the multiple-purpose programme.

By eliminating navigation $44,880,800 could be saved; or by eliminating flood
control $33,763,000 could be saved; or by eliminating power $108,884,965 could
be saved.

Taken all together, these direct costs leave $220,281,099 of the total multi-
purpose costs still unallocated. This remainder represents common costs and
may be considered as the cost of combining the three uses into one project and
is allocated by the following process.

2. For comparison with the direct costs as found in the multiple system,
the separate cost of alternative one-use systems were computed.

A system built for navigation alone, based mainly on the "18-dam plan"
suggested by the Army Engineers, would have cost $163,519,900.

A system built only for flood control would have cost $140,826,000.

A system built only for power production would have cost $250,096,000.
(These are, of course, on Tennessee Valley Authority estimates.)

3. The next step was to determine the sum of the alternative single purpose
costs remaining after deducting the direct costs identified in the multi-purpose
costs, in order to compare the remaining alternative costs with the corresponding
costs of the multi-purpose system.

The direct cost for navigation in the combined system is $118,639,100 less
than the cost of a system for navigation alone.

The direct cost for flood control in the combined system is $107,063,000 less
than the cost of a system for flood control alone.

The direct cost for power in the combined system is $141,211,035 less than
the cost of a system for power alone.

The sum of these differences is therefore $366,913,135; the common cost of
bringing them into combination, as given in (1) is $220,281,099, called in the
report "remaining multiple use costs".

4. The remaining costs, $220,281,099, are allocated to the three purposes
in the ratios of the respective single purpose remaining alternative costs (3) to
the sum of those alternative costs.

Applying this principle, the Authority made the following
allocation, embodied first in a report to the President in 1938, and
covering the three-dam system of Wilson, Norris and Wheeler:

---

[1] *Op. cit.*, pp. 157-158.

	Allocation (in dollars)	Per cent. of total cost
Navigation	26,294,000	28
Flood control	18,470,000	20
Power	49,360,000	52
	94,124,000	100

A further report was submitted, as required by the Statute, in November 1940, based upon the same principles as the original one, but now applied to seven dams as a single system—Wilson, Norris, Wheeler, Pickwick, Guntersville, Chickamauga and Hiwassee. The Authority said: "The seven dams are so interrelated and interdependent in their operation that any significant assignment of costs to their several uses can be made only by considering them as a single system, rather than as separate projects". The amount invested in the seven-plant system, subject to allocation, was $210,279,469. Of this total, facilities installed exclusively for each special purpose were as follows:

	(in dollars)
Navigation	17,177,896
Flood control	4,871,000
Power	56,368,996

The remainder of the total investment, equal to $131,861,577, represented joint investment or common expenditure for the three purposes, and was allocated thus: navigation, 36 per cent.; flood control, 24 per cent.; power, 40 per cent.; nothing to national defence, and nothing to fertiliser. The Authority observed that these percentages could not be regarded as fixed with respect to future allocations; these must depend on varying circumstances relating to the additional multi-purpose structures, and wide differences in the circumstances raised the probability of difference in the allocations. When the direct facilities for the single purposes are added to the percentages stated above, that is, single purpose investment plus joint investment, the result is:

	Per cent. of total investment
Navigation	21.8
Flood control	12.4
Power	65.8

Until the time of the T.V.A.'s allocation there had never been more than a two purpose project, namely, navigation and power, requiring allocation.

PROFITABILITY OF SALES

Since the profitability of the T.V.A.'s power policy has been the subject of public controversy, involving the conflicting judgment of the most creditable experts, it is reasonable for the observer to follow the opinion of the majority report of the Joint Committee on the Investigation of the T.V.A. The Committee employed a number of engineering experts to guide it on this subject, headed by Mr. Tom Panter, chief of the Los Angeles Power System.

The majority believed that it was necessary to hold fast the principle that the Authority is a river control project, to which power generation is incidental. Under this assumption, in order to justify the cost of generating hydroelectric power it was necessary only to show that the added cost of power generation and transmission would be repaid by the revenues from power. It was thought that the estimates actually presented by the T.V.A. showed additional revenues far in excess of this necessary minimum.

In trying to answer the question whether the taxpayers of the nation were contributing to costs which should be borne by the consumers of the Authority's power, the Committee analysed the various elements of cost, constantly bearing in mind a comparison with all the items of cost met by any private utility. These items are:

1. Cost of dams as allocated to power;
2. Interest during construction;
3. Depreciation and amortisation;
4. Taxes and insurance;
5. Operation and maintenance.

1. *Cost of Dams as Allocated to Power*

This aspect of the matter has already been discussed.[1] The Engineer's Report for the Committee of Investigation increased the T.V.A.'s figure only a little, on account of the total cost, but thought that the percentage of allocation was sound.

2. *Interest during Construction*

Here, the T.V.A. allows for a rate of 3 per cent., basing this figure upon an estimate of the rate of interest for long-term money as reported by the Treasury for the years 1933 to 1937. The Committee's engineers, in order to take a conservative view, used the figure of 3¼ per cent. The minority of the Committee, hostile to the T.V.A., ignored the guidance of the Committee's engineers, and argued that the T.V.A. would be on a like basis with utility companies only if it paid 6 per cent., which on the minority's estimate of power-investment costs would total nearly $17 million. But in fact a Government agency whose credit stands high quite properly passes on the benefits of this credit to the power consumer or the general taxpayers. Knoxville City bonds readily sold at 3.39 per cent.

3. *Depreciation*

In the matter of depreciation, Dean Moreland, making estimates for evidence on behalf of the utilities, reckoned on a 30-year life for the equipment and 50 years for the dams. This, on a sinking-fund basis, gave a rate of 1.5 per cent., comparing rather unfavourably with such systems as the Ontario Hydro-electric and the great utilities operating in the Tennessee Valley. The T.V.A. made a more particular calculation, specifying the depreciation on the

---

[1] Cf. Chapter III.

expected service lives for the various items of depreciable property. Thus, machinery and equipment were assumed to have an average life of 35 years; dams and mass concrete structures, 85 years; superstructures and buildings, 75 years; transmission facilities, in six classifications, ranging from 15 to 50 years. The Committee's engineers followed Dean Moreland's rate, even adding a little.' They worked on the 50-year basis, and further calculated amortisation on a 50-year basis at $3\frac{1}{4}$ per cent. interest, which, in their judgment, adequately provided for obsolescence by returning the total investment in this period.[1] Thus, they allowed for both depreciation and amortisation, although privately owned utilities are not required to amortise their investments, and some have not even been required to provide for full depreciation. Actually, the T.V.A. does not use the sinking-fund basis for meeting depreciation, but the much more conservative "straight-line" method whereby investment is spread as uniformly as possible over expected useful life; this has the effect of penalising the early years of the power development.

4. *Taxes and Insurance*

The T.V.A., being a Government agency, was by general constitutional law not subject to taxation, but the Statute provided that the T.V.A. should pay to the States in which it operated 5 per cent. of its gross revenues.[2] This figure was smaller than the amount in taxes generally paid by utilities, and had been violently criticised on the ground that because they did not include the full tax amount as an item of cost, the Authority's accounts of true net profit were unfairly contrasted with those of the utilities. The Committee's engineers therefore investigated the amounts paid in total taxes by the privately owned utilities; and considered that $12\frac{1}{2}$ per cent. on the Authority's wholesale revenues would be a fair allowance. It was also observed that since the net receipts over cash payments are returned to the Federal Treasury, the fact that they are not returned in the form and under the name of taxes is immaterial. The Authority, in fact, took the figure of $12\frac{1}{2}$ per cent. into account when fixing its wholesale rates.

There was also computed by the Committee an amount of insurance equivalent to that paid by private companies.

5. *Operation and Maintenance*

On this item, the various parties in dispute found no occasion to differ seriously in their estimates. The only items upon which there was controversy were a number of elements which the Authority obtained free of charge or at less than the price asked of private firms, such as real estate taxes, gasoline taxes, postage and special freight rates from the land grant railroads, and workmen's compen-

---

[1] The T.V.A. made allowance for amortisation only for that part of its property that was non-depreciable and had an indefinite life, such as reservoir lands and rights which it proposed to amortise in 85 years; but even computing this item on the terms of the Committee's engineers the difference to costs is not important.

[2] Since 1940 these payments have been substantially raised. Cf. Chapter IX.

sation payments.[1] The amount for franked envelopes was found to be very small; and the amount saved by special freights on land grant railroads was practically negligible, being equivalent to one seventieth of a mill per kilowatt hour. On the other hand, the Committee thought that because the T.V.A. operated under Government regulation it was compelled to meet a number of expenses which tended to increase its costs; for instance, in purchase and inspection requirements, auditing, personnel policies, and public health. The engineers thought that the net effect was negligible.[2]

Having included these various items of cost, the Committee's engineers then made an estimate of power revenues for a ten-dam system with a 60 per cent. load factor. The result showed a substantial profit, though a little less than the expectations entertained by the T.V.A. The minority report of the investigating committee naturally took a different view of the estimates of revenue, considering that the calculations of the Authority and the Committee's engineers were unduly optimistic and that the T.V.A. was producing an amount of electricity for which it could never find a market.

It would seem on a reasonable survey of the facts that the estimates of the Committee's majority report were well founded, especially if it is taken into consideration that the Authority's interconnections with surrounding utility systems having a large steam generating capacity make possible the transformation of much of the Authority's secondary and dump power into first-grade continuous current. Referring to a ten-dam system, the Committee thought that the T.V.A. would have an annual surplus over costs of about $3.8 million, if it remained an independent hydro-system; about $6.3 million if its secondary capacity were supported by interconnection; and about $7 million if this, again, were supported by supplementary steam generation.

The Committee pointed out that the T.V.A. had been losing money during its period of development, which came to an end in 1938. It estimated the losses to 30 June 1939 as $11,310,000, which, with interest accruing at $3\frac{1}{4}$ per cent., amounted to a maximum of $13,000,000. The surplus on a seven-dam system would liquidate this in nine years; on a ten-dam system in five years; on a ten-dam system interconnected, in something like two years. The net conclusion was that for a ten-dam system with all charges paid, $3\frac{1}{4}$ per cent. interest amortisation and replacement, and a full tax-equivalent to the Treasury, the existing wholesale rates provided a balance of some $7 million a year, which could be applied to the maintenance and liquidation of the other Authority programmes. Such a power surplus would cover the annual expenses of navigation and flood control, and return the total investment in these programmes in less than 50 years. Thus, as hoped, hydroelectric power would be the "paying partner".

---

[1] T.V.A. employees come under the United States Federal Employees' Compensation system, and the compensation is paid by the Federal Government.

[2] The T.V.A. and the distributors who buy its power also have certain minor accountancy obligations to the Federal Power Commission, which has established forms of account for suppliers of electricity.

An analysis of the prices and the operations of the municipalities and co-operatives buying wholesale electricity from the T.V.A. showed that, of fourteen municipalities, twelve had a net profit and two a net loss, and of the co-operatives, six had a net profit and seven a net loss. (The Engineers' Report analysed only those distributors in service for eighteen months or more before 30 June 1938.) The results appear to show that after 18 months' service most of the municipalities could cover all fixed charges including a return of more than 6 per cent. on plant investments. But co-operatives, largely operating rural lines, need a longer period in which to attain profitability; some four or five years would be required to build up the necessary load.[1] It still remains to be seen, however, whether the rates at which the T.V.A. requires the rural co-operatives to resell the electricity can be generally applied without requiring supplementary contributions to capital account from the members of the co-operative.

"THE YARDSTICK"

A further question is whether the Authority's methods of operation may be regarded as providing a yardstick of equitable rates for comparison with private industry, in order to show in particular that a reduction of rates was possible from the standpoint of costs, and desirable for the stimulation of consumption. The Committee thought that it was not necessary to exhibit the Authority's internal costs and wholesale prices as the standard by which to challenge private utilities; it was enough to show that the T.V.A.'s own wholesale rates did not, in fact, undercut the costs charged by private utilities for wholesale power. (The cost of distribution of power, of course, is so large compared with wholesale costs, that the former is the crucial figure for analysis.) This was a simple task because it merely meant a comparison of the actual wholesale charges made by private utilities and the T.V.A. Such an analysis showed that the T.V.A. was not underselling the market by more than a mill or two per kilowatt hour, if at all. Therefore, the yardstick was not in the Authority, but in the distributing operations performed by the municipalities and co-operatives. On the one side there was the Authority with its internal costs, selling prices, and profit or loss. These were important to the Authority and to the general public which pays the bill, and, as already shown, the rates were more than sufficient to cover the Authority's power costs. They did not, however, affect the "retail yardstick", which became valid from the moment the municipalities and co-operatives began their operations with the purchase of wholesale power from the T.V.A. at rates which did not undersell the market.

These retail operations were a sound yardstick, because the only criticisms raised against them were fallacious or immaterial. Thus, for example, it was argued that the benefits of various pro-

---

[1] The accounts of the T.V.A. since this analysis was made tend to bear out the conclusions of the Committee's engineers. Thus, in the fiscal year 1941, of 34 co-operatives, 19 showed net losses for the year, due largely to heavy amortisation collections. Cf. *Report from Comptroller, T.V.A.;* Financial Statements, Municipalities and Co-operatives, Year ended June 30, 1941.

motional costs incurred by the T.V.A., such as advertising the uses of electricity, redounded cost free and unaccounted for to the distributors; but evidence showed that adequate accounts of these had been kept in the T.V.A. There had also been a proper charge to legal, engineering, accounting, and organisation costs. The advertising provided by the E.H.F.A. had been paid for by the Government, was not concealed, and had offered advantages to private utilities as well as to the T.V.A., for the result was an increase of electric sales generally and the benefits had spread over the whole area.

ESTIMATES OF POWER REVENUES BEFORE THE JOINT CONGRESSIONAL COMMITTEE

(in dollars)

Items	Moreland	T.V.A.	Congressional Committee
Total cost of 11 dams	521,854,373	486,669,540	
Navigation and flood	172,942,600	230,892,384	
Power	348,911,773	255,777,156	(10 dams) 281,710,000

ANNUAL COSTS

(in dollars)

Items	11 dams	11 dams	10 dams
Interest	12,212,000 (3.5 per cent.)	7,673,315 (3 per cent.)	(3¼ per cent.) 9,155,575
Depreciation	4,300,000	2,304,000	
Amortisation			(0.825 percent.) 2,324,108
Renewals and replacements			(0.95 per cent.) 2,653,000
Operations and maintenance			3,130,000
Taxes (5 per cent.)	1,193,000	1,198,400	(insurance 3,284,550 13.5 per cent.)
Power generation	17,633,000	11,805,315	
Transmission	7,341,000	5,195,260	
General equipment	858,000	205,000	
Development	150,000	120,000	
Administration	1,000,000	820,000	
Total	28,175,000	19,343,975	20,547,233
Estimated revenues	24,136,000	23,968,750	24,330,000
Profit or loss	− 4,039,000[2]	+ 4,624,775[2]	+ 3,782,767[1]

[1] If all primary power were sold for general service and not put into special contracts, revenue would be $22,925,000, and with slightly less annual cost surplus would be $2,822,000.
[2] Compare this estimate with T.V.A. actual results, 1938-1942, as given on pp. 242-3.

MINORITY REPORT ESTIMATE ON 10 DAMS

		(in dollars)
Total cost of projects, including transmission, all charged to power		494,092,864
Annual costs (as they should be):		
Interest at 6 per cent. on total cost		29,646,000
Taxes equal to those paid by utilities		7,506,000
Total		37,152,000
Actual annual costs:		
T.V.A. interest at 3½ per cent.		
T.V.A. taxes at 5 per cent.	Total	10,782,921
	Difference	26,369,079

T.V.A. deficit	Profits	1,737,479 on 10 dams on T.V.A. basis.
	Difference	26,369,079
	Loss	24,631,600

APPENDIX IV

INTERSTATE COMPACTS

The United States Congress, being convinced of the value of unified development of the Tennessee River, was able to establish an agency and give it the requisite continuing powers because it had the authority to act under the Constitution, in virtue of its powers to provide for national defence[1] and its powers over navigable rivers.[2] There was an alternative constitutional route by which a local agency for unified development might have been set up, namely the "Compact Clause", (Article 1, Section 10 of the Constitution), which reads: "No State shall, without the consent of Congress . . . enter into any Agreement or Compact with another State, or with a foreign Power". Although this looks like a prohibition, it is an authorisation with Congressional consent.

In the many decades before Congress acted the seven Valley States could have made a compact or contract among themselves to accomplish the aims that were ultimately embodied in the T.V.A. Statute. It is true that there might have been reluctance on the part of these States to make financial provision for navigation and flood control which would benefit other States—for instance, Louisiana and Arkansas—or the whole country as an economic unit, without a contribution from them, and this would doubtless have obstructed the plan. However, a careful search of the historical records shows that the compact method was never even contemplated. It may be surmised that, from the standpoint of each separate State, unity of administration of the Valley was desirable but not desperately necessary, since each had alternative methods of dealing with its own needs. There was plenty of water for all, and so no occasion for a compact to determine its distribution as in the Colorado River Compact. Floods were dealt with by local works, or, as on the Mississippi, with the aid of the United States Government through the Army Engineers. Thus the States saw no reason for a compact. What was needed for the common good was perceived more clearly by the national Government, which also foresaw the future, than by the local communities.

Far otherwise was it in the case of the Colorado Compact.[3]

---

[1] Implied by Article 1, Section 8, clause 11, "To declare war . . . ".

[2] Article 1, Section. 8, clause 3; "To regulate Commerce . . . among the several States".

[3] Cf. NATIONAL RESOURCES COMMITTEE: *Regional Factors in National Planning* (Dec. 1935), Part III, especially Chapter 7; also F. FRANKFURTER and J. M. LANDIS: "The Compact Clause of the Constitution", in *Yale Law Journal*, May 1925, pp. 685 *et seq.* and A. W. MACMAHON: "Interstate Compacts", in *Encyclopaedia of the Social Sciences*, Vol. II.

Here seven States—Arizona, Utah, Colorado, New Mexico, Wyoming, Nevada, and California, in order of their part in the area of 240,000 square miles drained by the river—were gravely concerned in the uses of the Colorado River, especially for irrigation, on which their agricultural economies depended. It was seen also that mining activity in these States would be assisted, and an electrochemical industry opened up, if the problems of water supply and hydroelectric potentialities, which were enormous, could be solved by planned use over the whole area. Since 1902 the United States Bureau of Reclamation had built many dams and canals in the river system, and the United States Government had conducted surveys. After the world war of 1914-1918, reclamation projects and plans for the use of the water by the States in the lower basin of the River (with Arizona, California and New Mexico chiefly concerned) caused the States in the upper basin (with Wyoming, Utah, and Colorado chiefly concerned), as well as the former, to see the urgent need for agreement. Meetings of representatives of the States resulted, in 1920, in a suggestion that the apportionment of the waters might be accomplished by interstate compact. The several States passed a Bill authorising a State commissioner to formulate the compact, and required a representative of the Federal Government to participate in the formulation. Prolonged and anxious proceedings resulted in a compact signed in November 1922, based upon the principle of assigning the water, not between several States, but between the upper and the lower basin. Article 1 of the compact reads:

> The major purposes of this compact are to provide for the equitable division and apportionment of the use of the waters of the Colorado River System; to establish the relative importance of different beneficial uses of water; to promote interstate comity; to remove causes of present and future controversies; and to secure the expeditious agricultural and industrial development of the Colorado River Basin, the storage of its waters, and the protection of life and property from floods. To these ends the Colorado River Basin is divided into two basins, and an apportionment of the use of part of the water of the Colorado River System is made to each of them with the provision that a further apportionment may be made.

Thus the problem of the rights of the individual States was put off till a later date. The upper basin States were to allow so many acre feet to flow through a given point which was held to connect the two basins.[1] The States ratified the compact (with the exception of Arizona, which anticipated being placed at a disadvantage in relation to California), and it was finally accepted by an Act of Congress—the Boulder Dam Act of December 1928—on the basis of the adherence of six States.

It appears that the compact method has by no means fully solved the problem, which was the division of the supply of water not merely in accordance with present needs, but with concern for future development. The settlement of future difficulties was left to *ad hoc* conferences of commissioners appointed for the purpose by each State. No authority was set up to consider all the needs

---

[1] Ratified in Apr. 1944.

in relation to the supply and the changing economy of the United States as a whole, and rivalry between the States was intensified.

It should be noted that the construction of Boulder Dam or any other dams on the Colorado system does not depend on a compact among the States, but derives directly from the power of the Federal authority to regulate navigable rivers, arising out of its power "to regulate commerce . . . among the several States".

The States of New Jersey and New York were also able to make a compact (1921) which enabled the New York Port Authority[1] to come into existence to administer the affairs of that great port. Up to that time, each State had sought to exploit for itself the fruits of the commerce passing into and out of the harbour. Neither alone could fully plan the terminals, the transport and other facilities required, or offer to all users the economies available from amalgamated government. The agreement ended a series of controversies and quarrels which began in the early nineteenth century and remained quiescent for some decades, but which flared up again when, from the turn of the century onwards, the remarkable growth in commerce produced an intolerable congestion. From 1911 onwards, there were many conferences and investigations, and strong public controls over the harbours were later established by each State; but such controls did not lessen competitive hostility, which was, indeed, promoted by discriminatory railroad rates and facilities to the rival parties of the harbour. The controversy over the discrimination in rates came before the Interstate Commerce Commission in 1917 at the instance of New Jersey. The proceedings showed clearly that New York Harbour was one, and should be governed as a unit; and the Interstate Commerce Commission reprimanded the private interests, the railroads, and others which had supported and fomented the hostility by their individual quests for their own convenience and profit. As a result of this open analysis, and after prolonged studies and plans, a compact was entered into, making it possible to set up a body corporate and politic, consisting of six commissioners, three from each State to be chosen as each State should determine, to govern a port district with boundaries roughly 20 miles from the lower end of Manhattan Island.

The method of treaty-making between the nations of Europe regarding European transport by railway, road, waterways, and air, and the exploitation of hydro and other electricity resources follows generally the United States interstate compact method rather than the T.V.A. method[2], and in consequence there are grave shortcomings in the conduct of those utilities from a European point of view. The larger the number of States which are parties to a common problem, the greater would seem to be the need for the establishment of a continuing agency through whose good offices the development of the sector of economic or social life in question might be promoted. Generally speaking, bi-partite compacts are easier to negotiate than multi-partite, but the bi-partite pact may throw burdens on those not included in it and may not solve the problem.

_____

[1] Cf. E. W. BARD: *The Port of New York Authority* (New York, 1942).
[2] Cf. for a comparative study, H. A. SMITH: *The Economic Uses of International Rivers* (London, 1931).

APPENDIX V

THE TENNESSEE VALLEY AUTHORITY ACT

[PUBLIC—No. 17—73D CONGRESS, 1ST SESSION]
[H. R. 5081]

18 May 1933, 48 Stat. 58, as amended to 21 November 1941

AN ACT

To improve the navigability and to provide for the flood control of the Tennessee River; to provide for reforestation and the proper use of marginal lands in the Tennessee Valley; to provide for the agricultural and industrial development of said valley; to provide for the national defense by the creation of a corporation for the operation of Government properties at and near Muscle Shoals in the State of Alabama, and for other purposes.

Be it enacted by the Senate and House of Representatives of the United States of America in Congress assembled, That for the purpose of maintaining and operating the properties now owned by the United States in the vicinity of Muscle Shoals, Alabama, in the interest of the national defense and for agricultural and industrial development, and to improve navigation in the Tennessee River and to control the destructive flood waters in the Tennessee River and Mississippi River Basins, there is hereby created a body corporate by the name of the "Tennessee Valley Authority" (hereinafter referred to as the "Corporation"). The board of directors first appointed shall be deemed the incorporators, and the incorporation shall be held to have been effected from the date of the first meeting of the board. This Act may be cited as the "Tennessee Valley Authority Act of 1933." [48 Stat. 58-59.] *

SEC. 2. (a) The board of directors of the Corporation (hereinafter referred to as the "board") shall be composed of three members, to be appointed by the President, by and with the advice and

---

*—For the purpose of identifying the sections which appeared in the original act of 1933 and those which have been brought into the act by amendment, references have been placed at the end of the sections. For example, the reference at the end of section 1, 48 Stat. 58-59, indicates that this section will be found in volume 48 of the Statutes at Large on pages 58 to 59. All sections will be found in volumes 48, 49, 53, and 54 of the Statutes at Large as indicated, with the exception of sections 4 (*k*) and 9 (*b*) which at the time of this printing were not available.

consent of the Senate. In appointing the members of the board, the President shall designate the chairman. All other officials, agents, and employees shall be designated and selected by the board.

(*b*) The terms of office of the members first taking office after the approval of this Act shall expire as designated by the President at the time of nomination, one at the end of the third year, one at the end of the sixth year, and one at the end of the ninth year, after the date of approval of this Act. A successor to a member of the board shall be appointed in the same manner as the original members and shall have a term of office expiring nine years from the date of the expiration of the term for which his predecessor was appointed.

(*c*) Any member appointed to fill a vacancy in the board occurring prior to the expiration of the term for which his predecessor was appointed shall be appointed for the remainder of such term.

(*d*) Vacancies in the board so long as there shall be two members in office shall not impair the powers of the board to execute the functions of the Corporation, and two of the members in office shall constitute a quorum for the transaction of the business of the board.

(*e*) Each of the members of the board shall be a citizen of the United States, and shall receive a salary at the rate of $10,000 a year, to be paid by the Corporation as current expenses. Each member of the board, in addition to his salary, shall be permitted to occupy as his residence one of the dwelling houses owned by the Government in the vicinity of Muscle Shoals, Alabama, the same to be designated by the President of the United States. Members of the board shall be reimbursed by the Corporation for actual expenses (including travelling and subsistence expenses) incurred by them in the performance of the duties vested in the board by this Act. No member of said board shall, during his continuance in office, be engaged in any other business, but each member shall devote himself to the work of the Corporation.

(*f*) No director shall have financial interest in any public utility corporation engaged in the business of distributing and selling power to the public nor in any corporation engaged in the manufacture, selling, or distribution of fixed nitrogen or fertilizer, or any ingredients thereof, nor shall any member have any interest in any business that may be adversely affected by the success of the Corporation as a producer of concentrated fertilizers or as a producer of electric power.

(*g*) The board shall direct the exercise of all the powers of the Corporation.

(*h*) All members of the board shall be persons who profess a belief in the feasibility and wisdom of this Act. [48 Stat. 59.]

Sec. 3. The board shall without regard to the provisions of Civil Service laws applicable to officers and employees of the United States, appoint such managers, assistant managers, officers, employees, attorneys, and agents, as are necessary for the transaction of its business, fix their compensation, define their duties, require bonds of such of them as the board may designate, and provide a system of organisation to fix responsibility and promote efficiency. Any appointee of the board may be removed in the discretion of the board. No regular officer or employee of the Corporation shall receive a salary in excess of that received by the members of the board.

All contracts to which the Corporation is a party and which require the employment of laborers and mechanics in the construction, alteration, maintenance, or repair of buildings, dams, locks, or other projects shall contain a provision that not less than the prevailing rate of wages for work of a similar nature prevailing in the vicinity shall be paid to such laborers or mechanics.

In the event any dispute arises as to what are the prevailing rates of wages, the question shall be referred to the Secretary of Labor for determination, and his decision shall be final. In the determination of such prevailing rate or rates, due regard shall be given to those rates which have been secured through collective agreement by representatives of employers and employees.

Where such work as is described in the two preceding paragraphs is done directly by the Corporation the prevailing rate of wages shall be paid in the same manner as though such work had been let by contract.

Insofar as applicable, the benefits of the Act entitled "An Act to provide compensation for employees of the United States suffering injuries while in the performance of their duties, and for other purposes", approved September 7, 1916, as amended, shall extend to persons given employment under the provisions of this Act. [48 Stat. 59-60.]

SEC. 4. Except as otherwise specifically provided in this Act, the Corporation—

(*a*) Shall have succession in its corporate name.

(*b*) May sue and be sued in its corporate name.

(*c*) May adopt and use a corporate seal, which shall be judicially noticed.

(*d*) May make contracts, as herein authorised.

(*e*) May adopt, amend, and repeal bylaws.

(*f*) May purchase or lease and hold such real and personal property as it deems necessary or convenient in the transaction of its business, and may dispose of any such personal property held by it.

The board shall select a treasurer and as many assistant treasurers as it deems proper, which treasurer and assistant treasurers shall give such bonds for the safe-keeping of the securities and moneys of the said Corporation as the board may require: *Provided,* That any member of said board may be removed from office at any time by a concurrent resolution of the Senate and the House of Representatives.

(*g*) Shall have such powers as may be necessary or appropriate for the exercise of the powers herein specifically conferred upon the Corporation.

(*h*) Shall have power in the name of the United States of America to exercise the right of eminent domain, and in the purchase of any real estate or the acquisition of real estate by condemnation proceedings, the title to such real estate shall be taken in the name of the United States of America, and thereupon all such real estate shall be entrusted to the Corporation as the agent of the United States to accomplish the purposes of this Act.

(*i*) Shall have power to acquire real estate for the construction of dams, reservoirs, transmission lines, power houses, and other structures, and navigation projects at any point along the Tennessee River, or any of its tributaries, and in the event that the owner or owners of such property shall fail and refuse to sell to the Corporation at a price deemed fair and reasonable by the board, then the Corporation may proceed to exercise the right of eminent domain, and to condemn all property that it deems necessary for carrying out the purposes of this Act, and all such condemnation proceedings shall be had pursuant to the provisions and requirements hereinafter specified, with reference to any and all condemnation proceedings [48 Stat. 60-61]: *Provided,* That nothing contained herein or elsewhere in this Act shall be construed to deprive the Corporation of the rights conferred by the Act of February 26, 1931 (46 Stat. 1422, ch. 307, secs. 1 to 5, inclusive), as now compiled in section 258a to 258e, inclusive, of Title 40 of the United States Code. [49 Stat. 1075.]

(*j*) Shall have power to construct such dams, and reservoirs, in the Tennessee River and its tributaries, as in conjunction with Wilson Dam, and Norris, Wheeler, and Pickwick Landing Dams, now under construction, will provide a nine-foot channel in the said river and maintain a water supply for the same, from Knoxville to its mouth, and will best serve to promote navigation on the Tennessee River and its tributaries and control destructive flood waters in the Tennessee and Mississippi River drainage basins; and shall have power to acquire or construct power houses, power structures, transmission lines, navigation projects, and incidental works in the Tennessee River and its tributaries, and to unite the various power installations into one or more systems by transmission lines. The directors of the Authority are hereby directed to report to Congress their recommendations not later than April 1, 1936, for the unified development of the Tennessee River system. [48 Stat. 61, as amended by 49 Stat. 1075.]

(*k*) Shall have power in the name of the United States—

  (*a*) to convey by deed, lease, or otherwise, any real property in the possession of or under the control of the Corporation to any person or persons, for the purpose of recreation or use as a summer residence, or for the operation on such premises of pleasure resorts for boating, fishing, bathing, or any similar purpose;

  (*b*) to convey by deed, lease, or otherwise, the possession and control of any such real property to any corporation, partnership, person, or persons for the purpose of erecting thereon docks and buildings for shipping purposes or the manufacture or storage thereon of products for the purpose of trading or shipping in transportation: *Provided,* That no transfer authorized herein in (*b*) shall be made without the approval of Congress: *And provided further,* That said Corporation, without further action of Congress, shall have power to convey by deed, lease, or otherwise, to the Ingalls Shipbuilding Corporation, a tract or tracts of land at or near Decatur, Alabama, and to the Commercial Barge Lines, Inc., a tract or tracts of land at or near Guntersville, Alabama;

(c) to transfer any part of the possession and control of the real estate now in possession of and under the control of said Corporation to any other department, agency, or instrumentality of the United States: *Provided, however,* That no land shall be conveyed, leased, or transferred, upon which there is located any permanent dam, hydroelectric power plant, or munitions plant heretofore or hereafter built by or for the United States or for the Authority, except that this prohibition shall not apply to the transfer of Nitrate Plant Numbered 1, at Muscle Shoals, Alabama, or to Waco Quarry: *And provided further,* That no transfer authorized herein in (a) or (c), except leases for terms of less than twenty years, shall be made without the approval of the President of the United States, if the property to be conveyed exceeds $500 in value; and

(d) to convey by warranty deed, or otherwise, lands, easements, and rights-of-way to States, counties, municipalities, school districts, railroad companies, telephone, telegraph, water, and power companies, where any such conveyance is necessary in order to replace any such lands, easements, or rights-of-way to be flooded or destroyed as the result of the construction of any dam or reservoir now under construction by the Corporation, or subsequently authorized by Congress, and easements and rights-of-way upon which are located transmission or distribution lines. The Corporation shall also have power to convey or lease Nitrate Plant Numbered 1, at Muscle Shoals, Alabama, and Waco Quarry, with the approval of the War Department and the President. [49 Stat. 1076, as amended by Public, No. 184, 77th Cong., 1st sess., H. R. 2097.]

(*l*) Shall have power to advise and cooperate in the readjustment of the population displaced by the construction of dams, the acquisition of reservoir areas, the protection of watersheds, the acquisition of rights-of-way, and other necessary acquisitions of land, in order to effectuate the purposes of the Act; and may cooperate with Federal, State, and local agencies to that end. [49 Stat. 1080.]

Sec. 5. The board is hereby authorized—

(a) To contract with commercial producers for the production of such fertilizers or fertilizer materials as may be needed in the Government's program of development and introduction in excess of that produced by Government plants. Such contracts may provide either for outright purchase of materials by the board or only for the payment of carrying charges on special materials manufactured at the board's request for its program.

(b) To arrange with farmers and farm organizations for large-scale practical use of the new forms of fertilizers under conditions permitting an accurate measure of the economic return they produce. [48 Stat. 61.]

(c) To cooperate with National, State, district, or county experimental stations or demonstration farms, with farmers, landowners, and associations of farmers or landowners, for the use of new forms of fertilizer or fertilizer practices during the initial or experimental period of their introduction, and for promoting the prevention of soil erosion by the use of fertilizers and otherwise. [48 Stat. 61, as amended by 49 Stat. 1076.].

(d) The board in order to improve and cheapen the production of fertilizer is authorized to manufacture and sell fixed nitrogen, fertilizer, and fertilizer ingredients at Muscle Shoals by the employment of existing facilities, by modernizing existing plants, or by any other process or processes that in its judgment shall appear wise and profitable for the fixation of atmospheric nitrogen or the cheapening of the production of fertilizer.

(e) Under the authority of this Act the board may make donations or sales of the product of the plant or plants operated by it to be fairly and equitably distributed through the agency of county demonstration agents, agricultural colleges, or otherwise as the board may direct, for experimentation, education, and introduction of the use of such products in cooperation with practical farmers so as to obtain information as to the value, effect, and best methods of their use.

(f) The board is authorized to make alterations, modifications, or improvements in existing plants and facilities, and to construct new plants.

(g) In the event it is not used for the fixation of nitrogen for agricultural purposes or leased, then the board shall maintain in stand-by condition nitrate plant numbered 2, or its equivalent, for the fixation of atmospheric nitrogen, for the production of explosives in the event of war or a national emergency, until the Congress shall by joint resolution release the board from this obligation, and if any part thereof be used by the board for the manufacture of phosphoric acid or potash, the balance of nitrate plant numbered 2 shall be kept in stand-by condition.

(h) To establish, maintain, and operate laboratories and experimental plants, and to undertake experiments for the purpose of enabling the Corporation to furnish nitrogen products for military purposes, and nitrogen and other fertilizer products for agricultural purposes in the most economical manner and at the highest standard of efficiency.

(i) To request the assistance and advice of any officer, agent, or employee of any executive department or of any independent office of the United States, to enable the Corporation the better to carry out its powers successfully, and as far as practicable shall utilize the services of such officers, agents, and employees, and the

President shall, if in his opinion, the public interest, service, or economy so require, direct that such assistance, advice, and service be rendered to the Corporation, and any individual that may be by the President directed to render such assistance, advice, and service shall be thereafter subject to the orders, rules, and regulations of the board: *Provided*, That any invention or discovery made by virtue of and incidental to such service by an employee of the Government of the United States serving under this section, or by any employee of the Corporation, together with any patents which may be granted thereon, shall be the sole and exclusive property of the Corporation, which is hereby authorized to grant such licenses thereunder as shall be authorized by the board: *Provided further*, That the board may pay to such inventor such sum from the income from sale of licenses as it may deem proper.

(*j*) Upon the requisition of the Secretary of War or the Secretary of the Navy to manufacture for and sell at cost to the United States explosives or their nitrogenous content.

(*k*) Upon the requisition of the Secretary of War the Corporation shall allot and deliver without charge to the War Department so much power as shall be necessary in the judgment of said Department for use in operation of all locks, lifts, or other facilities in aid of navigation.

(*l*) To produce, distribute, and sell electric power, as herein particularly specified.

(*m*) No products of the Corporation shall be sold for use outside of the United States, its Territories and possessions, except to the United States Government for the use of its Army and Navy, or to its allies in case of war.

(*n*) The President is authorized, within twelve months after the passage of this Act, to lease to any responsible farm organization or to any corporation organized by it nitrate plant numbered 2 and Waco Quarry, together with the railroad connecting said quarry with nitrate plant numbered 2, for a term not exceeding fifty years at a rental of not less than $1 per year, but such authority shall be subject to the express condition that the lessee shall use said property during the term of said lease exclusively for the manufacture of fertilizer and fertilizer ingredients to be used only in the manufacture of fertilizer by said lessee and sold for use as fertilizer. The said lessee shall covenant to keep said property in first-class condition, but the lessee shall be authorized to modernize said plant numbered 2 by the installation of such machinery as may be necessary, and is authorized to amortize the cost of said machinery and improvements over the term of said lease or any part thereof. Said lease shall also provide that the board shall sell to the lessee power for the operation of said plant at the same schedule of prices that it charges all other customers for power of the same class and quantity. Said lease shall also provide that, if the said lessee does not desire to buy power of the publicly owned plant, it shall have the right to purchase its power for the operation of said plant of the Alabama Power Company or any other publicly or privately owned corporation engaged in the generation and sale of electric power, and in such case the lease shall provide further that the said lessee shall have a free right of way to build a transmission line over

Goverament property to said plant paying the actual expenses and damages, if any, incurred by the Corporation on account of such line. Said lease shall also provide that the said lessee shall covenant that during the term of said lease the said lessee shall not enter into any illegal monopoly, combination, or trust with any privately owned corporation engaged in the manufacture, production, and sale of fertilizer with the object or effect of increasing the price of fertilizer to the farmer. [48 Stat. 61-63.]

SEC. 6. In the appointment of officials and the selection of employees for said Corporation, and in the promotion of any such employees or officials, no political test or qualification shall be permitted or given consideration, but all such appointments and promotions shall be given and made on the basis of merit and efficiency. Any member of said board who is found by the President of the United States to be guilty of a violation of this section shall be removed from office by the President of the United States, and any appointee of said board who is found by the board to be guilty of a violation of 'this section shall be removed from office by said board. [48 Stat. 63.]

SEC. 7. In order to enable the Corporation to exercise the powers and duties vested in it by this Act—

(a) The'exclusive use, possession, and control of the United States nitrate plants numbered 1 and 2, including steam plants, located, respectively, at Sheffield, Alabama, and Muscle Shoals, Alabama, together with all real estate and buildings connected therewith, all tools and machinery, equipment, accessories, and materials belonging thereto, and all laboratories and plants used as auxiliaries thereto; the fixed-nitrogen research laboratory, the Waco limestone quarry, in Alabama, and Dam Numbered 2, located at Muscle Shoals, its power house, and all hydroelectric and operating appurtenances (except the locks), and all machinery, lands, and buildings in connection therewith, and all appurtenances thereof, and all other property to be acquired by the Corporation in its own name or in the name of the United States of America, are hereby intrusted to the Corporation for the purposes of this Act.

(b) The President of the United States is authorized to provide for the transfer to the Corporation of the use, possession, and control of such other real or personal property of the United States as he may from time to time deem necessary and proper for the purposes of the Corporation as herein stated. [48 Stat. 63.]

SEC. 8. (a) The Corporation shall maintain its principal office in the immediate vicinity of Muscle Shoals, Alabama. The Corporation shall be held to be an inhabitant and resident of the northern judicial district of Alabama within the meaning of the laws of the United States relating to the venue of civil suits.

(b) The Corporation shall at all times maintain complete and accurate books of accounts.

(c) Each member of the board, before entering upon the duties of his office, shall subscribe to an oath (or affirmation) to support the Constitution of the United States and to faithfully and impartially perform the duties imposed upon him by this Act. [48 Stat. 63.]

SEC. 9. (a) The board shall file with the President and with the Congress, in December of each year, a financial statement and a complete report as to the business of the Corporation covering the preceding governmental fiscal year. This report shall include an itemized statement of the cost of power at each power station, the total number of employees and the names, salaries, and duties of those receiving compensation at the rate of more than $1,500 a year. [48 Stat. 63.]

(b) All purchases and contracts for supplies or services, except for personal services, made by the Corporation, shall be made after advertising, in such manner and at such times sufficiently in advance of opening bids, as the board shall determine to be adequate to insure notice and opportunity for competition: *Provided,* That advertisement shall not be required when, (1) an emergency requires immediate delivery of the supplies or performance of the services; or (2) repair parts, accessories, supplemental equipment, or services are required for supplies or services previously furnished or contracted for; or (3) the aggregate amount involved in any purchase of supplies or procurement of services does not exceed $500; in which cases such purchases of supplies or procurement of services may be made in the open market in the manner common among businessmen: *Provided further,* That in comparing bids and in making awards the board may consider such factors as relative quality and adaptability of supplies or services, the bidder's financial responsibility, skill, experience, record of integrity in dealing, ability to furnish repairs and maintenance services, the time of delivery or performance offered, and whether the bidder has complied with the specifications.

The Comptroller General of the United States shall audit the transactions of the Corporation at such times as he shall determine, but not less frequently than once each governmental fiscal year, with personnel of his selection. In such connection he and his representatives shall have free and open access to all papers, books, records, files, accounts, plants, warehouses, offices, and all other things, property, and places belonging to or under the control of or used or employed by the Corporation, and shall be afforded full facilities for counting all cash and verifying transactions with and balances in depositaries. He shall make report of each such audit in quadruplicate, one copy for the President of the United States, one for the chairman of the board, one for public inspection at the principal office of the Corporation, and the other to be retained by him for the uses of the Congress: *Provided,* That such report shall not be made until the Corporation shall have had reasonable opportunity to examine the exceptions and criticisms of the Comptroller General or the General Accounting Office, to point out errors therein, explain or answer the same, and to file a statement which shall be submitted by the Comptroller General with his report. The expenses for each such audit shall be paid from any appropriation or appropriations for the General Accounting Office, and such part of such expenses as may be allocated to the cost of generating, transmitting, and distributing electric energy shall be reimbursed promptly by the Corporation as billed by the Comptroller General. The Comptroller General shall make special report to the President of the United States and to the Congress of any transaction or condition found by him to be in conflict with the powers or duties entrusted to the Corporation by law. [48 Stat. 63-64, as amended by 49 Stat. 1080-1081.]

Nothing in this Act shall be construed to relieve the Treasurer or other accountable officers or employees of the Corporation from compliance with the provisions of existing law requiring the rendition of accounts for adjustment and settlement pursuant to section 236, Revised Statutes, as amended by section 305 of the Budget and Accounting Act, 1921 (42 Stat. 24), and accounts for all receipts and disbursements by or for the Corporation shall be rendered accordingly: *Provided*, That, subject only to the provisions of the Tennessee Valley Authority Act of 1933, as amended, the Corporation is authorized to make such expenditures and to enter into such contracts, agreements, and arrangements, upon such terms and conditions and in such manner as it may deem necessary, including the final settlement of all claims and litigation by or against the Corporation; and, notwithstanding the provisions of any other law governing the expenditure of public funds, the General Accounting Office, in the settlement of the accounts of the Treasurer or other accountable officer or employee of the Corporation, shall not disallow credit for, nor withhold funds because of, any expenditure which the board shall determine to have been necessary to carry out the provisions of said Act.

The Corporation shall determine its own system of administrative accounts and the forms and contents of its contracts and other business documents except as otherwise provided in the Tennessee Valley Authority Act of 1933, as amended. [Public, No. 306, 77th Cong., 1st sess., H. R. 4961.]

SEC. 9a. The board is hereby directed in the operation of any dam or reservoir in its possession and control to regulate the stream flow primarily for the purposes of promoting navigation and controlling floods. So far as may be consistent with such purposes, the board is authorized to provide and operate facilities for the generation of electric energy at any such dam for the use of the Corporation and for the use of the United States or any agency thereof, and the board is further authorized, whenever an opportunity is afforded, to 'provide and operate facilities for the generation of electric energy in order to avoid the waste of water power, to transmit and market such power as in this act provided, and thereby, so far as may be practicable, to assist in liquidating the cost or aid in the maintenance of the projects of the Authority. [49 Stat. 1076.]

SEC. 10. The board is hereby empowered and authorized to sell the surplus power not used in its operations, and for operation of locks and other works generated by it, to States, counties, municipalities, corporations, partnerships, or individuals, according to the policies hereinafter set forth; and to carry out said authority, the board is authorized to enter into contracts for such sale for a term not exceeding twenty years, and in the sale of such current by the board it shall give preference to States, counties, municipalities, and cooperative organizations of citizens or farmers, not organized or doing business for profit, but primarily for the purpose of supplying electricity to its own citizens or members: *Provided*, That all contracts made with private companies or individuals for the sale of power, which power is to be resold for a profit, shall contain a provision authorizing the board to cancel said contract upon five years' notice in writing, if the board needs said power to supply the demands of States, counties, or municipalities. In order to promote and encourage the fullest possible use of electric light and power on farms within reasonable distance of any of its transmission lines the board in its discretion shall have power to construct transmission lines to farms and small villages that are not otherwise supplied with electricity at reasonable rates, and to make such rules and regulations governing such sale and distribution of such electric power as in its judgment may be just and equitable: *Provided further*, That the board is hereby authorized and directed to make studies, experiments, and determinations to promote the wider and better use of electric power for agricultural and domestic use, or for small or local industries, and it may cooperate with State governments, or their subdivisions or agencies, with educational or research institutions, and with cooperatives or other organizations, in the application of electric power to the fuller and better balanced development of the resources of the region [48 Stat. 64]: *Provided further*, That the Board is authorized to include in any contract for the sale of power such terms and conditions, including resale rate schedules, and to provide for such rules and regulations as in its judgment may be necessary or desirable for carrying out the purposes of this Act, and in case the purchaser shall fail to comply with any such terms and conditions, or violate any such rules and regulations, said contract may provide that it shall be voidable at the election of the board: *Provided further*, That in order to supply farms and small villages with electric power directly as contemplated by this section, the board in its discretion shall have power to acquire existing electric facilities used in serving such farms and small villages: *And provided further*, That the terms "States," "counties", and "municipalities" as used in this Act shall be construed to include the public agencies of any of them unless the context requires a different construction. [49 Stat. 1076.]

SEC. 11. It is hereby declared to be the policy of the Government so far as practical to distribute and sell the surplus power generated at Muscle Shoals equitably among the States, counties, and municipalities within transmission distance. This policy is further declared to be that the projects herein provided for shall be considered primarily as for the benefit of the people of the section as a whole and particularly the domestic and rural consumers to whom the power can economically be made available, and accordingly that sale to and use by industry shall be a secondary purpose, to be utilized principally to secure a sufficiently high load factor and revenue returns which will permit domestic and rural use at the lowest possible rates and in such manner as to encourage increased domestic and rural use of electricity. It is further hereby declared to be the policy of the Government to utilize the Muscle Shoals properties so far as may be necessary to improve, increase, and cheapen the production of fertilizer and fertilizer ingredients by carrying out the provisions of this Act. [48 Stat. 64-65.]

SEC. 12. In order to place the board upon a fair basis for making such contracts and for receiving bids for the sale of such power, it is hereby expressly authorized, either from appropriations made by Congress or from funds secured from the sale of such power, or from funds secured by the sale of bonds hereafter provided for, to construct, lease, purchase, or authorize the construction of transmission lines within transmission distance from the place where generated, and to interconnect with other systems. The board is also authorized to lease to any person, persons, or corporation the use of any transmission line owned by the Government and operated by the board, but no such lease shall be made that in any way interferes with the use of such transmission line by the board: *Provided*, That if any State, county, municipality, or other public or cooperative organization of citizens or farmers, not organized or doing business for profit, but primarily for the purpose of supplying electricity to its own citizens or members, or any two or more of such municipalities or organizations, shall construct or agree to construct and maintain a properly designed and built transmission line to the Government reservation upon which is located a Government generating plant, or to a main transmission line owned by the Government or leased by the board and under the control of the board, the board is hereby authorized and directed to contract with such State, county, municipality, or other organization, or two or more of them, for the sale of electricity for a term not exceeding thirty years; and in any such case the board shall give to such State, county, municipality, or other organization ample time to fully comply with any local law now in existence or hereafter enacted providing for the necessary legal authority for such State, county, municipality, or other organization to contract with the board for such power: *Provided further*, That all contracts entered into between the Corporation and any municipality or other political subdivision or cooperative organization shall provide that the electric power shall be sold and distributed to the ultimate consumer without discrimination as between consumers of the same class, and such contract shall be voidable at the election of the board if a discriminatory rate, rebate, or other special concession is made or given to any consumer or user by the municipality or other political subdivision or cooperative organization: *And provided further*, That as to any surplus power not so sold as above provided to States, counties, municipalities, or other said organizations, before the board shall sell the same to any person or corporation engaged in the distribution and resale of electricity for profit, it shall require said person or corporation to agree that any resale of such electric power by said person or corporation shall be made to the ultimate consumer of such electric power at prices that shall not exceed a schedule fixed by the board from time to time as reasonable, just, and fair; and in case of any such sale, if an amount is charged the ultimate consumer which is in excess of the price so deemed to be just, reasonable, and fair by the board, the contract for such sale between the board and such distributor of electricity shall be voidable at the election of the board: *And provided further*, That the board is hereby authorized to enter into contracts with other power systems for the mutual exchange of unused excess power upon suitable terms, for the conservation of stored water, and as an emergency or break-down relief. [48 Stat. 65-66.]

SEC. 12a. In order (1) to facilitate the disposition of the surplus power of the Corporation according to the policies set forth in this Act; (2) to give effect to the priority herein accorded to States, counties, municipalities, and nonprofit organizations in the purchase of such power by enabling them to acquire facilities for the distribution of such power; and (3) at the same time to preserve existing distribution facilities as going concerns and avoid duplication of such facilities, the board is authorized to advise and cooperate with and assist, by extending credit for a period of not exceeding five years to, States, counties, municipalities and nonprofit organizations situated within transmission distance from any dam where such power is generated by the Corporation in acquiring, improving, and operating (a) existing distribution facilities and incidental works, including generating plants; and (b) interconnecting transmission lines; or in acquiring any interest in such facilities, incidental works, and lines. [49 Stat. 1076-1077.]

SEC. 13. In order to render financial assistance to those States and local governments in which the power operations of the Corporation are carried on and in which the Corporation has acquired properties previously subject to State and local taxation, the board is authorized and directed to pay to said States, and the counties therein, for each fiscal year, beginning July 1, 1940, the following percentages of the gross proceeds derived from the sale of power by the Corporation for the preceding fiscal year as hereinafter provided, together with such additional amounts as may be payable pursuant to the provisions hereinafter set forth, said payments to constitute a charge against the power operations of the Corporation: For the fiscal year (beginning July 1) 1940, 10 per centum; 1941, 9 per centum; 1942, 8 per centum; 1943, 7½ per centum; 1944, 7 per centum; 1945, 6½ per centum; 1946, 6 per centum; 1947, 5½ per centum; 1948 and each fiscal year thereafter, 5 per centum. "Gross proceeds", as used in this section, is defined as the total gross proceeds derived by the Corporation from the sale of power for the preceding fiscal year, excluding power used by the Corporation or sold or delivered to any other department or agency of the Government of the United States for any purpose other than the resale thereof. The payments herein authorized are in lieu of taxation, and the Corporation, its property, franchise and income, are hereby expressly exempted from taxation in any manner or form by any State, county, municipality, or any subdivision or district thereof.

The payment for each fiscal year shall be apportioned among said States in the following manner: One-half of said payment shall be apportioned by paying to each State the percentage thereof which the gross proceeds of the power sales by the Corporation within said State during the preceding fiscal year bears to the total gross proceeds from all power sales by the Corporation during the preceding fiscal year; the remaining one-half of said payment shall be apportioned by paying to each State the percentage thereof which the book value of the power property held by the Corporation within said State at the end of the preceding fiscal year bears to the total book value of all such property held by the Corporation on the same date. The book value of power property shall include that portion of the investment allocated or estimated to be allocable to power: *Provided*, That the minimum annual payment to each State (including payments to counties therein) shall not be less than an amount equal to the two-year |average of the State and local *ad valorem* property taxes levied against power property purchased and operated by the Corporation in said State and against that portion of reservoir lands related to dams constructed by or on behalf of the United States Government and held or operated by the Corporation and allocated or estimated to be allocable to power. The said two-year average shall be calculated for the last two tax years during which said property was privately owned and operated or said land was privately owned: *Provided further*, That the minimum annual payment to each State in which the Corporation owns and operates power property (including payments to counties therein) shall not be less than $10,000 in any case: *Provided further*, That the corporation shall pay directly to the respective counties the two-year average of county *ad valorem* property taxes (including taxes levied by taxing districts within the respective counties) upon power property and reservoir lands allocable to power, determined as above provided, and all payments to any such county within a State shall be deducted from the payment otherwise due to such State under the provisions of this section. The determination of the board of the amounts due hereunder to the respective States and counties shall be final.

The payments above provided shall in each case be made to the State or county in equal monthly installments beginning not later than July 31, 1940.

Nothing herein shall be construed to limit the authority of the Corporation in its contracts for the sale of power to municipalities, to permit or provide for the resale of power at rates which may include an amount to cover tax-equivalent payments to the municipality in lieu of State, county, and municipal taxes upon any distribution system or property owned by the municipality or any agency thereof, conditioned upon a proper distribution by the municipality of any amounts collected by it in lieu of State or county taxes upon any such distribution system or property; it being the intention of Congress that either the municipality or the State in which the municipality is situated shall provide for the proper distribution to the State and county of any portion of tax equivalent so collected by the municipality in lieu of State or county taxes upon any such distribution system or property.

The Corporation shall, not later than January 1, 1945, submit to the Congress a report on the operation of the provisions of this section, including a statement of the distribution to the various States and counties hereunder; the effect of the operation of the provisions of this section on State and local finances; an appraisal of the benefits of the program of the Corporation to the States and counties receiving payments hereunder, and the effect of such benefits in increasing taxable values within such States and counties; and such other data, information, and recommendations as may be pertinent to future legislation. [48 Stat. 66, as amended by 54 Stat. 626-627.]

SEC. 14. The board shall make a thorough investigation as to the present value of Dam Numbered 2, and the steam plants at nitrate plant numbered 1, and nitrate plant numbered 2, and as to the cost of Cove Creek Dam, for the purpose of ascertaining how much of the value or the cost of said properties shall be allocated and charged up to (1) flood control, (2) navigation, (3) fertilizer, (4) national defense, and (5) the development of power. The findings thus made by the board, when approved by the President of the United States, shall be final, and such findings shall thereafter be used in all allocation of value for the purpose of keeping the book value of said properties. In like manner, the cost and book value of any dams, steam plants, or other similar improvements hereafter constructed and turned over to said board for the purpose of control and management shall be ascertained and allocated. [48 Stat. 66.]

The board shall, on or before January 1, 1937, file with Congress a statement of its allocation of the value of all such properties turned over to said board, and which have been completed prior to the end of the preceding fiscal year, and shall thereafter in its annual report to Congress file a statement of its allocation of the value of such properties as have been completed during the preceding fiscal year.

For the purpose of accumulating data useful to the Congress in the formulation of legislative policy in matters relating to the generation, transmission, and distribution of electric energy and the production of chemicals necessary to national defense and useful in agriculture, and to the Federal Power Commission and other Federal and State agencies, and to the public, the board shall keep complete accounts of its costs of generation, transmission, and distribution of electric energy and shall keep a complete account of the total cost of generating and transmission facilities constructed or otherwise acquired by the Corporation, and of producing such chemicals, and a description of the major components of such costs according to such uniform system of accounting for public utilities as the Federal Power Commission has, and if it have none, then it is hereby empowered and directed to prescribe such uniform system of accounting, together with records of such other physical data and operating statistics of the Authority as may be helpful in determining the actual cost and value of services, and the practices, methods, facilities, equipment, appliances, and standards and sizes, types, location, and geographical and economic integration of plants and systems best suited to promote the public interest, efficiency, and the wider and more economical use of electric energy. Such data shall be reported to the Congress by the board from time to time with appropriate analyses and recommendations, and, so far as practicable, shall be made available to the Federal Power Commission and other Federal and State agencies which may be concerned with the administration of legislation relating to the generation, transmission, or distribution of electric energy and chemicals useful to agriculture. It is hereby declared to be the policy of this Act that, in order, as soon as practicable, to make the power projects self-supporting and self-liquidating, the surplus power shall be sold at rates which, in the opinion of the board, when applied to the normal capacity of the Authority's power facilities, will produce gross revenues in excess of the cost of production of said power and in addition to the statement of the cost of power at each power station as required by section 9 (*a*) of the "Tennessee Valley Act of 1933", the board shall file with each annual report, a statement of the total cost of all power generated by it at all power stations during each year, the average cost of such power per kilowatt-hour, the rates at which sold, and to whom sold, and copies of all contracts for the sale of power. [49 Stat. 1077.]

Sec. 15. In the construction of any future dam, steam plant, or other facility, to be used in whole or in part for the generation or transmission of electric power the board is hereby authorized and empowered to issue on the credit of the United States and to sell serial bonds not exceeding $50,000,000 in amount, having a maturity not more than fifty years from the date of issue thereof, and bearing interest not exceeding 3½ per centum per annum. Said bonds shall be issued and sold in amounts and prices approved by the Secretary of the Treasury, but all such bonds as may be so issued and sold shall have equal rank. None of said bonds shall be sold below par, and no fee, commission, or compensation whatever shall be paid to any person, firm, or corporation for handling, negotiating the sale, or selling the said bonds. All of such bonds so issued and sold shall have all the rights and privileges accorded by law to Panama Canal bonds, authorized by section 8 of the Act of June 28, 1902, chapter 1302, as amended by the Act of December 21, 1905 (ch. 3, sec. 1, 34 Stat. 5), as now compiled in section 743 of title 31 of the United States Code. All funds derived from the sale of such bonds shall be paid over to the Corporation. [48 Stat. 66-67.]

Sec. 15a. With the approval of the Secretary of the Treasury, the Corporation is authorized to issue bonds not to exceed in the aggregate $50,000,000 outstanding at any one time. which bonds may be sold by the Corporation to obtain funds to carry out the provisions of section 12a of this Act. Such bonds shall be in such forms and denominations, shall mature within such periods not more than fifty years from the date of their issue, may be redeemable at the option of the Corporation before maturity in such manner as may be stipulated therein, shall bear such rates of interest not exceeding 3½ per centum per annum, shall be subject to such terms and conditions, shall be issued in such manner and amount, and sold at such prices, as may be prescribed by the Corporation, with the approval of the Secretary of the Treasury: *Provided*, That such bonds shall not be sold at such prices or on such terms as to afford an investment yield to the holders in excess of 3½ per centum per annum. Such bonds shall be fully and unconditionally guaranteed both as to interest and principal by the United States, and such guaranty shall be expressed on the face thereof, and such bonds shall be lawful investments, and may be accepted as security, for all fiduciary, trust, and public funds, the investment or deposit of which shall be under the authority or control of the United States or any officer or officers thereof. In the event that the Corporation should not pay upon demand, when due, the principal of, or interest on, such bonds, the Secretary of the Treasury shall pay to the holder the amount thereof, which is hereby authorized to be appropriated out of any moneys in the Treasury not otherwise appropriated, and thereupon to the extent of the amount so paid the Secretary of the Treasury shall succeed to all the rights of the holders of such bonds. The Secretary of the Treasury, in his discretion, is authorized to purchase any bonds issued hereunder, and for such purpose the Secretary of the Treasury is authorized to use as a public-debt transaction the proceeds from the sale of any securities hereafter issued under the Second Liberty Bond Act, as amended, and the purposes for which securities may be issued under such Act, as amended, are extended to include any purchases of the Corporation's bonds hereunder. The Secretary of the Treasury may, at any time, sell any of the bonds of the Corporation acquired by him under this section. All redemptions, purchases, and sales by the Secretary of the Treasury of the bonds of the Corporation shall be treated as public-debt transactions of the United States. With the approval of the Secretary of the Treasury, the Corporation shall have power to purchase such bonds in the open market at any time and at any price. No bonds shall be issued hereunder to provide funds or bonds necessary for the performance of any proposed contract negotiated by the Corporation under the authority of section 12a of this Act until the proposed contract shall have been submitted to and approved by the Federal Power Commission. When any such proposed contract shall have been submitted to the said Commission, the matter shall be given precedence and shall be in every way expedited and the Commission's determination of the matter shall be final. The authority of the Corporation to issue bonds hereunder shall expire at the end of five years from the date when this section as amended herein becomes law, except that such bonds may be issued at any time after the expiration of said period to provide bonds or funds necessary for the performance of any contract entered into by the Corporation, prior to the expiration of said period, under the authority of section 12a of this Act. [49 Stat. 1078.]

SEC. 15b. No bonds shall be issued by the Corporation after the date of enactment of this section under section 15 or section 15a.

SEC. 15c. With the approval of the Secretary of the Treasury the Corporation is authorized, after the date of enactment of this section, to issue bonds not to exceed in the aggregate $61,500,000. Such bonds may be sold by the Corporation to obtain funds which may be used for the following purposes only:

(1) Not to exceed $46,000,000 may be used for the purchase of electric utility properties of the Tennessee Electric Power Company and Southern Tennessee Power Company, as contemplated in the contract between the Corporation and the Commonwealth and Southern Corporation and others, dated as of May 12, 1939.

(2) Not to exceed $6,500,000 may be used for the purchase and rehabilitation of electric utility properties of the Alabama Power Company and Mississippi Power Company in the following named counties in northern Alabama and northern Mississippi: The counties of Jackson, Madison, Limestone, Lauderdale, Colbert, Lawrence, Morgan, Marshall, De Kalb, Cherokee,

Cullman, Winston, Franklin, Marion, and Lamar in northern Alabama, and the counties of Calhoun, Chickasaw, Monroe, Clay, Lowndes, Oktibbeha, Choctaw, Webster, Noxubee, Winston, Neshoba, and Kemper in northern Mississippi.

(3) Not to exceed $3,500,000 may be used for rebuilding, replacing, and repairing electric utility properties purchased by the Corporation in accordance with the foregoing provisions of this section.

(4) Not to exceed $3,500,000 may be used for constructing electric transmission lines, substations, and other electrical facilities necessary to connect the electric utility properties purchased by the Corporation in accordance with the foregoing provisions of this section with the electric power system of the Corporation.

(5) Not to exceed $2,000,000 may be used for making loans under section 12a to States, counties, municipalities, and non-profit organizations to enable them to purchase any electric utility properties referred to in the contract between the Corporation and the Commonwealth and Southern Corporation and others, dated as of May 12, 1939, or any electric utility properties of the Alabama Power Company or Mississippi Power Company in any of the counties in northern Alabama or northern Mississippi named in paragraph (2).

The Corporation shall file with the President and with the Congress in December of each year a financial statement and complete report as to the expenditure of funds derived from the sale of bonds under this section covering the period not covered by any such previous statement or report. Such bonds shall be in such forms and denominations, shall mature within such periods not more than fifty years from the date of their issue, may be redeemable at the option of the Corporation before maturity in such manner as may be stipulated therein, shall bear such rates of interest not exceeding $3\frac{1}{2}$ per centum per annum, shall be subject to such terms and conditions, shall be issued in such manner and amount, and sold at such prices, as may be prescribed by the Corporation with the approval of the Secretary of the Treasury: *Provided*, That such bonds shall not be sold at such prices or on such terms as to afford an investment yield to the holders in excess of $3\frac{1}{2}$ per centum per annum. Such bonds shall be fully and unconditionally guaranteed both as to interest and principal by the United States, and such guaranty shall be expressed on the face thereof, and such bonds shall be lawful investments, and may be accepted as security, for all fiduciary, trust, and public funds, the investment or deposit of which shall be under the authority or control of the United States or any officer or officers thereof. In the event that the Corporation should not pay upon demand when due, the principal of, or interest on, such bonds, the Secretary of the Treasury shall pay to the holder the amount thereof, which is hereby authorized to be appropriated out of any moneys in the Treasury not otherwise appropriated, and thereupon to the extent of the amount so paid the Secretary of the Treasury shall succeed to all the rights of the holders of such bonds. The Secretary of the Treasury, in his discretion, is authorized to purchase any bonds issued hereunder, and for such purpose the Secretary of the Treasury is authorized to use as a public-debt transaction the proceeds from the sale of any securities hereafter issued under the Second Liberty Bond Act, as amended, and the purposes for which securities may be issued under such Act, as amended, are extended to include any purchases of the Corporation's bonds hereunder. The Secretary of the Treasury may, at any time, sell any of the bonds of the Corporation acquired by him under this section. All redemptions, purchases, and sales by the Secretary of the Treasury of the bonds of the Corporation shall be treated as public-debt transactions of the United States. With the approval of the Secretary of the Treasury, the Corporation shall have power to purchase such bonds in the open market at any time and at any price. None of the proceeds of the bonds shall be used for the performance of any proposed contract negotiated by the Corporation under the authority of section 12a of this Act until the proposed contract shall have been submitted to and approved by the Federal Power Commission. When any such proposed contract shall have been submitted to the said Commission, the matter shall be given precedence and shall be in every way expedited and the Commission's determination of the matter shall be final. The authority of the Corporation to issue bonds under this section shall expire January 1, 1941, except that if at the time such authority expires the amount of bonds issued by the Corporation under this section is less than $61,500,000, the Corporation may, subject to the foregoing provisions of this section, issue, after the expiration of such period, bonds in an amount not in excess of the amount by which the bonds so issued prior to the expiration of such period is less than $61,500,000, for refunding purposes, or, subject to the provisions of paragraph (5) of this section (limiting the purposes for which loans under section 12a of funds derived from bond proceeds may be made) to provide funds found necessary in the performance of any contract entered into by the Corporation prior to the expiration of such period, under the authority of section 12a. [53 Stat. 1083-1085.]

SEC. 16. The board, whenever the President deems it advisable, is hereby empowered and directed to complete Dam Numbered 2 at Muscle Shoals, Alabama, and the steam plant at nitrate plant numbered 2, in the vicinity of Muscle Shoals, by installing in Dam Numbered 2 the additional power units according to the plans and specifications of said dam, and the additional power unit in the steam plant at nitrate plant numbered 2. [48 Stat. 67.]

SEC. 17. The Secretary of War, or the Secretary of the Interior, is hereby authorized to construct, either directly or by contract to the lowest responsible bidder, after due advertisement, a dam in and across Clinch River in the State of Tennessee, which has by long custom become known and designated as the Cove Creek Dam, together with a transmission line from Muscle Shoals, according to the latest and most approved designs, including power house and hydroelectric installations and equipment for the generation of power, in order that the waters of the said Clinch River may be impounded and stored above said dam for the purpose of increasing and regulating the flow of the Clinch River and the Tennessee River below, so that the maximum amount of primary power may be developed at Dam Numbered 2 and at any and all other dams below the said Cove Creek Dam: *Provided, however,* That the President is hereby authorized by appropriate order to direct the employment by the Secretary of War, or by the Secretary of the Interior, of such engineer or engineers as he may designate, to perform such duties and obligations as he may deem proper, either in the drawing of plans and specifications for said dam, or to perform any other work in the building or construction of the same. The President may, by such order, place the control of the construction of said dam in the hands of such engineer or engineers taken from private life as he may desire: *And provided further,* That the President is hereby expressly authorized, without regard to the restriction or limitation of any other statute, to select attorneys and assistants for the purpose of making any investigation he may deem proper to ascertain whether, in the control and management of Dam Numbered 2, or any other dam or property owned by the Government in the Tennessee River Basin, or in the authorization of any improvement therein, there has been any undue or unfair advantage given to private persons, partnerships, or corporations, by any officials or employees of the Government, or whether in any such matters the Government has been injured or unjustly deprived of any of its rights. [48 Stat. 67.]

SEC. 18. In order to enable and empower the Secretary of War, the Secretary of the Interior, or the board to carry out the authority hereby conferred, in the most economical and efficient manner, he or it is hereby authorized and empowered in the exercise of the powers of national defense in aid of navigation, and in the control of the flood waters of the Tennessee and Mississippi Rivers, constituting channels of interstate commerce, to exercise the right of eminent domain for all purposes of this Act, and to condemn all lands, easements, rights of way, and other area necessary in order to obtain a site for said Cove Creek Dam, and the flowage rights for the reservoir of water above said dam, and to negotiate and conclude contracts with States, counties, municipalities, and all State agencies and with railroads, railroad corporations, common carriers, and all public utility commissions and any other person, firm, or corporation, for the relocation of railroad tracks, highways, highway bridges, mills, ferries, electric-light plants, and any and all other properties, enterprises, and projects whose removal may be necessary in order to carry out the provisions of this Act. When said Cove Creek Dam, transmission line, and power house shall have been completed, the possession, use, and control thereof shall be entrusted to the Corporation for use and operation in connection with the general Tennessee Valley project, and to promote flood control and navigation in the Tennessee River. [48 Stat. 67-68.]

SEC. 19. The Corporation, as an instrumentality and agency of the Government of the United States for the purpose of executing its constitutional powers, shall have access to the Patent Office of the United States for the purpose of studying, ascertaining, and copying all methods, formulae, and scientific information (not including access to pending applications for patents) necessary to enable the Corporation to use and employ the most efficacious and economical process for the production of fixed nitrogen, or any essential ingredient of fertilizer, or any method of improving and cheapening the production of hydroelectric power, and any owner of a patent whose patent rights may have been thus in any way copied, used, infringed, or employed by the exercise of this authority by the Corporation shall have as the exclusive remedy a cause of action against the Corporation to be instituted and prosecuted on the equity side of the appropriate district court of the United States, for the recovery of reasonable compensation for such infringement. The Commissioner of Patents shall furnish to the Corporation, at its request and without payment of fees, copies of documents on file in his office: *Provided*, That the benefits of this section shall not apply to any art, machine, method of manufacture, or composition of matter, discovered or invented by such employee during the time of his employment or service with the Corporation or with the Government of the United States. [48 Stat. 68.]

SEC. 20. The Government of the United States hereby reserves the right, in case of war or national emergency declared by Congress, to take possession of all or any part of the property described or referred to in this Act for the purpose of manufacturing explosives or for other war purposes; but, if this right is exercised by the Government, it shall pay the reasonable and fair damages that may be suffered by any party whose contract for the purchase of electric power or fixed nitrogen or fertilizer ingredients is hereby violated, after the amount of the damages has been fixed by the United States Court of Claims in proceedings instituted and conducted for that purpose under rules prescribed by the court. [48 Stat. 68.]

SEC. 21. (*a*) All general penal statutes relating to the larceny, embezzlement, conversion, or to the improper handling, retention, use, or disposal of public moneys or property of the United States, shall apply to the moneys and property of the Corporation and to moneys and properties of the United States entrusted to the Corporation.

(*b*) Any person who, with intent to defraud the Corporation, or to deceive any director, officer, or employee of the Corporation or any officer or employee of the United States (1) makes any false entry in any book of the Corporation, or (2) makes any false report or statement for the Corporation, shall, upon conviction thereof, be fined not more than $10,000 or imprisoned not more than five years, or both.

(*c*) Any person who shall receive any compensation, rebate, or reward, or shall enter into any conspiracy, collusion, or agreement, express or implied, with intent to defraud the Corporation or wrongfully and unlawfully to defeat its purposes, shall, on conviction thereof, be fined not more than $5,000 or imprisoned not more than five years, or both. [48 Stat. 68-69.]

SEC. 22. To aid further the proper use, conservation, and development of the natural resources of the Tennessee River drainage basin and of such adjoining territory as may be related to or materially affected by the development consequent to this Act, and to provide for the general welfare of the citizens of said areas, the President is hereby authorized, by such means or methods as he may deem proper within the limits of appropriations made therefor by Congress, to make such surveys of and general plans for said Tennessee basin and adjoining territory as may be useful to the Congress and to the several States in guiding and controlling the extent, sequence, and nature of development that may be equitably and economically advanced through the expenditure of public funds, or through the guidance or control of public authority, all for the general purpose of fostering an orderly and proper physical, economic, and social development of said areas; and the President is further authorized in making said surveys and plans to cooperate with the States affected thereby, or subdivisions or agencies of such States, or with cooperative or other organizations, and to make such studies, experiments, or demonstrations as may be necessary and suitable to that end. [48 Stat. 69.]

SEC. 23. The President shall, from time to time, as the work provided for in the preceding section progresses, recommend to Congress such legislation as he deems proper to carry out the general purposes stated in said section, and for the especial purpose of bringing about in said Tennessee drainage basin and adjoining territory in conformity with said general purposes (1) the maximum amount of flood control; (2) the maximum development of said Tennessee River for navigation purposes; (3) the maximum generation of electric power consistent with flood control and navigation; (4) the proper use of marginal lands; (5) the proper method of reforestation of all lands in said drainage basin suitable for reforestation; and (6) the economic and social well-being of the people living in said river basin. [48 Stat. 69.]

SEC. 24. For the purpose of securing any rights of flowage, or obtaining title to or possession of any property, real or personal, that may be necessary or may become necessary, in the carrying out of any of the provisions of this Act, the President of the United States for a period of three years from the date of the enactment of this Act, is hereby authorized to acquire title in the name of the United States to such rights or such property, and to provide for the payment for same by directing the board to contract to deliver power generated at any of the plants now owned or hereafter owned or constructed by the Government or by said Corporation, such future delivery of power to continue for a period not exceeding thirty years. Likewise, for one year after the enactment of this Act, the President is further authorized to sell or lease any parcel or part of any vacant real estate now owned by the Government in said Tennessee River Basin, to persons, firms, or corporations who shall contract to erect thereon factories or manufacturing establishments, and who shall contract to purchase of said Corporation electric power for the operation of any such factory or manufacturing establishment. No contract shall be made by the President for the sale of any of such real estate as may be necessary for present or future use on the part of the Government for any of the purposes of this Act. Any such contract made by the President of the United States shall be carried out by the board: *Provided*, That no such contract shall be made that will in any way abridge or take away the preference right to purchase power given in this Act to States, counties, municipalities, or farm organizations: *Provided further*,

That no lease shall be for a term to exceed fifty years: *Provided further*, That any sale shall be on condition that said land shall be used for industrial purposes only. [48 Stat. 69-70.]

SEC. 25. The Corporation may cause proceedings to be instituted for the acquisition by condemnation of any lands, easements, or rights of way which, in the opinion of the Corporation, are necessary to carry out the provisions of this Act. The proceedings shall be instituted in the United States district court for the district in which the land, easement, right of way, or other interest, or any part thereof, is located, and such court shall have full jurisdiction to divest the complete title to the property sought to be acquired out of all persons or claimants and vest the same in the United States in fee simple, and to enter a decree quieting the title thereto in the United States of America.

Upon the filing of a petition for condemnation and for the purpose of ascertaining the value of the property to be acquired, and assessing the compensation to be paid, the court shall appoint three commissioners who shall be disinterested persons and who shall take and subscribe an oath that they do not own any lands, or interest or easement in any lands, which it may be desirable for the United States to acquire in the furtherance of said project, and such commissioners shall not be selected from the locality wherein the land sought to be condemned lies. Such commissioners shall receive a per diem of not to exceed $15 for their services, together with an additional amount of $5 per day for subsistence for time actually spent in performing their duties as commissioners.

It shall be the duty of such commissioners to examine into the value of the lands sought to be condemned, to conduct hearings and receive evidence, and generally to take such appropriate steps as may be proper for the determination of the value of the said lands sought to be condemned, and for such purpose the commissioners are authorized to administer oaths and subpoena witnesses, which said witnesses shall receive the same fees as are provided for witnesses in the Federal courts. The said commissioners shall thereupon file a report setting forth their conclusions as to the value of the said property sought to be condemned, making a separate award and valuation in the premises with respect to each separate parcel involved. Upon the filing of such award in court the clerk of said court shall give notice of the filing of such award to the parties to said proceeding, in manner and form as directed by the judge of said court.

Either or both parties may file exceptions to the award of said commissioners within twenty days from the date of the filing of said award in court. Exceptions filed to such award shall be heard before three Federal district judges unless the parties, in writing, in person, or by their attorneys, stipulate that the exceptions may be heard before a lesser number of judges. On such hearing such judges shall pass *de novo* upon the proceedings had before the commissioners, may view the property, and may take additional evidence. Upon such hearings the said judges shall file their own award, fixing therein the value of the property sought to be condemned, regardless of the award previously made by the said commissioners.

At any time within thirty days from the filing of the decision of the district judges upon the hearing on exceptions to the award made by the commissioners, either party may appeal from such decision of the said judges to the circuit court of appeals, and the said circuit court of appeals shall upon the hearing on said appeal dispose of the same upon the record, without regard to the awards or findings theretofore made by the commissioners or the district judges, and such circuit court of appeals shall thereupon fix the value of the said property sought to be condemned.

Upon acceptance of an award by the owner of any property herein provided to be appropriated, and the payment of the money awarded or upon the failure of either party to file exceptions to the award of the commissioners within the time specified, or upon the award of the commissioners, and the payment of the money by the United States pursuant thereto, or the payment of the money awarded into the registry of the court by the Corporation, the title to said property and the right to the possession thereof shall pass to the United States, and the United States shall be entitled to a writ in the same proceeding to dispossess the former owner of said property, and all lessees, agents, and attorneys of such former owner, and to put the United States, by its corporate creature and agent, the Corporation, into possession of said property.

In the event of any property owned in whole or in part by minors, or insane persons, or incompetent persons, or estates of deceased persons, then the legal representatives of such minors, insane persons, incompetent persons, or estates shall have power, by and with the consent and approval of the trial judge in whose court said matter is for determination, to consent to or reject the awards of the commissioners herein provided for, and in the event that there be no legal representatives, or that the legal representatives for such minors, insane persons, or incompetent persons shall fail or decline to act, then such trial judge may, upon motion, appoint a guardian *ad litem* to act for such minors, insane persons, or incompetent persons, and such guardian *ad litem* shall act to the full extent and to the same purpose and effect as his ward could act, if competent, and such guardian *ad litem* shall be deemed to have full power and authority to respond, to conduct, or to maintain any proceeding herein provided for affecting his said ward.   [48 Stat. 70-71.]

SEC. 26. Commencing July 1, 1936, the proceeds for each fiscal year derived by the board from the sale of power or any other products manufactured by the Corporation, and from any other activities of the Corporation including the disposition of any real or personal property, shall be paid into the Treasury of the United States at the end of each calendar year, save and except such part of such proceeds as in the opinion of the board shall be necessary for the Corporation in the operation of dams and reservoirs, in conducting its business in generating, transmitting, and distributing electric energy and in manufacturing, selling, and distributing fertilizer and fertilizer ingredients.   A continuing fund of $1,000,000 is also excepted from the requirements of this section and may be withheld by the board to defray emergency expenses and to insure continuous operation: *Provided*, That nothing in this section shall be construed to prevent the use by the board, after June 30, 1936, of proceeds accruing prior to July 1, 1936, for the payment of obligations lawfully incurred prior to such latter date. [48 Stat. 71, as amended by 49 Stat. 1079.]

SEC. 26a. The unified development and regulation of the Tennessee River system requires that no dam, appurtenant works, or other obstruction, affecting navigation, flood control, or public lands or reservations shall be constructed, and thereafter operated or maintained across, along, or in the said river or any of its tributaries until plans for such construction, operation, and maintenance shall have been submitted to and approved by the board; and the construction, commencement of construction, operation, or maintenance of such structures without such approval is hereby prohibited. When such plans shall have been approved, deviation therefrom either before or after completion of such structures is prohibited unless the modification of such plans has previously been submitted to and approved by the board.

In the event the board shall, within sixty days after their formal submission to the board, fail to approve any plans or modifications, as the case may be, for construction, operation, or maintenance of any such structures on the Little Tennessee River, the above requirements shall be deemed satisfied, if upon application to the Secretary of War, with due notice to the Corporation, and hearing thereon, such plans or modifications are approved by the said Secretary of War as reasonably adequate and effective for the unified development and regulation of the Tennessee River system.

Such construction, commencement of construction, operation, or maintenance of any structures or parts thereof in violation of the provisions of this section may be prevented, and the removal or discontinuation thereof required by the injunction or order of any district court exercising jurisdiction in any district in which such structures or parts thereof may be situated, and the Corporation is hereby authorized to bring appropriate proceedings to this end.

The requirements of this section shall not be construed to be a substitute for the requirements of any other law of the United States or of any State, now in effect or hereafter enacted, but shall be in addition thereto, so that any approval, license, permit, or other sanction now or hereafter required by the provisions of any such law for the construction, operation, or maintenance of any structures whatever, except such as may be constructed, operated, or maintained by the Corporation, shall be required, notwithstanding the provisions of this section. [49 Stat. 1079.]

SEC. 27. All appropriations necessary to carry out the provisions of this Act are hereby authorised. [48 Stat. 71.]

SEC. 28. That all Acts or parts of Acts in conflict herewith are hereby repealed, so far as they affect the operations contemplated by this Act. [48 Stat. 71.]

SEC. 29. The right to alter, amend, or repeal this Act is hereby expressly declared and reserved, but no such amendment or repeal shall operate to impair the obligation of any contract made by said Corporation under any power conferred by this Act. [48 Stat. 72.]

SEC. 30. That the sections of this Act are hereby declared to be separable, and in the event of any one or more sections of this Act, or parts thereof, be held to be unconstitutional, such holding shall not affect the validity of other sections or parts of this Act. [48 Stat. 72, as amended by 49 Stat. 1081.]

SEC. 31. This Act shall be liberally construed to carry out the purposes of Congress to provide for the disposition of and make needful rules and regulations respecting Government properties entrusted to the Authority, provide for the national defense, improve navigation, control destructive floods, and promote interstate commerce and the general welfare, but no real estate shall be held except what is necessary in the opinion of the board to carry out plans and projects actually decided upon requiring the use of such land: *Provided*, That any land purchased by the Authority and not necessary to carry out plans and projects actually decided upon shall be sold by the Authority as agent of the United States, after due advertisement, at public auction to the highest bidder, or at private sale as provided in section 4 (*k*) of this Act. [49 Stat. 1080.]